Praise for

THE REPUBLIC OF PIRATES

"Fascinating . . . beyond rip-roaring adventure stories from the distant past, [the book offers] an opportunity to understand pirates as they truly were—and to be grateful that the worst of them, at least, are gone." —*The New York Times Book Review*

"Brilliant . . . Meticulously researched and thrillingly told . . . Woodard brings this slice of outlaw history gloriously to life, realizing a worthy tome for anyone who's so much as muttered a tiny 'arrrr.'" —*Baltimore City Paper*

"In a beautifully researched book, *The Republic of Pirates*, Woodard chronicles a brief chapter in piracy in the 18th century, when pirates of many nationalities banded together as a political group, to foster everything from racial tolerance to the revival of the Stuarts in England. For my money, it makes a better story than *Treasure Island*. And it's true!" —Dave Wood, *River Falls Journal* (WI)

"Forget Jack Sparrow and the buccaneers of Disney's cinematic thrill ride. The best pirate entertainment of the summer is one you can haul to the beach, and the story is true." —*Journal Register*

"Using archive material from England, Spain, and the Americas, Woodard tells the real story, brief as it was, of the Caribbean pirates as they fought nature and empire." —*The Denver Post*

"Well-written."   —EW.com

"Contain[s] passages that are absolutely riveting, sometimes for their high-seas action, sometimes for their wicked illumination of life aboard an antiquated vessel at sea for months on end."   —*The Toronto Star*

"If you love pirates, well-researched history and a good story, Woodard's book is the right read."   —*The Daily Advance* (Elizabeth City, NC)

"Narrative history at its best."   —*Winston-Salem Journal*

"Moviegoers eager to meet some real-life 'Pirates of the Caribbean' can now pick up *The Republic of Pirates* by Colin Woodard. Journalist and author Woodard tells the fascinating story of pirate captains Edward 'Blackbeard' Teach and 'Black Sam' Bellamy who set up a form of pirates' cooperative in the Caribbean in the 1700s. *The Republic of the Pirates* is the ultimate in beach reading—breezy, colorful, and rich in history and action."   —*The Christian Science Monitor*

"Disregard Robert Louis Stevenson's rowdy buccaneers, the Disney factory's lively rascals and those musical lads from Penzance: Here are the real pirates of the Caribbean, and the facts are as colorful and exciting as fiction."   —*Kirkus Reviews* (starred review)

"Woodard's book explains how this fragile democracy came about, and why the pirates who populated it were actually better suited for such organization than their legends would have us believe."
                                             —*Alexandria Gazette Packet*

"Challenges what we think we know about these ruffians, dispelling notions of dictatorial rule aboard ship in favor of an image of egalitarianism."
                                             —*Boston Magazine*

The Republic of PIRATES

The Republic *of* PIRATES

BEING THE TRUE AND SURPRISING STORY OF THE CARIBBEAN PIRATES AND THE MAN WHO BROUGHT THEM DOWN

COLIN WOODARD

MARINER BOOKS
HOUGHTON MIFFLIN HARCOURT
Boston   New York

For Sarah
My wife and true love

For information about permission to reproduce selections from this book,
write to Permissions, Houghton Mifflin Harcourt Publishing Company,
215 Park Avenue South, New York, New York 10003.

www.hmhco.com

Maps by Jojo Gragasin/LoganFrancis, Inc.

The Library of Congress has cataloged the hardcover edition as follows:
Woodard, Colin, 1968–
The republic of pirates: being the true and surprising story of the Caribbean
pirates and the man who brought them down/Colin Woodard.
p. cm.
Includes bibliographical references and index.
1. Buccaneers—History—18th century.   2. Pirates—Caribbean Area—
History—18th century.   I. Title.
F2161.W56   2007
910.4′5—dc22   2006037389
ISBN 978-0-15-101302-9
ISBN 978-0-15-603462-3 (pbk.)

Text set in Adobe Jenson
Designed by April Ward

Printed in the United States of America
First Harvest edition 2008

DOC 20 19 18 17 16 15 14 13

CONTENTS

The
Republic
of
PIRATES

FLORIDA

Spanish
wrecks

Abaco

Harbour
Island

New Providence — Eleuther

Key Biscayne —

Nassau

Cat I

Andros

R

Exuma

Long
Island

Havana

Mariel

Bahia Honda

CUBA

YUCUTAN CHANNEL

FLORIDA STRAITS

DAHAMA I

Isla de los Pinos

Port Royal

Spanish Town —

Kings

Campeche

OCCUPIED BY BAY MEN

JAMAICA

Turneffe

Bay
of Honduras

Bay Islands

Caribbean Sea

MOSQUITO COAST

Ca

Portobelo

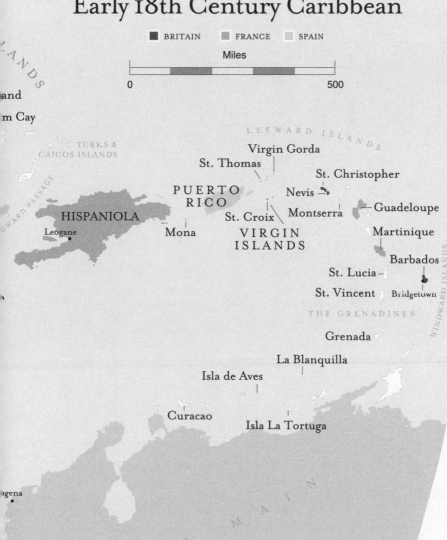

Early 18th Century Caribbean

BRITAIN　FRANCE　SPAIN

Miles

0　　　　　　　　　　　500

LEEWARD ISLANDS

...LANDS

...and

...m Cay

TURKS &
CAICOS ISLANDS

...WARD PASSAGE

Virgin Gorda

St. Thomas

St. Christopher

PUERTO
RICO

Nevis

Guadeloupe

HISPANIOLA

St. Croix

Montserra

Leogane

Mona

VIRGIN
ISLANDS

Martinique

Barbados

St. Lucia

WINDWARD ISLANDS

St. Vincent

Bridgetown

THE GRENADINES

Grenada

La Blanquilla

Isla de Aves

Curacao

Isla La Tortuga

...agena

SPANISH MAIN

THE GOLDEN AGE OF PIRACY

To their admirers, pirates are romantic villains: fearsome men willing to forge a life beyond the reach of law and government, liberated from their jobs and the constraints of society to pursue wealth, merriment, and adventure. Three centuries have passed since they disappeared from the seas, but the Golden Age pirates remain folk heroes and their fans are legion. They have been the models for some of fiction's greatest characters—Captain Hook and Long John Silver, Captain Blood and Jack Sparrow—conjuring images of sword fights, plank walking, treasure maps, and chests of gold and jewels.

Engaging as their legends are—particularly as enhanced by Robert Louis Stevenson and Walt Disney—the true story of the pirates of the Caribbean is even more captivating: a long-lost tale of tyranny and resistance, a maritime revolt that shook the very foundations of the newly formed British Empire, bringing transatlantic commerce to a standstill and fueling the democratic sentiments that would later drive the American revolution. At its center was a pirate republic, a zone of freedom in the midst of an authoritarian age.

The Golden Age of Piracy lasted only ten years, from 1715 to 1725, and was conducted by a clique of twenty to thirty pirate commodores and a few thousand crewmen. Virtually all of the commodores knew one another, having served side by side aboard merchant or pirate vessels or crossed paths in their shared base, the failed British colony of the

Bahamas. While most pirates were English or Irish, there were large numbers of Scots, French, and Africans as well as a smattering of other nationalities: Dutch, Danes, Swedes, and Native Americans. Despite differences in nation, race, religion, and even language, they forged a common culture. When meeting at sea, pirate vessels frequently joined forces and came to one another's aid, even when one crew was largely French and the other dominated by their traditional enemies, the English. They ran their ships democratically, electing and deposing their captains by popular vote, sharing plunder equally, and making important decisions in an open council—all in sharp contrast to the dictatorial regimes in place aboard other ships. At a time when ordinary sailors received no social protections of any kind, the Bahamian pirates provided disability benefits for their crews.

Pirates have existed for a long time. There were pirates in Ancient Greece and during the Roman Empire, in medieval Europe, and during the Qing Dynasty in China. Even today, pirates plague the world's sea lanes, seizing freighters, container ships, even passenger liners, looting their contents, and, not infrequently, killing their crews. They are distinct from privateers, individuals who in wartime plunder enemy shipping under license from their government. Some mistake Sir Francis Drake and Sir Henry Morgan for pirates, but they were, in fact, privateers, and undertook their depredations with the full support of their sovereigns, Queen Elizabeth and King Charles II. Far from being considered outlaws, both were knighted for their services, and Morgan was appointed lieutenant governor of Jamaica. William Dampier was a privateer, as were most of the English buccaneers of the late 1600s.* Even the infamous Captain William Kidd was a well-born privateer who be-

---

* Buccaneer is an imprecise term referring to the pirates and privateers who operated out of the West Indies in the seventeenth century, particularly in the 1670s and 1680s. The word originally referred to bands of lawless men, most of them French, who roamed the island of Hispaniola, hunting wild cattle and drying the meat on a *boucan*, an Indian-style meat-smoker; in addition to cattle, they occasionally hunted small vessels. The English later adopted the term *buccaneer* to refer to maritime raiders in the Caribbean in general, though this was not how the word was used at the time.

came a pirate accidentally, by running afoul of the directors of the East India Company, England's largest corporation.

The Golden Age Pirates were distinct from both the buccaneers of Morgan's generation and the pirates who preceded them. In contrast with the buccaneers, they were notorious outlaws, regarded as thieves and criminals by every nation, including their own. Unlike their pirate predecessors, they were engaged in more than simple crime and undertook nothing less than a social and political revolt. They were sailors, indentured servants, and runaway slaves rebelling against their oppressors: captains, ship owners, and the autocrats of the great slave plantations of America and the West Indies.

Dissatisfaction was so great aboard merchant vessels that typically when the pirates captured one, a portion of its crew enthusiastically joined their ranks. Even the Royal Navy was vulnerable; when HMS *Phoenix* confronted the pirates at their Bahamian lair in 1718, a number of the frigate's sailors defected, sneaking off in the night to serve under the black flag. Indeed, the pirates' expansion was fueled in large part by the defections of sailors, in direct proportion to the brutal treatment in both the navy and merchant marine.

Not all pirates were disgruntled sailors. Runaway slaves migrated to the pirate republic in significant numbers, as word spread of the pirates attacking slave ships and initiating many aboard to participate as equal members of their crews. At the height of the Golden Age, it was not unusual for escaped slaves to account for a quarter or more of a pirate vessel's crew, and several mulattos rose to become full-fledged pirate captains. This zone of freedom threatened the slave plantation colonies surrounding the Bahamas. In 1718, the acting governor of Bermuda reported that the "negro men [have] grown so impudent and insulting of late that we have reason to suspect their rising [against us and] . . . fear their joining with the pirates."

Some pirates had political motivations as well. The Golden Age erupted shortly after the death of Queen Anne, whose half-brother and would-be successor, James Stuart, was denied the throne because he was Catholic. The new king of England and Scotland, Protestant George I, was a distant cousin of the deceased queen, a German prince who didn't care much for England and couldn't speak its language. Many Britons, including a number of future pirates, found this unacceptable and remained loyal to James and the House of Stuart. Several of the early Golden Age pirates were set up by the governor of Jamaica, Archibald Hamilton, a Stuart sympathizer who apparently intended to use them as a rebel navy to support a subsequent uprising against King George. As Kenneth J. Kinkor of the Expedition Whydah Museum in Provincetown, Massachusetts, puts it, "these were more than just a few thugs knocking over liquor stores."

The pirate gangs of the Bahamas were enormously successful. At their zenith they succeeded in severing Britain, France, and Spain from their New World empires, cutting off trade routes, stifling the supply of slaves to the sugar plantations of America and the West Indies, and disrupting the flow of information between the continents. The Royal Navy went from being unable to catch the pirates to being afraid to encounter them at all. Although the twenty-two-gun frigate HMS *Seaford* was assigned to protect the Leeward Islands, her captain reported he was "in danger of being overpowered" if he were to cruise against the pirates. By 1717, the pirates had become so powerful they were able to threaten not only ships, but entire colonies. They occupied British outposts in the Leeward Islands, threatened to invade Bermuda, and repeatedly blockaded South Carolina. In the process, some accumulated staggering fortunes, with which they bought the loyalty of merchants, plantation owners, even the colonial governors themselves.

The authorities made the pirates out to be cruel and dangerous monsters, rapists and murderers who killed men on a whim and tortured children for pleasure, and indeed some were. Many of these tales were intentionally exaggerated, however, to sway a skeptical public. To the consternation of the ship and plantation owners of the Americas, many ordinary colonists regarded the pirates as folk heroes. Cotton Mather,

Massachusetts' leading Puritan minister, fumed about the level of support for the pirates among the "sinful" commoners of Boston. In 1718, as South Carolina authorities prepared to bring a pirate gang to trial, their sympathizers broke the pirates' leader out of prison and nearly took control of the capital, Charleston. "People are easily led to favor these Pests of Mankind when they have hopes of sharing in their ill-gotten wealth," Virginia governor Alexander Spotswood complained in the same year, adding that there were "many favorers of the pirates" in his colony.

I first thought of writing about these particular pirates while sitting under a palm tree with my future wife on an island off the coast of Belize, a Central American nation founded by English pirates and buccaneers, whose late-seventeenth-century words and phrases are still part of everyday speech. Three hundred years ago, this, like my native Maine, was a no-man's-land, a wilderness coastline studded with islands, its scant indigenous population still ungoverned by Europeans. I imagined a bowsprit coming into view around the end of the island, then the patched sails and tar-seamed hull of a small ship, her sides pierced with gun ports, and a death's-head flag flying from her mainmast. The vessel appeared real enough, all the way down to the scent of canvas and the abrasive nap of her thick hemp ropes. The crew was less clear, a jumble of pop culture references—bandanas and earrings, an eye patch for this one, a peg leg for that, a parrot on the captain's shoulder, knives and rum bottles all around—decorating men with mildly sinister smiles, barking out clichés frequently punctuated by the signature "Arrrr!" Realizing that for all of their popularity, through movies and merchandising, I still had no real sense of who the pirates really were. Where did they come from, what drove them to do what they did, how did they dispose of their plunder, and had any of them gotten away with it?

Good answers were not readily available. Most pirate books, movies, and television shows continue to trade on the pirate myths, failing to distinguish between documented and demonstrably fabricated events, most of which are traceable to *A General History of the Robberies and Murders of the Most Notorious Pyrates*, a 1724 book whose author* wrote under the alias Captain Charles Johnson. Those that do, tend to focus not on the true pirates, but on the buccaneers and privateers of an earlier era— more respectable men, most of whose activities were legally sanctioned. The lives of these individuals—Henry Morgan, William Kidd, or William Dampier—are documented by far more voluminous paper trails. A few excellent overviews remain, but they focus on piracy as an institution, not on the lives of specific pirates. The biographical approach, I would find in writing this book, poses an entirely different suite of questions, revealing connections, motivations, and events that would otherwise be missed.

What follows is based on material found in the archives of Britain and the Americas. No dialogue has been made up, and descriptions of everything from cities and events to clothing, vessels, and the weather are based on primary documents. Previously lost aspects of the pirates' history were recovered by integrating legal testimony and trial documents; the letters of English and Spanish governors, colonial officials, and naval captains; accounts in period pamphlets, newspapers, and books, scrawling in customs house ledgers, parish registers, and the logbooks of His Majesty's warships.

When quoting from seventeenth- and eighteenth-century sources, modern punctuation and, occasionally, spelling, have been applied to ensure they are comprehensible to twenty-first-century readers. All dates in the text correspond to the Julian calendar that was then in use in the English-speaking world; this has required subtracting ten or eleven days† from the dates in French and Spanish sources, wherein

---

* As later discussed, this author was not Daniel Defoe, as asserted by generations of well-intentioned scholars and librarians.

† Most Catholic nations adopted the Gregorian calendar in 1582, when the two systems were ten days apart. By 1700, the discrepancy had widened to eleven days, where it remained until 1752, when Britain finally adopted the new calendar.

today's Gregorian calendar was already in use. The original sources will be found in the notes in the back of this book.

My research led me to many of the settings included herein: London, Bristol, Boston, Charleston, and the Bahamas. I visited pirate haunts in eastern North Carolina, where divers from the state's Department of Cultural Resources are exploring what is believed to be the wreck of Blackbeard's flagship. Artifacts from another Golden Age pirate ship, the *Whydah*, are still being discovered off the beaches of Cape Cod. I have benefited greatly from conversations and correspondence with archeologists and historians in these and other places, who continue to sift through evidence for more clues to the pirates' past.

⌘

This book tells the story of the Golden Age of Piracy through the lives of four of its leading figures. Three were pirates: Samuel "Black Sam" Bellamy, Edward "Blackbeard" Thatch, and Charles Vane, all of whom knew one another. Bellamy and Blackbeard were friends, having served together under their mentor, Benjamin Hornigold, who founded the pirate republic at Nassau on New Providence Island. Both were also well acquainted with Vane, the protégé of Hornigold's rival, Henry Jennings, a blustery privateersman declared an outlaw by King George. Vane shared many of his master's characteristics: a penchant for unnecessary cruelty and violence, and a sadistic streak that eventually undermined his own authority. Bellamy and Blackbeard, following Hornigold's lead, were more circumspect in their use of force, generally using terror only to compel their victims to surrender, thereby avoiding the need for violence. In the voluminous descriptions of Bellamy's and Blackbeard's attacks on shipping—nearly 300 vessels in all—there is not one recorded instance of them killing a captive. More often than not, their victims would later report having been treated fairly by these pirates, who typically returned ships and cargo that did not serve their purposes.

In the process, these pirates built powerful followings, sailing or recreating with virtually all of the leading pirates of the era: the flamboyantly dressed John "Calico Jack" Rackham, the eccentric Stede Bonnet, the infamous Olivier La Buse, the wig-wearing Paulsgrave Williams, and the female pirate Anne Bonny. At the height of their careers, each commanded a small fleet of pirate vessels, a company consisting of hundreds of men, and, in Bellamy's and Blackbeard's cases, a flagship capable of challenging any man-of-war in the Americas. So successful were their campaigns that soon governors, slave merchants, plantation owners, and shipping magnates—the entire power structure of British America—was clamoring for something to be done.

This brings us to our fourth and final subject, Woodes Rogers, the man the Crown sent to confront the pirates and pacify the Bahamas. More than anyone else, Rogers put an end to the Golden Age of Piracy. He was not a pirate, of course, but had served as a privateer during England's most recent war with France and Spain and knew how the pirates thought and operated. A war hero and celebrated author, Rogers had led a successful assault on a Spanish city, been disfigured during a pitched battle with a massive treasure galleon in the Pacific, and was one of only a handful of men who had circumnavigated the world. Despite his swashbuckling past, Rogers held no sympathy for pirates. He represented everything the pirates were rebelling against. Unlike many of his peers, Rogers was courageous, selfless, and surprisingly patriotic, selflessly devoted to king and country. While many other governors, naval officers, and government ministers routinely lined their pockets at the Crown's expense, Rogers emptied his pockets in support of projects he believed would further the public good and the established order of the young British Empire. Despite his heroic service, Rogers would suffer at the hands of his superiors and colleagues.

Bellamy, Blackbeard, and Vane didn't start their pirate society from scratch. They had a role model in Henry Avery,* a "pirate king" who was said to have led his fellow crewmen from oppression between the decks to a life of unimaginable luxury in a pirate kingdom of their own.

---

* Also spelled "Every" or "Evarie" in documents from the period.

Avery's feats were accomplished while Bellamy, Blackbeard, and Vane were still children, and had become legendary by the time they were young men. His adventures inspired plays and novels, historians and newspaper writers, and, ultimately, the Golden Age pirates themselves. The romantic myth of piracy didn't follow the Golden Age, it helped create it. The pirates' tale, therefore, starts with Henry Avery, and the arrival of a mysterious ship in Nassau three centuries ago.

THE LEGEND

1696

T HE SLOOP ARRIVED in the afternoon of April Fool's Day 1696, swinging around the low, sandy expanse of Hog Island and into Nassau's wide, dazzlingly blue harbor.

At first, the villagers on the beach and the sailors in the harbor took little notice. Small and nondescript, this sloop was a familiar sight, a trading vessel from the nearby island of Eleuthera, fifty miles to the east. She came to Nassau, the capital of the Bahamas, on a regular basis to trade salt and produce for cloth and sugar, and to get news brought in from England, Jamaica, and the Carolinas. The bystanders expected to see her crew drop anchor, load their goods into their longboat, and row toward the beach, as the capital had no wharves or piers. Later, their cargoes disposed of, the crew would go drinking in one of Nassau's public houses, trading updates of the ongoing war, the movements of the infernal French, and cursing the absence of the Royal Navy.

But not on this day.

The sloop's crew rowed ashore. Its captain, a local man familiar to all, jumped onto the beach, followed by several strangers. The latter wore unusual clothing: silks from India, perhaps, a kerchief in bright African patterns, headgear from Arabia, as rank and dirty as the cheap woolens worn by any common seaman. Those who came near enough to overhear their speech or peer into their tanned faces could tell they were English and Irish mariners not unlike those from other large ships that came from the far side of the Atlantic.

The party made its way through the tiny village, a few dozen houses clustered along the shore in the shadow of a modest stone fortress. They crossed the newly cleared town square, passing the island's humble wooden church, eventually arriving at the recently built home of Governor Nicholas Trott. They stood barefoot on the sun-baked sand and dirt, the fecund smell of the tropics filling their nostrils. Townspeople stopped to stare at the wild-looking men waiting on the governor's doorstep. A servant opened the door and, upon exchanging a few words with the sloop's master, rushed off to inform His Excellency that an urgent message had arrived.

✦✦✦

Nicholas Trott already had his hands full that morning. His colony was in trouble. England had been at war with France for eight years, disrupting the Bahamas' trade and supply lines. Trott received a report that the French had captured the island of Exuma, 140 miles away, and were headed for Nassau with three warships and 320 men. Nassau had no warships at its disposal; in fact, no ships of the Royal Navy had passed this way in several years, there not being nearly enough of them to protect England's sprawling empire. There was Fort Nassau, newly built from local stone, with twenty-eight cannon mounted on its ramparts, but with many settlers fleeing for the better protection of Jamaica, South Carolina, and Bermuda, Trott was finding it almost impossible to keep the structure manned. There were no more than seventy men left in town, including the elderly and disabled. Half the male population was serving guard duty at any one time in addition to attending to their usual occupations, which left many of them, in Trott's words, "terribly fatigued." Trott knew that if the French attacked in force, there was little hope of holding Nassau and the rest of New Providence, the island on which his tiny capital was perched. These were Trott's preoccupations when he received the merchant captain from Eleuthera and his mysterious companions.

The strangers' leader, Henry Adams, explained that he and his colleagues had recently arrived in the Bahamas aboard the *Fancy*, a private warship of forty-six guns and 113 men, and sought Trott's permission to come into Nassau's harbor. Adams handed over a letter from his captain, Henry Bridgeman, containing a most outlandish proposition. The *Fancy*, Bridgeman claimed, had just arrived in Eleuthera from the coast of Africa, where he had been slave trading without the permission of the Royal Africa Company, which owned a monopoly over such activities. Captain Bridgeman's letter explained that the *Fancy* had run low on provisions and its crew was in need of shore leave. Were the governor to be so kind as to allow the ship into the harbor, he would be amply rewarded. Every member of the crew would give Trott a personal gift of twenty Spanish pieces of eight and two pieces of gold, with Bridgeman, as commander, kicking in a double share. The strangers were offering him a bribe worth some £860 at a time when a governor's annual salary was but £300. To top it off, the crew would also give him the *Fancy* herself, once they had unloaded and disposed of the (as yet) unspecified cargo. He could pocket nearly three years of wages and become the owner of a sizeable warship simply by letting the strangers ashore and not asking any pointed questions.

Trott pocketed the letter and called an emergency meeting of the colony's governing council. The minutes of that meeting have since been lost, but from the testimony of others in Nassau at the time, it's clear that Governor Trott neglected to mention the bribes to the councilmen. Instead, he appealed to their shared interest in the colony's security. The *Fancy*, he pointed out, was as large as a fifth-rate frigate of the Royal Navy, and her presence might deter a French attack. The addition of her crew would nearly double the number of able-bodied men on New Providence, ensuring that Fort Nassau's guns would be manned in the event of an invasion. And besides, where would they be if Bridgeman chose to refit his vessel at the French port of Martinique or, worse, decided to attack Nassau itself? Violating the Royal Africa Company's monopoly was a fairly minor crime, an insufficient reason to deny him entry.

The members of the council concurred. The governor gave Henry Adams a "very civil" letter welcoming the *Fancy* to Nassau, where she and her crew "were welcome to come and to go as they pleased."

Not long thereafter, a great ship rounded Hog Island,* her decks crowded with sailors, her sides pierced with gun ports, and her hull sunk low in the water under the weight of her cargo. Adams and his party were the first to come ashore, their longboat filled with bags and chests. The promised loot was there: a fortune in silver pieces of eight and golden coins minted in Arabia and beyond. Longboats ferried the crew ashore throughout the day. The rest of the crew resembled the landing party: ordinary-looking mariners dressed in oriental finery, each bearing large parcels of gold, silver, and jewels. The man calling himself Captain Bridgeman also came ashore and, after a closed meeting with Trott, turned the great warship over to him. When the governor arrived aboard the *Fancy*, he found they had left him a tip: The hold contained more than fifty tons of elephant tusks, 100 barrels of gunpowder, several chests filled with guns and muskets, and a remarkable collection of ship's anchors.

Trott would later claim to have had no reason to suspect the *Fancy's* crew of being involved in piracy. "How could I know it?" he testified under oath. "Supposition is not proof." Captain Bridgeman and his men had claimed to be unlicensed merchants, he added, and the people of New Providence "saw no reason to disbelieve them." But Trott was no fool. He had been a merchant captain himself and well knew that treasures of the sort the *Fancy* carried were not the product of some unsanctioned bargaining with the people of Africa's Slave Coast. Standing aboard the *Fancy*, her hold filled with ivory and weapons, her sails patched from cannonball damage and musket balls embedded in her deck work, Trott was forced to make a choice: enforce the law or pocket the money. He didn't ponder very long.

---

* In 1962, the Bahamian legislature renamed it Paradise Island at the request of American supermarket tycoon Huntington Hartford. It is now taken up by luxury resort hotels.

On the governor's orders, boats began ferrying the *Fancy*'s remaining cargo ashore. Soon the beach was littered with chests of ivory tusks and firearms, piles of sails, anchors and tackle, barrels of gunpowder and provisions, heavy cannon and their ammunition. Trott put his personal boatswain and several African slaves aboard the ship. The ivory tusks, the pieces of eight and bags of gold coins were delivered to his private quarters. Captain Bridgeman and his men were free to drink and carouse in Nassau's two pubs and could leave whenever they wished.

So it was that England's most wanted man bought off the law and sold his pirate ship to one of His Majesty's own governors. Captain Bridgeman was in reality Henry Avery, the most successful pirate of his generation, a man whose exploits were already becoming the stuff of legend. At that moment, dozens of ships, hundreds of officials, thousands of sailors, informers, and soldiers around the world were searching for Avery, his crew, and a king's ransom in stolen treasure. East India Company agents were following up rumors about his having been sighted near Bombay and Calcutta. Royal Navy captains were hunting for the *Fancy* off the shores of West Africa, Madagascar, and Arabia. Bounty hunters sailed the Indian Ocean and the approaches to the English Channel. Few would guess that Avery and his men were, at that moment, relaxing in the shadow of an English fort.

✥

Henry Avery had spent most of his thirty-six years at sea. Born outside the coastal town of Plymouth in the English West Country, he went to sea as a young man and served as mate on a number of trading vessels. Shortly after England went to war with France in 1688, Avery enlisted in the Royal Navy, serving as a junior officer aboard HMS *Rupert* and HMS *Albemarle* and seeing combat on both frigates. Along the way, he and his fellow sailors had experienced beatings and humiliations from officers, eaten rotten or substandard food courtesy of corrupt pursers, and their salaries had gone unpaid for years on end. It was a beggar's life for shipmates who lost arms, legs, hands, feet, or eyes in accidents or battle. Sailors said that prisoners led a better life, and after more than two decades at sea, Avery had to agree.

In the spring of 1693, he thought he'd found a better deal. He heard that a group of wealthy merchants was assembling a squadron of merchant ships for an unusually daring mission. Four heavily armed ships were to leave England, collect necessary documents in Spain, and sail for the Caribbean. Once there, they would conduct trade with the Spanish colonies and attack and plunder French ships and plantations. The merchants were paying well and, most importantly, their contract promised more certain prospects: a guaranteed monthly wage at fair rates, with one month's pay advanced before the ships even left England. Avery knew there would be better food and drink than aboard the king's ships, as well as the possibility of pocketing a small share of the plunder along the way. He applied for a position and, with his top-notch references and distinguished service record, was hired as first mate aboard the expedition's forty-six-gun flagship, *Charles II*, under Captain Charles Gibson.

In early August, before the squadron sailed, the men received, as promised, their first month's wages. More encouraging, the squadron's chief owner, Sir James Houblon, personally came aboard the ships, assuring the men that they or their families would be paid every six months throughout their deployment. With that, the *Charles II* and her three consorts, the *James*, *Dove*, and *Seventh Son* pulled up anchor and floated down the River Thames. For Avery and his shipmates, it appeared to be the beginning of a profitable adventure.

Things went badly from the start. The journey to La Coruña in northern Spain should have taken two weeks, but for some reason it took the *Charles II* and her consorts five months. Upon arrival they discovered that the privateering documents they needed had yet to arrive from Madrid, so they sat at anchor and waited. A week passed, then two, and then a month, with no indication that the wheels of Spanish bureaucracy were turning. Aboard the crowded ships, the men grew restless, and some began asking why their promised semiannual salary payment had not yet been made. They sent a petition to Sir James Houblon, asking that salaries be paid out to the sailors or their wives, as previously agreed. In response, Houblon told his agent to put several petitioners in irons and lock them in the ships' dank brigs.

Such reaction did not put the sailors' minds at rest. While visiting other vessels in La Coruña's sleepy harbor, some of the married sailors were able to send word back to their wives in England. A letter informed the women of their husbands' plight and urged them to meet Houblon in person to demand the wages they no doubt needed to survive. The women then confronted Houblon, a wealthy merchant and founding deputy governor of the Bank of England, whose brother was chief governor of the Bank and would soon become Lord Mayor of London. His response chilled them to the bone. The ships and their men were now under the king of Spain's control and as far as he was concerned the king could "pay them or hang them if he pleased."

When word of Houblon's response got back to La Coruña, the sailors began to panic. Several pleaded with the captain of a visiting English warship to take them back, but were refused. Captain Gibson's personal steward, William May, offered to forsake £30 in back wages were he allowed to leave the *Charles II*; Gibson told him to return to duty or he would be thrown in jail. The ship's company concluded they had been sold into the service of the king of Spain for "all the dayes of their lives."

Henry Avery came up with a solution. On May 6, 1694, four months after arriving in La Coruña, he and some of his fellow sailors rowed into town. Wandering the narrow, winding streets, they gathered up men from the other English ships in the harbor. He had a plan to gain their freedom.

At nine o'clock the following evening, several of these recruits set out from the *Charles II* in a small boat. When they came alongside the *James*, one of the sailors hailed a figure on deck using a prearranged password: "Is your drunken boatswain on board?" This failed to elicit the expected response, so they spoke more plainly, something along the lines of: "We're part of the secret plan to seize control of the *Charles*, so all you mutineers hop on board and we'll row you over there." Unfortunately the man on the deck of the *James* was not a member of the conspiracy and he ran off to alert his captain. Before the captain sounded the general alarm, however, twenty-five conspirators from the *James* launched the ship's pinnace—the largest of her boats—and rowed off after their colleagues in the direction of the *Charles*.

Back on the *Charles*, Avery heard the sounds of commotion echoing across the harbor from the *James*. He knew they could wait no longer. He and two dozen of his men rushed out on deck, seized the watchman, and took control of the quarterdeck, where the helm and many of a ship's other controls were located. As their co-conspirators from the other ship arrived in boats, the captain of the *James* opened fire, sending two cannonballs splashing into the harbor next to the *Charles*. The cannon fire alerted the Spaniards manning La Coruña's medieval fortress, who were now readying its guns. Avery barked out orders. Men rushed forward to cut the ship's thick anchor lines or clambered up the ratlines to unfurl the sails; the helmsman brought the ship off the wind, while others hauled the sails into place. Slowly, the *Charles* pulled out of the harbor, under the guns of the fort, and into the open Atlantic.

A few miles out of port, Avery went below decks to speak with Captain Gibson, who was ill and bedridden, and the second mate, Jonathan Gravet, both of whom were now under guard in their respective cabins. By their accounts, Avery treated them with courtesy and even offered Gibson command of the *Charles* if he joined their conspiracy. He refused. Avery nonetheless promised to let both men go ashore come morning in one of the boats, along with any other men who wished to leave. Avery gave Gravet three parting gifts: a coat, a waistcoat, and his own commission as first mate. Gravet later recalled that Gibson's steward, William May, "took me by the hand and wished me well home and bid me remember him to his wife."

In the morning, Gibson, Gravet, and fifteen other men got into one of the *Charles II*'s launches and rowed off toward the mainland. "I am a man of fortune, and must seek my fortune," Avery told Gibson before they parted.

❦

Later that day, Avery held a general meeting of the ship's company: eighty-five men in all, each of them there voluntarily except for the ship's doctor, whose services they were unwilling to part with. Avery proposed a new and better way of providing for themselves and their families: They would raid ships and settlements as originally planned, only not in the Caribbean, and not for the profit of Houblon. Instead they would sail for the Indian Ocean, where they would go after the richly laden merchantmen of the Orient and keep the plunder for themselves. He'd heard that the island of Madagascar would make a perfect base of operations; located off the southeastern coast of Africa it had no European presence, hundreds of miles of secluded coastline, and natives who would happily trade food and other necessities. When it was all over, Avery told them, they could quietly slip back into England with their riches.

Avery must have been persuasive because the men agreed to his plan and appointed him as their captain. Collectively they laid out an equitable scheme for sharing future plunder. While on most privateering vessels, the captain got between six and fourteen shares to the ordinary seaman's one, Avery would receive only one extra share, his mate an extra half. They would make all major decisions democratically, except during combat, when Avery's command would be absolute. They also voted to rename the ship: From here on out she would be called the *Fancy*.

They spent the month of May sailing down the Atlantic, stopping at the island of Moia in the Cape Verde Islands, 350 miles off the West African coast. Moia was a depressing place, a treeless island baking under the tropical sun. It was frequented by mariners for its expansive inland salt ponds, salt being the main food preservative of the era. In the bleak cove that served as Moia's harbor, they found three English merchant ships loading salt the natives had piled for them on the beach. Faced with the *Fancy*'s overwhelming firepower, the captains surrendered without a fight. Avery relieved them of provisions and an anchor to replace the one he'd left on the bottom of La Coruña harbor, but politely gave them a receipt for everything he had stolen. Less thoughtfully, he forced nine members of their crew to join his pirate band, probably because they, like the doctor, had special skills required to keep the *Fancy* operational.

Avery apparently regretted looting English ships in time of war. A few months later he wrote an open letter to all English shipmasters, in which he told them they had nothing to fear from the *Fancy* and her men. "I have never as yet wronged any English or Dutch [vessels]," he wrote, "nor ever intend to whilst I am Commander." He signed it "As yet an Englishman's Friend." One can see why Avery would become a hero to the poor and downtrodden, a sort of maritime Robin Hood. He'd risen up against injustice and handled his prisoners with remarkable humanity, taking only what he and his band required for survival.

Not all of Avery's subsequent actions were particularly honorable. His later admirers made much of his upstanding behavior toward English and European captives, but they tended to skip over or make light of his treatment of nonwhite foreigners who fell into his clutches. His crew and captives would later describe many acts of cruelty. Once, on the coast of West Africa, Avery lured a band of local tribesmen aboard his ship with the promise of trade, then stole their gold, clapped them into irons, and sold at least seven of them into slavery. There were numerous instances when his crew captured small, unarmed Arab trading vessels and, after seizing their humble cargoes of rice and fish, proceeded to burn them rather than return them to their captains. While cruising off what is now Somalia, the *Fancy*'s crew burned the town of Mayd to the ground because the residents refused to trade with them. Before leaving Asia, Avery and his men would do far worse.

By June 1695, thirteen months after the mutiny in Spain, Avery's gang had captured at least nine vessels and sailed from Maio to Madagascar, from the Cape of Good Hope to the coast of India. They had set up camp in the secluded harbors of Madagascar, given the *Fancy* a thorough overhaul in the Comoros Islands, and gorged themselves on pots of honey purchased from traders in Gabon. Their numbers had swollen to over one hundred, including fourteen volunteers from a Danish merchant vessel and a party of French privateers found stranded on an island near the Mozambique Straits. They had stolen large parcels of rice, grain, brandy, wool, linen, and silks, but only very small quantities of gold, silver, and other easily transportable valuables. If they were to make a real fortune, they had to go after a bigger prize. From their captives they learned that a great fleet would soon be sailing from Mocha, a port on the Red Sea in what is now Yemen, and would pass out of the Red Sea's entrance on its way to Surat, India. Aboard the ships would be thousands of Muslims returning from their annual pilgrimage to the holy shrines of Mecca and dozens of merchants repatriating the profits of their annual trading mission. The convoy's treasure ships—property of the Grand Moghul of India—were the most valuable vessels to sail the Indian Ocean.

Avery and his crew sailed north for the mouth of the Red Sea, where they planned to lie in wait for the Mocha fleet. But they were not the only English raiders with this in mind. Along the way they came across two armed sloops—small, nimble, single-masted sailing vessels—flying English colors. Their captains turned out to be privateers from Rhode Island and Delaware, men who had been given a license to raid enemy shipping in time of war, but had decided, like Avery, to attack the neutral treasure fleet. A day after arriving at the narrows, three more American privateers showed up, including Thomas Tew of New York, who had been a famous pirate himself. Avery and the captains of the five privateers agreed to attack the treasure fleet together and to share the resulting plunder. They lay in ambush behind a tiny island in the passage of Bab-al-Mandab under the blazing sun: four six-gun sloops, the forty-six-gun *Fancy*, and a six-gun brigantine.

The treasure fleet, consisting of twenty-five ships, passed the straits late one Saturday night in August, their lamps unlit, moving so stealth-ily that the pirates and privateers failed to see the first twenty-four. However they did capture the very last vessel, a slow-moving ketch and, upon interrogating the crew, realized they would have to chase the rest of the fleet across the Gulf of Aden and the Arabian Sea. For three days Avery's squadron pursued their quarry. The smaller vessels had trouble keeping pace with the *Fancy*. They burned the slowest of them so as not to be slowed down; a second sloop fell so far behind that it was never seen again.

Finally, near the Indian coast, the pirates spotted a sail on the hori-zon. This turned out to be the *Fath Mahmamadi*, a ship larger than the *Fancy*, but also slower and armed with only six guns. The crew of the *Fath Mahmamadi* fired one pathetic three-gun salvo as the pirate ships gathered around them. The *Fancy* responded with a deafening twenty-three-gun broadside and a volley of musket fire. The Indian captain sur-rendered, the *Fancy* came alongside, and Avery's crew poured onto their 350-ton prize. In the holds they found the proceeds of the *Fath Mahma-madi*'s trade in Mocha: £50,000 to £60,000 in gold and silver belonging to the ship's owner, the merchant Abd-ul-Ghafur. It was an impressive haul, enough to purchase the *Fancy* fifty times over, but Avery wanted more. He placed the vessel under the control of a detachment of his men—a prize crew—and, together with his fellow captains, continued his pursuit of the great fleet.

Two days later, along the shores of eastern India, a lookout spotted another ship in the distance bound for the Indian port of Surat. The pirates soon caught up with what turned out to be the *Ganj-i-sawai*, a gigantic trading vessel that belonged to Grand Moghul Aurangzeb him-self. She was far and away the largest ship operating out of Surat, with eighty guns, 400 muskets, and 800 able-bodied men aboard. Her cap-tain, Muhammad Ibrahim, had reason to be confident of fending off the raiders, having more guns and more than twice as many men as the *Fancy* and the three American privateers combined. The stakes were high, however, for *Ganj-i-sawai* was heavily laden with passengers and treasure.

As soon as the *Fancy* came into range, Captain Ibrahim ordered a gun crew into action. They loaded their heavy weapon and rolled it out of its port. The gunner took aim, lit the fuse, and stood back with the rest of his team, awaiting the cannon's recoil. Instead of a loud report and a burst of smoke, there came a horrifying flash. Owing to some internal defect, the heavy cannon exploded, sending shards in all directions. The gun crew was blown to bits. As Ibrahim was taking in the gruesome spectacle, the *Fancy* returned fire. One of her cannonballs struck the *Ganj-i-sawai* in the lower part of her mainmast, the most critical of locations. The mast partially collapsed, throwing sails and rigging into disarray and compounding the chaos aboard the ship. The loss of sail area meant the *Ganj-i-sawai* began to slow. Her pursuers closed in.

Swords drawn and muskets at the ready, over 100 pirates crouched behind the *Fancy*'s rails, waiting for the ships to come together. When they did, lines snapping, sails tearing, their wooden hulls moaning and creaking with the stress, Avery and company rushed over the side and onto the decks of the crippled vessel.

An Indian historian named Muhammad Hashim Khafi Khan, who was in Surat at the time, wrote that given there were so many weapons aboard the *Ganj-i-sawai*, the crew would certainly have defeated the English pirates "if the captain had made any resistance." Captain Ibrahim apparently panicked and fled below decks to the quarters of a group of Turkish girls he had purchased in Mocha to serve as his personal concubines. "He put turbans on their heads and swords into their hands and incited them to fight," Khafi Khan wrote. Resistance aboard the Indian ship collapsed. Avery's men began their plunder.

According to the stories that would later circulate in the waterfront pubs of England, Avery behaved chivalrously. One of the most popular accounts told of how he found "something more pleasing than jewels" aboard the captured ship: the Moghul Emperor's granddaughter, en route to her wedding with a vast dowry and a gaggle of beautiful handmaidens. Avery, it was said, proposed to the princess and, upon receiving her consent, married her right then and there with the assistance of a Muslim cleric. In this version of the story, which was published in London in 1709, "The rest of the crew then drew lots for her servants and, to follow the example of their commander, even stay'd their stomachs 'till the same priest had said Grace for them." The happy newlyweds were said to have spent the whole trip back to Madagascar engaged in conjugal bliss.

The true story is less romantic. Trial documents and accounts of Indian witnesses and English officials make it clear that Avery presided over an orgy of violence. For several days, the pirates raped female passengers of all ages. Among the victims was one of the Moghul emperor's relatives—not a young princess, but the elderly wife of one of his courtiers. Khafi Khan reported that a number of women killed themselves to avoid such a fate, some by jumping into the sea, others stabbing themselves with daggers. Survivors said the pirates treated many of the captives "very barbarously" in an effort to make them confess where they had hidden their valuables. One of Avery's crew, Philip Middleton, later testified that they murdered several men aboard the captured ship. Fact and legend only agree on the scale of the treasure the pirates loaded aboard the *Fancy*: a trove of gold, silver, ivory, and jewels worth £150,000 or more.

Once the pirates were satisfied, the *Ganj-i-sawai* was allowed to sail on to Surat with her surviving crew and passengers. The pirates left in the opposite direction, heading south toward Madagascar and the Cape of Good Hope. On the island of Réunion, halfway to the Cape, Avery and the privateer captains divided their plunder and went their separate ways. Most of the crew received an individual share of £1,000, the equivalent of twenty years' wages aboard a merchant ship. Avery put to his crew that they sail directly for Nassau to avoid the emperor's revenge. In November 1695 the *Fancy* began its long journey, halfway around the world, to New Providence Island.

～≈～

Having concluded their deal with Governor Trott, Avery and his men spent several days in Nassau, drinking Trott's refreshments and debating what to do next. A few men—seven or eight at least—resolved to stay right where they were and soon married local women. The remaining pirates split into three parties, each with its own idea of how best to slide into obscurity with their plunder. Twenty-three men, led by Thomas Hollingsworth, purchased a thirty-ton sloop called the *Isaac* from the islanders and sailed for England in the second week of April 1696, apparently wishing to quietly slip back to their homes. The second party of approximately fifty made their way to Charleston in Carolina, the nearest English colony, 400 miles to the north. The third group consisted of Avery and twenty others, who paid £600 for a fifty-ton ocean-going sloop, the *Sea Flower*, armed with four small cannon. Around the first of June, they loaded their possessions and treasure and made ready to depart. Henry Adams, the man who had carried Avery's messages to Governor Trott, married a Nassau girl and brought her with him aboard the sloop. Avery ordered the sails raised and the *Sea Flower* began making its way north with the Gulf Stream, bound for the north of Ireland.

Nicholas Trott spent the early part of June picking the *Fancy* clean. To make this process easier—and because the ship was in poor condition already—he ordered her run aground on Hog Island shortly before the *Sea Flower*'s departure. Whether he knew the ship's true identity is unclear, but sometime that summer, other mariners passed through Nassau and recognized the beached hulk as the *Charles II*. Trott brought a few men in for questioning but claimed "they could give no information." In December he received a letter from his counterpart in Jamaica, informing him that Bridgeman was none other than the outlaw Henry Avery. Trott brought a few of Avery's colleagues in for questioning. He soon released them, noting that the governor of Jamaica "gave no proof." Months later he disingenuously ordered the *Fancy* be "seized . . . in the hope that evidence might be found." Trott would ultimately lose his governorship over the incident, but ended his days prosperously enough.

Some of Avery's men found shelter in other ports. Several of those who had gone to Charleston continued on to Philadelphia, where they bought the allegiance of another governor, William Markham of Pennsylvania, for £100 per man. Markham, who apparently knew who they were, not only neglected to arrest them, he entertained them at his home and allowed one of them to marry his daughter. When one of the king's magistrates, Robert Snead, attempted to arrest the pirates, the governor had him disarmed and threatened with imprisonment. Snead, unperturbed, apprehended two of the pirates, but they "escaped" from Markham's prison within hours. The incident, Snead wrote back to authorities in London, had allowed "all the people [to] see how Arabian gold works with some consciences."

The *Isaac*, the first of the sloops carrying the England-bound pirates, landed on remote Achill Island off the west coast of Ireland during the first week in June. About a dozen pirates came ashore at the foot of Achill Head, piling bags of gold and silver coins onto the wide beach. They later made their way to Dublin and there vanished without a trace. The rest of the *Isaac*'s company sailed down to Westport, County Mayo, where they hastily unloaded and broke company. They offered townspeople £10 each for nags worth not one-fifth of that, and exchanged bags of Spanish silver for purses of gold guineas at a discount, simply to lighten their loads. On small Irish horses laden down with guineas, silks, and other valuables, many rode out of town in the direction of Dublin. Hollingsworth, their leader, sold the *Isaac* to local merchants and took off himself. Local officials estimated the sloop had arrived in Westport with £20,000 in gold and silver, plus several tons of valuable Bahamian logwood, a tropical species from which dyes were extracted. Only two men, James Trumble and Edward Foreside, were apprehended, though others were seen in Dublin later that summer.

Avery and the *Sea Flower* arrived at the end of June, landing at Dunfanaghy, County Donegal, in the northeast. They were confronted by the local customs official, Maurice Cuttle, who they handled in their usual fashion; each gave Mr. Cuttle about £3 in gold and, in exchange, he not only issued them passes to go to Dublin, he escorted them part of the way there. Six miles out of Dunfanaghy, Avery parted ways with the rest of the men, saying he was bound for Scotland and, ultimately, Exeter in his native Devonshire. Only one person accompanied the pirate: Henry Adams's wife. Together Avery and Mrs. Adams made their way from Donegal Town.

The other men of the *Sea Flower* traveled to Dublin. One of them, John Dan, booked passage to England and then ventured overland to London. While passing through the town of St. Albans, Hertfordshire, he ran into Mrs. Adams, who was boarding a stagecoach. She told Dan that she was going to meet Avery, but refused to take him along or tell him where he was. A few days later, at an inn in Rochester, Kent, outside London, a maid discovered the £1,100 Dan had sewn into his quilted jacket. He wound up in prison, as did seven of his former shipmates. Five of them, including the steward William May, were hanged at the Execution Dock in London on November 25, 1696.

Avery was never heard from again.

❧❧❧

Rumors of Avery's fate circulated the English-speaking world for decades afterward, passing from deckhand to deckhand within the ships and pubs of the empire. It was said that he was literally the King of the Pirates, and had returned to Madagascar with his accomplices to reign over his own pirate domain. There he lived with his wife, the granddaughter of the Grand Moghul, in a sumptuous and well-defended palace, beyond the reach of English law. Pirates were drawing to him from the four corners of the world.

The legend gained credence in 1709, when a London bookseller published *The Life and Adventure of Capt. John Avery*, allegedly based on the journal of a man who had escaped from his pirate kingdom. The anonymous author claimed Avery presided over a fleet of more than forty large warships and an army of 15,000 men. "Towns were built, communities established, fortifications built, and entrenchments flung up, as rendered his Dominions impregnable and inaccessible by sea and land." Avery had so much silver and gold that he'd begun minting his own coins bearing his likeness. "The famous English pirate," he wrote, had gone "from a Cabin Boy to a King." The story so captivated the English public that within a few years, London's Theatre Royal staged a play based on Avery's life. In *The Successful Pyrate*, Avery lived in a vast palace, "a sceptered robber at the head of a hundred thousand . . . brother-thieves . . . burning cities, ravaging countries, and depopulating nations."

To abused young sailors and cabin boys, Avery had become a hero. He was one of their own, a man who stuck up for his fellow sailors and led them to a promised land, a sailor's heaven on earth. A champion of the ordinary man, the Avery of legend was a symbol of hope for a new generation of oppressed mariners, as well as a role model for the men who would one day become the most famous and fearsome pirates in history.

Only years later, as the Golden Age of Piracy was coming to an end, would a competing account of Avery's fate be published. According to *A General History of the Pyrates*, published in London in 1724, Avery never made it back to Madagascar. After taking leave of his shipmates in Ireland, he headed to his native Devon bearing a large quantity of diamonds. Through friends in Biddeford, he arranged to sell the gems to some Bristol merchants, men who, unlike Avery, were sufficiently wealthy that "no enquiry would be made [of] how they came by them." According to this account, Avery handed over the jewels, with the understanding that he would be sent most of the proceeds of their sale, and relaxed with kin in Biddeford. The payments he eventually received from Bristol "were not sufficient to give him bread." He confronted the merchants and they threatened to turn him in to the authorities, showing themselves to be "as good Pyrates at Land as he was at Sea." Reduced to beggary, Avery fell sick and died on his return to Biddeford, "not being worth as much as would buy him a coffin."

But that version of the story was to be written a quarter-century hence. For those alive in the year 1700, the only versions of the Avery story were those of a robber king and his republic of pirates.

CHAPTER TWO

GOING TO SEA

1697–1702

WHEN HENRY AVERY vanished into the Irish night, the men who would shape the Golden Age of Piracy were boys or very young men. Of the early lives of those who became bona fide pirates, we know very little.

Most people in late-seventeenth-century England left little record of their time on earth. An honest, law-abiding commoner's birth, marriage, and death might be recorded by a priest in the register of the local parish church. Were they fortunate enough to own property, a will with an inventory of the person's possessions and to whom they were bequeathed might survive. If the person had committed or had been the victim of a crime, the records of that person would likely be more voluminous, particularly if the case had gone to trial. In fact, much of what we know about the great pirates comes from depositions, trial transcripts, and other legal records stored in the archives of Great Britain, Spain, and their former colonies in the New World. Before they turned to piracy, in other words, history has little to say about them.

❧

Samuel Bellamy, the man who would call himself the Robin Hood of the seas, was likely the child of Stephen and Elizabeth Pain Bellamy, born March 18, 1689, in the hamlet of Hittisleigh, Devon. If so, he was the youngest of five children, the eldest son having died in infancy five years before Samuel's birth. As the only remaining son, he stood to inherit the family estate, which probably didn't amount to much. Hittisleigh was an extremely modest place, a handful of cottages scattered over hills on the northern fringe of the stark wastes of Dartmoor, the setting of Arthur Conan Doyle's *Hound of the Baskervilles*. The soil was heavy with clay, complicating both the plowing and drainage of fields; the inhabitants did their best to eke out a living farming wheat, barley, and potatoes. The region's soil, Daniel Defoe reported in the 1720s, was "barren by nature" and "very unhealthy, especially to sheep, which in those parts are of a small kind, and very subject to rot which destroys them in great numbers." The soil grew "nothing but rushes, or a coarse, sour kind of pasturage which the cattle will not feed upon."

Like many boys, Bellamy probably left his farm as soon as he could to escape the growing social and economic catastrophe that was engulfing the English countryside. The old medieval system was being supplanted by capitalism, and the pain of that transition was being borne by the country's peasant farmers. Beginning in the 1500s, English lords began driving peasants off their lands, either by purchasing their medieval tenancy rights for cash or simply refusing to renew their leases. All over England, fields and pastures once used in common by local villagers were seized by feudal lords, enclosed with walls, fences, and hedgerows, and incorporated into large private farms and sheep ranches. This "enclosure movement" turned feudal lords into landed aristocrats and turned millions of self-sufficient farmers into landless paupers.

Rural English life was increasingly perilous as a result. Without land, peasants could no longer raise livestock, meaning they could no longer produce their own milk, cheese, wool, or meat. Since they had to pay cash rents to their landlords to use their fields and live in their cottages, most were forced to hire themselves and their children out as laborers. For the typical peasant family, this represented a huge loss in real income; the annual dairy production of just one cow was worth as much as a full-grown man's annual wages as a laborer. "The poor tenants," one traveler observed, "cannot afford to eat the eggs their hens lay, nor the apples and pears that grow on their trees . . . but must make

money of all." Sir Francis Bacon described the tenant farmers as little
better than "housed beggars." By the year of Bellamy's birth, three million Englishmen—roughly half the country's population—were poised
on or below the level of subsistence, and most lived in the countryside.
Malnutrition and disease left their mark on this submerged half of England's population: On average they stood six inches shorter and lived
less than half as long as their middle- and upper-class countrymen.

Large numbers of them abandoned their ancestral lands and headed
for England's towns and cities in search of work. The young Sam Bellamy was likely one of them. Although we don't know his itinerary, we
do know he ultimately made his way to one of England's ports. Perhaps
he was inspired by the exploits of Henry Avery, whose stories had spread
out across Devon from Avery's hometown of Newton Ferrers, just thirty
miles from Hittisleigh. Dreams of swashbuckling adventure and kingly
riches may have swum in the young man's head as he walked across the
moors toward Plymouth, over the hills in the direction of Bristol, or
down the long road to London, making his way toward the sea.

～≈～

Of Charles Vane, who would one day challenge an entire squadron of
His Majesty's warships, we know even less. There is a portrait of him in
the 1725 edition of *A General History of the Pyrates*, a woodcutting whose
creator would have worked from what he had heard or read, not by
what he had seen; it depicts Vane in a shoulder-length wig and soldierly
long coat, sword drawn, pointing purposefully toward an unseen objec-
tive; he is of middle stature, with an aquiline nose, dark hair, a thin
goatee standing out from a few days' growth of facial hair. His birth-
place and childhood have been lost to history, leaving us to guess at his
origins. He is thought to be English, though his name holds out the
possibility of French ancestry. Before turning pirate, he resided for a
time in Port Royal, Jamaica, but was not originally from there. He was
likely about the same age as Bellamy and probably went to sea around
the same time. The best guess is that he was from London, which his-

torian Marcus Rediker estimates was home to nearly a third of the pirates of Vane's generation. Bellamy also may have sailed from there; later in his pirate career, he once claimed to have been from London.

In 1700, London dominated England like no other time before or since. It had 550,000 residents, more than a tenth of the nation's population, and fifteen times larger than England's second city, Norwich. It was the center of trade, commerce, society, and politics for England's growing empire. It was also far and away its greatest port.

The city had already jumped its ancient walls and spread across the fields to the village of Westminster, three miles up the Thames, home to both Queen Anne and Parliament, and downriver as far as the Royal Navy shipyard in Rotherhithe. Its center was rebuilt on a magnificent scale after the Great Fire of 1666, the skyline punctuated by the spires of Sir Christopher Wren's churches and the half-finished dome of Wren's greatest project, St. Paul's Cathedral. Tidy brick buildings on paved streets of uniform width were replacing the crooked alleys and irregular wooden homes of the medieval period. Commerce pulsed through the streets, the cobblestones echoing under wheels of tradesmen's carts and street vendors' wheelbarrows, the hooves of gentlemen's carriage horses and the herds of cattle and sheep bound for slaughter in the downtown meat markets. Shops and stalls not only lined the streets and squares, they spilled out into thoroughfares and even choked the flow of traffic crossing London Bridge, the only span across the River Thames. Many of London's fine churches were "so crowded up with shops and dwelling houses," one writer lamented, "that one would think religion in danger of being smothered up by the growth of trade."

The city's main artery, the Thames, was even more crowded than the streets. Upriver from London Bridge—under whose narrow arches the tides poured like waterfalls—hundreds of watermen rowed boats ferrying passengers and cargo up, down, and across the river, into which flowed the contents of a half million chamber pots; the blood and guts of thousands of slaughtered livestock; and the bodies of cats, dogs, horses, rats, and just about anything else wanting disposal. Downriver from the bridge, hundreds, sometimes thousands of seagoing vessels waited to load and unload their cargoes, often tying up three or four abreast, a floating forest of masts extending nearly a mile. Coastal trading sloops brought heaps of coal from Newcastle; two- and three-masted ships disgorged lumber from the Baltic, tobacco from Virginia, sugar from Jamaica and Barbados, and salt cod from New England and Newfoundland. Further downriver, on the outskirts of the metropolis at the naval yards of Deptford and Rotherhithe, the warships of the Royal Navy gathered for orders, repairs, or reinforcements.

Had they come to London, Charles Vane and Samuel Bellamy would have wound up in the neighborhood of Wapping, sandwiched on the riverfront between the naval yards and London Bridge. Wapping was a crowded warren of crumbling homes and dreary alehouses interspersed with wharves, lumberyards, and warehouses. Built on ground squeezed between marshes and the river, the neighborhood had long been known as "Wapping on the Ooze," and was home to those who couldn't afford to live anyplace else.

Life in Wapping and the other poorer districts of London was dirty and dangerous. People often lived fifteen or twenty to a room, in cold, dimly lit, and unstable houses. There was no organized trash collection; chamber pots were dumped out of windows, splattering everyone and everything on the streets below. Manure from horses and other livestock piled up on the thoroughfares, as did the corpses of the animals themselves. London's frequent rains carried away some of the muck, but made the overpowering stench from the churchyards even worse; paupers were buried in mass graves, which remained open until fully occupied. Cold weather brought its own atmospheric hazards, as what little home heating there was came from burning poor-quality coal.

Disease was rampant. Eight thousand people moved to London each year, but the influx barely kept up with the mortality rate. Food poisoning and dysentery carried off on average a thousand a year, and more than eight thousand were consumed by fevers and convulsions. Measles and smallpox killed a thousand more, many of them children, most of whom were already ravaged by rickets and intestinal worms. Between a quarter and a third of all babies died in their first year of life, and barely half survived to see the age of sixteen.

The streets swarmed with parentless children, some of them orphaned by accidents or disease, others simply abandoned on the church steps by parents who were unable to feed them. Overwhelmed parish officials rented babies out to beggars for use as props for four pence (£.016) a day and sold hundreds of five- to eight-year-olds into seven years of slavery for twenty or thirty shillings (£1 to £1.5) apiece. These small children were purchased by chimney sweepers, who sent them down the flues to do the actual cleaning, sometimes while fires were still burning below them, cleaning coal dust without masks or protective clothing. These "climbing boys" soon succumbed to lung ailments and blindness or simply fell to their deaths. Church officials put the children they could not sell back out on the street "to beg about in the daytime and at night [to] sleep at doors, and in holes and corners about the streets," as one witness reported. Large numbers of these hungry, bedraggled urchins roamed the streets together in bands called the Blackguards, so called because they would shine the boots of cavalrymen for small change. "From beggary they proceed to theft," the same Londoner concluded, "and from theft to the gallows."

Not everyone in Wapping was destitute. There were pub keepers and dockworkers, merchants and sailmakers, brothel owners and boardinghouse keepers, even officers and ship captains of modest means. A few prominent craftsmen also lived in the precinct, including a Mr. Lash, who built the queen's carriages, and the brewer Altoway, in whose barrels upward of £1,500 in beer and ale were stored at any given time, awaiting distribution to a thirsty city. London's water supplies were so unhealthy that the entire population drank beer instead, children included. Nearby was Roberts's boatyard, which afforded its workers a grandstand view of the neighborhood's greatest attraction: Execution Dock, where the Admiralty Court sent condemned sailors and captured pirates to meet their maker.

Early Eighteenth-Century Prices and Wages

PRICES

Cod, whole, twelve pounds,
Boston £0.01

Beef, fresh, one pound,
Boston £0.03–0.05

Cider, one barrel £0.15

Rum, one gallon £0.20

Sailor's canvas trousers £0.06

Sailor's waist coat £0.45

Gentleman's wig £10–30

Cutlass £0.30

Musket £3

Cannon, 4-pounder £16

Alleged cure, venereal disease,
one pot, London £0.15

Doctor, annual retainer
for a family, Boston £5

Postage, letter,
England to Boston £0.05

Book, *General History
of the Pyrates*, 1st ed. £0.2

Subscription, *Jamaica Weekly
Courant*, 3 months £0.38

Spanish silver, one ounce £0.45

Gold, one ounce, London £4.3

Coach ride from edge
of London to center £0.05

Budget transportation,
England to Americas £5–6

Rent, attic room, Oxford £3/year

Rent, shop,
central Boston £20/year

Rent, gentleman's
townhouse, Charleston £46/year

Indentured servant,
adult European, Virginia £12

Slave, adult African,
Americas £25–40

Sugar plantation, 100 acres,
Jamaica, total value £5,625

Sloop, ten-ton trader £30

Frigate, 350 tons, 36 guns,
fully fitted £8,200

WAGES

Housemaid, London £5/year

Sailor, navy £11.5–15/year

Teacher, England £16/year

Farm laborer, England £18/year

Able sailor, merchant
marine £33/year

First mate, merchant
marine £44/year

Shopkeeper, England £45/year

Surgeon, England £52/year

Captain, merchant marine . . £65/year

Attorney, England £113/year

Governor, North Carolina . . £300/year

Country squire, England . . . £300/year

Governor, New York £1,200/year

Gentleman, England
. . . . £1,000–5,000/year

Duke of Newcastle £25,000/year

OTHER

Book advance, Defoe's
Robinson Crusoe £50

Profit, 100-acre sugar
plantation, Jamaica £540/year

Tax revenue, Government
of New Hampshire £1,300/year

Profit, 500-acre sugar
plantation, Barbados £7,500/year

Spending, Government of
Massachusetts £17,000/year

If Charles Vane grew up in Wapping, he would have seen numerous pirate hangings, including those of five of Henry Avery's crew in the fall of 1696, and William Kidd and four other pirates in May of 1701. Vane would have been a boy, but in those days nobody missed an execution: It was one of the most popular forms of entertainment.

The fun started days or weeks ahead of time at Marshalsea or Newgate Prison, where visitors tipped the guards for a chance to gawk at the condemned. On the day of execution, thousands lined the streets along the route to Wapping, waiting for the prisoners to roll by, lashed inside carts and escorted by guards and the Admiralty marshal. So many people tried to get a glimpse of the prisoners that the three-mile trip often took as long as two hours. By the time the procession reached Execution Dock, festive crowds massed on the riverbank and wharves, choking Wapping Stairs and spreading out on the stinking mud exposed at low tide. The gallows stood out in the mud, and behind them hundreds of passenger boats jockeyed for the best view of the impending event.

Vane would have watched Avery's men say their final words. According to witnesses, each of the pirates expressed penitence, but John Sparcks clarified that his regret was confined to the "horrid barbarities" they'd committed aboard the Grand Moghul's ship. "Stealing and running away with [the *Charles II*]" was, Sparcks said, a "lesser concern." Their speeches completed, they were led to the gallows one by one and hanged, kicking and gagging. When the last man finished twitching, the sheriff's deputies dragged the bodies into the mudflats, lashed them to posts, and left them to be slowly engulfed by the incoming tide. Early the next morning, the retreating tide exposed their bloated bodies for a few hours until the next flood tide submerged them again. By custom, the Admiralty authorities only took the bodies away after they had been washed by three tides. The deputies buried most pirates in shallow graves or turned them over to surgeons for dissection, but the prominent ones they covered in tar and placed in iron cages hung at prominent points along the river. Sailors and watermen sailing up and down the Thames would see these ghoulish scarecrows, intended to strike fear in the hearts of would-be pirates. Time would tell just how ineffective they were.

∼✍∼

Plenty of people were trying to lure young men like Bellamy and Vane aboard their ships. Professional seamen were in short supply, and the captains of both merchant vessels and Royal Navy warships were continually shorthanded. By some estimates, even if all of England's sailors were healthy and working at the same time, they would have accounted for only about two-thirds of the manpower needed for her merchant and naval fleets. Either service welcomed volunteers—the navy offered a bounty of two month's pay to any who would sign up—but they got few takers. There was a saying: "Those who would go to sea for pleasure would go to hell as a pastime." Only the ignorant and naïve joined either service voluntarily, country boys like Sam Bellamy, itching for adventure, but there weren't nearly enough of them.

Merchants were compelled to adopt aggressive tactics to fill their crews. Some hired "spirits," or men who, in the words of sailor Edward Barlow, went about inns and taverns looking to "entice any who they think are country people or strangers . . . or any who they think are out of place and cannot get work and are walking idly about the streets." The spirits promised these idlers high wages and advances of money if they signed on the dotted line. Those who did found themselves on an outbound ship as an underpaid sailor's apprentice, the spirit pocketing several months of their pay as commission. Other captains hired men called "crimps" who sought out drunk or indebted seamen and tried to persuade them to sign on in exchange for drinks or the payment of their debts. If and when that failed, particularly unscrupulous crimps simply handcuffed and kidnapped drunken sailors, locking them up overnight before selling them to merchant captains. Whatever the circumstances, the new sailor was legally bound to serve the vessel until it completed a journey that would last for months, sometimes years.

The Royal Navy had a reputation for offering poorer pay and harsher discipline than merchant service and resorted to a more sweeping and violent approach: the press gang. Led by a naval officer, press gangs stalked the streets, rounding up any seamen they came across with the aid of clubs. Mariners were easy to pick out because of their distinct way of speaking, dressing, and walking. Edward Ward, a writer and sometime tavern keeper, encountered a pack of sailors in London around this time and likened them to "a litter of squab rhinoceroses, dressed in human apparel." In their tarred jackets, the sailors catcalled women and bashed every horse-hitching post they passed with their cudgels, causing any stray dog they came across to run away with "his tail between his legs to avoid the danger of the approaching evil."

Tough as they were, the sailors fled in terror when a press gang was near. Seamen would hide in their rooms above alehouses for days at a time. One sailor fled from London to Dover only to find gangs operating there as well. "I was still terrified [of] the press, for I could not walk the streets without danger, nor sleep in safety," the sailor later recalled, describing his as "a prisoner's life." Other men pretended to marry pub or coffeehouse owners so they could claim to be homeowners, who were exempt from naval service. Others avoided it by getting themselves appointed as constables or neighborhood officials, or simply signed on board a merchant vessel. Large numbers of sailors fled England altogether.

The press gangs were persistent, not least because their leaders received twenty shillings (£1) for every man they captured. They would break into homes and boarding houses in the middle of the night in search of sailors, and regularly raided merchant ships entering London and other ports. Men who had been at sea for months or years were dragged off their merchant vessels and onto warships before they could set foot on land, catch a glimpse of their families, or collect their pay. Some merchant ships were left so shorthanded they were barely able to make it to port. Occasionally, sailors returning from particularly long voyages mutinied to avoid being pressed; once in control, they either abandoned their vessel in one of its boats or took up arms and attempted to fight off the gangs when they tried to board. On colliers, the small vessels that hugged the coast, carrying coal to London and other cities, the most able-bodied sailors would hide as soon as the press gang's ketch pulled alongside. Frustrated gang leaders responded by seizing the ship's boys and whipping them until they revealed the location of the hidden men. When sailors were particularly scarce, the gangs would break into homes of potters, weavers, tailors, and other poor tradesmen, seizing the men and their apprentices who were, according to a 1705 tract by playwright and pamphleteer John Dennis, "driven from their families like dogs or the worst of criminals," often without even letting them dress. Many died of exposure for lack of clothing, "and those that remained were of little use" for lack of skills. Beggars, vagabonds, and street children were relentlessly pursued by the press. Many of these landlubbers would never see England again.

By these varied methods, thousands of boys and men left England for the sea every year. Somewhere among this mass of the naïve, the unlucky, and the desperate, were two boys who would help to bring the commerce of the British Empire to a grinding halt.

❧❧

By 1700, Edward Thatch, the man who would become Blackbeard, was already an experienced seaman. He was born about 1680 in or around Bristol, England's second-largest port and the center of its transatlantic trade. He was apparently from a reasonably comfortable family, possibly even a reputable one: He had received an education and so, unlike most of his fellow mariners, could read and write. No "Thatches" (or "Taches," "Teaches," or "Thaches") appear in the Bristol tax records for 1696—the only complete one of that city to survive this period—and this has led historians to speculate that Edward Thatch was an assumed name. He may have taken pains to obscure his true identity in order to avoid bringing dishonor upon his relations. That said, it is possible he was related to the Thatches of nearby Gloucester, one of whom,

Thomas Thatch, moved to Bristol in 1712 and leased a house a mere block from the city docks.

Thatch was tall and thin and—as you might expect—heavily bearded. These characteristics, reported by people who had met him, are reflected in three posthumous portraits prepared by engraver B. Cole for the various editions of *A General History of the Pyrates*. Thatch is shown in the same confident pose in all three, one hand on his hip, the other holding aloft a cutlass while his men battle their way aboard a large merchant ship in the harbor behind him. In another eighteenth-century engraving by Thomas Nicholls and James Basire, Thatch has a wild-eyed expression and fuses burning from the ends of his dread-locked beard.

Thatch was intelligent, capable, and charismatic, characteristics that helped him rise quickly through the ranks of the merchant or naval vessels he served on. In the process, he picked up the skills necessary to operate large armed sailing ships: sail handling, gunnery, combat tactics and, most importantly, navigation. Like Avery, Thatch had the experience to assume control of what were the most powerful and sophisticated vessels of the day.

In Thatch's youth, Bristol was still England's primary gateway to the Americas. In the sixteenth and seventeenth centuries, its merchants had pioneered the exploration of Newfoundland's fisheries and the Gulf of Maine. By the beginning of the eighteenth century, the American trade permeated almost every aspect of life in Bristol. The small city of 20,000 was still ringed by medieval walls, but its downtown was now girded with stone quays, against which were tied scores of oceangoing vessels. Shops and warehouses overflowed with American goods. The city's craftsmen grew prosperous supplying the merchants with woven cloth, cured provisions, and manufactured goods. Most of these products were sent straight back to the Americas, but some were loaded aboard ships bound for Africa, where local chiefs were happy to exchange them for slaves. The ships then carried the slaves to Barbados and Jamaica and their captains traded them for sugar, which was brought back to

Bristol to complete the triangular trade. Signs of the Americas were everywhere: visiting merchants from Boston and New York, flamboyantly dressed sugar plantation owners from Barbados and Jamaica, and country squires from Virginia and the Carolinas. The great gothic seaman's church of St. Mary Redcliffe contained an entire chapel dedicated to the Americas, featuring a whale rib donated by John Cabot, the explorer who "discovered" the North American mainland in 1497. America seemed to be the place where fortunes were made. Thatch discovered that being a sailor was not the way to make it.

❧

Sailors stood below even farm laborers in England's pecking order. The historian David Ogg described their treatment as being "barely distinguishable from the criminal," while the eighteenth-century essayist Samuel Johnson wrote that their lot was very much the same as that of a prisoner, only with the added possibility of drowning.

The sailor's work was extremely hazardous. Seamen got "bursted bellies," hernias, while manhandling heavy cargoes, which were transported in casks and barrels that occasionally rolled free, slicing off fingers or crushing limbs. While underway, the ship's assorted canvas sails had to be regularly adjusted, either by hauling on ropes from the deck or by climbing high up the mast. "We were often waked up before we had slept half an hour and forced to go to the maintop or foretop to take in our topsails, half awayke and half asleep, with one shoe on and the other off," sailor Edward Barlow recalled in about 1703. "In stormy weather, when the ship rolled and tumbled, as though some great millstone were rolling up one hill and down another, we [had to] . . . haul and pull to make fast the sail, seeing nothing but air above us and water beneath us, and that so raging as though every wave would make a grave of us." Men fell to their deaths, while others were washed off the decks by crashing waves or crushed beneath falling rigging.

Sailors wrapped themselves in woolen clothing against the cold and wore leather caps and tar-dipped jackets against the spray and rain. Still, it was not unusual to spend days on end in the soaking wet clothing in winter weather, resulting in sickness or death. In the tropics, they worked shirtless, leading to terrible sunburns. Dr. Hans Sloane, traveling to Jamaica in 1687, reported that the entire company of HMS *Assistance* had turned a bright red and were "breaking out all over into little whales, pimples, and pustules."

There wasn't much solace belowdecks. Merchant seamen were crammed into a communal cabin in the bow, where the movement of the vessel was most violent. They slept in densely packed rows of hammocks in this dark and poorly ventilated space, which reeked of bilge water and unwashed flesh. Lice, rats, and cockroaches swarmed the vessel, spreading diseases like typhus, typhoid, and the plague. Gottlieb Mittelberger, who crossed the Atlantic in 1750, reported that the cabins were a place of "stench, fumes, horror, vomiting, many kinds of seasickness, fever, dysentery, headache, heat, consumption, boils, scurvy, cancer, mouth rot and the like, all of which come from old and sharply salted food and meat, also from very bad and foul water, so that many die miserably."

The food they were fed was literally sickening. The salted beef and pork that were the staples of the seaman's diet came out of barrels dry and hard at best, putrid and maggoty at worst. Sailors closed their eyes before eating the "mouldy and stinking" ship's biscuits to avoid seeing the maggots and weevils wiggling through them. After a few weeks at sea, the fresh-water supply turned green and reeking and fueled deadly outbreaks of dysentery and bloody flux. Sailors drank huge quantities of alcohol instead; Royal Navy rations gave each man a half pint of rum and a gallon of beer every day, meaning the crew was drunk most of the time.

Bad as these victuals were, they were better than nothing, as not a few crews painfully discovered. Especially greedy merchant shipowners regularly tried to boost their profits by understocking the crew's food supply, leaving them to face starvation if storms or adverse winds caused their passage to take longer than expected. Vessels carrying poor immigrants or African slaves to the Americas were particularly vulnerable.

On passenger vessels, people starved to death in large numbers. One ship, the *Katharine*, left Londonderry for Boston in 1729 with 123 crew and passengers, but limped ashore six months later in western Ireland with only fourteen left alive. Later that year, the *Lothrop* showed up in Philadelphia with only ninety survivors; thirty children and seventy adults had starved to death en route including all but three of the crew. When food ran low on slave ships, the captain would throw human cargo overboard.

The captain ruled with absolute authority, and many of them exercised it with shocking brutality. The Admiralty's trial records are filled with accounts of sailors being flogged or clubbed for minor mistakes: losing an oar, forgetting a chore, or unsteady helmsmanship. More than a few lost teeth, eyes, arms, and fingers during beatings. Others lost their lives. When sailor Richard Baker became bedridden from dysentery on a passage from St. Christopher to London, his captain forced him to man the helm for four hours, then had him whipped and lashed to the mizenmast; he died four days later. Anthony Comerford, accused of stealing a live bird on the merchantman *Ridge*, was tied to the rigging and whipped to death.

Then there were the truly sadistic captains. On a journey from Charleston to Bristol, Captain John Jeane took a dislike to his cabin boy, whom he had whipped "several times in a very cruel manner" and increased the pain by pouring pickle brine into the wounds. Jeane strung the child up to the mast for nine days and nights with his arms and legs fully extended. He then dragged him to the gangway and trod up and down over his body, and ordered the rest of the crew to do the same. The other sailors refused, so he kicked the boy repeatedly and "stamped upon his breast so violently that his excrement came involuntarily from him"; Jeane finally scooped up the excrement and "forced it several times down his throat." The youngster took eighteen days to die, despite being whipped every day. Just before expiring he asked for water. Jeane rushed to his cabin and returned with a glass of his own urine and forced the boy to drink it. When sailors prepared the body to be thrown overboard, they found "it was as many colours as the rainbow" with "flesh in many places like jelly" and a "head swollen as big as two men's of the largest size." Jeane was eventually executed for his actions. Other captains got away with murdering men they disliked by denying them rations or beating them until they were barely able to stand and forcing them to climb the mainmast, while some disposed of unwanted men by turning them over to the navy, which could be tantamount to a death sentence.

Legally speaking, merchant captains were only supposed to employ "moderate" discipline on their crews. Not so in the Royal Navy, where captains were under standing orders to mete out brutal punishments. Petty officers whacked slow-moving crewmen across the shoulders with rattan canes. A crewman caught stealing small objects was made to "run the gauntlet," forced to walk between parallel lines of crewmen as they lashed his bare back. Major thefts resulted in a full-on flogging with a knotted cat-o'-nine tails, as also befell "he that pisseth between decks." The commission of serious crimes resulted in potentially fatal floggings of seventy-two to three hundred lashings, or outright hanging.

It's a wonder any sailors survived. Mortality rates among the crews of vessels employed in the African slave trade were comparable to those of the slaves themselves. It was not unusual for 40 percent of the crew to perish during a single voyage, most from tropical diseases against which they had no resistance. About half the sailors pressed into the Royal Navy died at sea. Captains of both types of vessels had to carry extra men as insurance against the inevitable loss of hands.

Even sailors who managed to survive their terms of service rarely received the wages they were due. Merchant captains used a variety of ruses to shortchange their crews. Sailors often found their earnings had been docked for damages to the cargo, even when the damage was caused by storms or poor packaging by the merchants themselves. Edward Barlow, who was one of the few ordinary sailors of the age to record his experiences, reported that his captain typically deducted £3 from each man's salary, the equivalent of two months of an ordinary sailor's wage. Some captains would pay in colonial currencies, which were worth only 25 to 50 percent of pounds sterling. Men whose ships were wrecked or who were pressed into the navy at sea rarely received any of the wages they were owed, spelling disaster for the families they left behind.

The navy had a semiofficial policy summed up in the maxim "Keep the pay, keep the man." On arrival in port, sailors were often not paid until just before the vessel sailed again, and any who left before that moment automatically sacrificed all of their back wages. Payment was often made in the form of "tickets," official IOUs issued by the government that would be honored at some unspecified time in the future. Sailors in need of ready cash were forced to sell their tickets to loan sharks at a fraction of their face value. Finally there were those who served for years on end without being paid at all.

No wonder, then, that young sailors like Samuel Bellamy, Charles Vane, and Edward Thatch regarded Henry Avery as a hero.

❦

Woodes Rogers, the man who would confront the pirates, knew there was money to be made in merchant shipping, provided, that is, that one *owned* the vessels. Like Bellamy, Vane, and Thatch, Rogers went to sea at a young age. He did so from a different starting point, however; his father was a successful merchant captain and owned shares in numerous ships. Woodes was his heir.

The Rogers family was among the leading families of Poole, a modest seaport on the English Channel, sixty miles south of Bristol in County Dorset. Several of Woodes's ancestors had served as mayor. Woodes's father, Captain Woods Rogers, became successful in the Newfoundland fishing trade, and as a merchant captain he had been to Spain, the Red Sea, and the coast of Africa. He would regale listeners with tales of hippopotami attacking his ship's boats. Woodes, born in 1679, was the eldest of Captain Rogers's three children, a year older than Mary Rogers, and nine years older than John.

He spent his childhood in Poole, which sat at the head of a large, well-protected bay. The town was famous for two things: oysters and fish. Poole oysters were said to be the best and biggest in the region and the finest in all of England for their pearls; the townspeople pickled huge numbers of these oysters every year, shipping them by the barrel to London, Spain, Italy, and the West Indies. The fish—split, sun-dried salt cod—came from farther away; Woodes's father and other merchants led a small fleet of fishing vessels across the North Atlantic to Newfoundland every year. These fleets could be gone for nine months or more at a time, hauling hooked cod up from the deep and drying them on Newfoundland's cold, stark shores. While his father was away, young Woodes likely attended the local school, for his later writings reveal a man of considerable education. On Sundays, he and his siblings listened to the sermons of their Puritan pastor, Samuel Hardy, in St. James Church. As he grew older, Woodes likely accompanied his father on short trips up the channel, helping him unload salt cod on the London docks and load salt and other provisions for his father's next voyage.

Sometime between 1690 and 1696, Woodes's father moved the family to Bristol, probably to expand his trade with Newfoundland. His father had friends in Bristol, as well as a probable relative, an influential merchant named Francis Rogers, who would invest in many of their later adventures. By the time the poll-tax collector made his rounds in June 1696, the Rogers family was living in the seafarer's neighborhood of Redcliffe, across the river from central Bristol.

Bristol was a strange location for a port. It was located seven miles from the sea up a narrow, winding river—the Avon—beset by tides so powerful the watercraft of the day stood no chance of proceeding against them. The spring tides rose and fell by as much as forty-five feet, and at low tide much of the serpentine harbor turned to mudflats. Vessels under 150 tons had to wait until the tides were flowing in the direction of travel, and even then had difficulty rounding St. Vincent's Rock, halfway down the river. Larger ships were almost certain to wind up grounded on a mud bank if they tried to sail the gauntlet, and had to be towed to and from Bristol's docks by large rowboats. Many ship captains elected not to make the trip at all, anchoring instead at the mouth of the Avon, where they loaded and unloaded their cargoes onto a series of rafts and tenders that could more easily navigate the river's tides. Bristol stood on a bend in the Avon that was congested with vessels. Visiting Bristol in 1739, Alexander Pope said they extended along the riverfront as far as the eye could see, "their masts as thick as they can stand by one another, which is the oddest and most surprising sight imaginable."

The city itself was still medieval in character. Inside its walls, timber-framed, Tudor-style houses perched on streets so narrow people could shake hands across them from their upstairs windows. Principal roads were no more than twenty feet across and were the only ones paved. Other roads were surfaced in mud and garbage, in which pigs rooted about. Even the center of the city was separated by only a few hundred yards from the farms and fields that surrounded it. The focus of commerce was an artificial anchorage—the River Frome—where the ocean-going ships disgorged their cargoes onto The Quay in full view of counting houses. Only a few blocks' walk south of The Quay were the gates leading into a marsh. From there, among grazing cows, one could look across the river and see the bluffs of Redcliffe, where the Rogers family made its home.

Growing up in Redcliffe, Woodes Rogers may well have rubbed shoulders with Edward Thatch, or even been acquainted with him. They were almost the same age, engaged in the same profession, and probably lived within a few blocks of each other. Rogers the Pirate Hunter and Blackbeard the Pirate may have prayed together as teenagers, beneath John Cabot's great whalebone in the cool interior of Redcliffe's cathedral-sized parish church.

Henry Avery's exploits were well known within the Rogers household by way of one of Captain Rogers's closest friends, the mariner William Dampier, a former buccaneer who had circumnavigated the world. Dampier renewed their friendship in the mid-1690s, while preparing two books for publication. The first, *A New Voyage Round the World*, an account of his circumnavigation, would make him a national celebrity following its publication in the spring of 1697. The second, *Voyages and Descriptions* (1699), contained extracts of several letters from Captain Rogers, whom Dampier referred to as "my ingenious friend." The elder Rogers had shared his knowledge of the Red Sea and African coast; Dampier, in turn, had intimate, firsthand knowledge of Henry Avery and his fellow pirates, whose adventures were just then captivating the English public.

Dampier had spent months holed up with Avery and his men in the harbor of La Coruña in 1694. While Avery was serving as first mate of the *Charles II*, Dampier was second mate on one of her consorts, the *Dove*. Dampier may have provided Avery with sailing directions to Madagascar, the Red Sea, and the Indian Ocean, as he was one of the only people in La Coruña with firsthand knowledge of those waters. Dampier had shared Avery's frustrations with how the fleet's owners were treating them, but refused to join the mutiny itself. Back in England, he joined the crewmen's lawsuit against James Houblon and the other owners and later testified in court on behalf of one of Avery's six captured crewmen, Joseph Dawson, the only one to avoid the gallows. Years later, while serving as commander of the forty-gun frigate HMS *Roebuck*, he encountered several of Avery's fugitive crewmen during a port call in Brazil. Rather than placing them under arrest, he socialized with them and signed one on to serve aboard his ship.

As the heir of a growing shipping concern, the young Woodes Rogers likely looked on Avery as a villain, not a hero. But he also may have internalized some important lessons from Dampier's story of Avery's mutiny and its aftermath. In an era when most captains ruled their ships through terror, Rogers would eventually take a more lenient, fair-minded approach. Winning the crew's respect proved a much more reliable method of control than keeping them in a state of fear.

In November of 1697, Rogers started an apprenticeship to the mariner John Yeamans, who lived just a few doors away. At eighteen, he was a bit old to be starting a seven-year tutelage, particularly given his family's seafaring background. Rogers had probably already traveled to Newfoundland with his father, and learned the essential elements of seamanship, commerce, and the art of command. Bryan Little, the best of Rogers's twentieth-century biographers, suspected that young Rogers entered Yeamans's tutelage for political purposes. Such an apprenticeship gave the newcomers from Poole an entrée into the closed circles of Bristol's merchant elite and a way of establishing the contacts and relationships essential to successful maritime trade. It was also a means by which Rogers could become a freeman, or voting citizen, although, as it turned out, the Rogers family was able to secure this coveted privilege for their son by other means.

∽≈∾

While Rogers was sailing with Yeamans, his father was amassing a small fortune from Bristol's growing transatlantic trade. Like many English merchants, Captain Rogers spread his risk by purchasing shares in a few different vessels, and rarely owned any vessel outright. Should one ship sink, Rogers would share the losses with other merchants and still count on profits from other ships. He also reduced uncertainty—and increased his income—by captaining some of the vessels he invested in. Captain Rogers sailed regularly to Newfoundland, spending the entire spring and summer of 1700 aboard the sixty-ton *Elizabeth*, buying oil from whale hunters in Trinity Bay, Newfoundland, where the fish merchants of Poole had based their North American operations. He may have left servants behind to maintain the docks, storage houses, and fish-drying racks they had built there, helping to settle Newfoundland.

It was in Newfoundland that the elder Rogers probably solidified his most important alliance. In 1696 or 1697 he met the ambitious Royal Navy captain William Whetstone. Whetstone, who was also from Bristol, was a former merchant captain with close business ties to Woods Rogers. In the mid-1690s, Captain Rogers and other fish merchants in Poole and Bristol had become increasingly concerned about an aggressive expansion of French fishing outposts in Newfoundland and French attacks on their own fishing stations. The merchants cried for help. The Admiralty responded by ordering Whetstone to sail the fourth-rate man-of-war HMS *Dreadnought* to Newfoundland with the fishing fleet, and once there, to protect their facilities at Trinity Bay. During the long weeks at sea, Captain Rogers and Whetstone had plenty of time to cement their friendship.

By 1702, Captain Rogers was wealthy enough to buy property in Bristol's most fashionable new subdivision. The town fathers had decided to tear down the walls separating the town center from the marshes at the river's bend. Where the marshes had been, they built Queen's Square, Bristol's first preplanned neighborhood. It was to be a thoroughly modern place. Instead of cramped and dirty alleys, its residences would face a great square—the second largest in England—with lime trees and formal gardens, and accessed by wide, paved boulevards. Rather than frame, all the buildings would be constructed of red brick, with sash windows and stone ornamentation. In short, it would be as comfortable and uniform a district as any built in London after the Great Fire of 1666. Shortly before Christmas 1702, Captain Rogers purchased a double-sized lot at Number 31–32 Queen's Square, where workers began work on an elegant new mansion. The Whetstones, who lived on fashionable St. Michael's Hill, purchased the lot at Number 29, two doors down, along the square's southern promenade.

William Whetstone did not have the opportunity to oversee the construction of his home, as the navy had called him back to sea. Whetstone, now a commodore, spent most of 1701 trying to sail a squadron of warships to Jamaica, but his vessels were repeatedly battered by storms and never got further than Ireland. In February 1702, he set out again, and while he was crossing the Atlantic, England went to war against France and Spain. He would not return home for nearly two years.

War had been brewing for some time due to the political and genetic complications of royal inbreeding. For more than twenty years, the most powerful throne in Europe had been occupied by the drooling and disfigured King Charles II of Spain, who was not only mentally and physically handicapped, but impotent. Spanish authorities did their best to rehabilitate their king, but no matter how many exorcisms they subjected Charles to, he remained barely able to walk or speak. He was an overgrown child who spent his reign wallowing in his own filth, shooting firearms at animals, and gazing at his ancestors' decomposed corpses, which he had ordered his courtiers to exhume for that purpose. When he died in November 1700, the Spanish Habsburg line died with him. His out-of-town relatives immediately started squabbling over who would inherit the estate, which, in addition to Spain, included Italy, the Philippines, and most of the Western Hemisphere. Unfortunately for the people of Europe, these same out-of-town relatives were the French King Louis XIV and the Holy Roman Emperor, Leopold I. Pretty soon armies were clashing and, for various geopolitical and genealogical reasons of their own, most of Europe's rulers were drawn in. In the spring of 1702, England went to war, siding with the Dutch, Austrians, and Prussians against France and Spain. By doing so, they were setting the stage for the greatest outbreak of piracy the Atlantic would ever know.

The War of the Spanish Succession made life more hazardous for Captain Rogers, whose merchant ships were easy prey for French raiders. He and other merchants may have also lost ships in the horrific storm of 1703, the worst in English history, which destroyed thirteen warships and over 700 merchantmen. Despite their losses, his business must have remained profitable in the war's early years because construction continued on the Queen's Square mansion. It was completed in 1704 (the same year young Woodes finished his apprenticeship); three stories tall, with an attic for servants, the back windows looking out over the River Avon. Sometime during this period, Woodes took notice of the girl next door: eighteen-year-old Sarah Whetstone, the commodore's eldest daughter and heir.

In January of 1705, the Rogers family and the Whetstones traveled to London and witnessed three important ceremonies. On the eighteenth, William Whetstone was appointed rear admiral of the blue by the queen's husband, Prince George, the lord high admiral of the navy. The newly appointed admiral hosted the next event six days later: the wedding of Sarah and Woodes Rogers, held at the church of St. Mary Magdalene in central London. Not long thereafter, Admiral Whetstone was reappointed commander in chief of the West Indies and began preparing to sail again for Jamaica. The newlyweds probably stayed in London through February to see Admiral Whetstone off and to witness a third ceremony: his knighthood by Queen Anne.

At the end of February, Sir William sailed for Jamaica, whose citizens expected an enemy attack at any moment. The Rogers and Whetstone families headed back to Bristol, where their merchant empire awaited. Captain Rogers was in a good place: his son married to the daughter of a knight and an admiral, who was also a dear friend. Little did he know he would never see Sir William again.

A year later, Captain Rogers was dead. In the winter of 1705–1706, he died at sea and was committed to the ocean where he had spent so much of his life. His fortune, his company, and his home would pass to his widow and twenty-five-year-old son, by then a freeman of Bristol by dint of a noble marriage.

The young gentleman merchant of Bristol was tall and strongly built, with dark brown hair and a prominent nose and strong chin. Before war's end, intelligent and ambitious Woodes Rogers would be a household name from London to Edinburgh, from Boston to Barbados. But in France and Spain, they would know him by just one word: pirate.

~~~~ CHAPTER THREE ~~~~

WAR

1702–1712

THE ONSET of the War of Spanish Succession (1702–1712) made Sam Bellamy's life more uncertain than it already was. He was thirteen years old when the conflict began, a ship's boy on either a merchant vessel or Royal Navy warship. By the time it ended, he was a skilled mariner, able to guide a vessel a thousand miles, handle grappling hooks, firearms, and cannon.

In the early years of the conflict, the English and French navies clashed in two massive fleet engagements. These battles involved only the Royal Navy's largest vessels, the ships of the line: enormous, lumbering, wooden fortresses bristling with three stories of heavy cannon. These ships, the first-, second-, and third-rates, were too slow and cumbersome to use in more subtle operations such as convoying merchantmen, attacking enemy shipping, or patrolling the unmarked reefs and shoals of the Caribbean. They were built for one purpose: to join a line of battle in a massive set-piece engagement.

Had the teenage Bellamy been unlucky enough to be grabbed by a press gang, he may well have ended up aboard one of these ships of the line, for they soaked up much of the available manpower. Each of the navy's seven first-rate ships had a crew of 800 men, who were crammed into a 200-foot-long hull with a hundred heavy cannon, and months of supplies and food stores, including live cows, sheep, pigs, goats, and poultry. Bellamy would have awoken in his hammock to the rolling of drums, the cries calling all hands to stations as the massive ship maneuvered into the line of battle, two hundred yards ahead of one ship, two hundred yards behind another. The enemy ships lined up in similar fashion and, after hours or even days of maneuvers, the two lines passed each other, discharging broadsides. The ships would sometimes pass within a few feet, blasting thirty-two-pound cannonballs into each other's hulls. These balls punched straight through people, eviscerating or decapitating, and spraying the cramped gun decks with body parts and wooden splinters. Cannon trained on exposed decks were generally loaded with grapeshot or with a pair of cannonballs chained together, either of which could reduce a crowd of men into a splay of mangled flesh. From the rigging, sharpshooters picked off enemy officers or, if the ships came together, dropped primitive grenades on their opponent's deck. Above and below, every surface was soon covered with blood and body parts, which oozed out of the scuppers and drains when the ship heeled in the wind. "I fancied myself in the infernal regions," a veteran of such a battle recalled, "where every man appeared a devil."

These early engagements took the lives of thousands of men but they were hardly conclusive. Seven English and four French ships of the line fought a six-day battle off Colombia in August 1702, for example, with neither side losing a single ship. Two years later, fifty-three English and Dutch ships of the line squared off with some fifty French vessels off Málaga, Spain, in the largest naval engagement of the war; the day-long bout of fleet-scale carnage ending in a draw.

By happenstance, the Royal Navy wiped out its French and Spanish rivals early in the war. In October 1702, an English battle fleet trapped twelve French ships of the line and most of the Spanish navy in a fjordlike inlet on Spain's northern coast, destroying or capturing all of them. Five years later, an Anglo-Dutch force captured the French port of Toulon and so many men-of-war that the French were unable to engage in further fleet actions. Thereafter on many English ships of the line, crewmen had substantially reduced odds of dying in battle, though disease, accident, and abuse still carried off nearly half the men who enlisted.

Early Eighteenth-Century Merchant Vessels

SPANISH TREASURE GALLEON
2,000 tons | 170 feet | 100 guns

SHIP (frigate-rigged)
250 tons | 95 feet | 22 guns

SHIP (galley-rigged)
250 tons | 98 feet | 22 guns

BRIGANTINE
100 tons | 65 feet | 8 guns

LARGE SLOOP
100 tons | 65 feet | 8 guns

SNOW
60 tons | 55 feet | 8 guns

SCHOONER
60 tons | 55 feet

SMALL SLOOP
20 tons | 40 feet

PERIAGUA (Sailing Canoe)
30 feet

Were Bellamy serving in the merchant marine rather than the navy, these early English victories would have made his life a good deal *more* hazardous. After these defeats, the French and Spanish decided to focus their war at sea not on the English navy, but on its merchant vessels, hoping to cut off the island kingdom from its sources of wealth and supplies. The French navy assembled a few squadrons of swift warships for the purpose. However, King Louis XIV decided it would be cheaper to outsource most of the work to the private sector, offering generous subsidies to encourage subjects to build their own privateers. After the Battle of Málaga, the French sent out huge numbers of heavily manned privateers, which typically carried anywhere from ten to forty guns. Over 100 privateers operated out of the French channel port of Dunkirk alone. Together with their counterparts in dozens of other French ports from Calais to Martinique, French privateers took 500 English and Dutch vessels every year; dozens more fell victim to Spanish privateers operating out of Cuba and other parts of the Spanish West Indies. English merchant vessels couldn't leave Dover and other English ports for fear of being captured.

France and Spain were soon to get a taste of their own medicine, and Thatch and Rogers would be among those administering it.

✦❦✦

At some point before or during the War of Spanish Succession, Edward Thatch made his way to the Americas in search of better fortunes, and on some unidentified vessel he sailed into the capacious harbor of Port Royal, Jamaica.

Jamaica had been an English colony for half a century. Nonetheless, it was about as un-English a place as one could find. The sun was overpowering. Instead of fog and chill, the sea carried in hot, heavy air, smothering its wool-wearing English residents. Thatch found nothing resembling the gently rolling hills of the Avon valley. The ridges of volcanic mountains sliced through their jungled skin, belching steam and sulfur. En route from Europe, the sea had lost its pigment, becoming so

Royal Navy Warships

SHIP-OF-THE-LINE (First Rate)
1,800 tons | 172 feet | 100 guns

SHIP-OF-THE-LINE (Third Rate)
1,220 tons | 150 feet | 70 guns

FRIGATE (Fifth Rate)
500 tons | 118 feet | 40 guns

FRIGATE (Sixth Rate)
250 tons | 94 feet | 24 guns

SLOOP-OF-WAR
100 tons | 65 feet | 10 guns

clear one could see her sandy, coral-studded footings and colorful inhabitants, even at a depth of a hundred feet or more. There were fish
that could fly and birds that could speak. Legions of gigantic turtles
crawled from the sea by the thousands, laying piles of eggs, each as big
as a grown pheasant. In the fall, storms lashed the island, some so powerful they would flatten towns and leave the beaches littered with broken ships. Sometimes the island itself awoke in an earthquake, shaking
off towns, plantations, and people like so many bedbugs. Moreover, Jamaica and her fellow islands welcomed their new residents with invis-
ible contagions: malaria and yellow fever, dysentery, and plague.

To enter the colony's main harbor, Thatch's vessel sailed around a long sandy spit protecting the anchorage's southern approaches. At its tip stood Port Royal, once the largest and wealthiest English settlement in the Americas, whose merchants achieved the "height of splendor" through a brisk trade in sugar and slaves. When Thatch arrived, much of Port Royal was underwater, the result of a devastating earthquake in 1692 that swallowed part of the town and flattened most of the rest, killing at least 2,000 of its 7,000 residents. In 1703, a fire burned what was left to the ground, sparing only the stone forts guarding the harbor entrance and one house, which lay stranded on what was now an island, part of the sand spit having collapsed during the earthquake. A city once known for its splendor and decadence, Port Royal was, by Thatch's time, little more than a slum with "low, little, and irregular" houses and streets that visitors compared unfavorably with those of London's poorest neighborhoods. To make matters worse, Jamaican authorities forced local slaves to carry their chamber pots to a central waste heap located upwind from Port Royal, creating a terrible stench that overpowered residents when the sea breezes kicked up in the afternoon.

Circling Port Royal and its foul-smelling wind, incoming ships crossed Jamaica's busy harbor, passing coastal trading sloops, ocean-going slave ships and naval frigates. Most ships anchored near the north shore, where the survivors of the 1703 fire had founded the new settlement of Kingston at the foot of the Blue Mountains. To the east, a dirt road wound past slaves' hovels and fields of sugarcane in the direction of the settlement of St. Jago de la Vega or Spanish Town, five miles away, which Queen Anne had recently designated as the colony's new capital.

Jamaica had a dubious reputation. After a visit in 1697, the London writer Edward Ward had nothing nice to say about it. "The receptacle of vagabounds, the sanctuary of bankrupts, and a [toilet] stool for the purges of our prisons," he declared. Jamaica was "as sickly as a hospital, as dangerous as the plague, as hot as hell, and as wicked as the Devil." It was "the Dunghill of the Universe" the "shameless Pile of Rubbish . . . neglected by [God] when he formed the world into its admirable order."

Its people, he harangued, "regard nothing but money, and value not how they get it, there being no other felicity to be enjoyed, but purely riches."

Beyond the docks of Kingston and Port Royal, the island was carved up into huge cattle ranches and sugar plantations, many of them the property of absentee owners who lived in the comparative safety and comfort of England on the profits sent home to them. For decades, English authorities had used the island's plantations as a dumping ground for people they found undesirable: Puritans and other religious deviants, Scottish and Irish nationalists, followers of failed rebellions against the crown, landless peasants, beggars, and large numbers of common criminals all found themselves in bondage to the sugar and cotton planters. Hoards of these indentured servants died, overwhelmed by tropical diseases as they worked the planters' fields under the unrelenting sun; others simply ran off and joined the privateers who used Port Royal as a base to attack Spanish shipping during the wars of the 1660s and 1670s.

In the early 1700s, when Thatch arrived, the plantation owners had given up on indentured servants altogether, replacing them with armies of enslaved Africans brought to the island. Jamaica had already become more than just a society that allowed slavery, it was the slave society perfected. Every year, dozens of ships arrived from West Africa, disgorging thousands of them. Despite the fact that the Africans' mortality rate far exceeded their birth rate, the island's slave population had doubled since 1689, to 55,000, and by the early 1700s, it had exceeded the English population by a ratio of eight to one. Outside of Kingston and Port Royal, Jamaica was a land where a tiny cadre of white planters, supervisors, and servants lived in constant fear of an uprising by the sea of Africans manning their fields, pastures, and sugar works. To maintain order, the English passed draconian slave laws under which masters could discipline their black captives in pretty much any way they wished, though murdering one without cause carried a fine of £25. Slaves could be punished by castration, having their limbs cut off, or being burned alive, punishments that were meted out without a court trial. Any three landowners could join with two justices of the peace to pass most any sentence they pleased. A resident caught hiding a runaway slave suspected of having committed a crime faced a fine of £100, more than most people earned in four years. Even so, dozens of blacks did escape each year. They established rogue settlements in the mountains, where they grew crops, raised families, practiced their religions, and trained bands of swift and effective jungle warriors to raid the plantations, free slaves, and kill Englishmen. In their capital, Nanny Town, the runaways were said to be led by an ancient and powerful witch, Granny Nanny, who protected her warriors with magical spells.

With the outbreak of war in 1702, Jamaica's plantation owners had to worry about not just a slave rebellion, but an enemy invasion as well. Jamaica was an island in a Spanish sea, located near Spanish Cuba, hundreds of miles from any other English possession. In 1703, French and Spanish forces sacked and destroyed Nassau, Jamaica's nearest English neighbor, obliterating the government and forcing the settlers into the woods. There was good reason to fear Jamaica would be next.

From the Spanish point of view, the English should never have settled in the New World in the first place. Christopher Columbus had "discovered" the Americas for Spain in 1492, although he never set foot on either the North or South American mainland. The year after Columbus's discovery, Pope Alexander VI, acting on God's behalf, had given the entire Western Hemisphere to Spain, even though virtually none of it had been discovered yet. From Newfoundland to the tip of South America, the pope gave it all to Spain, save for the eastern part of what is now Brazil, which he bequeathed to the king of Portugal. Unfortunately, Pope Alexander had granted the king of Spain far more territory than he could possibly manage: sixteen million square miles, an area eighty times the size of Spain itself—two continents already populated by millions of people, some organized into powerful empires. Conquering and colonizing South and Central America during the sixteenth and seventeenth centuries stretched Spanish resources to the limit, and the kings of Spain were forced to leave the cold, gold-less forests of the northeastern Americas to the colonists of New England, New Holland, and New France. Everything south of Virginia, however, the Spanish regarded as an integral part of their empire, including Spanish Florida, the Bahamas, and the vast archipelago of the West Indies.

By the early 1600s, it was clear that even this parcel was too big a place for the Spanish to colonize and defend, and other European powers wormed into the Caribbean basin. With an overall population of only seven million, Spain could colonize only the choicest parts of the Caribbean—the mainland coasts of South America (the so-called Spanish Main) and the big islands of Cuba, Puerto Rico, Jamaica, and Hispaniola. They did their best to patrol the scraps—thousands of smaller, less valuable islands stretching from the Bahama Banks off Florida to Trinidad on the South American coast—but their rivals still managed to occupy a few, building forts to defend their infant colonies. The French grabbed tiny Martinique, St. Lucia, and Guadeloupe, the Dutch took Curaçao and Bonaire, just off the Spanish Main. The English concentrated on the tiny islands at the far eastern end of the West Indies, settling St. Christopher in 1624, Nevis in 1628, Barbados in 1627, Antigua and Montserrat in the early 1630s, and some of the islets of the Bahamas in the 1640s. In 1655, an English expeditionary force attacked and conquered Jamaica, which had a landmass larger than all of these other islands combined (4,400 square miles, a bit smaller than Connecticut or Northern Ireland). Straddling the Windward Passage—one of the primary trade routes between Europe and the Spanish Main— English Jamaica was a threat to Spain's commerce and the Spanish had wanted to recover the place ever since.

During the War of Spanish Succession, Jamaica's planters had reason to worry about a Spanish or French invasion. With most of its warships tied up protecting the English Channel or convoying merchantmen, England's Royal Navy could spare few resources to defend its scattered Caribbean colonies. For most of the war, the Leeward Islands colony (St. Christopher, Nevis, Antigua, and Montserrat) was protected by a single fifth-rate frigate and for long periods had no naval protection at all. Barbados, located dangerously close to the French colonies of Martinique and Guadeloupe, had only a fourth- and fifth-rate in the best of times. The Bahamian settlements had no protection at all and were repeatedly burned by French and Spanish invaders. Even Jamaica, the navy's regional headquarters, generally had only a half dozen warships on station, and rarely were these larger than a fourth-rate.

Nor could the frigates stationed at the various colonies help one another effectively. Simply getting from one place to another could be next to impossible. The square-rigged warships of the day could not sail into the wind any closer than sixty-eight degrees, and with the wind and waves pushing the ships away from their destination, might make little or no progress at all. Since the trade winds blew from the east, it was very easy for ships to sail from, say, Barbados or the Leeward Islands to Jamaica with the wind at their backs—which was the direction all incoming trips from Europe sailed; sailing from Jamaica toward Barbados, on the other hand, was extremely difficult, which is why ships bound for Europe sailed up the Atlantic seaboard in the Gulf Stream instead, eventually catching prevailing westerlies back across the North Atlantic. Were Barbados to come under attack, there was little hope of anyone in Jamaica helping them. Smaller, more nimble sloops and schooners could sail closer into the wind, and carry messages back and forth between islands, but even that could take weeks, so each colony's naval detachment was usually on its own.

The warships were, in any case, rarely in any condition to sail, let alone engage an enemy. The tropical climate rotted the sails and rigging and corroded fittings and anchors, none of which could be easily replaced in the West Indies. If a mainmast were lost in a lightning storm or battle, the ship would have to sail all the way to New England for a replacement, there being no suitable trees left in the islands. Worse yet, the sea itself was home to shipworm, a ravenous wood-eating parasite that would bore through the warships' oaken hulls, causing them to leak. The only effective means of fighting the parasite was to careen the ship every three months: emptying the entire vessel and, in shallow water, turning it first on one side, then the other, scraping and cleaning all the parasites and bottom growth that had accumulated there. Smaller vessels could do this on a gradually sloping beach, but the larger ones, like navy frigates, required some sort of base against which to rest the ship—a specially constructed wharf or the hulk of an old ship, for instance—which were generally unavailable in the islands. As a result, when the Jamaican squadron attempted to sail out of Port Royal in 1704 to beat off a rumored French attack, the twenty-gun sixth-rate HMS *Seahorse* was so leaky she had to immediately return to harbor, the fifth-rate *Experiment* was found unseaworthy, and two Jamaican support ships were judged too structurally unsound to go into combat. In 1711, the governor of the Leeward Islands reported that the sole station ship there was "so foul, her sails and riggings much worn, in short everything [so] out of order for want of stores that should she go to Leeward" to protect a convoy of outgoing merchantmen "it would be impossible for her to turn to the windward again [and] she would be obliged to go either for Jamaica or New England."

The crews were often in worse shape than the ships. Men already suffering from a poor diet, harsh discipline, exposure, and disease had difficulty acclimatizing themselves to the heat and humidity of the Caribbean. It didn't help that they wore woolen clothes and subsisted on salted meats, heavy biscuits, and large quantities of beer and rum. Once exposed to the diseases of the tropics—malaria and yellow fever, smallpox and leprosy—the sailors began dropping like flies. Commodore William Kerr, the commander at Jamaica in 1706, had lost so many men to disease he was unable to leave Port Royal's harbor to carry out a planned attack on the annual Spanish treasure fleet. In the months that followed, the English fleet ran out of food and was unable to procure sufficient provisions from the Jamaicans, who, like other

English colonists, refused to grow or eat tropical produce, relying instead on imported flour and salt meats from England or North America. By the time Kerr's official supply arrived in July 1707, most of his men were dead, and he had to take large numbers of men from the newly arrived ships just to make it home.

Even when operative, the warships couldn't contend with the nimble French privateers swarming across the Caribbean from Martinique and Guadalupe. Privateers used swift sloops and two-masted brigantines that could sail much closer into the wind than a square-rigger. Captain Charles Constable, stationed at Barbados in 1711, warned its governor that the French privateers sailed "so very well" that it was usually impossible for any man-of-war to catch them. "Upon seeing any Man of War . . . they only stretch farther to windward and continue cruising for our merchant vessels and often do take them." The governor, he suggested, needed to get himself "an extraordinary sailing sloop" that could challenge the privateers.

The English needed to fight fire with fire, and the merchants of Jamaica were eager to do just that.

❧❦❧

Privateering had a long history in Port Royal. In the 1660s and 1670s, Henry Morgan and other buccaneers raided Spanish shipping under commissions from the governor of Jamaica. The privateers captured hundreds of Spanish ships, bringing them into Port Royal to be condemned by the Vice-Admiralty Court as legal prizes of war. The buccaneers surrendered 10 percent of the prize's value to the Admiralty, which was a small impediment to amassing incredible wealth. Individual buccaneers were said to have spent 2,000 to 3,000 pieces of eight (£500 to £750) in a single binge. While the buccaneers had faded away in the intervening decades, the Jamaican merchants were well aware of just how profitable privateering could be. They began fitting out privateering vessels as soon as they knew their nation was at war. In the summer of 1702, nine such vessels sailed from Jamaica for the Spanish Main with more than 500 men aboard. They returned to Jamaica the following spring, their ships laden with slaves, silver, gold dust, and other precious goods, having burnt and plundered several Spanish settlements in Panama and Trinidad. In 1704, a Jamaican privateer defeated a twenty-four-gun French ship and, in conjunction with Royal Navy frigates, began clearing the shipping lanes of enemy privateers.

As the war progressed, the Jamaican privateer fleet grew to thirty vessels, carrying between seventy and 150 men each, the equivalent of three-fourths of the island's white male population. "The people of this island were intent on nothing so much as encouraging the Privateers, and though they sometimes suffered considerable losses . . . the many rich prizes that were daily brought in made a sufficient return," a resident recalled a quarter century later.

Edward Thatch served aboard one of these privateering vessels, which cruised the waters around nearby Cuba and Hispaniola,* attacking poorly defended Spanish merchantmen. Occasionally they cruised in Leeward Islands, the Straits of Florida, or off Vera Cruz and other parts of the Spanish Main. In his years of service aboard the privateers, Thatch never made captain, though he probably rose to a skilled position such as mate (the captain's chief lieutenant), quartermaster (in charge of ship's operations), boatswain (commanding landing parties), or gunner. He certainly learned his way around the Caribbean: how to sail the treacherous, unmarked passages between islands, where to find hidden anchorages from which one could hunt for food, water, a good beach to careen a sloop's hull, and, most important, where to find and catch richly laden prizes.

～≈✤≈～

Meanwhile, on the other side of the Atlantic, Woodes Rogers had also turned to privateering. The merchants of Bristol were losing large num-

---

* An island now split between the nations of Haiti and the Dominican Republic.

bers of vessels to French privateers; many wanted both revenge and a chance to recover some of their losses. Dozens applied for commissions to fit out privateering vessels or, at the very least, to let them keep any prizes their armed merchantmen happened to take in their travels. The applications found a receptive audience in London. Queen Anne was sufficiently concerned about the loss of shipping to issue a 1708 decree revoking the Admiralty's share of the prize money; henceforth, the privateers' owners and crew could divide all the spoils among themselves. Privateering commissions—or letters of marque—were granted to 127 Bristol vessels during the war, including at least four partially owned by Rogers.

Rogers was an active slave trader throughout his life, and his earliest privateering venture was no exception. He received his first commission for the 130-ton *Whetstone Galley*, which he co-owned with three Bristol merchants. While she carried sixteen cannon, the vessel Rogers named for his father-in-law was not a private warship per se, but rather an armed slave ship. Bristol customs records show the *Whetstone Galley* leaving that city on February 3, 1708, bound for the Slave Coast of Africa, with £1,000 worth of trade goods. On arrival in Guinea, Captain Thomas Robbins was to use the goods to buy 270 slaves and then carry them to Jamaica to be sold. He never made it to Africa. On the way out of England, the *Whetstone Galley* was captured by French privateers.

In March 1707, Rogers received letters of marque for the *Eugene Prize*, an outright privateer that he co-owned with another merchant. This 100-ton vessel carried eight guns and twenty well-armed men, and apparently cruised close to home; Rogers had provided only one ball for each of the *Eugene Prize*'s cannon. The next privateers he would invest in would cruise farther afield.

Rogers spent the early years of the war in Bristol, starting a family and managing his growing business. At the end of 1707, he received a visitor, one of his father's old friends, the navigator William Dampier. Dampier had left Bristol four and a half years earlier, at the start of the war, on a most daring and unusual privateering mission to the Pacific

Ocean. He had come to Bristol in the hopes of convincing merchants to bankroll another such mission. The fifty-one-year-old sea captain would have been upset to learn of the elder Woods Rogers's death, but found an even more capable backer in his son.

For most English merchants, the Pacific Ocean was still terra incognita. Spain monopolized all European trade on this vast ocean, having colonized the Philippines, Guam, and the entire Pacific coast of the Americas, from the glaciated fjords of southern Chile to the arid missionary pueblos of Nuestro Señora de Loreto on the Baja peninsula. The Spanish considered their Pacific holdings to be safe from attack, particularly from the east, where ships could access it only by braving the horrific conditions in the Drake Passage at the southern tip of South America, home to the world's most frequent and ferocious storms. Englishmen agreed, calling the Pacific "the Spanish Lake."

Dampier knew this was not entirely true. He had sailed around the world three times, twice via the Drake Passage, plundering towns in Panama and Peru, and, as captain of HMS *Roebuck*, exploring Australia and New Guinea. Great riches, Dampier knew, awaited those who found a way into the Spanish Lake.

The Spanish Empire was fueled by the gold and silver mines of Mexico and Peru, where armies of enslaved Indians were worked to death. The Peruvian "silver mountain" at Potosi alone produced two million pesos' (£500,000) worth of that precious metal each year, and the other gold and silver mines of Mexico and Peru added another 8.7 million (£2,175,000). There was little to buy in the new world, so all those riches had to be shipped to Spain. Thus the need for the great treasure fleets.

By the time of the War of Spanish Succession, Spain had three treasure fleets in all. The first two sailed across the Atlantic every year or so from Cádiz, Spain, their holds filled with the soldiers, weapons, wines, mining equipment, and manufactured goods needed in their American colonies. One, the Tierra Firma (or mainland) fleet, sailed to Cartagena, in what is now Colombia, where it exchanged its cargo for millions of pesos' worth of Potosi silver. The other, the New Spain fleet, made for Veracruz, Mexico, where it loaded gold and silver from the mines of Mexico and the cargoes brought in from the third fleet. This latter fleet sailed across the Pacific from Acapulco, on Mexico's Pacific coast, to Manila in the Philippines, 9,000 miles away, carrying silver and gold. There, the captains of these "Manila galleons"—normally only one or two—bought huge quantities of silks, porcelain, and other high-end products from Asian merchants. The galleons then turned around, carrying the luxuries back across the Pacific to Acapulco. These goods were transported across Mexico to Veracruz in armed mule trains and loaded aboard the galleons of the New Spain fleet, which joined the Tierra Firma fleet in Havana before sailing through the Straits of Florida and back to Cádiz.

Filled with the treasures of Mexico, Peru, and the Orient, the Atlantic treasure fleets had always offered tempting targets for English buccaneers, privateers, and Royal Navy warships. The Manila galleons were another story. They were built to be impregnable: floating fortresses of 500 to 2,000 tons, bearing hundreds of men and tiers of heavy cannon. Only one Englishman had ever captured one—the buccaneer Thomas Cavendish in 1587—and that had been a relatively small 700-tonner. Dampier himself had attacked a Manila galleon during his last cruise, but, in the words of one of his crewmen, "They were too hard for us." His ship's five-pound cannonballs hardly made a dent in the treasure galleon's tropical hardwood hull, while the Spaniards' twenty-four-pounders smashed into his ship's worm-infested hull. Nonetheless, in the words of another contemporary, Dampier "never gave over the project" and was eager to win young Rogers's support for his plan.

Dampier was more desperate to leave England than Rogers could possibly have known. Despite his fame, his career was in shambles. His command of HMS *Roebuck* had been a disaster: The 290-ton frigate sank on the way back to England, and when he and his marooned crew

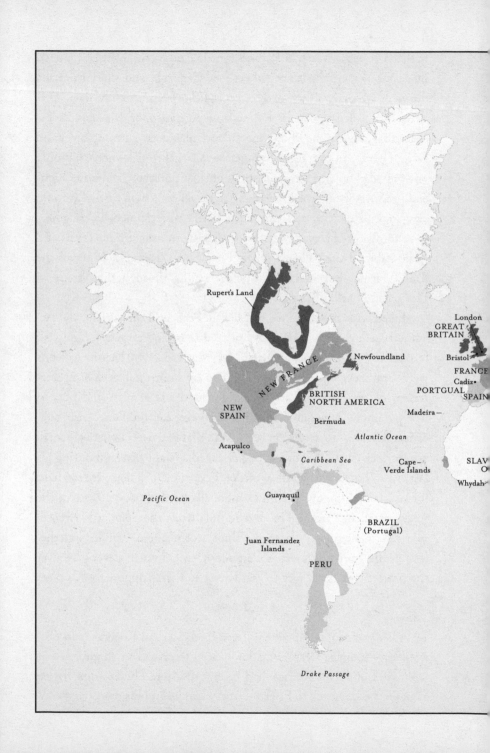

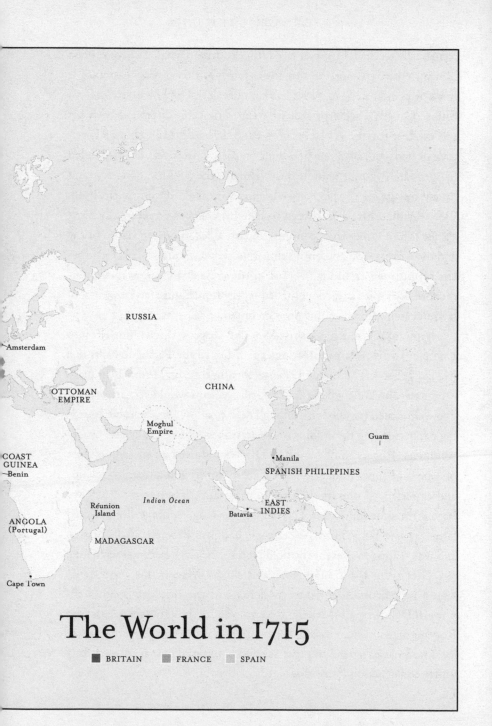

RUSSIA

Amsterdam

OTTOMAN
EMPIRE

CHINA

Moghul
Empire

Guam

COAST
GUINEA
Benin

•Manila

SPANISH PHILIPPINES

Indian Ocean

EAST
INDIES

Réunion
Island

Batavia

ANGOLA
(Portugal)

MADAGASCAR

Cape Town

The World in 1715

■ BRITAIN   ■ FRANCE   ■ SPAIN

were finally rescued, Dampier faced three courts-martial. The court fined him his entire pay for the three-year journey, ruling that "Dampier is not a fit person to be employed as commander of any of Her Majesty's Ships." On his Pacific privateering expedition, he quarreled with his officers, lost the respect of his crews and, in battle, hid behind a barricade of beds and blankets he'd built on the quarterdeck. He had failed to adequately clean the hulls of his ships—the 200-ton *St. George* and ninety-ton galley *Cinque Ports*—leaving worms to devour them both. One crewman had even chosen to take his chances on an uninhabited Pacific island rather than continue aboard a decomposing vessel. In the end the worms won and both ships went down, though not before a series of mutinies resulting in most of the crew abandoning their commodore. Dampier somehow made his way home and faced a variety of lawsuits stemming from his poor command performance.

Ignorant of much of this, Woodes Rogers threw himself into Dampier's scheme, a privateering expedition to the Pacific to capture a Manila galleon. The main challenge was fundraising. From Dampier's experience, he knew taking on a Manila galleon would require at least two well-armed frigates with enough men to allow for a sizeable boarding party. Sending these ships to the Pacific would be expensive, far beyond what Rogers could bankroll. They would need an enormous store of food and supplies to sail that far from home, and a team of reliable and experienced officers who could maintain discipline on a journey lasting three or four years. Fortunately for Rogers, his well-connected father-in-law, Sir William Whetstone, had just arrived back in Bristol, and was willing to present the bold plan to the city's leading merchants.

They went for it, hook, line, and sinker. Mayors, former mayors, would-be mayors, sheriffs, town clerks and the head of Bristol's all-powerful Society of Merchant Venturers all bought shares, as did Rogers's friend and possible relative, Francis Rogers. Together these local luminaries agreed to purchase and equip two new frigates already under construction in the dockyards of Bristol.

The *Duke* was the larger of the two, a 350-ton ship with thirty-six guns, the *Dutchess* slightly smaller at 260 tons and twenty-six guns. Rogers invested in the ships and was appointed as both commodore of the expedition and captain of the *Duke*. Another investor, noble-born merchant Stephen Courtney, commanded the *Dutchess*. Dampier was hired as the expedition's indispensable Pacific Ocean pilot. Other officers included Rogers's younger brother, John, and the *Dutchess*'s executive officer Edward Cooke, a Bristol merchant captain who had been attacked twice by French ships in the preceding year. One of the largest investors, Dr. Thomas Dover, also came along as the expedition's president, a position that allowed him considerable say over strategic decisions, such as where to sail and what to attack. An Oxford-educated physician, Dover had earned the nickname Dr. Quicksilver for his propensity to administer mercury to his patients to treat a wide range of illnesses. The owners made him chief medical officer and also captain of the marines, with ultimate authority over military operations ashore, which was odd, given that he had neither military experience nor, as subsequent events would show, a knack for leadership.

Rogers's expedition would make him famous among his contemporaries, but it has also provided historians with the only detailed account of life aboard an early-eighteenth-century privateering vessel. Both Rogers and Cooke kept detailed, daily diaries of their experiences on the three-year journey and published them as competing books shortly after their return. Together with other letters and documents, they not only afford a comprehensive picture of some of Rogers's formative command challenges, but also a sense of those faced by Thatch, Vane, and other privateersmen during the War of Spanish Succession.

The expedition departed on August 1, 1708, the ships flying the new Union Jack ensign of Great Britain, a nation that had been created in 1707 with the union of England and Scotland. Rogers was forced to spend a month in Ireland, retrofitting the ships, stocking supplies, and recruiting crewmen. They left Ireland with a complement of 333, a third of whom were Irish, Danish, Dutch, or other foreigners. The expedition council met soon thereafter to discuss an important problem: a shortage of alcohol and cold-weather clothing for the frigid journey through the Drake Passage. Rogers argued that alcohol was the more important of the two, as "good liquor to sailors is preferable to clothing," so the council resolved to stop at Madeira to stock up on the island's namesake wine.

Along the way, a large number of the *Duke*'s crew mutinied after Rogers refused to take a neutral Swedish ship as a prize, a decision that, in their view, deprived them of plunder. The *Duke*'s officers broke out muskets and cutlasses and kept control of the quarterdeck throughout the night and, in the morning, managed to seize the ringleaders. Many captains would have executed the mutineers, but Rogers knew terror was not always the best way to win the respect and loyalty of a crew. He had the leading rebels placed into irons and their top instigators "soundly whipped" and sent back to England on a passing ship. The others he let off with light punishments—fines or reduced rations— and returned to duty. He even took the trouble to address the entire crew, explaining why it would be unwise to seize a neutral ship, which would probably result in legal proceedings against them. These actions broke the mutineers' resolve, though the atmosphere on the *Duke* remained tense for many days. Had the ship not had double the ordinary number of officers, Rogers noted in his diary, the mutiny might have succeeded.

They spent December 1708 sailing down the Atlantic coast of South America, the weather turning colder as they moved south. Rogers set six tailors to work making the crew cold-weather clothing from blankets, trade cloth, and the officers' hand-me-downs. The winds strengthened as they passed into the latitudes known as the Roaring Forties, and great waves swamped the decks of the smaller *Dutchess*. At times the ships were surrounded by breaching whales or great troops of exuberant dolphins, which, Rogers wrote, "often leaped a good height out of the water, turning their white bellies uppermost." There were large numbers of seals, the occasional penguin, and soaring albatross. By January 5, 1709, the ships had entered the Southern Ocean, and the seas grew to thirty feet or more, lifting the ships so quickly that the men could feel the blood swelling their feet, and then dropping them into the trough so fast they felt almost weightless. As the wind speeds increased, the captains sent men up into the rigging to lower the upper sails and reef the lower ones to prevent them from being torn to shreds. Suddenly there was a terrible mishap aboard the *Dutchess*. As the men lowered the main yard—the crosswise timber suspending the main sail—one side slipped, dropping part of the big sail into the water. At the speed the *Dutchess* was moving, the sail acted like a gigantic anchor, pulling the port side down so far that the frigid gray ocean began pouring onto the main deck. Captain Courtney ordered the other sails loosened. The *Dutchess* swung into the wind, sails flapping like flags, her bow facing into the towering seas. "We expected the ship would sink every moment," Edward Cooke recounted, "floundered with the weight of the water that was in her." The crew secured the main sail; Courtney swung her around, stern to the screaming wind. The vessel began drifting rapidly to the south, toward the still undiscovered continent of Antarctica. Rogers, watching these events from the *Duke*, became increasingly worried as he followed the *Dutchess* further and further toward the bergs and pack ice Dampier had warned lay in these southern waters.

At nine P.M.—the spring sun still high above the horizon—the *Dutchess's* exhausted officers went down to the great cabin for dinner. Just before their food was served, a massive wave crashed into her stern, smashing through the windows and carrying everything it picked up, human and otherwise, forward through the ship. Edward Cooke was certain all of them would have drowned in the submerged cabin had its interior wall not been torn down by the force of the wave. An officer's sword was found driven straight through the hammock belonging to Cooke's servant who, fortunately, was not in it at the time. Amazingly, only two men were injured, but the entire middle of the ship was filled with water, soaking every bit of clothing, bedding, and cargo in ice-cold seawater.

Somehow the *Dutchess* stayed afloat through the night, during which time the storm abated. In the morning, Rogers and Dampier rowed over from the *Duke* and found the crew "in a very orderly pickle," busying themselves with pumping water from the hold and lowering some of the heavy cannon into storage to make the ship less top-heavy. Her masts and rigging were covered in wet clothes, bedding, and hammocks hung out to dry in the icy wind. The captains agreed that the two ships had been pushed to nearly sixty-two degrees south (almost to Antarctica), slightly shy of the farthest point south any person had yet been known to travel. By the end of the day, they had swung around to the northwest and beat their way toward the Pacific in the mouth of yet another Drake Passage gale.

As they crawled out of the Antarctic, toward the warmth of the southern spring, the crew began to fall sick. Some suffered from exposure after spending days in soaked or frozen clothing; others were stricken with scurvy, the disease mariners feared more than any other. An affliction caused by a lack of vitamin C, scurvy is thought to have carried off more mariners in the age of sail than all other causes combined. Without vitamin C, the sailors' bodies could no longer maintain connective tissues, causing gums to turn black and spongy, teeth to fall out, and bruises to form beneath scaly skin. Toward the end, as the sailors withered and wheezed in their hammocks, bones broken long before became unhealed and old scars opened into wounds again. Most mariners believed it was caused by exposure to cold and damp clothing, but Rogers and Dover were aware it had more to do with the lack of fresh fruit and vegetables on long ocean passages. At a time when the Royal Navy had no treatment for the disease, Rogers stocked his ships with limes, which were rich in vitamin C. This supply was now exhausted, so the ships were in a race against time to get fresh produce. The first man, John Veal of the *Duke*, died on January 7 and was buried at sea in the Drake Passage.

From his prior travels, Dampier knew of a sanctuary where they would find ample provisions without alerting the Spaniards of Chile to their presence: the uninhabited island of Juan Fernández,* 400 miles off the coast. By the time the jagged peaks of Juan Fernández were sighted on January 31, more than thirty men were sick and seven men had perished. There, to their surprise, they saw a fire on the shore, an indication that a Spanish vessel was visiting the remote island.

The next morning the *Duke* and *Dutchess* sailed into the harbor entrance, their guns ready for action. It was deserted. Rogers anchored the ships a mile from shore, while Dr. Dover, eager to secure provisions, led a landing party ashore in one of the ship's boats. As they approached the beach, they were shocked to see a solitary man, clad in goatskin, waving a white cloth and yelling exuberantly to them in English. Alexander Selkirk, the castaway whose story would inspire Daniel Defoe to write *Robinson Crusoe*, was about to be rescued.

～～～

Selkirk had been stranded on Juan Fernández Island for four years and four months, indeed ever since William Dampier's ill-fated privateering mission had passed through these parts in the latter part of 1704. Selkirk, a Scotsman, had been the mate aboard Dampier's consort, the *Cinque Ports*, whose captain and officers had lost faith in their commodore's leadership and sailed off on their own. Unfortunately, the

---

* Renamed Robinson Crusoe Island in 1966 by the Chilean government.

Cinque Ports' hull was already infested by shipworm, so much so that when the galley stopped at Juan Fernández for water and fresh provisions, young Selkirk decided to stay—to take his chances on the island rather than try to cross the Pacific in a deteriorating vessel. According to the extended account he gave Rogers, Selkirk spent the better part of a year in deep despair, scanning the horizon for friendly vessels that never appeared. Slowly he adapted to his solitary world. The island was home to hundreds of goats, descendents of those left behind when the Spanish abandoned a halfhearted colonization attempt. He eventually learned to chase them down and catch them with his bare hands. He built two huts with goatskin walls and grass roofs, one serving as a kitchen, the other as his living quarters, where he read the Bible, sang psalms, and fought off the armies of rats that came to nibble his toes as he slept. He defeated the rodents by feeding and befriending many of the island's feral cats, which lay about his hut by the hundreds. As insurance against starvation in case of accident or illness, Selkirk had managed to domesticate a number of goats, which he raised by hand and, on occasion, would dance with in his lonely hut. When his clothes wore out, he stitched together new goatskin ones, using a knife and an old nail, and grew calluses on his feet as a substitute for shoes. He was rarely sick and ate a healthful diet of turnips, goats, crayfish, and wild cabbage. He'd barely evaded a Spanish landing party by hiding at the top of a tree, against which some of his pursuers pissed, unaware of his presence.

Although Selkirk greeted Rogers's men with enthusiasm, he was reluctant to join them after learning that his old commodore, William Dampier, was serving with them. Cooke wrote that Selkirk distrusted Dampier so much that he "would rather have chosen to remain in his solitude than come away with [Dampier] 'till informed that he did not command" the expedition. Dr. Dover and his landing party were only able to rescue the castaway by promising they would return him to the island were he not satisfied with the situation. Selkirk, in turn, helped them catch crayfish, piling them into the ship's boat before they rowed him out to the *Duke*. On seeing Selkirk for the first time, Rogers said he looked wilder than the original owners of his goatskin coverings. "At his first coming on board us, he had so much forgot his language for want of use that we could scarce understand him, for he seemed to speak by halves," Rogers wrote in his journal. "We offer'd him a Dram, but he would not touch it, having drank nothing but water since his being there, and 'twas some time before he could relish our victuals." Selkirk was remarkably healthy and alert at first, but Rogers noted that "this man, when he came to our ordinary method of diet and life, though he was sober enough, lost much of his strength and agility."

The expedition stayed on the island for twelve days. A tent city was set up on shore, and there the sick men were nursed to health with turnip greens and Selkirk's special goat broth; only two of the fifty patients died. Rogers lived in a tent on the beach, overseeing the repair of rigging, barrels, and sails. Selkirk ran down three or four goats each day, while the officers shot some of the seals and sea lions that lolled about on the shore by the thousands. "The men who worked ashore on the rigging eat young seals, which they prefer'd to our ship's victuals and said was as good as English lamb," Rogers wrote, "though for my own part I should have been glad of such an exchange."

Selkirk decided he enjoyed the company of men and joined the expedition as mate. On the thirteenth of February, he helped load the last firewood, water barrels, and freshly salted fish on board and bid farewell to his island home.

❧⁓❧

The next month proved frustrating. The privateers prowled the coast of Peru under an intense sun for weeks on end without seeing a single vessel. Rogers became increasingly concerned about the crew's darkening temperament. It didn't help that that some men were showing renewed signs of scurvy, or that one of the *Dutchess*'s boys whimpered in his hammock, having broken his leg in a fall from the mizzenmast. Rogers's lookouts didn't sight a sail until the afternoon of March 16. It proved a pathetic prize: a sixteen-ton coastal trading bark carrying fifty pounds, a seven-man crew, and eight black and Incan slaves. Rogers's prize crew took over the vessel, to which he gave the hopeful name *Beginning*.

After that, the prizes finally started coming in. Based out of the desolate, guano-covered Lobos Islands, thirty miles off the Peruvian coast, Rogers's ships captured four Spanish vessels, one of them a 500-ton ship carrying a cargo familiar to Rogers: slaves. There were seventy-three of them, mostly women and children, whose names were later added to the expedition's account ledgers, carefully sorted by gender and categories: from the two "useful men" (mariners Jacob and Quasshee) to two infant girls, Teresia and Molly. Amid the stink of Lobos, Rogers now presided over a sizeable flotilla and a growing army of prisoners and slaves, all taken without a shot.

With some 200 captives to provide for, the expedition's water supply was vanishing fast, and Rogers realized they would have to make a trip to the mainland. The privateers held an official council and agreed that if they had to betray their presence, they might as well surprise attack a wealthy town at the same time. They chose the shipbuilding port of Guayaquil, in today's Ecuador, which Dampier had sacked as a buccaneer in 1684.

En route, however, they gave chase to a large French ship and, in the ensuing battle, Woodes's brother, John, took a musket ball to the head and died, an event that Rogers took with "unspeakable sorrow." The only consolation was that the prize, the French-built *Havre de Grace*, carried "a considerable quantity of pearls," seventy-four slaves, and a number of wealthy Spanish passengers, improving his crews' morale.

The siege of Guayaquil was a comedy of errors. Under cover of darkness, the invaders paddled up the Guaya River in the boats, while the ships remained outside its mouth. Rogers, Dover, and Courtney each led a detachment of sixty-five men, but Dover, as captain of the marines, was the overall commander. It took two nights to reach the city, the intervening day spent hiding among mosquito-infested mangroves. On approaching the city, they mistook a festive celebration for the cheers of a defending army. Rogers counseled an immediate attack, but Dover preferred to spend another day hiding in the mangroves. The next evening, Dover insisted on negotiating with the Spanish, thereby losing the element of surprise altogether. The governor of Guayaquil, Don Jeronimo Bosa y Solis y Pacheco, dithered for days over the payment of a ransom while his staff evacuated some £100,000 in valuables out of the area. Finally Rogers, disgusted with both the doctor and the governor, usurped command and launched an assault on the city. He captured it with the loss of only two men.

As most of Guayaquil's valuables had been spirited away, the privateers found only bulky goods and barrels of alcohol. Many of the men got drunk and, in their search for plunder, started digging up corpses in the churchyard, unaware that Guayaquil had recently been stricken by bubonic plague. While the sailors rifled through the corpses, exposing themselves to the black death, Rogers and his officers enjoyed a dinner hosted by Don Jeronimo, who eventually ransomed his city for 26,810 pesos (£6,703), a fraction of what a more timely assault might have captured.

Any celebration of the assault's success was shortlived. On May 10, 1709, two days out to sea, Rogers's men began falling sick by the dozens. Within a week 140 men were down with the plague and two had died. The fleet had trouble finding water on the rocky islands they stopped at, and the crew of one of the prize ships barely staved off a slave uprising. By June 14, when they reached the island sanctuary of Gorgona, part of modern Colombia, both Rogers and Courtney were sick, and half a dozen men had died.

They spent six weeks recovering at Gorgona, during which time the crews cleaned and repaired the ships and fitted the *Havre de Grace* with new masts, rigging, and weapons, while the officers ransomed off some of the prize ships to their captains. A number of slaves were sold to local merchants who came by in canoes, and two black boys were given to

Cooke and another officer as rewards for their bravery in attacking the *Havre de Grace*. An unlucky black girl was turned over to a lecherous Spanish priest, a reward for having helped the privateers trade goods. Rogers wrote that he was sure the priest "will crack a Commandment with her, and wipe off the sin with the Church's indulgence."

Most of the plague-ridden men recovered in tents ashore, but the morale of the crew did not improve. Indeed, the men believed that Rogers and the officers were cheating them; sixty of them signed a document attesting that they would stop work unless the plunder were more equitably divided. Imbued by Henry Avery perhaps, they didn't feel that Rogers should get fourteen shares to an ordinary seaman's one. Rogers and Courtney had already surrendered their customary right to all plunder found in the captains' cabins of prize vessels, which Rogers reckoned had slashed their personal take by 90 percent. Now they were forced to further increase the crew's portion of the plunder. To make matters worse, the officers were still quarrelling over who should have done what at Guayaquil. Tensions mounted to the point where Rogers felt compelled to have them swear an oath on the Bible that each would come to the aid of the other in case of battle.

Under these uneasy truces, the privateers left Gorgona in early August 1709, and by early November were off the coast of Baja California, awaiting the arrival of the Manila galleons. Weeks passed. Water and supplies dwindled, and the officers worried they wouldn't have enough to make the 7,000-mile run to Guam. Riddled with shipworm, the *Duke* and *Havre de Grace* were leaking, and each passing day made them less likely to survive the long Pacific crossing. On December 20, the officers decided to call it quits and head home while they still could. "We all looked very melancholy and dispirited," Rogers wrote in his journal.

As the ships prepared for their departure, a sail appeared on the western horizon: large, multimasted, and coming from the direction of far-off Manila.

The men worked all night, preparing the *Duke* and *Dutchess* for action as they sailed through the darkness in the direction of the galleon. Daybreak found the Spanish ship to be just three miles off the *Duke's* bow. The *Dutchess* had overshot her prey in the dark and would have to tack a mile back to her. Looking over the Spanish vessel, Rogers realized that the *Duke* might be able to take her alone. The *Nuestra Señora de la Incarnación Disenganio* was not a typical galleon, but rather a lumbering ship-rigged vessel of 450 tons and twenty guns. Rogers had a tub of hot chocolate set out on deck for the men and, with this comforting beverage in hand, the crew said their prayers as the first of the *Incarnación's* cannonballs splashed into the water.

Rogers ordered the *Duke* alongside the Spanish vessel and gave the command to fire. His ship rocked as the guns discharged, one after another. The muzzles of the *Incarnación's* cannon flared in response. A musket ball tore into Rogers's left cheek, splattering much of his upper jaw and a number of his teeth on the deck. As he lay in a growing pool of blood, he could see the enemy's raised forecastle passing along the length of his rail. He tried to bark out an order, but the pain was too excruciating, so he scribbled a command on a scrap of paper. Accordingly, the *Duke* turned sharply, passed ahead of the *Incarnación's* bowsprit, and discharged her guns to deadly effect. The *Incarnación's* French-born captain, Jean Pichberty, struck his colors and the English clambered aboard their greatest prize.

Captain Pichberty provided his captors with a fascinating piece of information: Two treasure ships had left Manila that year, and the *Incarnación* was by far the smaller of them. The other, the *Nuestra Señora de Begoña*, was a proper treasure galleon, a mighty vessel of 900 tons, with twin gun decks and a vast store of oriental luxuries. Rogers issued further written orders for the fleet to escort the *Incarnación* into the secluded Baja harbor they'd been using as a base, and for the officers to prepare to intercept the *Begoña*. He then retreated to his cabin, his face and throat grotesquely swollen, barely able to drink. He was not yet aware that a Spanish musket ball was lodged deeply in the roof of his mouth. His colleagues tried to persuade Rogers to stay aboard the *Incarnación* while they sailed off to find the *Begoña*, but he refused to leave the *Duke*.

The crew of the *Duke* was still repairing the ship from its battle with the *Incarnación* on Christmas Day when the *Begoña* appeared on the horizon. By the time Rogers got the *Duke* out of the harbor that evening, the *Dutchess* and *Havre de Grace* were already miles out to sea, closing in on the enormous galleon. All night long, he watched the flashes of ships' cannons exchanging broadsides. In the morning, he could see that the *Dutchess* had been hard hit, her masts damaged and rigging in disorder. That afternoon, Rogers watched the *Dutchess* and *Havre de Grace* engage the galleon for hours, only to retreat again. The *Duke* didn't catch up to the running battle until late afternoon on the twenty-seventh, at which point all three privateers circled the *Begoña*, bombarding her with cannon fire. In the action, a wood splinter tore through Rogers's left foot, leaving his heel bone sticking out and half of his ankle missing.

Cooke, commanding the *Havre de Grace*, estimated the fleet had unloaded three hundred cannonballs and fifty rounds of sail-wrecking bar shot on the *Begoña*, but their six-pound cannon had little effect on her thick, rock-hard hull. "We might as well have fought a castle of fifty guns as this ship," Cooke lamented. The *Begoña*'s heavy cannon blasted the English ships, punching holes in their hulls and killing or wounding thirty-three. Running low on ammunition, the privateers had to admit they were outmatched and abandoned the *Begoña* to continue her run to Acapulco. Rogers, unable to speak or walk, prepared the fleet for the long trip home.

❧❧❧

It took another twenty-two months to reach England, during which time relations between the officers deteriorated. They fought over who would take command of the *Incarnación*, whose holds were packed with silk, spices, jewels, silver, and other finery, later found to be worth over £100,000. Amazingly, Courtney and Cooke were willing to allow Dr. Dover to command the ship. Still in unbearable pain, Rogers mustered the other officers to block the appointment, declaring Dover "utterly uncapable of the office." In the "paper war" that followed, the officers agreed to a compromise, whereby Selkirk and others would actually operate the *Incarnación*, while Dover held the ceremonial title of Chief Captain. The skirmish made Rogers some bitter enemies.

In late June 1710, they arrived at the Dutch East Indies capital of Batavia (now Jakarta, Indonesia), the first friendly port they'd seen in a year and a half. There they cleaned the weakening hulls of the *Duke*, *Dutchess*, and *Incarnación*, and sold the now worm-eaten *Havre de Grace* for scrap. Courtney and some of the other officers in Dover's faction would later claim that the *Duke* was still dangerously leaky and in need of a new keel, and that Rogers had refused to address the problem. They also suspected that Rogers had "insideous designs" to sail to Newfoundland or Brazil and trade in contraband East Indian goods. This was a serious allegation, for the British East India Company had a legal monopoly over all British trade with Southeast Asia. Crossing the powerful East India Company, they noted, "may endamage" the expedition. Many in the crew came to believe Rogers had stolen a large quantity of treasure and hid it at Batavia, though this seems both improbable and out of character. We do know that during his six-month stay at Batavia, he underwent surgery to repair his heel and remove the musket ball from the roof of his mouth. He also closely supervised the purchase of necessities for the trip home to avoid any entanglements with the East India Company, though even these precautions didn't save the Bristol men from the insatiable greed of the company's directors.

When the three ships finally dropped anchor in the Thames on October 14, 1711, the East India Company's agents were waiting for them. The privateers' purchase of provisions at Batavia, they argued, constituted a violation of the company's monopoly. They seized the great "Acapulco ship," already made famous by the London newspapers, and embroiled the privateers' owners in a lengthy legal dispute. In the end, over £6,000 of the £147,975 in proceeds was paid to the company's directors. Once expenses were deducted, each of the owners had doubled his investment. Rogers, his face mutilated, his foot mangled, his brother dead, received about £1,600, much of which was probably consumed by his family's debts back in Bristol. Many of the crew received nothing at all, having been pressed aboard Royal Navy ships as soon as the *Duke* and *Dutchess* reached London.

Rogers returned to his wife and children in Bristol to mend his wounds and prepare his journal for publication. His circumnavigation and successful capture of a Manila ship had made him a national hero, but it had also left him maimed, aggrieved, and little wealthier than the day he'd left home three years earlier.

❧

Rogers wasn't the only one recovering from trauma in the late summer of 1712. Across the Atlantic in Jamaica, Edward Thatch and Charles Vane had been witnesses to far worse. On August 28, 1712, Jamaica was struck by one of the most powerful hurricanes in its history.

Of Charles Vane, we know three things: During the War of Spanish Succession he came to reside in Port Royal, he was a professional mariner, and he was acquainted with the soon-to-be-infamous Captain Henry Jennings. When the winds suddenly shifted from north to south on the fateful August night, Vane may well have been aboard Captain Jennings's four-gun sloop *Diamond*, which was anchored among hundreds of other ships in Port Royal's harbor.

The harbor, that evening, was particularly crowded due to an embargo on shipping; a French attack was deemed imminent. Because of this, Edward Thatch was probably there as well, resting ashore at Port Royal. Also in Port Royal was the London slave ship captain Lawrence Prince and the Massachusetts merchant master William Wyer, both of whom would one day run afoul of the pirates. Jennings, an established

Jamaican merchant captain "of good standing and estate" commanded a vessel with empty holds, whatever cargoes she'd been carrying having long since been unloaded during the island's weeks-long embargo.

The storm struck around eight at night, "a furious hurricane of lightning, wind, and rain without thunder." It blew down trees, flattened homes and warehouses, toppled sugar works, and tore apart entire fields of sugar cane. A number of people ashore lost their lives when their houses, the hospital, and half of Kingston's main church collapsed, but the greatest carnage took place out in the harbor. At least fifty-four vessels sank, capsized, or were driven ashore, including the sloop-of-war HMS *Jamaica* and the slaver *Joseph Galley*, which lost every member of her crew and all 107 slaves chained in her hold. Captain Wyer was on land when the storm sank his slaver, the *Ann Galley*, drowning 100 slaves and half of his twenty-eight crewmen. Lawrence Prince lost the vessel under his command, the brigantine *Adventure*, as did Henry Jennings, though neither lost any men. When the sun came up the next morning, it revealed beaches and salt marshes strewn with smashed and dismasted vessels and dozens of corpses. In addition to the slaves, an estimated 400 sailors had lost their lives.

As Jennings, Vane, Thatch, and other mariners took stock of the destruction in the following weeks, a ship arrived bearing dramatic news from Europe. Queen Anne had declared a cessation of hostilities with France and Spain. The war was coming to an end, and with it, the stream of wealth and plunder brought to Jamaica by the privateering trade. With much of the Jamaican merchant fleet lying wrecked on the shores, hundreds of seamen were out of work, left to fend for themselves amid the wreckage of Kingston and Port Royal. Ironically, another hurricane would bring them riches on a scale the wartime privateers could have only dreamed of.

CHAPTER FOUR

PEACE

1713–1715

Wide-The end of the War of the Spanish Succession in 1713, tens of thousands of sailors suddenly found themselves out of a job. The Royal Navy, bankrupted by the twelve-year-long world war, rapidly demobilized, mothballing ships and dumping nearly three-quarters of its manpower, over 36,000 men, in the first twenty-four months following the signing of the Peace of Utrecht. Privateering commissions ceased to have any value, their owners compelled to tie their warships up and turn the crews out onto the wharves of England and the Americas. With thousands of sailors begging for work in every port, merchant captains slashed wages by 50 percent; those lucky enough to find work had to survive on twenty-two to twenty-eight shillings (£1.1 to £1.4) a month.

Peace did not bring safety to those English sailors who found work in the West Indies. Spanish coast guard vessels, the *guardas costas*, continued to seize English vessels passing to and from Jamaica, declaring them smugglers if so much as a single Spanish coin were found aboard. They always found the "illicit" coins because they were the de facto currency of all of England's Caribbean colonies. Thirty-eight Jamaican vessels were so seized in the first two years of peace, costing the vessel owners nearly £76,000. When the crews resisted, the *guardas costas* often killed a few in retribution; the rest spent months or years in Cuban prisons. "The seas," the governor of Jamaica would later recall, had become "more dangerous than in time of war."

As the months passed, the streets, taverns and boarding houses of Port Royal grew crowded with angry, destitute mariners. Merchants, stung by their losses, sent out fewer vessels, further reducing the number of jobs for sailors. Those sailors who had been captured—some more than once—were physically abused by the Spanish and financially pinched by their employers, who reduced their losses by not paying them for the time they were serving in prison. "Resentment and the want of employ," one resident later recalled, "were certainly the motives to a course of life which I am of [the] opinion that most or many of them would not have taken up had they been redressed or could by any lawful mean have supported themselves."

Benjamin Hornigold was one of the very first to turn to this other "course of life," and he took Edward Thatch with him. They had both served aboard Jamaican privateers during the war and now found themselves stuck in Port Royal Harbor. By the summer of 1713, they had had enough of poverty and the Spanish coast guard. Hornigold suggested to a number of former shipmates and drinking buddies that they put their skills together to solve both problems. They should go back to attacking Spanish shipping, avenging and enriching themselves at the same time. All they needed was a small vessel, a few good men, and a secure nest from which to launch their raids. Hornigold knew just the place.

The Bahamas, every Jamaican knew, was a perfect buccaneering base. The western end of the 700-island archipelago stood alongside the Straits of Florida, the primary shipping channel for every Europe-bound vessel in South America, Mexico, and the Greater Antilles, including Spanish Cuba, English Jamaica, and the new French colony on the island of Hispaniola. Sailing vessels had little choice but to pass this way in order to reach the colonies of the Eastern seaboard, or to catch the tradewinds back to Europe. Pirates could hide among the maze of islands, taking advantage of a hundred little-known anchorages where water and fresh fruit could be collected, vessels careened and repaired, and plunder safely divided. Nobody would have dared to follow them into the tight channels between those islands without an experienced Bahamian pilot aboard; with hundreds of low, sandy scraps of land, one could easily become lost and subject their craft to sharp reefs and uncharted shoals. More importantly, since attacking the Spaniards was technically against the law, the Bahamas didn't have a government, and hadn't since the Franco-Spanish invasion of July 1703. Thus, late in that first peacetime summer of 1713, Hornigold and a small band of followers left Port Royal and sailed 450 miles north, passing between Cuba and Hispaniola, and into the coral-studded labyrinth of the Bahamas.

During the war, the Spanish and French sacked New Providence Island four times, burning Nassau to the ground, spiking the fort's guns, carrying off the governor as well as most of the island's African slaves, and forcing the rest of the population into the woods. In the aftermath, most survivors abandoned the island, leaving only a handful of settlers who, according to resident John Graves, lived "scatteringly in little hutts, ready upon any assault to secure themselves in the woods." When word of the first raid got back to London, the aristocrats who owned the Bahamas appointed a new governor, Edward Birch, and sent him across the Atlantic to reestablish order in the backwater colony. When Birch arrived in January 1704, he found New Providence almost completely deserted and, according to contemporary historian John Oldmixon, "did not give himself the trouble to open his commission." Birch tarried for three or four months, sleeping in the woods, before leaving his "government" to its own devices.

Nine years later, little had changed. When Hornigold and his companions stepped onto the beach at Nassau, they found not a town, but a collection of partially collapsed buildings overgrown with scrub and tropical vegetation gathered around the burned-out shells of a church and fort that Nicholas Trott had constructed a quarter-century earlier. On the whole island there were probably fewer than thirty families living in hovels and rudimentary houses, eking out a living by catching fish, cutting trees, or picking the bones of ships unfortunate enough to wreck on the islands' treacherous shores. Hornigold took a good look around and realized he'd made the right choice.

It began humbly enough. Hornigold and his men built or "acquired" three large wooden boats called periaguas, or canoes, capable of carrying thirty men and an ample supply of cargo. Equipped with banks of oars and a single fore-and-aft rigged sail, they were well suited to small-scale piracy: swift, able to row straight into the wind to catch or escape from a square-rigged vessel, and drawing so little water they could be rowed or sailed over shoals, coral heads, and other hazards to give would-be pursuers the slip. Armed with cutlasses, muskets, pikes and cudgels, Hornigold's men could count on easily overwhelming a lightly crewed trading sloop or the overseers of a remote Spanish or French plantation. Cuba lay just 175 miles to the south, Spanish Florida 160 miles west, and French Hispaniola 400 miles to the southeast. The little pirate gang was perfectly poised to descend on their wartime enemies.

The men organized themselves into three bands, each with twenty-five men and a canoe. Hornigold led one and John West, about whom little is known, and John Cockram, an ambitious young mariner with a head for trade, led the others. Over the next six months, they attacked small Spanish trading vessels and isolated sugar plantations from the Straits of Florida to the shores of Cuba. Hornigold's band returned to Nassau laden with bales of expensive linens from Silesia and Prussia; Cockram brought back Asian silks, copper, rum, sugar, and silver coins stolen from Spanish vessels off Florida and elsewhere; West came home with fourteen African slaves stolen from a Cuban plantation. Together they brought cargoes worth £13,175 into the ruins of Nassau, ten times the value of the annual imports of the entire colony of Bermuda.

The fledgling pirate gangs needed someone to sell these stolen goods to, preferably without undertaking the long journey to Jamaica, where officials might demand a share under threat of legal entanglements. Fortunately, they appear to have found ready buyers among the relatively stable settlers of Harbour Island, fifty miles north of Nassau, which had a population of about 200. Richard Thompson, the island's largest and wealthiest landowner and merchant, had no scruples about fencing the Nassau pirates' goods and little sympathy for the Spanish, who had done Bahamians so much harm. He and John Cockram seem to have hit it off particularly well. In fact, by March 1714 Cockram had married one of Thompson's daughters and was living contentedly with her on Eleuthera, Harbour Island's larger, less-developed neighbor. Thompson even made his new son-in-law master of one of his trading sloops, sending him on smuggling runs to the Dutch spice island of Curaçao, a thousand miles away, with loads of brasiletto wood, from which a valuable red dye could be extracted. Thompson presumably purchased most of the pirates' cargo; it wouldn't be long before he and Cockram would emerge as the leading black market traders of the Golden Age of Piracy.

By late winter 1714, rumors began circulating on New Providence that Spanish authorities in Havana were preparing a retaliatory raid on the island. The pirates consulted with one another and decided to divide their plunder—now £60,000 worth—and split up. West and many of the rank-and-file pirates apparently chose to quit while they were ahead and scattered off to Jamaica and beyond. A handful stayed on in the Bahamas, including Hornigold, who joined John Cockram and others in the relative safety of Harbour Island, with its snug, easily defended harbor and battery of cannon. Edward Thatch was very likely among them, laying low and waiting for the Spaniards' anger to subside.

❧❧

The Peace of Utrecht had also put Sam Bellamy out of work. According to 300 years of oral history, he made his way to Eastham, Massachusetts, located on the outermost reaches of Cape Cod, in 1714 or early 1715. There's no documentary evidence to confirm their stories, though the people of the Outer Cape have been telling them in more or less the same form since the days of the great pirates; nor is there any proof to the contrary. In fact, the evidence we do have fits the Cape legend tantalizingly well.

Families who were living in and around Eastham had close ties with the English West Country, where Bellamy is believed to have been from, and some had surnames and pedigrees that suggest they might have been his mother's kinsmen. Most importantly, the primary character in the legend, the figure on which the story turns, was in fact a real person whose life details are consistent with the folk traditions of the Cape.

⁓❦⁓

Between 1713 and early 1715, Sam Bellamy very likely arrived in Boston, where most inbound ships cleared customs before proceeding to other New England ports. With 10,000 people, Boston was the largest city in British North America, and the port through which most of the transatlantic commerce of the Eastern Seaboard passed. The city rose from the center of the harbor, a mass of brick and clapboard buildings around the foot of Beacon Hill, which was crowned by its namesake beacon mast. Bellamy's ship would have docked at the end of Long Wharf, a newly completed pier jutting out sixteen hundred feet into the harbor, allowing thirty ocean-going ships to tie up simultaneously in water so deep they could unload their cargoes directly onto the docks in any tide. This was more than could be said of Boston's other gateways. The city was perched on a hilly peninsula, two miles long and a half-mile wide, connected to the mainland by a neck of land so low and slender that it would be submerged during storms and spring tides. Going from Boston to Roxbury on the peninsular road was always treacherous, and numerous people drowned crossing it in fog or darkness. There were no bridges yet, and so aside from the three ferries crossing the mouth of the Charles River, Long Wharf was the city's front door. Bellamy stepped through it, passing between the warehouses constructed along its length, and onto the foot of King Street.

Climbing the freshly paved street, a visitor knew he had arrived in a particularly cultured city. In the half-mile walk up to the brand-new

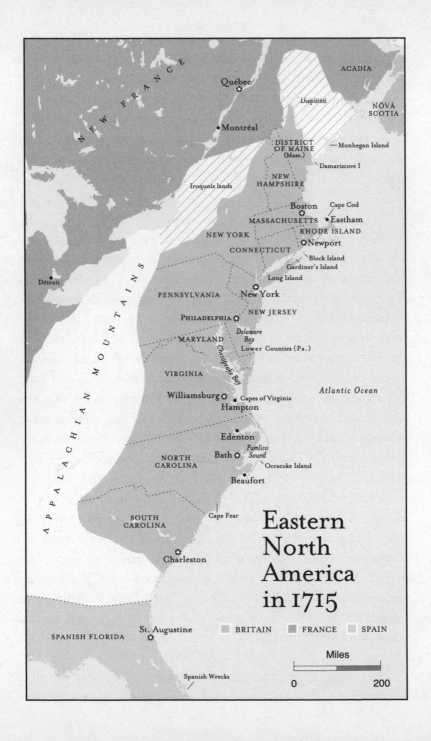

New France

Québec

ACADIA

Disputed

NOVA SCOTIA

Montréal

DISTRICT OF MAINE (Mass.)

— Monhegan Island

Damariscove I

NEW HAMPSHIRE

Iroquois lands

Boston

Cape Cod

MASSACHUSETTS

Eastham

RHODE ISLAND

NEW YORK

Newport

CONNECTICUT

Block Island

Gardiner's Island

Long Island

Détroit

APPALACHIAN MOUNTAINS

PENNSYLVANIA

New York

NEW JERSEY

PHILADELPHIA

MARYLAND

Delaware Bay

Lower Counties (Pa.)

Chesapeake Bay

VIRGINIA

Atlantic Ocean

Williamsburg

Capes of Virginia

Hampton

Edenton

Pamlico Sound

NORTH CAROLINA

Bath

Ocracoke Island

Beaufort

Cape Fear

SOUTH CAROLINA

Eastern North America in 1715

Charleston

SPANISH FLORIDA

St. Augustine

BRITAIN   FRANCE   SPAIN

Miles

Spanish Wrecks

0   200

brick Town House,* with its impressive bell tower, Bellamy would have passed no less than five printers and nineteen booksellers, including Nicholas Boone, who sold copies of the weekly *Boston News-Letter*, the only newspaper in British America. If he paused to read the *News-Letter*—indeed if he could read at all—he would have gotten the latest news from Europe and the other colonies as reported by newly arrived ship captains and passengers, including, perhaps, word of the marauding activities of Hornigold's men. The existence of the *News-Letter* made Boston the hub of eighteenth-century America's information infrastructure. It was published by the city postmaster, John Campbell, who was first to greet the weekly post rider from New York; the dangerous weeklong journey was the longest leg in the continent's nascent postal system, which stretched from Philadelphia to Portsmouth. Were there news of relevance to the inhabitants of Boston—a pirate attack for instance—the *News-Letter* was where most of them would first hear of it. If the newspaper didn't catch Bellamy's eye, he could look at the wares in Andrew Faneuil's King Street shop,† stocked with Venetian silks, French salts, and other European fineries. More likely he stopped in the Royal Exchange, a tavern at the top of the hill, well known for its food and drink. There he might have asked around about how best to book onward passage to Cape Cod, on the other side of Massachusetts Bay.

As a sailor, Bellamy would have felt at home on the Outer Cape. The sea's presence was everywhere in Eastham, its principal settlement: in the breezes that blew over town, in the roar of the surf rumbling from the east, and in the townspeople's household possessions, scavenged from a hundred ships wrecked on the Atlantic shore. Not all of the wrecks were purely accidental. On a dark night, a ship could be lured

---

* The Town House (1713) still stands today, surrounded by skyscrapers, and is known as the Old State House. King Street is now known as State Street. The tidal flats that Long Wharf once traversed have been filled in to make the Boston waterfront.

† Andrew Faneuil, for whom Boston's famed Faneuil Hall is named.

onto the Cape's stark, harborless eastern shore by a man standing on the beach, gently swinging his lamp. An inexperienced ship captain, nervous about navigating the dangerous Outer Cape, would follow the lamp, thinking it the stern light of another ship, discovering his mistake only when it was too late to save his ship. Of course, there could be no witnesses to such deceptions, and an unusually large number of ships were later found on these beaches with neither survivors nor cargo.

Eastham was literally an island in those days. A marshy creek south of town in the area of Nauset Harbor cut the Outer Cape off from the rest of Massachusetts. The marsh provided plenty of healthy fodder for cows, and the area quickly became known for the high quality of its dairy products. To the east, between the village and the open Atlantic, were the otherworldly tablelands—bleak, scrubby, windswept dunes that ended with frightening suddenness in sheer cliffs of sand dropping ninety feet or more to the Atlantic beaches.

According to Cape legend, Bellamy took to hanging about the taproom of an Eastham tavern. One spring night in 1715, he met a sixteen-year-old girl named Mary or Maria Hallett, charming her with tales of maritime adventure. Sam and Mary had a roll in the hay that very night and, in most versions of the story, were sufficiently smitten with each other to begin talking of marriage. Mary's parents were wealthy farmers, however, and refused to allow their daughter to marry a penniless sailor, the lowest of the low. Sam, furious, vowed that he would make his fortune and return to claim his bride. After his departure in September of 1715, the terrified girl discovered she was pregnant, and later that winter was said to have been discovered in a barn with a dead baby in her arms. The good people of Eastham, descendants of the Pilgrims, subjected Mary to a public whipping before tossing her in the town jail to await trial for her infant's murder. By some accounts, she lost her mind during her incarceration, and (with the possible assistance of the Devil) escaped to live a hermit's life on the stark tablelands above the Atlantic beach. There she roamed, scaring children, searching for Bellamy, and bringing nasty storms down on passing mariners, hobbies that earned her the epithet Sea Witch of Billingsgate, the latter being the old name for the north end of town now known as Wellfleet.

While embellished, the legend may have been based on historical events. In recent years, historians have discovered there was a young girl named Mary Hallett living in Eastham in 1715, and what we know of her life is surprisingly consistent with the legend. The historical Mary Hallett was about twenty-two years old in 1715, the daughter of one of the wealthiest settlers in the area, John Hallett of Yarmouth. Like his legendary counterpart, Hallett, a former constable and a veteran of the Indian Wars, appears to have cared deeply about property, having been involved in a bitter and protracted dispute with his brother over the division of their late father's pastureland. In March of 1715, Mary's older brother, John Hallett Jr., married an Eastham girl named Mehitable Brown, whose family is believed to have operated the Great Island Tavern, a Billingsgate establishment catering to mariners. Mary, the sixth of ten Hallett children, may well have been living with her brother and his wife in 1715, helping out in the kitchen, serving customers in the taproom, and cleaning the upstairs rooms they let to sailors. Furthermore, records show that Mary Hallett never married and died childless in her sixties in April 1751. In her last will and testament, discovered by Kenneth Kinkor of the Expedition Whydah Museum in Provincetown, she bequeathed all her possessions to her surviving siblings and their children; she had appointed her brother, John Jr., to execute her will, suggesting they were indeed close, even after the events of 1715, if they occurred at all.

Whatever the truth about Mary Hallett, we do know that Sam Bellamy made another, more lasting acquaintance while in New England. Thirty-nine years old when they met, Paulsgrave Williams was a silversmith from an influential Rhode Island family, with a wife and two young boys at home. At first glance, Williams would have seemed the most unlikely pirate. His father, John Williams, was the attorney general of Rhode Island, an exceptionally wealthy merchant who split his time between a Boston mansion and estates in Newport and Block

Island. His mother, Anna Alcock, was a descendent of the Plantagenet kings of England and the daughter of a Harvard-trained physician. Yet Paulsgrave would choose the life of an outlaw, joining a society of impoverished mariners fighting for the wealth and freedom that he had enjoyed since birth. It makes no sense, until you take his stepfather and childhood neighbors into account.

John Williams died in 1687, when his son was eleven years old, leaving the execution of his will and the guardianship of his children in the hands of his friend, a Scottish exile named Robert Guthrie. Guthrie married Paulsgrave's mother a year and a half later, permanently settling the family on their estate at Block Island in Rhode Island's Narragansett Bay, a move that profoundly altered the trajectory of young Williams's life. Guthrie's father had been a famous Scottish nationalist and preacher and had been executed by the English in front of his family when Guthrie was still an infant. Guthrie's mother and siblings were banished from the country, joining a large contingent of Scottish prisoners of war transported to New England to slave in the ironworks of Lynn and Braintree, Massachusetts. A large number of these Scots eventually relocated to Block Island, becoming part of a community with a reputation for organized crime. Through Guthrie, young Williams likely was introduced to some unpleasant truths about the English conquest of Scotland, and some radical notions about who should be sitting on the British throne. On Block Island, Paulsgrave's family became connected with some of the leading smugglers, money launderers, and black marketers in New England. His eldest sister, Mary, married Edward Sands, a personal friend of Captain Kidd; the couple had helped hide some of Kidd's contraband at their home while he was on the run from the law. His younger sister, Elizabeth, had also been implicated in helping Kidd; her husband, Thomas Paine, was likely the nephew and namesake of a retired pirate, Thomas Paine the elder, who also lived in the area and had a long history of buying and selling plunder. In this company, Williams may have become inclined to pursue extralegal ventures. All he needed was a willing partner, someone who knew more than he did about sailing ships and the sea.

Bellamy and Williams became fast friends and formed a partnership. With his wealth and connections, Williams was the senior partner, able to secure supplies and a seaworthy vessel for use in a maritime undertaking. Bellamy brought mariner's skills and knowledge of the West Indies. If Williams hired Bellamy to be the master of his vessel, he was entitled to shares of the profits of whatever commercial or smuggling scheme he was contemplating. Any plans they were hatching went out the window when news of a greater opportunity arrived.

❧❧❧

In the Bahamas, the Spanish attack everyone expected had failed to materialize and the pirates began to regroup. On Eleuthera, Hornigold began recruiting a new gang from the ranks of willing colonists. He was helped along by one of the island's old salts, Jonathan Darvell, who as a young sailor had joined a mutiny, seized a slave ship, and sold her living cargo to Dutch merchants on Curaçao. Darvell was now too old to join a pirating venture, but he was happy to invest in one. He contributed his sloop, the *Happy Return*, as well as his seventeen-year-old son, Zacheus, and his son-in-law, Daniel Stillwell. A handful of strangers came as well, most of them from Jamaica, including Ralph Blackenshire and possibly Edward Thatch.

In the summer of 1714, Hornigold sailed the *Happy Return* out of Harbour Island for the coasts of the Spanish colonies of Florida and Cuba. The little sloop was probably no greater than fifteen tons, but it was a considerable improvement over the sailing canoes: safer, faster, and capable of carrying more men and plunder. When they returned, Darvell made out well. By lending his vessel for a short cruise, he received a share of the plunder—barrels of dry goods, tallow, and a slave worth £2,000, which was enough to buy the *Happy Return* four times over. Within a few weeks, he sent the *Happy Return* out again. Hornigold sat that voyage out, perhaps disappointed with the size of his share. He probably didn't feel particularly jealous when the *Happy Return* came back from the north coast of Cuba with only a load of pungent hides and other goods worth just £350.

In the late fall, Hornigold and two other men purchased an open boat from an Eleutheran settler. They sailed to the coast of Cuba and, in early December, intercepted a sailing canoe and a small launch belonging to the Cuban noble Señor Barrihone. The Cuban vessels were nearly as tiny as their own, but they were laden with coins and valuables worth 46,000 pieces of eight (£11,500). The capture made Hornigold and his colleagues the most respected pirates in the Bahamas. It also drew the attention of authorities from three empires.

Thomas Walker was the only official representative still living in the islands. He had been an important figure in the Bahamas since the reign of King William, having served as His Majesty's justice for the Vice-Admiralty Court. He was probably living on New Providence when the pirate Henry Avery bribed Governor Trott with his treasures. With the collapse of the colony during the War of Spanish Succession, Walker had assumed the role of acting deputy governor, although it's not entirely clear that the lords proprietor of the Bahamas had ever approved this arrangement. He had somehow survived the war on New Providence, continuing to live on his homestead three miles outside of Nassau with his wife, Sarah, who was a free black, and his mulatto children: Thomas Jr., Neal, Charles, and fifteen-year-old Sarah.*

Thomas Walker didn't like the arrival of the pirates one bit. The last thing he and his neighbors needed was to bring the wrath of Spain

---

* Young Sarah Walker (c. 1700–1731) would eventually marry William Fairfax, for whom Fairfax County, Virginia is named. Her daughter, Anne, married George Washington's older brother, Lawrence, who built her Mount Vernon; the future president would later rent this Virginia estate from Anne, and inherit the estate on her death. Anne's own brother, George Fairfax, apparently had some African features; he suffered humiliation during a childhood visit to England when his paternal relatives began speculating aloud as to whether his skin would turn black at puberty.

down on them once again. Hornigold and his colleagues had to be stopped, and Walker figured he was the only man to do it.

First he called for reinforcements, dispatching letters to everyone he could think of—the lords of the admiralty, the lords of trade, the Duke of Beaufort, and the other Proprietors of the Bahamas, even the *Boston News-Letter*—informing them of the increasingly dangerous situation. He assured the lords proprietor that he was a "prosecutor and disturber of all pirates, robbers, and villains that do expect to shelter themselves or take up their abode in these, their Lordships' Islands." Until a new governor was appointed, he would take it upon himself "to curb the exorbitant tempers of some people of these islands and to execute justice upon Piratts."

Soon every sea captain from Boston to Port Royal was aware of the exploits of Hornigold and Cockram. The acting governor of Bermuda, Henry Pulleine, sent letters back to London warning that the two men were turning the Bahamas into a "nest for pyrates." Pulleine even offered to annex the Bahamas to his government, promising to destroy the "infamous rascals, who do an infinite mischiefe to trade, by making us scandalous to our neighbors."

After the pirate depredations of 1713, Walker decided letter-writing was not enough. Just after Christmas, he gathered some men together, boarded a vessel, and sailed up to Harbour Island to administer justice himself.

Walker's campaign had an auspicious start. At Harbour Island, he surprised the pirates, capturing Daniel Stillwell, teenager Zacheus Darvell, and one of their accomplices, Matthew Low. The other sea robbers fled into the woods and defended themselves "by force of Armes," but Walker was able to seize the *Happy Return*, ending her career as a pirate vessel. He compelled Low and the Darvell boy to turn on Daniel Stillwell, signing written depositions implicating him in the recent pirate raids on the Spaniards. Walker had no authority to try Stillwell, however, his commission as an Admiralty judge having expired decades before. Instead, he would have to send Stillwell to the nearest court of justice at Jamaica, a course of action the prisoner actually begged him to follow. Walker had his concerns the long sea voyage offered the prisoner an easy chance of escape—but he didn't have a lot of other options. He placed Stillwell and copies of the damning depositions in the hands of Jonathan Chase, the captain of the sloop *Portsmouth*, who agreed to deliver them directly to the governor of Jamaica, Lord Archibald Hamilton. He departed on January 2, 1715.

Walker sailed the *Happy Return* back to Nassau and hired men to help him capture Hornigold and other fugitives now hiding amid the lignum vitae and logwood trees of Eleuthera. Shortly thereafter, he received reports that the Spanish in Cuba were preparing a massive assault on the Bahamas in retribution for the piracies committed by Hornigold and his outlaw friends. A local man who had been held captive by the Spaniards told Walker that a fleet of warships were sailing from Havana with orders to "cut off" every man, woman, and child on New Providence. Walker promptly boarded the *Happy Return*, and set sail for Havana, hoping to talk the Spaniards out of invading his wayward colony.

Fortunately, the Spanish governor of Cuba, Laureano de Torres y Ayala, the Marquis Cassa Torres, was in a forgiving mood. He received the nervous Bahamian graciously, accepting his stories of having captured eight of the offending pirates and sending them to justice in Jamaica. "I return you grateful thanks and likewise [to] all the inhabitants of Providence [because] you have taken care to detect such villains who make it their evil practice to rob those who follow honest means to live," the Marquis proclaimed. Walker and his party remained at Havana for much of February, smoothing relations with their powerful neighbor for "the future safety and peace of all the inhabitants" of the Bahamas.

Walker returned home to Nassau to discover that the pirates were far from pacified. The prisoner Daniel Stillwell never made it to Jamaica. Somehow, Benjamin Hornigold and his men had managed to rescue him and were preparing to take care of Walker himself. All the colony's inhabitants knew that if Walker were out of the way, the Bahamas would belong to the pirates and to the pirates alone.

⚜

In Jamaica, Governor Archibald Hamilton had little time to wonder why Daniel Stillwell had failed to be delivered to him, to worry about Bahamian pirates, or, indeed, the petty colony of the Bahamas. He was involved in a far weightier and dangerous project: helping to orchestrate a secret plot to overthrow and replace the king of Britain. His efforts, strangely enough, would dramatically swell the ranks of pirates operating out of the Bahamas.

Queen Anne had died, childless, in August of 1714. Under normal circumstances, the crown would have passed to her half-brother, James Stuart, the next in the line of dynastic succession, a situation that, to the thinking of many at the time, was ordained by God himself. James was a Catholic, however, and under a law passed in 1701, no Catholic could sit on the throne. Unfortunately, there weren't any other members of the House of Stuart who weren't also Catholics. The best Protestant anyone could come up with was one of Anne's second cousins, George Ludwig, Elector of the German state of Hanover. Although he didn't speak English and wasn't interested in learning, George Ludwig was brought over to England and crowned King George I, becoming the founding member of a new ruling family, the House of Hanover, which still occupies the throne today. Many Britons were unhappy with this turn of events, especially in Scotland. The Scots were already upset about losing their independence under the 1707 Treaty of Union, but at least the Stuarts—that is, the Stewarts—had been the legitimate royal family of Scotland. Now, just seven years after the merging of the English and Scottish monarchies, the English had placed a German prince on the throne, one extremely hostile to Scottish Presbyterianism. Other Britons were upset by the coming of the Hanoverians, such as Catholics, adherents to the Church of England, and divine right enthusiasts, but it was the noble families of Scotland that spearheaded efforts to put James Stuart on the throne.

Lord Hamilton was a member of just such a family. His eldest brother, James, the fourth Duke of Hamilton, had headed opposition to Scotland's union with England, and was arrested on numerous occasions for pro-Stuart activities. His older brother, George, the Earl of Orkney, was deeply involved in plans for a military uprising in support of James Stuart, an effort that at least two of his nephews were also involved in. Governor Hamilton intended to do his part. Since taking up his post in 1711, he had purged Jamaica's governing council, militia, and civil service of Stuart opponents, replacing them with Catholics, Scotsmen, and other Jacobites, as supporters of James Stuart were called. He placed a fellow Scotsman in charge of Port Royal's fortifications, the chief defenses of the island, and refused to account for either the gunpowder hoarded there or the contents of merchant vessels he seized, allegedly for smuggling. The planters and merchants who sat in the Jamaican assembly were terrified at "the number of Papists and Jacobites" employed in Hamilton's administration. And as preparations unfolded toward a major Jacobite uprising back in Britain, Hamilton began assembling a fleet of private warships in Port Royal, a force that may have been intended for use as a colonial Jacobite navy.

Hamilton denied being anything but a loyal servant of George I. The small fleet he assembled in the summer and early fall of 1715, he later insisted, was for the sole purpose of defending the island's shipping against Spanish privateers, and this is what the commissions he issued his fleet stated. Hamilton would explain that Jamaican merchants had begged his administration to protect them from the Spaniards. "We had only one man of war and one sloop [of war] left on the Jamaica station, both foul [and] unfit to go after those nimble vessels which infested us," Hamilton wrote. With those two naval ships about to leave for Britain, he added, there was little choice but to replace them with vessels of his own. Thus Hamilton contacted a number of his allies on the island, urging them to join him in investing in a flotilla of ten armed privateers. All they needed were some trustworthy and experienced mariners to operate them. One of those mariners would be Charles Vane.

It's reasonable to assume Vane was unemployed, roaming the docks of Port Royal and Kingston in search of work. He eventually found it, being hired by his future mentor, Captain Henry Jennings, to serve on the crew of a privateer.

Jennings was offered the command of one of Governor Hamilton's privateers, a forty-ton sloop called the *Barsheba*. The *Barsheba* could carry eight guns and eighty men. The investors who owned her selected Jennings based on his reputation: a veteran merchant captain with wartime experience and a Jamaican estate that reliably earned him £400 annually, above and beyond what he earned at sea. Dependable, experienced, and fearless, Jennings was just the sort of man they wanted to command their warship.

By late July, as they prepared to sail, the skies around Jamaica darkened and the wind began to blow hard from the southeast. A great storm was brewing, one that would change the fortunes of Jennings and Hornigold, Thatch and Vane, Williams and Bellamy. Indeed, after it passed, the Caribbean and the Americas would never be the same.

✒✧✒

On July 13, 1715,* a Spanish treasure fleet left Havana, bound for Cádiz. On account of the war, it had been several years since the Spanish had dispatched their treasure fleets to the New World, so the galleons were carrying an unusually valuable haul: coins, silks, porcelain, ingots, and jewels worth an estimated seven million pieces of eight (£1,750,000). They were also departing unusually late in the season.

The combined fleet's commander, Captain-General Don Juan Esteban

---

* For consistency, all dates in this book correspond to the Julian calendar that was then in use in Great Britain. Spain (and France) were already using the modern Gregorian calendar that, during this time period, was eleven days ahead of the Julian, meaning that Spanish documents record the 1715 treasure fleet departing on July 24.

de Ubilla, had been fretting about the delays for months. First the Tierra Firma fleet under General Don Antonio de Echeverz had been delayed in Cartagena, waiting for the silver-laden llama caravans to arrive from Potosi, on the other side of the Andes. Then Ubilla's New Spain fleet had been stuck in Vera Cruz for months on end, waiting for the Manila galleons to arrive in Acapulco. By the time the two fleets joined forces in Havana, Ubilla began worrying that they might not make it out of the tropics before the onset of hurricane season. There were further delays in Cuba as Havana merchants loaded their wares and Governor Torres y Ayala insisted on the officers' attendance at his lavish parties. At the last minute, an extra vessel, the French-owned frigate El Grifon, joined the fleet because its commander feared his treasure-laden vessel would be easy prey for the pirate gang known to be operating out of the Bahamas. Ubilla was worried about departing so late, but he had no other choice. The court of King Philip V, the grandson of Louis XIV whose control of the Spanish throne was endorsed in the Treaty of Utrecht, desperately needed an influx of cash and had been exerting pressure on Ubilla for more than a year. Reluctantly, the Spanish commodore gave the order to set sail, clinging to the hope that no hurricanes would strike so early in the season.

The eleven-ship armada sailed out of Havana and into the Straits of Florida, their sails full and flags waving. Ubilla and Echeverz's massive fighting galleons took the lead, their raised aft decks towering above both the main deck and the ocean waves like wooden skyscrapers. Six treasure galleons made up the body of the fleet, their cargo-laden hulls riding low in the water. El Grifon, the French frigate, darted back and forth, being more nimble than her fortresslike consorts. Two more fighting galleons brought up the rear, dozens of heavy bronze cannon concealed behind their gun ports.

On Friday, July 19, the easterly winds blowing off the Florida coast began to fail. The air turned unusually hot and humid and some of the veteran sailors began feeling pains in their joints. Slowly the winds began picking up, but this time from the eastern horizon, where thin, wispy clouds had been hovering since morning. By midafternoon the skies had darkened, rain squalls passed over the galleons, and the winds began to strengthen from the east-northeast. First to twenty miles an hour, then to thirty, and forty. Sailors clung to the masts in the growing seas as they struggled to shorten sail. On every ship, cannons were secured, hatches battened down, and cargo double-checked as the Spaniards prepared to meet the coming storm.

By midnight, the Spanish vessels were plowing into hurricane-force winds. Fear turned to terror as the clumsy galleons began climbing mountainous waves, forty and fifty feet tall. As the winds reached a hundred miles an hour, the furled sails loosened and were torn to ribbons, and bits of heavy rigging began crashing onto the decks. All the while, Ubilla and his fellow officers kept looking over their shoulders, knowing that the wind and waves were driving the fleet toward the treacherous Florida coast. They were also aware that there wasn't a single refuge between Key West and the great Spanish outpost of St. Augustine, and there was little hope of making it that far.

In the small hours of the morning, the men spotted roaring surf off their ship's aft port quarters. Struggle as they might, the crew could do nothing to prevent the galleons from being driven onto the reefs and sand by the mountainous seas. One by one the ships struck. Ubilla's 471-ton flagship, *Nuestra Señora de la Regla*, had her bottom torn off by a reef and sank in thirty feet of water. One of the rear galleons vanished under a wave, while another, the 450-ton *Santo Cristo de San Roman*, capsized in the surf a few miles south of the *Regla* and disintegrated. The commander of one of the treasure galleons, the *Urca de Lima*, managed to run his ship aground in the shelter of a river mouth, but she was still battered apart by the storm. In the end, all ten were destroyed, littering the beaches with hundreds of bodies. Only *El Grifon*, which had sailed ahead of the fleet, was able to escape the hurricane.*

---

* *El Grifon* arrived in Brest, France, on September 2 (of the Gregorian calendar), her passengers unaware of the fate that had befallen the fleet.

Fewer than half of the 2,000 men aboard the doomed ships made it to the beaches alive, crawling in terror through the stinging rain and darkness to shelter themselves amid the dunes. Dozens more died from their wounds and dehydration over the next few days while they huddled on the beach, looking out for hostile Indians. Both Ubilla and Echeverz had drowned, but Admiral Don Francisco Salmon made it to shore and put the survivors to work digging for water and building crude shelters from the wreckage of their ships. Several men made for St. Augustine in one of the surviving ship's boats. A week later they made it into that harbor, rowing beneath the giant fort, Castillo de San Marcos,* to break the news of one of the greatest maritime disasters in the history of the Americas. Along with the remains of ten ships and a thousand corpses, seven million pesos in treasure lay scattered off the beaches of east Florida, most of it in water so shallow that a good diver could reach it all.

❧❧❧

The news spread across the Americas faster than the plague, from St. Augustine and Havana to Jamaica and the Bahamas. Ship captains carried the word to Charleston, Williamsburg, Newport, and Boston. The *Boston News-Letter* did the rest, its late summer editions carried far and wide by ships, sloops, and post riders alerting readers from Cape Cod to London of the disaster. Soon, from every corner of British America, men were piling onto vessels of all sorts bound "to fish upon ye wrecks."

For Williams and Bellamy, it was a dream come true. Sometime in the early fall they headed for the Florida wreck sites. Perhaps there were tearful good-byes between Sam and Mary Hallett, between Paulsgrave and his wife, Anna. When the two men eventually returned to New England, it would be under far different circumstances.

---

* This fort was completed in 1695 and survives today, entirely intact, the oldest masonry fort in the continental United States.

When the news of the wreck of the treasure fleet reached Jamaica, all hell broke loose. Every mariner in town seemed to be readying himself to sail to get his bit of Spanish treasure. Sailors were soon deserting the Port Royal-based naval frigate HMS *Diamond* at a rate of five a day, even as she was preparing to sail home to England. "If I had stayed a week longer I do believe I should not have had men enough to have brought me home," the *Diamond*'s commanding officer, John Balchen, reported. The mariners were "all mad to go a wrecking, as they term it, for the generality of the island think they have [the] right to fish upon the wrecks, though the Spaniards have not quitted them."

Rather than suppressing the wreckers, Governor Hamilton tried to get in on the action. He approached Captain Davis of HMS *Jamaica*, suggesting the young officer sail his sloop-of-war up to Florida, loot the wrecks, and share the proceeds with Hamilton. Davis was offended by the request, as was Commodore Balchen, who informed the governor in no uncertain terms that he would not permit his ships to be used in such an ignoble errand. Rebuffed by the navy, Hamilton quickly moved to purchase shares in the privateers he had commissioned. His official orders to the privateers were to "execute all manner of acts of hostility" against pirates. Privately, he directed them to go straight to the Spanish wrecks and to bring back whatever treasure they could.

Henry Jennings took his mission to heart. He signed on fourteen skilled divers—some black, some white—and loaded the *Barsheba* with "warlike stores." In December, he sailed out of Bluefields, Jamaica, in the company of another privateer, the thirty-five-ton sloop *Eagle* commanded by one John Wills. Jennings's *Barsheba* had eighty men and eight guns. The *Eagle* was even stronger, with twelve guns and 100 men. Together they could hold their own against the Spanish *guardas costas* and easily overwhelm the Spaniards' lightly manned trading vessels. They sailed along the mountainous shores of Cuba, stopping in the wild harbors of Honda and Mariel until, sometime after Christmas, they began making their way into the Florida Straits, searching for the signs of the ruined treasure fleet.

On Christmas morning 1715, the privateers stood just off Key Biscayne,* a well-known watering hole at the mouth of the Florida Straits. Around eight o'clock, a small sailing launch approached them from the north, bucking the warm flow of the Gulf Stream. It turned out to be the *San Nicolas de Vari y San Joseph*, an official Spanish mail boat on her way from St. Augustine to Havana. Her master, a forty-six-year-old seaman named Pedro de la Vega, offered no resistance. Yes, he knew where the treasure wrecks were: His vessel had stopped at the main Spanish salvage camp on the way down from St. Augustine. No, Jennings wasn't the first person to ask; the *San Nicolas* had been looted the day before by a pair of English sloops at the site of one of the wrecked treasure galleons. Those Englishmen had also wanted to know about the strength of the Spanish camp, the nature of its defenses, and the quantity of treasure accumulated there. Pedro de la Vega told Jennings, Wills, and Vane what he had told the others: that he'd only anchored off the shores of the camp for a few hours and knew little of the proceedings there. If de la Vega did know more, he wasn't volunteering. He also neglected to mention the 1,200 pieces of eight hidden aboard the *San Nicolas*.

De la Vega and his crew were imprisoned aboard the *Barsheba*, relieved of two gold pieces (worth £8) and some of their clothing, but not abused in any way. It helped that de la Vega had agreed to show the privateers the way to the Spanish salvage camp. It was easy, he told them: Just let the Gulf Stream push you along the flat, featureless Florida shore for a hundred miles and you can't miss it. There's really nothing else between here and there.

It was as the Spaniard said. All day long and through the night the three vessels made their way up the deserted Florida shore, flying Spanish colors. The following morning, they witnessed the first signs of the destroyed treasure fleet. Bits and pieces of the patrol ship, *Nuestra Señora de las Nieves*, were scattered high up a barrier island beach a few miles

---

* Now adjacent to the city of Miami, but then next to an uninhabited marsh. At this time, there were no Spanish settlements between Cuba and St. Augustine.

north of the St. Lucie Inlet. The vessel's hull was visible in the shallow water a few hundred yards off the beach. It was clear that it had already been thoroughly salvaged by the Spaniards. On the shore were signs of their operations: remains of campfires and crude crosses marking the graves of those who hadn't survived. The flotilla continued northward, passing the remains of the *Urca de Lima*, run aground in the mouth of Fort Pierce Inlet; the galleon had also been picked clean by her surviving crew, then burned to the waterline to discourage freelance salvors.

The campfires of the Spanish salvage camps flickered red against the pitch black shore. It was, again, as de la Vega outlined: two camps, six miles apart, near a grove of palm trees planted by Florida's natives, the Ayz Indians. Palmar de Ayz, as de la Vega called it, was the final resting place of the late General Ubilla's flagship as well as one of the treasure-laden fighting galleons, the *San Cristo de San Roman*. Any treasure the Spaniards had salvaged would be in the main camp, the northernmost clump of light on the shore. Jennings ordered all lamps doused, hands turned out of their hammocks, and the boats prepared for a landing.

Admiral Francisco Salmon, the commander of the camp, was lucky to be alive. The hurricane had dismasted his ship and smashed her into three pieces on the shoals; the middle section sank, carrying a hundred men to their deaths, but the bow and stern were thrown ashore, sparing Salmon and half of his crew. By the time help arrived from St. Augustine and Havana, the survivors had already eaten the last of the dogs, cats, and horses that had made it ashore, and had moved on to devour the bitter berries of the palmetto trees growing along the beach. Salmon was ill, but refused to leave the wreck site. "I will stay on this island [*sic*] . . . in bad health and half dressed," he wrote his king, "even if it means sacrificing my life." He had posted his strongest men as sentries near the hulk of the *Regla* in an attempt to prevent the other men from looting the chests of treasure within. Then he set about trying to recover as much of the fleet's cargo as possible. It was clear that a great deal of dangerous diving work would need to be done, but few of Salmon's men were eager to enter the shark-infested water. Those who did sickened within a few weeks under the strain of the heavy work. With hundreds of tons of treasure to salvage from the ocean floor, another solution was clearly called for. Salmon sent a man to Havana with orders to round up African and Indian divers.

Early-eighteenth-century diving techniques were primitive and extremely hazardous. Free divers—almost all of them slaves—were sent out over the wreck sites on simple rafts. Each took a large rock and a very deep breath before jumping overboard and sinking to the ocean floor twenty to fifty feet down. There they scampered about for a few minutes, scooping up coins and small objects, and marking the locations of chests, boxes, cannon and other desirable objects. On the surface they were searched, then sent back to the bottom with ropes or chains to attach to the larger objects, so they could be raised with ship-mounted windlasses. In deeper water, the divers couldn't stay down long enough to be useful, so a large bell was lowered down with them. When a diver ran out of breath, he could stick his face under the bell and take another from the pocket of air there. If they didn't take care to exhale completely before heading to the surface their lungs could rupture, resulting in an agonizing death. Others were forced to stay down so long that they built up dangerous levels of nitrogen in their blood; when they resurfaced the dissolved gas bubbled in their veins—the bends—leading to permanent paralysis, nerve damage, and death. Mortality rates were extremely high among enslaved divers, and a third of the 300 divers at Palmar de Ayz did not survive their servitude.

No matter the human cost, Admiral Salmon was pleased with the results. Over four million pesos (£1 million) in coins and cargo had already been salvaged, most of it from the *Regla* and *Roman*, which lay in relatively shallow water near his camp. To expedite operations, he'd set up an auxiliary camp next to the *Roman*, a mile down the beach from the main camp. The vast majority of the treasure Salmon recovered was already in Havana under heavy guard, yet some 350,000 pieces of eight (£87,500) were buried in the sand within his fortified main camp. These chests of silver must have been the first thing that came to mind when his aides shook him awake in the wee hours of December 27 to tell him the camps were under attack.

✥

As his ships tossed in the darkness, Jennings selected 150 men, armed them to the teeth, and divided them into three equal companies. Each company boarded a large boat and, at two in the morning, rowed ashore. They landed midway between the two Spanish camps. At daybreak, they marched up the beach toward the main camp, a drummer and flag bearer at the head of each company. Panic spread within the camp. Admiral Salmon's men had built a sand embankment to defend against attacks by the Ayz, but they knew it would be little match for the musket-toting English. They were also outnumbered; Salmon had only sixty soldiers and a few cannon at his command. A dozen of his men fled the scene as the rat-a-tat-tat of Jennings's drummers grew closer. Salmon, reading the writing on the wall, took a white flag and went out alone to meet the English.

Jennings and Salmon faced each other: Is this war, Salmon asked? No, we came to fish the wrecks, to claim the "mountain of wealth," the Englishman responded. There is nothing for you here, Salmon insisted. The wrecks "belonged to His Catholic Majesty," King Philip V, and Salmon's men were securing them for him. This line of reasoning got Salmon nowhere so he offered them 25,000 pieces of eight to leave peacefully. Jennings refused. Salmon, knowing resistance would be futile, surrendered, giving up the location of the buried treasure. Vane and Jennings's men loaded the silver into a launch, adding four bronze swivel guns and various sundries stolen from Salmon's staff. They sabotaged three cannons that were too large to carry away and returned to their sloop with £87,000 in Spanish gold and silver.

After releasing the Spanish mail boat, the English sailed off to the southeast. They needed somewhere safe to divide their plunder. Jennings suspected the Bahamas would serve that purpose well.

❧❧❦

In the Bahamas, things had gotten much busier since the destruction of the treasure fleet. The wrecks were attracting rogues, adventurers, and unemployed seamen from across the English-speaking world. Most used the Bahamas as their base of operations, it being the closest nominally British territory to Palmar de Ayz. For these raiders, treasure hunters, and pirates, the absence of government in the Bahamas was an added attraction.

In the late summer and fall of 1715, Hornigold and Thatch continued to raid Spanish trading vessels along the coasts of Cuba and Florida. They let it be known that they refused to respect the Treaty of Utrecht and considered the Spanish and French to be enemies still. The English and Dutch, they claimed, had nothing to fear from them, as they were merely avenging their countrymen for the ravages done by Spanish coastguardsmen. While they maintained this policy through the spring and summer of 1715, it began to falter by the fall. In early November, Hornigold and Thatch seized an English sloop, the *Mary* of Jamaica, off the coast of Cuba. The *Mary* represented a significant improvement for the pirates; the sloop was large enough to accommodate 140 men and six cannon, which meant she was probably thirty-five to forty tons, the size of Jennings's *Barsheba* and Lord Hamilton's other privateers. Hornigold and Thatch treated the sailors well, and a few of them may have even volunteered to join them, attracted by higher wages and greater freedom.

In November, Hornigold sailed the *Mary* back to the Bahamas, along with a Spanish sloop he'd captured whose hold was filled with barreled sugar and dry goods. This time however he did not return to the safety of Harbour Island but rather dropped anchor right in Nassau Harbor. He rallied the pirates, wreckers, and other ne'er-do-wells living in the ruined capital to announce that they were all under his personal protection. The pirates, who were starting to outnumber New Providence's law-abiding residents, began sauntering around the town as if they owned it. They had even taken a name for themselves: the Flying Gang.

At that time Thomas Walker had returned to Nassau from a trading voyage to Cuba with his twenty-year-old son, Thomas Jr. One day while Walker was attending to business around the house, he sent his son into town to run errands. The young man immediately sensed the changed atmosphere. Some of his friends told him of being shaken down for money by the Flying Gang brutes. Others said it was no longer safe to let their wives and daughters walk around unescorted. The pirates, it was said, had gotten "an abundance of money" out of the Spanish wrecks, and were using it to arm themselves and to buy the loyalty of whomever they needed. Then, somewhere in town, Walker came face-to-face with Benjamin Hornigold.

"Where's that old rogue, your father?" he angrily asked Thomas Jr.

"My father is at home," the young man replied, according to a deposition he later gave to officials in Charleston.

"He is a troublesome old fart," Hornigold exclaimed, "and if I see him I will shoot and kill him."

"My father is at home, and if you have anything to say to him the best way would be to go and speak to his face," the son responded.

Hornigold warned that if the Walkers didn't mind their own business, he would burn their house down, kill the old man, and whip the rest of them senseless. With over 100 men and a well-armed sloop at his command, Hornigold was unopposed in his authority.

The Walkers' situation became more dire by the week. In December, Hornigold and the captains of at least two other pirate sloops cruised the Florida shore to intercept Spanish shipping between Cuba and the wrecks. To the Walkers' horror, Hornigold returned at the end of the month with an even larger Spanish sloop. He renamed it the *Benjamin* after himself and transferred arms and material to her from the

Mary. Witnesses later described the *Benjamin* as a "great sloop" or sloop-of-war, capable of carrying 200 men and a variety of weapons. With such a warship, Hornigold had no need for the *Mary.* He sent the English sloop back to Jamaica with the crew members who did not wish to join the Flying Gang.

On or about the first of January, the Walkers watched, mouths agape, as Jennings's privateers sailed into the harbor, their holds filled with looted Spanish silver. The senior Thomas Walker gazed out at the growing fleet of warships in Nassau Harbor, and, for the first time, understood that a new age had begun.

CHAPTER FIVE

PIRATES GATHER

January–June 1716

SINCE RETURNING from his round-the-world voyage, Woodes Rogers had weathered one disappointment after another.

In Bristol he learned that his father-in-law, William Whetstone, had died. His wife and children had been living with the Whetstones during Rogers's long absence. They were compelled to turn over ownership of their Queen Square mansion to Lady Whetstone to defray the costs of supporting them all. With little to show for three years of dangerous work, Rogers also moved in with his in-laws, nursing his wounded face and leg and grieving the loss of his brother.

Within weeks, his convalescence was interrupted by a court summons. A man named Stephen Creagh was suing Rogers on behalf of 209 of the *Duke* and *Dutchess*'s former crewmen. Creagh's clients were convinced that the treasure galleon *Incarnación* had cargo worth not £140,000, but £3 million, and that Rogers had hidden much of the "missing" treasure in Batavia. The sailors must have felt slighted and abused. Many had been forced into the Royal Navy before they even set foot on dry land, and it was Creagh who paid the legal fees and charges to release them. In January 1712, Rogers journeyed to London to defend himself and to watch over the auction of his expedition's plunder.

While in London, Rogers learned that his wife was pregnant with their fourth child. Perhaps buoyed by this knowledge, he threw himself into preparing his journals for publication. He was beaten even in this, by Edward Cooke's account of the voyage, which appeared in London bookstores a few months before his own. He ultimately won out, however, when his *A Cruising Voyage Around the World* came out and quickly outsold its hastily written competitor. Readers were particularly captivated by Rogers's account of the castaway, Alexander Selkirk, who had received scant attention in Cooke's book. Among them was writer and journalist Daniel Defoe, who sought out Selkirk in Bristol and used him as the model for the hero of his most famous novel, *Robinson Crusoe*. *A Cruising Voyage* would go through two editions and numerous reprints, providing Woodes with a much-needed source of income.

In August there was another cause for happiness when Sarah gave birth to a son. The boy was christened Woodes, after his father, grandfather, and great-grandfather. The war was also coming to a close, raising the prospect of better times ahead for the financially troubled family.

Then their fortunes changed yet again. In December, Lord Chancellor Simon Harcourt announced his ruling in the case of *Creagh v. Rogers*. Rogers had lost, and the terms of the judgment forced him into bankruptcy. A few months later, while Rogers was still spinning from this disaster, his eight-month-old son died and was buried in St. Michael's churchyard. The stress of these losses seems to have finally undone the Rogers' marriage. Sarah and Woodes began living apart, he in London, she in Bristol, and soon weren't speaking at all. Within a few years, they were pretending each other were dead.

True to form, Rogers threw himself into another daring project. With the end of the war, piracy was bound to rear its ugly head, and nowhere more so than that most famous den of pirates, Madagascar. Madagascar, the fabled kingdom of Henry Avery, the haunt of Thomas Tew and the late Captain Kidd, was a nest of anarchy and disorder perched astride the primary shipping lanes connecting Europe with India and the Dutch Indies. Rogers had heard the tales from Dampier and others, and he'd undoubtedly heard a lot more from Dutch merchants, officers, and officials in Batavia and Cape Town. He must have sweated a bit, back in December 1710, when his worm-eaten, treasure-laden ships passed around the south end of Madagascar on their long journey home, expecting at any moment to see a pack of pirate sloops appear over the horizon. Rogers was a merchant, after all, and nothing was worse for trade than piracy. In the summer of 1713, Rogers began hatching a scheme to suppress the pirates and, ultimately, to bring their rogue state under the control of the proper authorities.

The first phase of this effort would involve a stealth mission to the island, where he would make contact with the pirates, assess their strength and numbers, and try to negotiate their peaceful surrender. If successful, Rogers may have intended to approach the king, volunteering to oversee the peaceful settlement of the island as its first governor. The benefits of this colony to Britain would be legion. Not only would it displace one of the primary threats to the empire's Asian trade, it would serve as a vital sanctuary and naval and resupply base halfway between England and the East Indies. At this stage, though, Rogers knew he needed to lie low. The British East India Company had already demonstrated that it would go to any lengths to maintain its royal monopoly on the lucrative Asia trade. Rogers couldn't risk having them squash his project before it even got off the ground.

His first trip to Madagascar would, therefore, proceed under cover of trade. He approached his old business partners in Bristol—and probably some new ones in London as well—and negotiated the purchase of a suitable ship. The result was the *Delicia*, a 460-ton merchantman armed with thirty-six-guns, slightly larger than the *Dutchess* and roughly equivalent to one of the navy's larger fifth-rate frigates. With a large rounded hull, the *Delicia* was capable of carrying large cargoes, making her perfect for long-distance trade and supply. She would become Rogers's constant companion for the next eight years. The penniless but well-connected young captain had to confront a more difficult challenge: securing a trading contract with his old enemies at the East India Company.

On October 2, 1713, Rogers traveled down Leadenhall Street, past the sprawling central city market, and rolled up to the entrance of the

East India House, the company's global headquarters. His nose likely stung from the stench of the adjacent market, where hundreds of animals were butchered daily, their entrails lying in huge piles just a few yards away. He stood on a cobblestone sidewalk before the imposing, four-story edifice. The company's sixty-five-year-old mansion was built of wood, and was opulently paned and ornamented. A balcony overhung the street, on which company officials could observe the comings and goings in the courtyards of the market below. Leaden-glass windows in patterns of tiny, diamond-shaped panes faced out onto the street from the second and third floors, except for the center of the third floor, which was adorned with a ten-foot-tall carving of the company's coat of arms. The building was crowned by an enormous mural, twenty-five feet long and fifteen high, of three of the company's great ships under sail, as well as two carvings of angry sea monsters and an Englishman leaning on a rapier. At street level, a doorman stood behind a counter. He would have asked Rogers if he had an appointment before leading him into the sprawling headquarters.

Rogers's proposal was simple. He asked the company officials to allow him to carry slaves from Madagascar to the company's base at Benkoelen, Sumatra.* The *Delicia* would undertake the journey as a "separate stock ship," meaning its owners would finance the journey themselves. The company would either buy the slaves Rogers had rounded up or pay him a per capita shipping fee for his services. Either way, the company would get a good return without any investment at all. The company men, perhaps tickled at having the famous author and war hero begging them for work, granted him a contract. Several weeks later, Rogers was on his way south astride the quarterdeck of his new command.

The *Delicia* arrived on the eastern coast of Madagascar in March 1714. At the time there were a dozen or so English pirates living in the harbor he visited, apparently led by a Thomas Collins, one of Henry

---

* Today part of Indonesia.

Avery's crewmen. Their "Kingdom of Pirates" was a far more modest affair than the novelists and playwrights were making it out to be back in London. Most of them had been on the island for a decade or more, a collection of pirates, ex-cons, and deserters enjoying an easier, simpler existence in this tropical no-man's-land. The local Malagasy people practiced polygamy, which seemed sensible to the English outlaws. Most of them had several wives and large numbers of mulatto children as well as a small army of slaves, whom they had acquired through trade or by intervening in the tribal wars that plagued the island. They sheltered their extended families in fortified houses hidden in the woods near the shore, which they encircled with high wooden walls and ditches. Paths to and from these compounds were made intentionally confusing and convoluted, to give their owners plenty of time to scatter into the woods if they were discovered. That's exactly what they did when Woodes Rogers arrived in the harbor. They no doubt feared his ship, which looked, with its long rows of guns, like one of His Majesty's frigates.

When Rogers and his men first came ashore there were only Malagasy tribesmen to greet them, and no sign of the pirates. Rogers offered to trade for slaves, knowing that a slave could be had here for ten shillings (£0.50) in trade goods, a seventh or eighth the going price in West Africa. Seeing that the visitors had come to buy people, the pirates came out of the woods. "I cannot say that they were ragged, since they had no clothes," recalled the author of A General History of the Pyrates, who later interviewed Rogers about his exploits. "They had nothing to cover them but the skins of beasts without any tanning . . . nor a shoe or stocking, so they looked like the pictures of Hercules in the Lion's Skin . . . the most savage figures that a man's imagination can frame." A lucrative trade ensued, with Rogers buying "great numbers" of the pirates' Malagasy slaves in return for clothes, gunpowder, and metal tools.

Rogers tarried on the island for nearly two months, entertaining the pirates and gathering intelligence on their society. He learned that the natives were involved in continuous warfare and would present little resistance to would-be colonizers. The pirates were, for the moment, weak and disorganized, lacking an ocean-going vessel to wreak any havoc. Morale was low, and Rogers felt they could easily be persuaded to surrender in return for clemency. It would need to be done quickly, however: Fifty sailors from the Dutch ship *Schoonouwen* were stranded on the island's western shore and were planning to join the pirates.

The pirates, for their part, kept a close eye on the *Delicia* and her crew, hoping for a chance to seize the powerful ship. The plan was to wait until nightfall, then swarm onto the decks from their little boats, overwhelming the watch. They even developed friendly relations with some of Rogers's crew, and may have recruited a few conspirators among them. But Rogers had enough experience to sniff out the brewing danger. He cut off contact between the pirates and his men and organized a strong watch aboard the *Delicia*, day and night. The pirates "found it vain to make any attempt," and by the time Rogers departed had even told him what they'd been contemplating.

Rogers had managed to convince many of the pirates that their best hope was to return to England. He helped them draw up a formal petition to Queen Anne, begging her forgiveness and pardon and declaring their wish to come home and live peacefully as honest men. Petition in hand and a shipload of slaves chained in the hold, Rogers ordered the anchors raised and a course set back to Cape Town. He arrived there in May 1714, put the pirates' petition on a London-bound ship, and sailed for Sumatra, where he needed to sell his slave cargo.

Slave ships of this period weren't purpose-built like their nineteenth-century descendents, their holds split into low-ceilinged slave decks. Captains regarded slaves as just another cargo to pack in the hold, albeit one that needed feeding. As a veteran of the African trade, Rogers probably followed its practices on the *Delicia*. The slaves were typically shackled two-by-two and packed into the hold so tightly that each had barely enough space to lie down. Women and girls were confined separately from the men and boys, probably through the use of a tarp or temporary partition. An armed crewman stood sentinel at each hatchway, ready to fire upon any of the people who tried to rush the deck where a chest of loaded muskets and several explosive grenades were kept. If the slaves made for the main deck, the officers could kill great numbers of them from the raised aft deck, whose rails were mounted with small swivel cannon. When the slaves were taken out to be fed, gunners kept these swivel guns trained and ready to spray them with partridge shot. In poor weather the slaves remained confined in the hot, poorly ventilated hold, gasping amid the sweat, feces, and urine. Some inevitably came down with dysentery, which could result in the deck becoming "so covered with the blood and mucus which had proceeded from [the slaves' sickness] that it resembled a slaughter-house." Disease spread quickly in such circumstances, and mortality was high among slaves and the crew, with both populations losing roughly 40 percent of their numbers on a typical passage. And if smallpox, malaria, dengue fever, measles, and dysentery didn't carry them off, there was also the risk of suicide: The imprisoned people were often so terrified and despondent that they had to be watched closely while on deck lest they throw themselves into the ocean, chains and all.

Few were troubled by slavery then—Europeans, Africans, or Malagasy—for they all participated in the slave trade as buyers or sellers. Rogers was no exception. His family fortune had been largely built on the African slave trade, and slaves were a lucrative part of the spoils of his round-the-world privateering expedition. The miserable Malagasy in his ship's hold were just another way of paying the bills, a way of earning capital to invest in larger schemes. We don't know how many slaves the *Delicia* carried to Sumatra, only that Rogers delivered them there in the summer of 1714, loaded his ship with company freight, and headed back to England. He was eager to get home, eager to get on with his plan to flush out a pirate's nest and seize it for the empire.

He never saw Madagascar again.

———

Back in the Bahamas, Benjamin Hornigold and Henry Jennings were getting off to a bad start. There may have been bad blood from their privateering days in Jamaica; or Jennings, an educated ship captain with a comfortable estate, may have looked down on Hornigold, who was likely a penniless sailor. Jennings apparently felt that only those who had one of Lord Hamilton's privateering commissions should be attacking the Spaniards. Otherwise, you would be participating in little better than piracy.

Shortly after arriving in Nassau, Jennings relieved Hornigold of one of his prizes, a small Spanish trading sloop. Having nearly 200 well-armed men and at least two sloops under his command, there was little Hornigold could do to stop him. Some of Jennings's men moved aboard the prize vessel, relieving the crowding on the other sloops. After a few days of revelry and the orderly distribution of the crew's portion of the prize money, the flotilla left for Jamaica. They were privateers, after all, and had to condemn their prizes at the Vice-Admiralty Court, an office presided over by none other than Governor Hamilton himself.

They would be back sooner than they thought.

On their way to Jamaica, Jennings's flotilla was recognized by Cuban mariners. The Spaniards followed Jennings all the way down Cuba's shore, through the Windward Passage, and right to the mouth of Port Royal Harbor. Governor Torres y Ayala would hear of it, and when he did, he would be furious.

The *Barsheba* dropped anchor in Jamaica on January 26, 1716. Thatch, Jennings, and Wills had only been away for about two months, but in that time, Lord Hamilton's situation had changed drastically. Around New Year's, word had reached the colonies that a "Terrible, Hellish Plot and Conspiracy" against King George had been put down back in Britain. "The Tower, Exchequer, and Bank of England were all to be seized," the *Boston News-Letter* breathlessly reported, "the city of London to be set fire in many places [and] insurrections to have been in several places of England." James Stuart was to invade with an army from France, "all on the 25th of September last." The main Jacobite army had risen up in Scotland, with 2,000 rebels commanded by Lord Hamilton's brother, Lieutenant General George Hamilton, but they had lost the initiative to the king's forces. Simultaneous risings had been planned in Wales and Devonshire, but the authorities had gotten wind of them and arrested the plotters. By late January, the news from Britain was bad for Hamilton. The uprising was clearly failing, and the king had placed a price on his brother George's head. The governor knew the time had come to start covering his tracks.

Jennings and Wills brought their treasure to Hamilton in accordance with their commissions. They may not have volunteered that they had seized the treasure from the salvage camp, as opposed to the wrecks themselves, but they didn't really need to. There was simply far too much money for the privateers to have salvaged in so brief a time. Still, it was in nobody's interest to ask. Hamilton later alleged that he didn't take the shares of the treasure that were due him, "for that I heard it was taken from the shoar." He didn't arrest Jennings and his colleagues, either. They went about, free and at liberty, enjoying the pleasures of the land and spending their ill-gotten gains, as did the crews of several other privateers Hamilton had commissioned. At the end of February, when Jennings approached the governor about obtaining permission to depart on another cruise, Hamilton personally signed his departure papers. As he awaited further news of the rebellion, Hamilton kept his privateers at arm's length, neither stopping them nor arresting them.

In early March, Jennings sent word to his men and fellow captains that he was making another cruise to the Spanish wrecks. Several responded, happy for a chance to get some treasure of their own. One was Leigh Ashworth, who had assumed the command of one of Hamilton's other privateers, the fifty-ton sloop-of-war *Mary*. Two others joined without commission—Samuel Liddell of the *Cocoa Nut* and James Carnegie of the *Discovery*—placing their small sloops under Jennings's overall command. Charles Vane, rough and mean, eagerly rejoined Jennings's crew.

The sloops left Bluefields on the morning of March 9, racing out of the harbor and away from Jamaica. That night the four vessels were separated by the wind, but a day or two later they regrouped at Isla de los Piños,* an uninhabited little island nestled behind Cuba's westernmost point. Their plan was to sail around the far end of Cuba, follow the Gulf Stream straight to the wrecks, and loot whatever was found. They rounded Cape Corrientes on April 2, and on the third were beating their way along Cuba's northwestern coast when the lookout on the *Barsheba* cried out.

∽∾∾

A few miles to the west, Sam Bellamy saw the unidentified sloop fall off the wind, bearing down toward him, followed by four consorts. He and Paulsgrave Williams didn't like the look of her.

Bellamy and Williams, deeply tanned, their hair bleached from months under the tropical sun, had likely arrived at the Spanish wrecks in January, shortly after Jennings's men had raided Palmar de Ayz. The work was hard, dangerous, and competitive. By the end of the month, there were seven or eight other English vessels anchored where the *Regla* and *San Roman* had gone down, but try as they might, none of them were able to locate the main hull sections of the great ships. Instead they had to content themselves with scattered cargo and coins; after weeks of work, the wreckers had scrounged up only 5,000 to 6,000 pieces of eight (£1,250–1,500) to share between hundreds of men. When Captain Ayala Escobar arrived from Havana with reinforcements on January 22 and dispersed the Englishmen, Bellamy and Williams were probably just as happy to have been driven off.

They made their way south, past the tip of Florida and the western end of Cuba, and down to the shores of Central America to the Bay of Honduras. They probably came to recruit men. The area was then a

---

* The "Island of Pines" later served as the model for Robert Louis Stevenson's *Treasure Island*. The second largest island in Cuba, it was renamed Isla de Juventud after the 1959 revolution.

rough no-man's-land inhabited by Mosquito Indians and gangs of rough and wild English loggers called Baymen. The latter lived in huts in the steaming swamps of what are now Belize, and the Yucatán and Campeche, in Mexico. They were in desperate shape, their food supplies having run short during the previous fall, causing the death by starvation of several loggers at their main camp in Campeche. At least 200 others decided to turn pirate, building great sailing canoes and heading out on the dangerous passage to New Providence or the Spanish wrecks at Palmar de Ayz. In February 1716, the Spanish attacked Campeche, capturing and killing many of the remaining loggers and dispersing the rest. By the time Bellamy and Williams reached the Bay of Honduras a few weeks later, most everyone in the logging camps was looking for a way out. The two had little trouble finding men willing to become pirates.

By late March, Bellamy and Williams were heading a pirate band operating out of a pair of periaguas, the very same type of sailing canoe that Hornigold and Thatch had started with two years earlier. Somewhere in the Bay of Honduras they boarded their first known prize, a Dutch vessel commanded by a John Cornelison. The band looted the vessel and forced a sailor to join them on pain of death, and shortly thereafter, seized control of an English sloop under a Captain Young. While their band of wreckers and Baymen searched the sloop for valuables, Bellamy and Williams tied their periaguas astern and forced Young to take them back over to Cuba. Unlike Hornigold and Jennings, they had no illusions about being privateers. They were pirates, pure and simple, and Bellamy had little sympathy for the shipowners and captains who had made his life so miserable. He argued that the band should act as Robin Hood's men, taking from the wealthy merchants and enriching the poor sailors. Williams, a wealthy merchant himself, was likely to have been motivated by sympathy for the Scots and their deposed Stuart king, or simply by the money.

When, off the coast of Cuba, Jennings's four sloops began bearing down on them, Bellamy and Williams saw their British colors and, fearing capture, decided to make a run for it. They ordered their men—who numbered around forty—to get all the valuables in the periaguas and prepare to abandon ship. As Jennings's *Barsheba* came up alongside, Bellamy's gang jumped into the sailing canoes, cast off the lines, and began rowing as hard as they could, straight into the wind.

◈

From the deck of the *Barsheba*, Jennings watched the periaguas cast off. He could see there was little point in pursuing them: Tacking against the wind, his sloops wouldn't be able to catch them before they made it inside the reefs protecting the Cuban shore. Instead, he came alongside the sloop and hailed its master, Captain Young. Young, expecting rescue, explained that the people in the two periaguas "were a parcel of villains" and had just made off with all his money. Young assumed that Governor Hamilton's privateers were there to fight pirates and protect merchants like him. He was soon disappointed.

Jennings was in no hurry to let Captain Young go. He put some of his men aboard and signaled to his consorts. The fleet would make its way to nearby Bahía Honda, a sheltered anchorage on a sparsely settled stretch of the Cuban coast. There they would decide what to do with Captain Young and his sloop.

Upon anchoring outside the narrow entrance of the anchorage a few hour later, Jennings and his men were greeted with a wonderful surprise. Lying in the keyhole-shaped harbor was a large armed merchant ship flying French colors, much of her crew on shore collecting water and firewood. With Jennings's fleet at the harbor entrance, there could be no escape. The wind was blowing off the land, however, and even in their nimble sloops it would be impossible for Jennings's fleet to tack into the narrow entrance. He gave orders for the five sloops to drop anchor while he tried to devise a plan.

Examining the ship through his eyeglass, Jennings could see it would be suicide to undertake a direct attack. Stealth, it seemed, was the best approach. He sent three of his men in a dory to assess the situation. They rowed into the harbor and up to the French ship and hailed the captain pleasantly. They were coming into the harbor to collect water, they told him. The French captain invited them onboard, and while engaging in small talk the Englishman had a look around.

They were aboard the frigate-rigged ship *St. Marie* of Rochelle under Captain D'Escoubet, a wealthy man who owned a quarter of the ship and cargo. The pirates guessed there were forty-five men aboard and fourteen to sixteen guns, though the ship was capable of carrying twice that. The *St. Marie* would make an excellent prize.

When the dory returned with this news, Jennings called a meeting of the captains. He declared his desire to ambush the *St. Marie*, label her a pirate, and take her back to Jamaica as a prize. Samuel Liddell, captain of the *Cocoa Nut*, argued this would be a terrible mistake. He told the other three captains that he'd seen the *St. Marie* in Vera Cruz, Mexico, some months before and that she was clearly "a trader on a lawful occasion."

The other men were not convinced by Liddell's argument. "What are you come out for?" one of them barked at him. "To look upon one another and return with your fingers in your mouth?" Jennings chimed in that he would be aboard the French ship that very night, but that his *Barsheba* "must not go only to be taken." If he went alongside the larger *St. Marie*, "we would probably be sunk," he declared. They would need to surprise the French ship and board her from their boats. Captains Ashworth and Carnegie agreed.

Liddell made a last ditch effort to save the situation. The *Cocoa Nut's* owners had sent him to dive the Spanish wrecks, not to engage in out-and-out piracy. Unless the *St. Marie* could be shown to be a pirate or to be carrying English goods illegally, the privateers had no grounds to seize her. He implored his colleagues to delay the attack until morning, offering to personally board the *St. Marie* to see if they could "make a lawfull prize of her." Liddell found himself outvoted, and made it clear he would have no part in this act of piracy.

Liddell's men watched enviously as the crews of the *Barsheba* and *Mary* gathered arms and prepared the boats for an assault. Finally his quartermaster announced he was joining them, abandoning Liddell with upward of a dozen men. It was going to be a risky venture rowing two miles across the bay to engage a heavily armed ship from small boats. At sunset something happened that changed the odds entirely.

~~~

As Bellamy and Williams escaped into the wind, they watched the English privateers board Captain Young's sloop for the inevitable consultation between captains. What happened next puzzled them. Young was clearly a legitimate trader, but instead of letting him go, the privateers put a prize crew aboard and took her along with them. Hidden amid the reefs and mangroves, they watched the little flotilla anchor at the entrance to Bahía Honda. The men in the periaguas began to realize that the men operating these sloops were not acting like sheriffs at all.

Around seven P.M., as the tropical sun set over the mellowing horizon, they rowed past Carnegie's and Young's sloops and among the *Barsheba*, *Mary*, and *Cocoa Nut*. Bellamy and Williams, who were aboard the same sailing canoe, hailed the captain of the *Barsheba*. Jennings, Vane, Bellamy, and Williams all laid eyes on one another for the first time. They needed each other, they realized, to capture this great French prize.

A little before ten o'clock, the *Barsheba* and *Mary* hauled up their anchors as their officers led a cheer: "All for one and one for all." The men let out a hurrah and somebody foolishly fired a musket. Whoever did that should be cut down, some of the men said, not wishing to place the *St. Marie* on alert.

Then amidst the flickering light of the sloops' lanterns, the privateers saw a most unusual thing. Bellamy's and Williams's great canoes rowed among the sloops, their crews stripped naked, pistols and cutlasses in their hands, like a pack of savages. The *Barsheba*'s men threw a bowline out to one of the periaguas; the crew of the *Mary* tossed theirs to the other. Bellamy's and Williams's canoes proceeded across the bay, their men straining at their oars, each canoe towing a sloop-of-war packed with heavily armed men.

They must have made a terrible sight to Captain d'Escoubet and the bewildered men aboard the *St. Marie*: two Indian-style war canoes filled with naked, wild-looking men tearing across the water, the sloops-of-war in tow. D'Escoubet had been suspicious of the English sloops from the start, and had even hidden a chest of treasure ashore, for fear they might attack. Even so, he was unprepared. As the periaguas closed in, Bellamy's men let go of the sloops and charged directly at his ship. "Where are you going?" one of Escoubet's men yelled at the men in the canoes. "Aboard, where do you think?!" came the reply, followed by a fusillade of musket shot. A blast of fire let loose from the *Barsheba*, and a cannonball tore over Escoubet's head. He was outnumbered by at least six to one. Escoubet ordered a number of his men aboard his dory, which then tried to make it ashore. One periagua overtook and captured them, while the men from the other charged onto her decks. From the second periagua, Bellamy warned the Frenchmen that if they resisted, they would all be slaughtered. Escoubet surrendered. His men hadn't fired a single musket.

For Sam Bellamy, it was a lesson in the value of terror. They had taken a well-armed, but lightly manned frigate, without harming the crew, ships, or cargo. They'd gone into battle looking like they were capable of anything and, as a result, they hadn't had to do anything at all. For Bellamy, it was a lesson on how to conduct piracy: that fear can be the most powerful of weapons.

As the *Barsheba* and *Mary* came to anchor alongside their prize, Jennings's men joined in the search of the *St. Marie*'s holds and the interrogation of her men. Charles Vane, hotheaded and violence prone, may have shaken hands and shared rum with Bellamy and Williams. This was not the sort of fellow Bellamy and Williams needed in their crew. They intended to fight smart, harm few, and score big.

The next morning, April 4, 1716, Jennings began questioning the French crew. Escoubet later reported that the English "tormented the crew to [such an] inhumane degree" and in "the vilest manner," forcing them to reveal where they had hid 30,000 pieces of eight (£7,500) ashore. Jennings also kept the *St. Marie*, appointing Carnegie as her master, and giving Escoubet and his men Carnegie's wayward *Discovery* instead. The pirates had captured a ship, treasure, and cargo worth 700,000 French livres or £30,300. Jennings also forced the French captain to write a letter to Lord Hamilton in Jamaica, absolving the privateers of any wrongdoing. "I must acquaint your Excellency that those gentlemen treated me very civilly and were very willing to give me so much per month for the hire or freight of my vessel," Escoubet wrote. The privateers only "took my vessel because she was fit for the expedition they were going on."

While the pirates and privateers busied themselves with dividing the plunder and transferring cargo and personnel from one ship to another, a large sailing canoe arrived in Bahía Honda. Its crew innocently made their way up to *St. Marie*, asking for Captain d'Escoubet. On board were a French merchant officer and eighteen men who had been sent from Mariel, twenty miles farther up the coast, where their vessel, the sloop *Marianne*, lay at anchor. They had come to trade with Escoubet, but found themselves prisoners of the English instead. Jennings "inflicted punishments" on his new captives, who, after "several torments," agreed to lead them back to their vessel. Jennings held a conference with Bellamy and Williams, who agreed to send one of their canoes to Mariel with the *Discovery* to capture this second French vessel.

The following morning, Bellamy's two periagua crews split up. One headed to Mariel with Carnegie. Bellamy and Williams stayed behind with the other to make sure their newfound colleagues didn't try to cheat them out of their share of the plunder on the *St. Marie*. A few hours later, the *Cocoa Nut* weighed anchor and headed out in the opposite direction; Liddell wanted nothing to do with these piracies and was headed back to Jamaica minus twenty-three members of his crew.

Jennings and his men waited in Bahía Honda, hoping their colleagues would soon return with another prize. A day and night passed, and in the morning light a pair of sloops was seen passing by the harbor entrance. One, the prisoners from Mariel confirmed, was their vessel, the *Marianne*. The other, an armed sloop of ten guns, flew a black flag. Jennings and Vane recognized it immediately. It was the great sloop of Captain Benjamin Hornigold.

❧❧❧

Hornigold had stayed at New Providence for two months after Jennings's departure, no doubt seething at the shoddy treatment he'd received at the privateer's hands and hoping to even the score.

Meanwhile, the outlaw population of Nassau was increasing by the day. Some fifty men had abandoned the sloops working on the nearby Spanish wrecks, most of them after waves of Spanish reinforcements arrived in February and early March. These men, resident John Vickers would later report, were committing "great disorders . . . plundering the inhabitants, burning their houses, and ravishing their wives." The wreckers were led by Thomas Barrow, formerly a mate on a Jamaican brigantine who had run off with a cache of valuables said to have belonged to "a Spanish marquis." Barrow had no vessel of his own, but swaggered about the island, claiming to be "Governor of Providence" and promising to "make it a second Madagascar." Dozens of logwood cutters arrived every week from Campeche, attracted by inflated tales of Spanish treasure, turning to piracy upon their arrival. Others came from New England, South Carolina, and Jamaica: unemployed seamen, indentured servants, criminals on the run, even a few escaped slaves from Cuba, Hispaniola, and beyond. Ordinary settlers grew increasingly fearful, and many of them were quietly making plans to leave. Others—prostitutes, smugglers, and arms dealers—were pouring in. New Providence had turned into an outlaw state.

Hornigold had started the Bahamas' burgeoning pirate republic, but between Barrow's wreckers and Hamilton's privateers, he must have felt his leadership of the Flying Gang was starting to slip. After all, unlike the privateers, his 200 crewmen didn't serve under legally sanctioned contracts that gave most of the plunder to the owners and captains. Apart from a few forced men, service aboard the pirate vessels was essentially voluntary. Most of the islands' pirates were mariners who long suffered abuse and exploitation in the navy and merchant marine. They had no intention of replicating that system, but rather turning it on its head. They took to electing their captains and, if dissatisfied with their selections, could vote to impeach them as well. The Flying Gang pirates gave their captains absolute authority while in combat, but most other decisions were made democratically in a general council of the crew, including where to go, what to attack, which prisoners to retain or set free, and how to punish transgressions within their companies. Hornigold and other pirate captains ate the same food as their men and had to share their cabins. The crew kept their authority further in check by electing another official, the quartermaster, who ensured that food, plunder, and assignments were doled out equitably. Captains typically received only 50 percent more plunder than an ordinary sailor, as opposed to perhaps 1400 percent more on a privateer. If the men trusted their leader and were satisfied with his performance, they would follow him to the bitter end. If not, they might depose him in the blink of an eye. Hornigold needed to show results, or his tenure as a pirate leader might soon be over.

With Thatch aboard, he set course for the sparsely settled coast of northwestern Cuba, which straddled the shipping lanes connecting Havana and the Spanish Main, New Orleans, and France. Along those poorly patrolled shores, prizes were waiting.

Hornigold made his way through the Straits of Florida, probably giving Havana a wide berth, and made landfall on Cuba around April 8, near the secluded harbor of Mariel. Sitting at anchor was a large merchant sloop flying French colors. This was the *Marianne* of Santo Domingo, en route from Hispaniola to the swampy French hamlet of New Orleans under the command of a French naval officer, Ensign Le Gardew. He had stopped to send a packet of mail to Havana and, while there, Le Gardew heard that his colleague, Captain d'Escoubet of the

St. Marie, was just down the shore. Eager to trade provisions and advice, Le Gardew sent half his crew down to Bahía Honda in the ship's boat. Undercrewed and lightly armed, she was no match for the *Benjamin*, with her ten guns and 200 men. Le Gardew promptly surrendered, and Hornigold took possession of the sloop and £12,500 in cargo. A prize crew was put aboard, and the two sloops made their way down the coast, perhaps hoping to take the *St. Marie*, as well.

At the entrance of Bahía Honda, a flotilla of English privateers had beaten them to the punch. Hornigold could see that one of them was that thorn in his side Henry Jennings.

❦

When Jennings gave the order for all vessels to weigh anchor and chase after Hornigold, Bellamy and Williams were aboard the *St. Marie*, their periagua tied astern. They helped the prize crew raise the French ship's anchors and watched as the *Barsheba* and *Mary* raced off. By the time the *St. Marie* was underway, the rest of the fleet had already passed out of sight. Opportunity, the two men could see, had come knocking.

As the *St. Marie* pulled out of the harbor, Bellamy and Williams gave the signal. Their men rose up in unison, surprising Jennings's prize crew and the French prisoners, and seized control of the ship. While some of Bellamy's men held their captives at gunpoint, the others quickly hauled their periagua alongside and threw sacks and chests of coins aboard. Keeping an eye on the *Barsheba* and *Mary*, six or eight miles off, Bellamy and Williams got their men aboard the canoe as well and rowed off into the wind. Their take: 28,500 pieces of eight (£7,125). To put it in perspective, the annual income of an early eighteenth-century merchant captain was about £65.

Meanwhile, Jennings, Vane, and the other men aboard the *Barsheba* knew they were never going to catch up to Hornigold and the *Marianne*. They could also see that the *St. Marie* had fallen dangerously far behind. Better to return to Bahía Honda, Jennings noted, than lose our own prize. At his signal, the *Barsheba* and *Mary* swung around. An hour or two later they approached the *St. Marie*. Her crew hailed them, clearly distraught. Bellamy's men had risen against them and made off with everything, they said. Murmurs of discontent spread through the *Barsheba*. Jennings had lost much of their plunder. The furious privateer ordered his men to seize the other periagua and, as the *Mary*'s carpenter, Joseph Eels, later recalled, had it "cut to pieces," apparently along with any of Bellamy's men who were aboard it at the time. During this rage, Jennings also ordered the hapless Captain Young's sloop burnt to the waterline.

Sometime later, his anger spent, Jennings gave out new orders. The fleet would sail for Nassau to divide up what remained of their spoils.

~~~

After the heist, Bellamy and Williams caught up with Hornigold. The pirates met face-to-face off the coast of Cuba. Hornigold must have been pleased to learn that the men in the canoes had managed to steal Jennings's treasure from right under his nose. He could use men like these. Bellamy and Williams, after the pirate articles were read, joined the crew of the *Benjamin*.

Mariners appreciate competence, and Bellamy must have inspired a great deal of it, for despite his youth, Hornigold appointed Bellamy as the captain of the newly captured *Marianne*, ahead of several older men in his own crew including Edward Thatch and his quartermaster, William Howard. Bellamy presumably manned the *Marianne* with his periagua crew of twenty or thirty, plus some thirty to forty of Hornigold's men. He and Williams now had a well-built ocean-going sloop at their disposal, a chest of treasure in the hold, and the most infamous English pirate of the day as their consort. All they needed were some cannon to arm their new raider.

For a week or more, they continued prowling the western end of Cuba, waiting to intercept Spanish or French traffic coming through the Yucatán Channel. But instead of a rich prize, they came across yet another pirate.

Olivier La Buse, captain of the armed sloop *Postillion*, joined the pirate squadron. La Buse and Hornigold made peculiar allies. La Buse and most of his crew were French, while Hornigold still saw himself as a patriot, carrying on a righteous war against England's enemies. La Buse and his men were bona fide pirates, happy to plunder anybody for a profit. Somehow, the French corsair and the English captains agreed to work together, cementing a transnational relationship that would last for many years.

It's likely that Bellamy had something to do with this arrangement. The young man wasn't fighting for Britain, he was fighting against the system: captains, shipowners, kings, the whole lot, and not a few of Hornigold's own company felt the same way. If Hornigold objected to sailing with the French pirate, his men overruled him. The *Postillion*, armed with eight guns, would be sailing with them.

Not long afterward, the three pirates—Hornigold, Bellamy, and La Buse—spotted a merchant ship coming across the Yucatán Channel from the direction of Campeche. This turned out to be an English ship bound for Holland with a load of logwood: a friendly vessel, not a prize. Unlike Hornigold, La Buse and Bellamy had no compunction about sacking an English ship. A vote was taken, and Hornigold's men again overruled him. While Bellamy and the unarmed *Marianne* held back, La Buse and Hornigold secured the prize. A crew was sent aboard to search and sail the ship. They took what odds and ends seemed useful—drink, coins, provisions, spare parts, a skilled crewman or two—and after eight or ten days let her go on her way, probably at Hornigold's insistence.

A few days later, at the western tip of Cuba, they made a capture everyone could be happy with: two Spanish brigantines loaded with cocoa, which they captured without firing a shot. After looting the vessels, they sailed to Isla de los Piños, where they found three or four English sloops topping off water and firewood supplies. The hulls of the pirate vessels needed cleaning, so the pirates announced to the masters of the small sloops that their vessels were to be commandeered to help with the careening process. Hornigold may have found an unpleasant surprise on the underside of the *Benjamin*. The shipworms appeared to have done her serious damage, something requiring the services of a proper shipyard to remedy. Hornigold began contemplating the disposal of his great sloop, the possession of which had caused so much alarm among the law-abiding citizenry of New Providence.

The careening completed, the pirates continued along the southern shore of Cuba, bound for the Windward Passage. La Buse knew of some good hideouts along the shores of sparsely populated French Hispaniola, and directed the fleet in that direction. Hispaniola was well placed for raiding commerce coming in and out of the Caribbean. A lair was found and agreed on, and the pirates resolved to work together to sack as many vessels as possible.

Hornigold wanted to get rid of the *Benjamin* first, and sometime around the end of May 1716 resolved to sail to Nassau for that purpose. The *Benjamin* was loaded up with bulky cargoes to sell to the Bahamas' growing cadre of unscrupulous smugglers. Bellamy and Williams may have come along as well in the interest of securing cannon for the *Marianne*. Hornigold, Thatch, and at least 150 others left La Buse, agreeing to return in a few weeks' time.

❧❧

On April 22, 1716, Henry Jennings's privateering fleet arrived in Nassau's expansive harbor. It was quite a sight: the *St. Marie*, now equipped with thirty-two guns, escorted by Jennings's own ten-gun *Barsheba* and Ashworth's ten-gun *Mary*. It was the most powerful naval force New Providence had seen since Henry Avery had shown up with the *Fancy* twenty years earlier.

Jennings, Ashworth, and Carnegie all went ashore to the bawdy town of Nassau, leaving their vessels left in the hands of trusted subordinates. After two or three days, the quartermaster of the *St. Marie*, the sickly Allen Bernard, rowed to town and interrupted Jennings's debauchery. Apart from four or five men, the entire complement of the *Barsheba* was aboard the *St. Marie* looting her remaining cargo. "This must not be," Jennings is said to have exclaimed. He told Bernard to "go on board and dissuade them" by claiming that none of them could afford to delay departure for the wrecks. "Between you and I," he confided, "if I can get her out to sea again with ye goods in her, I will run her up to Jamaica and secure her, for these fellows have drawn me into this [mess] and will doubtless, when they have shared the goods, leave me to answer all."

Bernard, suffering from a stomachache, begged the captain to go himself, to lend the weight of his authority. With both his authority and a large quantity of valuables at stake, it would have seemed a prudent measure. But Jennings refused, telling his quartermaster "he would not be concerned with such rogues." Apparently the captain had more important things to do between the taverns and whorehouses.

On his way to the shore, Bernard came across Carnegie and Ashworth and apprised them of the situation. The two captains took the situation more seriously than their commodore, each volunteering to help Bernard restore order on the *St. Marie*. Ashworth immediately rowed out to the *Mary* to make sure his crew hadn't joined the riot, while Carnegie and Bernard made their way to the *St. Marie*.

The French ship was a scene of chaos. A hundred men poured over her, hauling European goods and supplies from her holds, piling them in boats, and rowing them over to the desolate shore of Hog Island, not far from the rotting bones of Henry Avery's *Fancy*. None of them had the slightest interest in what Carnegie and Bernard had to say. Flummoxed, Bernard returned to shore to try to raise Jennings to action. The captain was once again unmoved and told Bernard to watch over them and to not take any of the cargo by force.

Bernard spent the rest of the day observing the men's actions on the Hog Island shore. They had divided the plunder into three lots, and contrary to the practice of privateers, had allocated two lots for themselves and one for the owners, rather than the other way around. They should have taken all the plunder back to Jamaica, to be distributed and taxed by the Vice-Admiralty Court. Instead, they immediately divided their portion among themselves. Only the owner's lot was to be sent to Jamaica. Not wanting to entrust the owners' share to Jennings, the crew contracted the services of a local sloop, the *Dolphin*. This ten-ton vessel, curiously enough, belonged to one of Thomas Walker's sons, Neal.

Before the *Dolphin's* departure, Jennings, Ashworth, and Carnegie decided their best course of action was to inform their vessels' owners of their taking the French ship and the insubordination of the men. They drew up a manifest of the *Dolphin's* contents and wrote detailed letters to their owners and business partners and entrusted them with Allen Bernard and the *Mary's* quartermaster, Joseph Eels. Bernard and Eels boarded the *Dolphin*, letters in hand, and began the journey home.

After the *Dolphin's* departure, Jennings managed to secure control of the *St. Marie* and mustered a crew for her, the *Barsheba*, and the *Mary* to sail for the Spanish wrecks. They arrived a few days later, their considerable firepower presumably scaring off the Spanish guard ships. A passing English merchantman later reported that the *St. Marie* was presiding over a total of twenty-four English vessels on the wrecks, half Jamaican, half Bermudan, which would "not permit either French or Spaniards to come there." According to the *Barsheba's* youthful doctor, John Cockrane, divers managed to take "some money out of ye water" before sailing back to Nassau. Not long thereafter, Jennings, still considering himself an honorable privateer, led the *Barsheba* and *St. Marie* back to Jamaica.

It's likely that Charles Vane did not return to Jamaica with the *Barsheba*. Nothing was there for him, except the possibility of legal proceedings. On the other hand, on New Providence he had his share of treasure, a good harbor at his disposal, and a town filled with brothers-in-arms. Given his personality, Vane was likely a ringleader of the looting of the *St. Marie*, in which case the owners would not have been pleased with him. It was better to stay in Nassau and enjoy a merry life until the money ran out.

———

Hornigold and Thatch sailed into Nassau in early June. They had been gone two months, and the pirate society on New Providence had grown in their absence. Dozens of periaguas, launches, and sloops sheltered inside Hog Island, their lines indicating a mix of origins: Spanish, French, English, and Dutch. Along the shore, the pirates had beached a couple of unwanted prize sloops, their looted hulls baking in the sun.

Amid the palms, palmettos, and tropical scrub, smoke rose from the cooking fires of a hundred huts, tents, and hovels. Most of these were made from whatever was handy: driftwood, old spars, decking, and worm-eaten hulls covered over with palmetto thatch or bits of old sailcloth. The ruder sort was home to groups of logwood cutters driven from Campeche, or black and Indian slaves on the run from their masters in Cuba, Hispaniola, or Jamaica. Slightly better were the hovels of the wreckers and former mariners. Nassau looked like an encampment of castaways, with sailors singing, dancing, drinking, and fornicating. Increasing numbers of wives and prostitutes were settling on the island, tending alehouses, mending clothes, cooking meals, and keeping the men company at night. One young sailor, James Bonny, had recently arrived from South Carolina with his sixteen-year-old wife, Anne; the latter quickly earned a reputation for libertine behavior. For most of the mariners it was a dream come true: ample food, drink, women, and leisure time. And when the money ran out, there was always another ship to capture, a plantation to loot, a treasure wreck to dive on.

The better homes—simple frame houses—belonged to the merchant-smugglers who bought the pirates' plunder with cheap rum, tobacco, and ammunition, and to the settlements' leading figures. Once these homes had belonged to New Providence's law-abiding colonists, but most had been forced to flee the town "for fear of being murdered." Thomas Barrow, the leader of the wreckers, had harassed them without mercy, shaking them down for drinking money and whipping anyone who refused him.

Even the merchants who came to trade with the pirates were not necessarily safe. In the harbor, Barrow robbed a brigantine from New

England and beat up the master of a Bermuda sloop. Some vessels were apparently off-limits, including the *Richard & John*, the fourteen-ton sloop owned by Hornigold and Thatch's old pirate buddy John Cockram and Cockram's influential father-in-law, Richard Thompson. Cockram and his brothers, Joseph and Phillip, were running a successful trading syndicate out of Harbour Island, shipping pirate goods to Charleston and sugar and provisions back to Nassau. They competed with Benjamin Sims, a forty-year veteran of New Providence, and Neal Walker, whose sloop *Dolphin* was said to be in Jamaica at that very time, bearing a load of Henry Jennings's plunder. Together these merchant-smugglers provided vital logistical support to the Bahamian pirates. "The pirates themselves have often told me that if they had not been supported by the traders [bringing them] ammunition and provisions according to their directions," a colonial official would report in 1718, "they could never have become so formidable, nor arrived to that degree [of strength] that they have."

⁓⁓⁓

While Hornigold looked for someone to sell the *Benjamin* to, the others bought and sold goods and personal items, and exchanged news and stories with the wreckers and logwood cutters. Along the way they learned that Jennings's own men had turned on him to loot the *St. Marie*. They ate fresh fish and pineapples, and pork and chicken that had never seen the inside of a barrel, and drank Madeira wine and Barbados rum. Bellamy may have felt he'd found paradise: a republic of sailors, freed from those who would exploit them, free to live the merry life as long as the agents of empire could be kept away.

Hornigold found a buyer for the *Benjamin*, a Virginian merchant by the name of Perrin, who also happily purchased most of his plunder. With the proceeds, the pirate commodore purchased another sloop, transferred his guns aboard, and christened her the *Adventure*. The *Adventure* was considerably smaller and less threatening than the *Benjamin*, probably only twenty tons or so. The trade, Thomas Walker reported, had weakened Hornigold and "in some measure has disabled him from doing such damages upon the high seas as he would have done if he had continued his command" of the *Benjamin*. The trade made, Hornigold oversaw the fitting out of his third pirate sloop-of-war.

He was also concerned about the future of the pirate republic. All it would take to do them in, he knew, was for the English, French, or Spanish to send three or four men-of-war to Nassau. But if the town could be better fortified, authority might be kept at bay. He looked at the assorted cannons poking from the sloops in the harbor, then up at the ruined shape of Fort Nassau. Yes, he realized, the time had come to arm the island, not just its vessels. He organized Thatch and others to obtain cannon, pulleys, shot, and powder, and began rearming the old fortress.

For Thomas Walker, this was the final straw. For nearly a year, he, his wife, and his children had been threatened and abused by these rogues. He had begged the outside world to quash the pirates before they grew too strong, but to no avail. He knew that he would be killed if he tried to stop them from fortifying the harbor. If they succeeded, it would be far harder to root them out. He gathered his family and fled to Charleston, leaving Nassau to the pirates.

❧❦❧

Back in Jamaica, Lord Archibald Hamilton's life was going from bad to worse. With each passing week, the news from Britain grew bleaker. By mid-March he knew that the main Jacobite army had suffered a devastating defeat near the English town of Preston and at least 4,000 had been taken prisoner. James Stuart and his entourage had reportedly landed in Scotland but "not finding things according to their expectation" had fled back to France four days later.* By the end of April, Lord Hamilton found his nephew Basil's name on a list of nobles captured at Preston and imprisoned in London. The uprising had failed before the colonies had even had a chance to join in.

---

* In reality, James Stuart had stayed for several weeks.

Lord Hamilton's Jacobite activities were catching up with him. In March, Samuel Page, the secretary of Jamaica's governing council, had sailed for England carrying a sheaf of damning documents, letters, and depositions that he intended to present to King George. The Assembly of Jamaica and the former commodore of the local naval detachment were submitting evidence against him. Peter Heywood, a member of the governing council, was maneuvering to replace Hamilton as governor, by professing his support of "King George's sacred person and family."

Hamilton's privateers were causing him further trouble. The activities of Jennings, Willis, Fernando, Ashworth, and others had generated a flurry of hostile letters from the governors of Cuba and French Hispaniola. Governor Torres y Ayala of Havana wrote that "several gentlemen of Jamaica" had told him that Hamilton "was part owner of all the vessels which have been sent to our camp" at Palmar de Ayz; all the treasure had to be returned and the perpetrators seized and punished. The Cuban governor's ambassador in Jamaica had traced some of the stolen money to Hamilton's own house. Recently there was the matter of the *Dolphin*, a little Bahamian sloop that had shown up filled with goods Jennings and his gang had recently plundered from a French ship. Then came Henry Jennings himself, the *St. Marie* in tow, though minus the coins and valuables she once carried. To top it off, an official French delegation arrived bearing a letter from the governor of Hispaniola, demanding the return of this ship and another French sloop supposedly captured by Jennings. "I believe, my Lord, all these actions must occasion horror," the governor had written Hamilton. "I know several of [the privateers] have estates in Jamaica. It is but just they should be sold, and the money employed to repair the wrong they have done. I demand it of your Excellency, in point of justice." The entourage included Captain Escoubet, who was extremely angry to see his ship, the *St. Marie*, anchored in Port Royal awaiting Hamilton's condemnation.

Alas, if the Jacobite uprising had succeeded, Hamilton could have used the privateers to fund his administration and secure the surrounding colonies for the rightful kings of England and Scotland. Instead, they had become a liability. They would have to be rounded up and sacrificed for the cause. He put out orders that Jennings and the other captains not be allowed to leave the island.

Shortly thereafter, in late July, there was a knock at Hamilton's door.

HMS *Adventure* had arrived from Britain bearing orders from King George. Lord Hamilton was to be arrested and delivered to England in chains. Peter Heywood, the leader of Hamilton's opponents on the governing council, had been appointed governor and he immediately launched a full investigation of Hamilton's privateers. Jennings's commission had been seized and he went into hiding.

A good thing, too, for in late August another ship arrived from London bearing an official proclamation from King George. It was printed and posted around the island on August 30, and distributed across the British Americas in the weeks that followed. The king had declared Jennings, Carnegie, Ashworth, Wills, and others to be pirates.

By then, Jennings and his men were already halfway to their sanctuary, beyond the reach of the law: the Bahamas.

CHAPTER SIX

BRETHREN OF THE COAST

June 1716–March 1717

IN LATE JUNE or early July 1716, the pirates regrouped at their Hispaniola hideaway: Bellamy and Williams in the *Marianne*, Hornigold and Thatch in the newly acquired sloop *Adventure*, and La Buse aboard the *Postillion*. All should have been well. The three sloops were freshly cleaned, and had plenty of fresh water, wine, ammunition, and powder stowed away below decks. There were nearly 200 men between them and a safe haven from which to sally forth and strike merchantmen as they passed through the Windward Passage.

But relations between the pirate companies were strained. Hornigold's rule over the little squadron was failing due to his reluctance to attack English and Dutch vessels. He thought himself a vigilante, settling old scores with the French and Spanish; friendly vessels were boarded only as a last resort to acquire vital supplies or skilled crewmen. Bellamy and Williams thought differently and La Buse and his largely French crew didn't see any reason to spare English shipping.

While Hornigold had been away in Nassau, Bellamy and La Buse had attacked several English vessels off the southern coast of Cuba, seizing men, provisions, and liquor. Hornigold was angry to learn of this upon returning. In the heat of August, tensions reached a breaking point. Bellamy and La Buse wished to plunder an English vessel; Hornigold again refused. Aboard the *Adventure*, many of Hornigold's men called for his impeachment. The commodore was overlooking valuable prizes, and he'd lost the *Benjamin* to boot; perhaps younger, more radical leadership was in order. The quartermaster likely called for a vote of the ship's company. Hornigold had lost the confidence of two-thirds of the crew. The majority was ready for no-holds-barred piracy and decided to join Bellamy and La Buse aboard their sloops. Hornigold, they decreed, could keep the *Adventure*, but was to leave the rendezvous immediately and not show his face there again. Humiliated, the deposed commodore headed back toward the Bahamas with twenty-six loyal men, including his protégé, Edward Thatch.

✦✦✦

Even for a pirate, the speed of Samuel Bellamy's ascent to power was striking. Only a year after leaving New England as a penniless sailor he had become the commodore of a gang of 170 pirates. He and Williams had already captured prizes worth thousands of pounds, more money than he and his fellow sailors could ever have hoped to see in a lifetime of legitimate service. He was twenty-seven and his career was just beginning.

Most of the ninety men in his own sloop's crew were English and Irish, with a few Scots, Welsh, Spaniards, and Dutchmen, a Swede, and at least two men of African descent. Most were in their midtwenties or early thirties, former seamen and privateers who had willingly entered piracy. A few had been forced to serve, at least at first. John Fletcher, whom Hornigold had kidnapped off the *Blackett* in October 1715, had come to embrace the pirate life; the crew liked and trusted him so much that they elected him to serve as the *Marianne*'s quartermaster. Others were unwilling captives, like Richard Caverley, seized from an English sloop on account of his navigational skills, and Peter Hoff, the thirty-four-year-old Swede with extensive knowledge of the southern Caribbean. Bellamy would need their expertise in the months ahead.

After Hornigold's departure, Bellamy and La Buse detained several sailing canoes, dinghies, and cargo boats, which kept their galleys stocked. They seem to have taken it easy through the end of the summer, eating, drinking, and making merry. By September, Bellamy reckoned it was time to expand their horizons. He proposed to his crew that they sail eastward, down the curving spine of the Antilles to the Spanish Main, chasing any sail crossing their path. The men agreed, as did those under La Buse. At the height of hurricane season, they began their trek from Hispaniola.

They sailed against the prevailing winds, tacking their way along the mountainous shores of Hispaniola and Puerto Rico. It was a quiet trip, punctuated only by whatever marine life passed their way: a curious pod of dolphins or a cascade of flying fish scattering fearfully before the sloop's hulls. But as they passed the far end of Puerto Rico and began the crossing to St. Thomas, a lookout spotted the telltale, triple-masted outline of a ship on the horizon. As they closed the distance, Bellamy could see it was quite large—a frigate, really—flying French colors. A long row of gun ports pierced her side, with a second, shorter row on her poop and forecastle. Forty guns all told, making her a smaller frigate similar to the *St. Marie*, the French ship they'd looted under Jennings's nose. Unlike the *St. Marie*, however, this ship was fully armed, and was not confined in a harbor, anchored to the seafloor. Her sails were up and her great guns were rolling out for action. A mighty prize, to be sure, one that could allow them to attack most anything in the West Indies, but not an easy one to capture. Bellamy consulted La Buse and his men and resolved to hazard a bold strike.

Bellamy and La Buse were outgunned two-to-one, so they had to count on outmaneuvering their powerful opponent. They weren't able to do so, unfortunately. The French ship delivered a broadside against the *Marianne*, cannonballs tearing through her decks, sending splinters in all directions. After an hour's engagement, Bellamy called off the attack. One of his men was dead and three were seriously wounded. The French ship proceeded on her way.

They spent October and November prowling the Virgin Islands, then a sparsely-populated archipelago contested by four nations. Five hundred Danish colonists lived on St. Thomas, overseeing the labor of more than 3,000 African slaves; several hundred English lived on Tortuga, the westernmost part of the sprawling British Leeward Islands colony, which stretched out 300 miles down the Antillies to Antigua and Nevis. The Danes and English both claimed uninhabited St. John, the French and Danes argued over St. Croix, while the Spaniards held onto several other islands. With so many rival nations squabbling over such a small area, the Virgin Islands provided ideal conditions for swift commerce raiders like Bellamy and La Buse. They could steal a merchantman and take off "over the border" if a warship or coast guard vessel tried to pursue them. The prizes proved small, but they kept themselves in food and drink by seizing a variety of hapless fishing vessels and a French cargo ship carrying flour and salted cod. On at least one occasion they forced unmarried men to join them, but let the married men go free, knowing their family bonds made them much harder to mold into committed bandits.

On the morning of November 9, as the pirates cruised the wide passage between St. Thomas and St. Croix, the rising sun revealed a sloop approaching from the west. It was a still morning, the wind barely filling their sails, but it was behind them. Bellamy and La Buse were able to overtake the vessel, a merchantman flying British colors. Bellamy ordered his gunner to fire a cannon over the sloop's bow, while La Buse had a large black flag "with a death's head and bones across" hoisted to the top of the *Postillion*'s mast.

The master of the sloop, Abijah Savage, saw there was no point in resisting. Each of the pirate sloops had eight guns and between eighty and ninety men. Savage's vessel, the *Bonetta*, was unarmed and crowded with passengers traveling from Jamaica to his home island of Antigua, the capital of the British Leeward Islands. There was an excitable nine- or ten-year-old traveling with his mother, an Antiguan planter heading home in the company of his Indian slave boy, a Negro or two, and some hired hands; no match for the approaching sloops, their decks packed with armed, wild-looking men. Savage did what virtually every shipmaster did when confronted with well-organized pirates. He struck his sails, pointing his vessel into the wind, where her sails flapped uselessly

like laundry hung out to dry—the universal maritime signal of submission. The Bonetta drifted to a stop, rolling gently in the swells. Savage
and his men hoisted a boat over the side, climbed in, and rowed over to
see what their captors wanted of them.

In council, the pirates resolved to detain the Bonetta and her complement for the time being. It wouldn't be long before the sloops would
need to be cleaned again, and they would need a spare vessel to careen
against. Savage and his men were confined aboard the Marianne while
the pirates took possession of his sloop and set course for the all-but-
deserted island of St. Croix. Savage and his crew remained prisoners for
fifteen days, almost all of which were spent at anchor in the harbor of
St. Croix. During this time, Savage later reported, Bellamy and La Buse
were primarily concerned with exchanging their sloops for a combat-
capable ship, which, with luck, they believed they "should be able to con-
quer and make a voyage." While the pirates cleaned the hulls of their
vessels, three of the forced men fled into the dense foliage surrounding
the harbor. The pirates recaptured one of the escapees, the Swede Peter
Hoff, whom they "severely whipped" for the infraction.

The sloops cleaned, Bellamy informed Savage that he, his men,
and cargo would be free to go. The pirates, whom one witness said
"pretended to be Robbin Hoods men," also had a penchant for fancy
dress and took the clothes of the wealthy passengers. They also seized
a black slave and an Indian boy belonging to an Antiguan planter, but
were prepared to let the remaining passengers and crew go. But one of
Savage's passengers, the nine- or ten-year-old child, John King, begged
the pirates to take him with them. When his mother tried to stop him,
King threatened her with violence and, according to Savage, "declared
he would kill himself if he was restrained" from joining Bellamy's crew.
The pirates must have been amused by the little boy, dressed in silk
stockings and fine leather shoes, for they took him aboard the Marianne. There were plenty of ten-year-old ship's boys on naval and merchant ships, and now they had two of their own. To Mrs. King's horror,
her son took an oath of loyalty to the pirates, promising not to steal

even a single piece of eight from the company, and sailed away with his new companions.

Bellamy was well aware that once Captain Savage reached Antigua, the alarm would spread across the Leeward Islands. The pirates needed to stay ahead of their former prisoners by quickly sailing down the chain toward the Spanish Main. From St. Croix they made for Saba, a tall, jagged, Dutch island seventy-five miles farther east, their eyes peeled for a combat-suitable ship.

They didn't wait long. The very next day, with Saba looming to the northeast, they spotted and overtook an armed merchantman. The *Sultana*, a British ship-rigged galley with twenty-six guns, was a formidable vessel but considerably smaller than the forty-gun French ship they'd tried to take several weeks earlier. Bellamy and La Buse raised the skull-and-crossbones, confident that this time they had found an opponent they could handle. Little did they know how easy the engagement would be. *Sultana*'s captain, John Richards, was in his cabin, suffering from wounds he'd received earlier in the voyage and entirely unable to organize her defense. The *Marianne* and *Postillion* quickly outmaneuvered her. The *Sultana* would never arrive at the Bay of Campeche to take on a cargo of logwood as planned. She would become a pirate ship instead.

With the approval of the crew, Bellamy assumed command of the *Sultana*. The ship represented a marked increase in power. As a galley, she was constructed for speed and maneuverability, with flush decks and a sleek and narrow hull. The *Sultana* was not as big as Bellamy would have liked, but she made an excellent stepping-stone, a tool that would win him a proper frigate. Bellamy's prestige among the crew was so great that they selected his friend and confidante, Paulsgrave Williams, to assume command of the *Marianne*. The silversmith and the farmer's boy were now in a position to do serious damage to the merchants of the Atlantic.

Within hours, the pirates captured a second ship, a clumsy merchant vessel under a Captain Tosor, who had been sailing for Campeche under the protection of the *Sultana*'s guns. Tosor's vessel was plundered and, because the pirates were running increasingly short of manpower, several of his men were forced into service. Tosor himself was allowed to proceed on his way to Campeche in his ship. One of Bellamy's crewmen, Simon Van Vorst, a twenty-four-year-old Dutchman born in the former Dutch city of New York, later recalled seeing many of the forced men "cry and express their grief" at their fate. More than a few would change their minds as the treasure piled up over the coming months.

~~~

The three-vessel squadron continued along the Leeward Islands, passing the British outposts on St. Christopher, Nevis, and Montserrat. Wishing to avoid entanglements with the Royal Navy, they gave Antigua a wide birth. They needn't have worried. At that time, there wasn't a single British warship between Jamaica and Barbados. On Antigua, the governor of the British Leeward Islands, Walter Hamilton,* had been apprised of the pirates' presence by the arrival of Captain Savage, but had no means to respond. At that moment, a merchant sloop was racing for Barbados with an urgent message for his counterpart there, asking that he dispatch his guardship, HMS *Scarborough*, to protect English shipping from the "vermine of pirates." But it was 250 miles to Barbados, and if his request was granted Hamilton knew it would be three weeks before help could get to his sprawling, poorly-defended colony.

In the second week of December, the pirates captured a pair of trading vessels within sight of the French island of Guadeloupe, which they looted of food and other necessities. Then they turned southsouthwest, letting the Lesser Antilles and their angry governors sink slowly behind the horizon. Bellamy knew it was time to find a hideaway to overhaul his new flagship and prepare for bigger things. They sailed for Spanish waters, for the remote island of La Blanquilla, where they could expect to conduct such business without disturbance.

---

* No relation to Lord Archibald Hamilton.

On December 19, twenty-seven miles short of La Blanquilla, they made yet another capture. They swarmed around the *St. Michael*, a British ocean-going merchant ship on its way from Bristol to Jamaica. Captain James Williams was carrying a cargo of provisions he had picked up in Cork three months earlier: barrels of flour, grains, salted pork, and the cured beef so prized by the people of Kingston and Port Royal. The *St. Michael* was lightly armed and resistance was pointless. Men from the *Marianne* and *Postillion* took control of the ship and set a course for La Blanquilla.

La Blanquilla, "the white one," lay 100 miles off the coast of what is now Venezuela, a low limestone island ringed with wide, gently sloping white sand beaches. A lonesome backwater, La Blanquilla had long been a favorite rest stop for mariners. Its beaches were perfect for careening and the only inhabitants were parrots and boobies. The pirates stayed for at least two weeks, through Christmas and New Year's, during which time they converted the *Sultana* into a man-of-war and added four of *St. Michael*'s guns to the *Marianne*. They intended to let Captain Williams and the *St. Michael* go, but forced fourteen of her men to help crew the *Sultana*. Bellamy must have been concerned about maintaining his new flagship because four of the pressed men were carpenters. Many of these men were horrified and begged the pirates to let them leave on the *St. Michael*. One, Tom South, was told by the ship's company that they "swore that they would shoot him before they should let him go from them"; when South persisted, Bellamy threatened to dump him on a desolate island to die of thirst or hunger. Another carpenter, Owen Williams, was promised that if he came quietly and helped the pirates with their ongoing repairs, they would release him on the next prize they plundered. Quietly or not, the forced men watched miserably as the *St. Michael* weighed anchor and continued on her way for Jamaica. Shortly thereafter, the *Postillion* raised her anchor as well. Olivier La Buse's men had decided to take their share of the plunder and head out on their own. They left on good terms with their English brethren, but must not have been interested in Bellamy's master plan: to

capture an even bigger ship and make a man-of-war capable of destroying HMS *Scarborough* or any other British warship serving in the West
Indies.

Bellamy and Williams reckoned things might have cooled off
enough for them to return up the Leeward Islands. They would make
their way back toward the Windward Passage, ready to intercept any
ships that crossed their paths. Then, perhaps, it would be time to return to the Bahamas. They swore in the new men taken from the *St.
Michael,* reading them the ship's articles and making them promise not
to steal from the communal plunder. This was kept in one large stash
aboard the *Sultana,* carefully inventoried by Bellamy's newly elected
quartermaster, Richard Noland. Captives later reported that Noland
declared, "If any man wanted Money, he might have it." Withdrawals
he marked in an account book, deducting them from the client's share
of the plunder, as if he were running a sort of pirate credit union. The
new men sworn, the two pirate vessels began their run back to the Virgin Islands.

The weather had been heretofore consistent: the trade winds blowing steadily from the northeast and east-northeast, sometimes carrying
patches of rain clouds, a welcome shower of fresh water to cool the
men's bodies and wash off days of accumulated salt and grime. But in
late January the winds began picking up, sculpting angry whitecaps in
the surface of the sea that grew into high waves. Hurricane season was
over, but the gale was becoming dangerous nonetheless. The pirates decided not to take any chances and sought shelter in the nearest harbor.
This turned out to be a familiar one: St. Croix, the uninhabited Virgin
Island where they'd spent much of November. But there was a surprise
waiting for them in the harbor.

The deserted anchorage was littered with the detritus of battle. On
the reef guarding the harbor entrance, the surf battered at the charred
remains of a vessel, which had apparently burned to the waterline. Another large sloop sat half-submerged inside the harbor, her hull riddled
with wounds from four- and six-pound cannonballs. As the *Sultana*

came alongside, Bellamy could see that someone had stripped her mast, bowsprit, anchors, cargo, and rigging. A small battery had been set up behind earthen ramparts on the shore, but it had clearly been bombarded from the sea.

Bellamy didn't have to wait long to find out what had happened. Ragged-looking men crept out of the woods and began waving and calling to them from the beach. Some were white, some black, others inbetween, but all looked tired and hungry. These men turned out to be pirates themselves, the 100 or so survivors of a six-vessel flotilla commanded by John Martel, another Jamaican privateer-turned-pirate. Like Bellamy and Williams, the Martel gang had been marauding the Antilles for months, capturing ships and sloops of all sorts, and had come to St. Croix in early January to clean their vessels. Unfortunately for them, on January 16 HMS *Scarborough** anchored at the mouth of the harbor and began battering their vessels with her guns. The pirates fought back from the four-gun battery they had set up on the shore, but the *Scarborough*'s guns soon took them out of action. For a short time, the pirates thought they might be spared: The fifth-rate frigate was too big to enter the harbor and retreated. The pirates piled aboard Martel's flagship, the twenty-two-gun galley *John & Marshall*, to make a run for it, only to run aground on the reef. Seeing the *Scarborough* tacking back toward them, Martel ordered the men to abandon and burn the galley, which carried forty black slaves the pirates had taken some weeks earlier. Twenty slaves burned to death, presumably because they were still chained in the hold. Martel and nineteen of the pirates made their escape in a small prize sloop before the *Scarborough* arrived, but the other 100 or so pirates and slaves were left to hide in the woods. The *Scarborough*'s sailors and marines recaptured eight of the slaves and looted the sloops of cargo and valuables before sailing off with the rest of their prizes.

---

* Captain Francis Hume of the *Scarborough* was actually looking for Bellamy and Williams, having responded to Governor Walter Hamilton's call to purge them from the Leeward Islands.

Martel's pirates were extremely happy to see Bellamy's men, knowing that it was only a matter of time before the authorities returned to hunt them down. The feelings of the twenty or so blacks in the Martel party is more difficult to ascertain. The fact that they survived suggests they had not been chained in the hold of the *John & Marshall* and, therefore, not regarded as cargo. When Martel captured the slave ship *Greyhound Galley*, some twenty or so of her crew may have been of African descent. It was not unusual for slavers to employ black sailors in their crews. Such men were usually born in the West Indies, some the children of Africans who had been freed by their masters. They were more resistant to the deadly tropical diseases of West Africa and the West Indies than British-born sailors, and since they (or their masters) were probably paid less, they made attractive hirelings. Pirates of this period were often known to free the Africans they found aboard slavers, finding them to be fierce and committed fighters; others treated them as cargo and sold them as such. The Martel gang may have done both: The English-speaking West Indian crew and servants were invited to join the pirate company, while the frightened Akan- and Igbo-speaking people remained in the hold. Whatever the status of the twenty blacks who survived, Bellamy and Williams appear to have welcomed them aboard as equal members of their company, along with the eighty or ninety white pirates who greeted them on that St. Croix beach.

Bellamy's manpower shortage had been solved in one fell swoop. But the sudden recruitment of some 130 men made veteran members of the crew a little uncomfortable. Bellamy and Williams's eighty original pirates, who had come to trust one another during the adventures of the past six months, were now outnumbered by nearly two to one by strangers, including the forced men. Could these new men be trusted in the heat of battle, or would they seize the first opportunity to make off with the company's treasure, as Bellamy himself had done to Henry Jennings the year before? Only time would tell.

Fearing the return of the *Scarborough*, the pirates resolved to leave St. Croix as soon as possible. They needed a new hideaway to ride out the stormy weather. Bellamy's solution was particularly audacious, and suggestive of the growing strength and confidence of his company. Rather than skulking off to some uninhabited island, the pirates made straight for the main British outpost in the Virgin Islands: Spanish Town, on the rocky shores of Virgin Gorda, sixty miles northeast of St. Croix.

Spanish Town, population 326, was the seat of the deputy governor of the British Leeward Islands, Thomas Hornby, the man who had tipped the *Scarborough* off to the Martel pirates' whereabouts. Hornby must have been alarmed when the two heavily armed pirate vessels sailed into the harbor, their cannon trained on his little town. There was little he could do to defend the settlement. A third of the population were black slaves, people more likely to join the pirates than repel them. The vast majority of the white population were children, there being only forty-two white men on the island. His defenses consisted of one unmounted, unfortified cannon. Hornby had no choice but to do as the pirates commanded, and hope that they left Virgin Gorda no worse than they found it.

Bellamy's gang took control for several days, and possibly as long as a week or two, treating the outpost as if it were one of their prizes. There wasn't a lot to plunder. Most of Virgin Gorda was barren and mountainous, restricting the settlers' production to corn, yams, potatoes, and some pathetic stands of sugar cane fit only for making cheap rum. A Royal Navy captain who visited the Virgin Islands a few months later concluded that none of them were "worthwhile to the government, either to settle them or be at any expense at all about them." Still, the pirates must have been amused by their changed circumstances, lording over one of His Majesty's possessions as if it were their own. Some of the less respectable colonists were happy to see the pirates and reportedly "caress[ed] them and gave them money." A few may have even joined Bellamy's gang, their prospects ashore as indentured servants looking less attractive by comparison. But while some of the colonists ingratiated themselves with the pirates, several of Bellamy's forced crewmen jumped ship, begging Deputy Governor Hornby to shelter them. Hornby agreed, but reneged on his promise when Bellamy sent word "that they would burn & destroy the town" if the deserters were not turned over. Hornby complied and the pirates left Spanish Town with more men than they arrived with.

Well fed, rested, and their numbers fortified, the pirates were ready to take on the *Scarborough* or any other vessel they came across. They conferred among themselves and decided that the Windward Passage would probably be the best place to ambush a large, combat-capable ship. Bellamy and Williams were returning to where they had started from, only with nearly three times the men and firepower. With each passing month, more and more of the less "respectable" sort of people seemed willing to join their gang: sailors, slaves, and servants. Bellamy and Williams had started out as thieves but were finding themselves leaders of a nascent revolution. What they really needed was a proper flagship.

❧

At that very moment, in Port Royal Harbor, the armed merchant ship *Whydah* was preparing to depart for London. The *Whydah* had everything a pirate might want. She was powerful, with eighteen six-pounders mounted and room for ten more in time of war. She was fast: a galley-built three-master capable of speeds of up to thirteen knots, perfect for transporting slaves across the Atlantic. Her 300-ton hull was capable of carrying between 500 and 700 slaves or a large cache of plundered treasure. It represented one of the most advanced weapons systems of its time, the sort of technology that could be extremely dangerous if it fell into the wrong hands.

The *Whydah*'s captain, Lawrence Prince, was eager to get home. He had been at sea for the better part of a year, first sailing from London to the Slave Coast of the Gulf of Guinea, where he succeeded in buying hundreds of slaves at bargain prices, paying "thirty iron bars" for each adult female. Prince had sailed across the Atlantic to Jamaica, selling his slaves at the Kingston docks. The crew was loading the proceeds into the *Whydah*: Jamaican sugar, indigo dyes, and chests of silver and gold. With luck, Captain Prince and his fifty-man crew would be back in London by early June, completing the lucrative "triangle trade" that could convert a cargo of iron and colored beads into heaps of gold.

The *Whydah* weighed anchor the last week in February and began what Captain Prince knew would be the most dangerous leg of her journey. Before reaching the open Atlantic, the ship would have to run a gauntlet of pirate haunts: eastern Cuba, Hispaniola, and, most infamously, the Bahamas. But Prince felt confident that his fast, powerful ship could hold off a few pirate sloops. He had sailed the *Whydah* through these waters before, in 1714, and none of the *guarda costas*, French privateers, or periagua-sailing brigands of the Bahamas had dared challenge him.

The first sign of trouble came just a few days out, as the *Whydah* tacked her way between Cuba and Hispaniola. A lookout noticed a pair of vessels were following them through the Windward Passage and appeared to be catching up. When Prince examined the vessels—a medium-sized warship and a sloop-of-war—he may have thought the Royal Navy was approaching. They bore the Union Jack ensign and seemed the right size to be the *Adventure* and the *Swift*, His Majesty's station ships in Jamaica. The warship was, in any case, too large to be a pirate vessel. But as the day wore on, Prince grew concerned. The hull of the larger ship was a galley, not a frigate, which ruled out HMS *Adventure*. Both the galley and the sloop appeared to have far too many men on deck to be innocent merchantmen, and the sloop's sails were covered in patches, as if she had not seen a proper shipyard in a year or more. Most worrying, they continued to follow an intercept course and were closing in. Prince ordered more sail and placed the crew on alert. The chase was on.

It lasted for three days. When the *Whydah* finally came into the range of the *Sultana* and *Marianne*'s guns, the vessels were halfway up the

Bahamas off Long Island, some 300 miles from where they had started. The *Whydah*, testing her range, fired a couple of shots at the *Marianne* with a small, stern-mounted chase cannon; they splashed in the warm sea. A bloody fight appeared imminent.

Bellamy assessed the situation. He felt confident he and Williams could take the larger ship, but a prolonged battle would cause extensive damage to all three vessels, damage the pirates might not be able to easily repair. They would first try psychological warfare instead. He and Williams and all their men put on a wild display with their muskets, cutlasses, and long-handled pikes. A few held up hand-made grenades: hollow iron spheres filled with gunpowder and plugged with a fuse. Many of them wore fine clothing stolen from the wealthy captains and passengers they had plundered—gentlemen's waistcoats, cuff links and collars, elaborate hats of silk and felt, perhaps even a wig or two. On these rough, wild-looking men, these could only be seen as trophies of war. Particularly terrifying to Captain Prince and his slaver crew were the twenty-five black men scattered among the pirates, their unshackled hands clutching swords and axes.

Prince surrendered, having fired but two shots. The pirates poured onto the *Whydah*, whooping and hollering in triumph. "Black Sam" Bellamy had acquired a ship worthy of Henry Avery. The poor boy from the West Country was now a pirate king himself.

᭤᭜᭤

While Bellamy was building his pirate fleet, Hornigold and Thatch were overseeing the development of the pirates' Bahamian base. They continued to attack shipping in the Florida Straits, piling the bones of their prize vessels onto the beaches of Nassau Harbor. But in between cruises, Hornigold continued to act as the Flying Gang's leader. He and his lieutenant organized the transfer of cannon to the crumbling battlements of Fort Nassau to help repel a Spanish or British assault. In the fall of 1716, one of the pirate gangs captured a large Spanish ship from Cádiz and brought it into Nassau to plunder. This Spanish vessel, too big and clumsy to make much of a pirate vessel, would normally have been beached and burned on the shore of Hog Island. But Hornigold realized that the ship could close a gap in the harbor's defenses. The pirates armed her with thirty-two cannon scavenged from various prizes, and by late winter it stood sentry near the harbor entrance, a floating gun platform capable of fending off unwanted visitors. Such precautions worked. When a group of concerned merchants sent a pair of ships over from London to see "how the pirates might best be dislodged," the pirates captured one and sent the second packing back to England.

Word of the pirate republic spread throughout the Western Hemisphere. Disaffected people continued streaming into Nassau from other colonies, and not all of them sailors. In plantation economies like Jamaica, Barbados, South Carolina, and Virginia, there was little room for small farmers, no way for the hundreds of poor people to make a living once they finished their terms of indentured servitude. But the Bahamas had never been a plantation colony, so there was plenty of cheap land available. Even before the pirates took control, blacks and mulattos had enjoyed considerable freedom in the Bahamas, intermarrying extensively with the white settlers, including top officials like Thomas Walker. Under the pirates, New Providence became a sanctuary for runaway slaves and free mulattos alike, as many moved in to join the pirate crews or the merchants, tradesmen, and farmers who supported them. The presence of this rogue state was destabilizing the slave societies around it. The "negro men [have] grown so impudent and insulting of late that we have reason to suspect their rising [against us]," the governor of Bermuda reported. "We can have no dependence on their assistance, but to the contrary, on occasion should fear their joining with the pirates."

Among the new residents was Henry Jennings, captain of the *Barsheba*. He may once have had pretensions of being better than the pirates, but now he was a wanted man himself. Relations between the Jennings and Hornigold remained strained, but there was room enough for both of them in the motley pirate enclave. Jennings earned the respect of the pirate rank-and-file because he was extremely good at what he did, equally capable of capturing French prizes or leading amphibious assaults on Spanish plantations. By the end of the winter, he was recognized as one of Nassau's leading pirates, with 100 men under his command. But in one respect, Jennings continued to set himself apart from the rest of the pirates. He still refused to attack English vessels. On a cruise of Cuba, Jennings did detain one English ship, the *Hamilton Galley* of Jamaica, but only out of dire necessity: Days from port, his men had run out of booze. His crew boarded the ship and seized twenty gallons of rum, leaving the rest of her cargo intact. Jennings treated the captain "civilly and told him they hurt no English men" and, in parting, gave him valuables worth far more than the rum itself.

As the outlaws poured in, Nassau's longtime residents were fleeing "to secure themselves from the pirates." Some went to Abaco, sixty miles northeast, where Thomas Walker and his family had resettled along with several other New Providence families seeking to escape "the rudeness of the pirates." Others moved to Harbour Island and Eleuthera, in part because it was so easy to get there. The Thompsons, Cockrams, and other merchants had boats sailing back and forth between Nassau and Harbour Island to bring the pirates supplies and provisions. For a while they shipped in supplies and special orders from Charleston and Jamaica with their own sloops, but by late winter 1717, they began to buy goods from third-party merchants, who came from as far away as Boston to keep the Harbour Islanders' warehouses stocked with enough supplies to keep the expanding pirate fleet in operation. The trade was so vital to the pirates that they organized a force of fifty men to staff the battery guarding the entrance to Harbour Island's anchorage.

One day in the fall of 1716, Hornigold's band captured a sloop of some twenty or thirty tons. Usually they brought their prizes back to Nassau to plunder the cargo, burn the vessel, and recruit as much of the crew as they could. But this sloop was swift, maneuverable, and capable of carrying a half-dozen cannon: an excellent pirate vessel. Hornigold called a council and suggested that they keep the sloop and place her in command of one of their most respected and reliable members: Edward Thatch. The company agreed. Thatch, the loyal lieutenant of the pirate republic's founder, finally had a pirate vessel of his own.

It was around this time that Thatch began calling himself Black-beard. In his years of piracy, he had let his beard grow wild, making a fear-some appearance. "This beard was black, which he suffered to grow of an extravagant length," an early eighteenth-century historian wrote. "As to breadth, it came up to his eyes" and "like a frightful meteor, covered his whole face, and frightened America more than any Comet that has ap-peared in a long time." He twisted it into many little braids, each tied off with a small ribbon, some of which he tucked behind his ears. This un-usual arrangement struck observers at the time as resembling the plaits that trailed down from the British infantryman's powdered Remellies wig; some late twentieth-century historians think it might be an indica-tion that Blackbeard was himself a light-skinned mulatto, with kinky hair inherited from his African ancestors. (Thatch, the late historian Hugo Prosper Leaming argued, was a slang term for bushy hair.) Either way, it was Thatch's "fierce and wild" eyes, not his beard, that commanded the respect of his men and struck fear into the hearts of his opponents.

By March 1717, Blackbeard had a company of seventy men aboard his six-gun sloop, making him the fourth most powerful pirate in Nas-sau after Hornigold, Jennings, and a sloop captain named Josiah Burgess. In a short time he would be the most powerful pirate in the Atlantic.

He continued to conduct joint operations with Hornigold through-out the winter and spring. His mentor was humbled by Bellamy's defec-tion and the forced sale of the *Benjamin*. For a few months, his men were placated by small thefts: a trading sloop here, a few barrels of rum there; but Hornigold needed gold and silver to keep the allegiance of his men, the merchants who bought his goods, and the rough and tumble crowd in Nassau. There were plenty of up-and-coming pirates operating out of Nassau. Burgess, a recent arrival to the island, already had an eight-gun sloop and a company of eighty men. Then there was that prodigy of Jennings, the impulsive Charles Vane, who enjoyed terrorizing old settlers and the ale tents alike. If Hornigold was to maintain his position, he needed a big score. Blackbeard, ever loyal, agreed to sail with him. In early March, the two sloops weighed anchor and sailed south into the shipping lanes.

Some time after leaving Nassau, one of Hornigold's crewmen, a "free Mullato," became critically ill. The man needed medical attention, but there wasn't a single doctor or surgeon among the 180 pirates. As they worked their way down the Florida Straits, Hornigold and Blackbeard stopped vessels of all sorts, looking for a doctor. In mid-March they finally found their man aboard a Jamaican vessel making her way around the southern end of Florida. John Howell, a gentle soul with a talent for the healing arts, begged the men in Hornigold's boarding party to let him go. The pirates refused: A good surgeon was hard to come by, and too many of their company had suffered needlessly from toothaches, infections, and venereal disease. Before the pirates dragged him into their boat, Howell begged his captain, Benjamin Blake, "to do him justice by declaring to his friends [and] the world, the manner of his being forced." Howell was dejected when he climbed aboard the *Adventure,* but he treated the mulatto sailor without hesitation. Although the man had been very sick, Howell's treatment worked marvelously; within a few days, he was back on his feet. Hornigold was overjoyed and insisted on giving the unhappy surgeon some broken silver buttons as a reward. Howell, not wanting to implicate himself in his crimes, later passed the buttons on to another man. It was a move that would one day help to save his neck.

The pirates continued south, past Havana, around the eastern end of Cuba, and down the Mosquito Coast of Central America. At the end of the month they arrived off Portobello, in what is now Panama, where merchants of all nations came to trade slaves for Spanish gold and silver. On April 1, the pirates finally hit pay dirt: the *Bonnet* of Jamaica, a large armed sloop, was heading home from trading in Portobello. Outgunned by the pirates, Captain Hickinsbottern surrendered his command. In his cabin, the pirates found a chest filled with gold coins. The *Bonnet* would make a worthy upgrade: She was larger, faster, and in better condition than the *Adventure*. As Hickinsbottern had been smart enough to surrender without a fight, they would give him the *Adventure* in exchange for his vessel. While the pirates transferred their cannon and other possessions to their new flagship, Howell begged Hornigold to let him leave with the *Adventure*, but the crew refused to let him go. As one of them later put it, he was "too narrowly valuable, being the only good surgeon which Hornigold and company had dependence on."

The pirates' luck held on their return home. On April 7, south of Jamaica, Blackbeard and Hornigold captured another treasure-laden sloop, the *Revenge*, which they plundered and released. Between the two sloops, the pirates had captured a stunning 400,000 pesos (£100,000). That was more than Jennings had taken in his raid on the Spanish salvage camp of Palmar de Ayz. For the black and mulatto members of the crew, it could only have been sweeter that much of the money had belonged to the largest slave cartel in the British West Indies. For Hornigold and Blackbeard, there would no longer be any fears of a coup against them. From now on, their only serious challengers would come from outside the Bahamas.

⚜

Woodes Rogers was obsessed with pirates. Since returning from Madagascar in the summer of 1715 he had thought of little else. He was sure that with a careful combination of carrot and stick, a pirates' nest could be quelled, and a productive, law-abiding colony would rise in its place. Assuming that most pirates were like his own privateering crews, they might occasionally do something rash like disobey commands or seize the ship from the captain; but most of them could be brought back into the fold with an offer of pardon and a gesture of understanding. The pirates of Madagascar struck him as lonely, forlorn men desperate to return to the motherly embrace of civilization, bowing again to the dictates of their country, Crown, and God. There would be some who would remain unrepentant, who would refuse a second chance. Such men would be dealt with harshly, to make an example for the rest.

Rogers lived in London, supporting himself from the proceeds of his book and the slave-trading journey to the East Indies. He had been appalled by the Jacobite uprising against King George in 1715 and had established friendships with some of the controversial king's leading supporters. These included Richard Steele and Joseph Addison,* childhood friends who had founded the influential Kit-Kat Club,† a circle of prominent members of the conservative Whig Party, which supported aristocratic interests. Steele, an Irish-born writer and journalist, had just been knighted by King George, while Addison was serving as the king's secretary of state for the Southern Department, which included the West Indies. Both men had considerable influence among the empire's leading decision makers, and access to the best information and intelligence. They would play a key role in furthering Rogers's antipiracy schemes.

Another of Rogers's acquaintances was Dr. Hans Sloane, physician to the king, who was credited with keeping Queen Anne alive long enough for the Whigs to organize the Hanoverian succession. Sloane was also an obsessive naturalist who collected specimens of plants, animals, and geological formations from around the world, which filled "every closet and chimney" of his sprawling Chelsea home, creating the greatest repository of natural history information in Britain.‡ In the spring of 1716 Rogers sent Sloane a letter, explaining that he was "ambitious to promote a settlement on Madagascar" and begging that Sloane send him "what accounts you have of that island."

Rogers also contacted the Society for Promoting Christian Knowledge, an Anglican missionary organization famous for its extensive pro-

---

* Author of the play Cato, a drama, a source of many Libertarian ideas.

† For which the Kit Kat candy bar is said to be named.

‡ After his death, Sloane's collection would form the core of the British Museum.

duction of religious pamphlets, books, and flyers. Hoping to reform the moral behavior of the pirates, Rogers asked for and received a shipment of Society books for distribution among "the English inhabitants of Madagascar." One wonders what the veterans of Henry Avery's 1696 campaign would have made of the Christian pamphlets, but in the end they were never distributed. In the latter part of 1716, Addison and Steele informed Rogers that his Madagascar plan had little hope of winning official support. Apparently the East India Company, which held a monopoly on British trade in the Indian Ocean, felt that a thriving royal colony would be a greater threat to their commercial interests than a few hardscrabble pirates hiding in their jungle huts. But Addison had good news as well: There was another pirate's nest in need of Rogers's services, one thousands of miles removed from the East India Company's jurisdiction.

Addison and other government officials were being bombarded by alarming reports about the pirates of the West Indies, who appeared to be gaining strength at a remarkable rate. The Bahamas, Virginia governor Alexander Spotswood warned in the summer of 1716, had become "a nest of pirates" and would "prove dangerous to British commerce if not timely suppressed." That December, the governor of Jamaica reported that the pirates "take more than half the ships and vessels" bound for Jamaica or Hispaniola, crippling his colony's trade. By midwinter, even the captains of His Majesty's warships feared for their safety. The captain of the six-gun sloop-of-war *Swift** was afraid to venture out of Port Royal, and Leeward Islands governor Walter Hamilton was forced to cancel an official tour of the Virgin Islands on the sixth-rate frigate HMS *Seaford* for fear they would be captured by "the pirate ship and sloop commanded by Bellamy." In the spring, London's top diplomats

---

* HMS *Swift* was capable of carrying eighty men and up to eighteen guns, most of them three-pounders, but only had six guns and forty men at Jamaica. She was a 128-ton sloop built in 1704. HMS *Seaford* was a large, 293-ton sixth-rate frigate with thirty-two six-pound guns.

informed Addison that the pirates had "grown so numerous that they infest not only the seas near Jamaica, but even those of the northern Continent." "Unless some effectual and immediate protection is sent," they warned, "the whole trade from Great Britain to those parts will not only be obstructed, but in imminent danger of being lost." With the empire's transatlantic trade at stake, something needed to be done about the pirates, and Addison knew just the man to do it.

Rogers took to the idea immediately. His plans for Madagascar were easily applicable to the Bahamas, he told Addison, and with proper support were sure to rid the Americas of piracy. Rogers envisioned a public-private partnership by which the government would outsource the management of the Bahamas to a corporation of private investors. The corporation would supply the necessary soldiers, colonists, and supplies, plus several private warships and a governor, in the person of Rogers himself. The Crown would contribute a squadron of frigates to support the initial landing and issue a pardon for those pirates who agreed to peacefully surrender to the new governor. The pirates expunged, Rogers and his fellow investors would recoup their investment from the colony's profits. All that was needed was the approval of the Crown and the acquiescence of the lords proprietor, the circle of aristocrats who still held title to the colony.

Rogers spent much of 1717 building political support for the venture. He called in every favor he could think of, exploiting his business network in Bristol, his personal relationships in London, and his late father-in-law's contacts within the Admiralty. He formed an alliance with the wealthy merchant Samuel Buck, the longtime agent of the lords proprietor for the Bahamas, who had personally lost over £2,700 to the pirates. Together they formed a corporation with the verbose name The Copartners for Carrying on a Trade & Settling the Bahama Islands, recruiting five other investors from across England. The two men got 163 leading merchants in London and Bristol to sign petitions to the king in support of the venture. "Woodes Rogers," petitioners informed the government, "is a person of integrity and capacity, well affected to his Majesty's government* . . . a person in every way qualified for such an undertaking."

Rogers and Buck managed to induce the lords proprietor to relinquish to the Crown their right to govern the Bahamas by pointing out that the pirates represented a grave threat to their far more valuable Carolina holdings. The proprietors may also have been swayed by the involvement of a well-known slave trader like Rogers, who would be likely to shape the wayward colony into a proper plantation society, making it harder for the slaves of South Carolina to make their escape. The proprietors would maintain their property and commercial rights in the Bahamas, but agreed to lease them to Rogers and his partners for twenty-one years for a token fee. Meanwhile, Joseph Addison shepherded the Copartners' proposal through the halls of power and onto King George's desk.

On September 3, 1717, Addison had the king's answer: Woodes Rogers would be appointed governor and garrison commander of the Bahamas. There was one small catch: If Rogers wanted the job, he would have to do it pro bono. There would be no salary. He had already committed £3,000—most of his estate—to the Copartners' corporation, but such was his enthusiasm for the project that he agreed to take it on without pay. It was a decision that would eventually bankrupt him, once again.

While the voluminous paperwork for these deals was being processed, Rogers and Buck scurried around London, making preparations for the expedition. Rogers's 460-ton ship *Delicia* would serve as flagship, backed by one of Buck's ships, the 135-ton *Samuel*, with six guns and twenty-six men; and the seventy-five-ton sloop-of-war *Buck*, also with six guns. They recruited an Independent Company consisting of 100 soldiers and 130 English, German, and Huguenot colonists. Thousands of pounds of provisions were ordered: lumber for houses and gun carriages; tools for repairing the fort and clearing land for farming; arms,

---

* That is, not a Jacobite like Governor Archibald Hamilton had turned out to be.

cannon, and clothing for the soldiers; and enough salt, bread, flower, and preserved food to feed the expedition's 530 people for more than a year. Much of the cargo would be carried by a fourth ship, a tubby 300-ton merchant ship called the *Willing Mind*, mounted with twenty guns. Before the year was out, Rogers and his five other Copartners had spent £11,000.

In late October, Rogers received word that the lords proprietor had signed the surrender of government papers. He happily offered to deliver the documents to St. James's Palace himself, which the proprietors agreed to. On November 6, his carriage made its way between the large brick homes lining the wide, straight dirt expanse of Pall Mall and up to the tall, Tudor-era guard tower of the Royal Palace. Guards ushered him into the first of a series of inner courtyards. There, at the heart of the British Empire, he was likely greeted by Addison, in his long wig of brown curls, with a shake of hands and a smile of accomplishment. The hard work was reaching fruition.

On January 6, 1718, King George issued Rogers his commission and official instructions. "Whereas by reason of the great neglect of the Proprietors of the Bahama Islands," the king proclaimed, "the said islands are exposed to be plundered and ravaged by pirates and others, and are in danger of being lost from our Crown of Great Britain . . . We . . . by these presents do constitute and appoint you, Woodes Rogers, to be Our Captain General and Governor in Chief."

Rogers had been granted his wish. It wouldn't be long before he would wish the king had turned him down.

CHAPTER SEVEN

BELLAMY

March–May 1717

WITHIN HOURS of capturing the *Whydah*, Sam Bellamy's men anchored the powerful ship off the nearest Bahamian island, Long Island, 160 miles southeast of Nassau. Bellamy headed the *Sultana* into the wind and, with sails flapping, ordered the men to drop her anchors as well. The heavy iron anchors plunged into the crystalline water and, as the wind pushed *Sultana* to the leeward, their heavy flukes dug into the sand and coral sea bottom. The vessel stopped moving and the two galleys lay side by side, one a miniature of the other, as the *Marianne* came to a stop a short distance away.

The pirates who had taken over the *Whydah* were happy and courteous, Captain Lawrence Prince was relieved to discover. A number of them probably knew Prince, at least by reputation. He had been to Jamaica several times and been stranded there for months after his previous command was sunk in the great hurricane of 1712. Both John Fletcher, the *Marianne*'s quartermaster, and Paulsgrave Williams's boatswain, Jeremiah Higgins, were from Jamaica, and may well have come across Prince during the grim aftermath of the disaster. They could vouch that Prince, unlike many other captains, treated his crews fairly. The pirates were in a generous mood. They were keeping the *Whydah*, but Prince could have the *Sultana* instead, along with £20 in silver and gold as a gesture of goodwill.

The pirates busied themselves transferring cargo and guns from the *Sultana* to the *Whydah*, trying to pack as many valuables as possible into the larger ship's holds. The most valuable items, silver, gold, and gems, were stored in a single heap of bags in the *Whydah*'s great cabin. The pirates bragged to the prisoners that this stash alone was worth between £20,000 and £30,000. At the time of the *Whydah*'s capture, Bellamy and Williams had over 120 men under their command, and each and every one, from nine-year-old John King to the Afro-Indian John Julian, were entitled to at least £100. In addition, the holds of the *Whydah* and *Marianne* overflowed with ivory, indigo, and other valuables. No wonder that when the time came, several of Prince's men asked to stay with the pirates and were welcomed into their ranks.

Days passed as the pirates hoisted more cannon into place on the *Whydah*'s gun deck, boosting her armament from eighteen to twenty-eight guns, and lowered extra cannon into *Marianne*'s hold. The pirates also loaded unwanted cargoes onto the *Sultana*, according to the desires of Captain Prince. As they prepared for departure, their stockpile of treasure was loaded into chests and taken out of the great cabin and stowed on the gun deck with the men. So great was the trust among the pirates, crewman Peter Hoff later reported, that the treasure was left there "without any guard, but none was to take any without the Quarter Master's leave." Before hoisting anchor, the pirates also forced two or three of Captain Prince's unmarried crewmen to join them, apparently finding themselves short of specialists.

In early March, Bellamy gathered the pirates together to decide what to do with their "ship of force." Spring was nigh, so they agreed to advance up the eastern coast of North America, seizing ships as they passed in and out of the gates of the Chesapeake and Delaware Bays, or the harbors of Charleston and New York. If separated by bad weather or unforeseen events, the *Whydah* and *Marianne* would regroup at Damariscove Island in Maine. En route, Williams would stop at his home on Block Island, Rhode Island, to visit family members there; he probably wished to give them a share of his plunder. The pirates knew his extended family could be counted on to purchase and discretely dispose of the pirates' bulkier cargo. Bellamy may have revealed an interest in making a similar stop on the Outer Cape, to return to his love, Mary Hallett.

❦

In early March, the *Whydah* and *Marianne* circled the southern end of Long Island until their bowsprits pointed toward Florida. They were embarking on what would be the most challenging cruise of their careers.

They captured their first prize off the north coast of Hispaniola a day or two after weighing anchor. The three-masted merchant ship *Tanner* had been only a few hours out of the French harbor of Petit Goave.* When the pirates boarded the *Tanner*, they discovered she was a peculiar vessel: a British ship under contract to France, carrying a mixed Anglo-French crew and an enormous consignment of Haitian sugar back to La Rochelle, France's greatest commercial port. While searching the *Tanner* for valuables, the pirates told her crew they were "Robin Hood's men." At least one of the *Tanner's* crew was impressed. John Shuan, a twenty-four-year-old sailor from Nantes, couldn't speak English, but declared loudly in French that he wanted to be a pirate as well. Bellamy relayed commands to him through a bilingual crewman. Shuan listened to his first order as a pirate: to climb high up the *Tanner's* rigging and take down her topmast; this would slow the vessel down when the pirates released her, making it impossible for her to raise a timely alarm. Shuan, eager to prove himself, scampered up the mast and unrigged this upper section, lowering it to the deck with pulleys. He also helped the pirates find 5,000 livres (£208) hidden in Captain John Stover's cabin and, with the help of an interpreter, was welcomed aboard the *Marianne*. The *Tanner* was then released.

Williams kept the *Tanner's* topmast because at this point the *Marianne* was in rough shape. The pirates had been in possession of the fifty-ton sloop for nearly a year, during which time they had weathered storms, fought at least one serious battle, and captured nearly fifty

---

* Then the principal port of French Hispaniola and now part of the nation of Haiti.

vessels. They kept her bottom clean, as best they could, by careening regularly and keeping the areas below the waterline covered in white lead paint. As pirates, however, they had had no access to proper ship-yards or port facilities. Above the waterline, the *Marianne* was becoming a wreck. The yellow and blue trim decorating her quarterdeck was peel-ing, as was the blue paint on her stern. Her single mast had broken just above the deck, a critical wound that had been shored up by lashing on an old spar against it like a splint on a broken leg. Her sails were old and covered in patches. The old English flag, the red cross of St. George, fluttered from her bowsprit, under which a large chunk of the upper part of the bow was missing. Williams could further reinforce his in-jured rigging with the *Tanner's* topmast, but pretty soon he would need to get the *Marianne* a new one.

As they picked their way north along the southern edge of the Ba-hamas, the pirates considered calling on Nassau, where they might scav-enge a mast off some derelict prize and overhaul the *Marianne* in safety. As attractive as that might have been, Bellamy and Williams counseled against this course. If they stopped now, they would miss the lucrative spring pirating season, when the East Coast teemed with shipping after the long, bitter winter. With a ship full of treasure, they would be wise to avoid potentially fractious encounters with either of the Bahamas' rival leaders, Benjamin Hornigold and Henry Jennings, as both had rea-son to be cross with Bellamy and Williams. Besides, with a ship like the *Whydah*, the pirates had the confidence to set up a seasonal pirate out-post of their own. The War of Spanish Succession, Williams told them, had left the coast of Maine in much the same condition as the Bahamas. The Indians and their French allies had burned most of the English settlements, leaving hundreds of miles of coastline uninhabited, includ-ing countless anchorages where an entire fleet of ships could refit un-observed by European eyes. Most important, the shores were covered in forests, with so many great pines that the Royal Navy itself relied on the region to supply its warships with pitch, lumber, and masts. Williams likely suggested they sweep up the East Coast, sell heavy cargoes at Block

Island, and rest and overhaul the *Marianne* on the central Maine coast. The pirates agreed and, a few days later, they watched the last of the Bahamas disappear astern.

They stayed well offshore of the Carolinas, intending to make a beeline for the entrance to Chesapeake Bay. Despite being more than 100 miles out to sea, they came upon a small merchant sloop out of Newport, Rhode Island. The sloop's master, Captain Beer, was bound for Charleston and had probably opted for the outside passage precisely to avoid the pirates said to be infesting the Florida Straits and Windward Passage. Instead, Beer found himself captive aboard the largest pirate ship he and his fellow sailors had ever seen.

Beer spent only two hours aboard the *Whydah*, but he subsequently wrote out everything that had transpired, including a transcription of his conversation with Samuel Bellamy, in which the pirate commodore expounded on the political motivations for his actions.

Beer was brought aboard the *Whydah* while the pirates were plundering his sloop of cargo and trying to decide whether to return the vessel to him or not. Both Williams and Bellamy were in favor of giving Beer his sloop, which was too small to be of any use to them, but their men, their egos inflated by their recent successes, refused. Bellamy ordered Beer brought before him so that he could, apologetically, give the hapless captain the bad news.

"Damn my blood, I am sorry they won't let you have your sloop again, for I scorn to do anyone a mischief when it is not for my advantage," Bellamy told Beer. "Damn the sloop, we must sink her and she might have been use to you." The pirate paused, looking the Rhode Islander over, his sympathy draining away by the second.

"Damn ye, you are a sneaking puppy, and so are all those who will submit to be governed by laws which rich men have made for their own security, for the cowardly whelps have not the courage otherwise to defend what they get by their knavery," he resumed, his anger building with every word. "But Damn ye altogether! Damn them [as] a pack of crafty Rascals. And you [captains and seamen], who serve them, [as] a parcel of hen-hearted numbskulls! They vilify us, the scoundrels do, when there is only this difference [between us]: they rob the poor under the cover of law . . . and we plunder the rich under the cover of our own courage."

Bellamy looked Beer over once again, carefully weighing the effect of his next words. "[Would] you not better make one of us," he asked the captain, "then sneak after the asses of those villains for employment?"

Beer took little time in responding. His conscience, he told the fiery pirate commodore, would not allow him to "break through the laws of God and man."

Bellamy looked at him with disgust. "You are a devilish consceint[tious] rascal, damn ye," he declared. "I am a free Prince, and I have as much authority to make war on the whole world as he who has a hundred ships at sea and an army of 100,000 men in the field. And *this* my conscience tells me: . . . There is no arguing with such sniveling puppies who allow superiors to kick them about [the] deck with pleasure, and [who] pin their faith upon a pimp of a Parson, a squab who neither practices nor believes what he [tells] the chuckle-headed fools he preaches to."*

With that, Bellamy ordered Beer away. He told crewmen to row the captain back over to the *Marianne*, so that Williams could leave him on Block Island. When the pirates finished transferring the last cider and foodstuffs onto the *Marianne*, they set Beer's sloop on fire. The smoke plume could be seen for miles around until the vessel burned down to the waterline, and the flames were quenched by the sea.

---

* Some writers have questioned whether this conversation, which was eventually published in *A General History of the Pyrates*, actually took place, asking who would have transcribed the conversation. The answer is Beer himself. After his audience with Bellamy, the captain was placed aboard the *Marianne*, where he had plenty of idle hours to record the historic conversation. He was released on Block Island a week or two later and, on April 29, showed up in Newport and reported what had happened to him to a correspondent of the *Boston News-Letter*. Details of the conversation were almost certainly recorded by Rhode Island authorities and forwarded to London, where they were made available to the author of the *General History*.

A few days later, the pirates noticed the skies were growing dark. It was early April, and a bank of air that had warmed itself over the sultry creeks and marshes of Chesapeake country migrated out over the colder sea, creating a fogbank as thick as pea soup. It appeared so quickly that Williams and Bellamy didn't have time to close ranks and quickly lost sight of each other. Bellamy's men rang the *Whydah*'s bronze bell but could hear no response from the *Marianne*. Night fell and, when the fog lifted to reveal the Capes of Virginia the following morning, the *Marianne* was nowhere to be found. Bellamy assured his crew that they would catch up with Williams at Block Island as planned or, failing that, at Damariscove Island, a few miles off the Maine coast. Meanwhile, it was time to hunt.

Out of the lifting haze, sails could be seen out to sea: at least three vessels, each with too many masts to belong to Paulsgrave Williams. Merchant ships, Bellamy suspected, and ordered the *Whydah* to swing around, her back to the wind, to bear down on them. Around eight A.M. they approached the first one, a worn-out-looking ship, the *Agnes* of Glasgow. Her captain, Andrew Turbett, wisely offered no resistance. Turbett was headed to Virginia from Barbados, with a load of that colony's signature products: sugar, molasses, and, most importantly for the pirates, rum. They made another discovery in the *Agnes*'s hold: The tired ship was leaking badly and could only be kept afloat by keeping men working the pumps for hours on end. *Agnes*, they knew, would be of no use to them. The *Whydah* bore down on her next target.

This was a 100-ton snow, the *Ann Galley*, a small but serviceable vessel Bellamy suggested they keep as an extra storage ship and to help careen the *Whydah* in Maine. The company agreed, put twenty-eight of their number aboard, and appointed quartermaster Richard Noland to command the new auxiliary. Meanwhile, the *Whydah* detained the third vessel, a modest ship called the *Endeavor*, which was sailing from Brighton, England, to Virginia. The captures completed, the pirate fleet stood offshore, where they finished their looting. The *Agnes* they would sink, her crew sent on their way to Virginia aboard with the *Endeavor*, which was too small for their purposes. Only the *Ann Galley* would be kept when the fleet continued their way northward toward Block Island, Cape Cod, and their Maine hideaway.

❧❦❧

At this time, the morning of April 9, 1717, the *Marianne* was just a few miles over the horizon, against the Capes of Virginia, searching for prey of their own. Williams no longer looked like the middle-aged son of a wealthy merchant. His white wig contrasted sharply with his skin, so deeply tanned after a year in the tropics that witnesses were struck by his "dark brown complexion." His motley crew—five Frenchmen, five Africans, an Indian, and nearly thirty Brits—looked as rough as the *Marianne* herself. Williams must have realized he would make quite an impression on his friends and family when he got to Block Island, but he was eager to see them. There was plenty of money to pass on to his mother, wife, and children, or to exchange with his smuggler friends for critical supplies.

Since becoming separated from Bellamy, Williams hadn't made a single capture. Without the *Whydah*'s firepower, he had to choose his targets carefully, staying clear of any vessel that might be well defended. While *Marianne* hid against the hilly shores of what is now Virginia Beach, Williams's lookout spotted a likely victim tacking toward the capes from the open sea. With the wind at their backs the pirates charged, and in less than an hour were alongside the hapless ship, the *Tryal*, also of Brighton, en route to Annapolis, Maryland. They yelled orders to the unarmed ship's captain, John Lucas, that if he did not row himself over to the *Marianne*, they would sink his ship. The pirates knew Lucas had no choice but to comply; he had only seven men and two boys against their forty men and ten cannon. The *Tryal* turned into the wind and drifted to a stop. Lucas made his way to the *Marianne*.

Still on the lookout for the *Whydah*, Williams took his time looting. With Captain Lucas incarcerated on the *Marianne*, Williams sent a number of his men back over to the *Tryal*. For eleven hours the pirates rummaged through her hold and cabins, breaking open chests and boxes, tearing into bales of goods, keeping some things and throwing others overboard. The *Tryal* had two more boats, and once the pirates had filled them with things they wished to keep, they rowed them back to the *Marianne*, put Lucas back aboard his ship, and ordered him to follow them on pain of death. Another ship had been sighted on the horizon and, in the hopes that it was the *Whydah*, the *Marianne* set a course to intercept. Shortly thereafter the wind began to stiffen, and the *Tryal* began moving faster than the smaller *Marianne*. Lucas, realizing his advantage, swung the *Tryal* around and made a successful dash to safety.

Williams's men had taken everything of value from the *Tryal*, but the last thing they needed was for Lucas to alert the whole Chesapeake region to their presence. From interrogating captured mariners, Williams knew that HMS *Shoreham*, a 360-ton, thirty-two-gun Royal Navy frigate, was stationed near Williamsburg, Virginia's capital. From then on, they would have to move with caution, to be sure they didn't put themselves in a position where the *Shoreham* might bring her guns to bear on their battered sloop.* To further their disappointment, the sails on the horizon turned out not to be Bellamy's. Williams's crew may have grown anxious about what was becoming a prolonged separation from the great treasure heap in the *Whydah*'s hold.

Williams tarried off the mouth of the Chesapeake for several more days, but his fear of encountering the *Shoreham* made him timid. Around April 13 the pirates captured an English ship out of Whitehaven, only to begin fighting among themselves as to whether to destroy it. During this argument, which seems to have pitched Williams against some of his officers, another sloop and ship came into the entrance of the bay. The pirates broke off their fight, left their prize at anchor, and took off into the

---

* Williams needn't have worried. While cruising the Carolina coast in May 1716, the *Shoreham* ran aground on a reef, causing extensive damage to her keel and hull sheathing. She limped into Charleston on May 29, and wasn't able to return to sea for nearly a year. While Williams and Bellamy were prowling the Capes of Virginia, the *Shoreham* was still loading supplies in Charleston; she wouldn't arrive at Kinquotan (Hampton Roads) until May 1, 1717.

bay in pursuit of these new prizes. Unfortunately, as they worked their way up the Virginia shore, they spotted a large frigate-rigged ship in Lynnhaven Bay and, fearing it was the *Shoreham*, beat a hasty retreat, abandoning even their anchored prize.

With tensions growing aboard his sloop, Williams decided to head for home. At Block Island his company could buy supplies; drink and fresh food would do a great deal to improve his crew's morale. With any luck, they would find the *Whydah* there.

Block Island, eleven square miles of windswept sand, lay twelve miles off the coast of Rhode Island. The colony of Rhode Island was noticeably poorer and more loosely governed than Massachusetts, with few roads and a great many smugglers. Even its capital, Newport, was still little more than an oversized village, its 3,000 residents having only started giving names to its streets five years earlier. Block Island was even rougher, an island kingdom of its own, far from the eyes, ears, and arms of the authorities in Newport and Boston. The islanders' first allegiance was to one another, and Williams was one of them, son of a leading landowner, stepson of one of the earliest settlers, related by law, blood, or marriage. It was as safe a haven as Williams could ask for, short of a war-wasted colony like the Bahamas or Maine.

The *Marianne* anchored off Block Island's main village on April 17 or 18. From Captain Beer, Richard Caverley, and other captives aboard the *Marianne* we know Williams went ashore to visit his mother, Anna Guthrie, and sisters Mary Westcott,* Catherine Sands, and Elizabeth Paine. He likely gave them part of his newfound wealth, perhaps asking them to forward some to his wife and children in Newport. He stayed ashore for a number of hours, and possibly a day or two, his activities masked to history by the complicity of his kith and kin.

Williams returned to the *Marianne*, anchored some distance from shore, and was accompanied by seven local men, including his brother-

---

* Mary's first husband, Edward Sands, friend of Captain Kidd, had died in 1708. Paulsgrave's half-sister Catherine (1690–1769) married his nephew John Sands (1683–1763), while Mary remarried one Robert Westcott.

in-laws, John Sands (the local warden and justice of the peace) and Thomas Paine (probable nephew of the great pirate of the same name), and one of his late stepfather's fellow Scots rebels John Rathbon. The men, according to an affidavit they drew up a month later, went aboard the *Marianne* for "about an hour or two," then boarded a boat "without any molestation" and began rowing back to the village. The men claimed that they were suddenly ordered to return to the *Marianne*, at which point three of the men in the boat—William Tosh, George Mitchell, and Dr. James Sweet, were "forcibly taken from us and commanded to come on board." Given that Sands, as justice of the peace, failed to report the incident for more than a month, it seems likely that the men actually volunteered to join the pirates, and that Williams's in-laws' business aboard the *Marianne* would not have born official scrutiny.

Before leaving Block Island, Williams released Captain Beer and his crewmen, who would eventually travel to Newport to report their capture. By the time Beer made it to the mainland, events had made his news of Bellamy irrelevant.

Williams cruised the mouth of Long Island Sound, calling at Gardiner's Island, a 3,500-acre island off the coast of Long Island, New York, and the feudal preserve of the family of the same name.* Captain Kidd, Williams knew, had visited the island in 1699 and had not only been entertained by John Gardiner and his Indian servants, he had managed to leave two chests and a number of bundles of treasure with him for safekeeping. Williams may have done the same, placing his wealth in the capable hands of "the 3rd Lord of the Manor" for later collection at the end of the summer season.

On the afternoon of April 26, the skies darkened and a powerful wind began blowing from the southeast. Long Island Sound roiled with angry whitecaps, and powerful gusts threatened to tear the *Marianne*'s

---

* The island, located off East Hampton, NY, has remained in the same family for four hundred years. Robert David Lion Gardiner, the last to hold the family name, called himself the "16th Lord of the Manor" until his death in 2004.

patched sails and splinted mast. A fearsome storm was striking New England. Williams was able to find shelter, probably nestled behind Gardiner's Island and between the two flukes of eastern Long Island. As the wind howled through the rigging, Williams was in a safe harbor. Out on the open ocean, he knew, it was going to be a dangerous night.

～≈～

Not 150 miles to the east, Bellamy was sailing over gentle seas, pushed along toward Cape Cod by a fair wind. The day had gotten off to a fine start. At nine that morning, while still out of sight of land, they had intercepted a two-masted vessel between Nantucket Shoals and Georges Bank, the most productive fishing grounds of southern New England. Bellamy ordered the craft to surrender, emphasizing the point by firing a cannon shot ahead of her bow. Seven of his men rowed over to the prize, the *Mary Anne* of Dublin, and ordered the captain and most of his crew to row themselves over to the *Whydah*. Bellamy questioned the captain, one Andrew Crumpsley, and was pleased to discover that he had been on his way from Boston to New York with a load of wine. He sent four more crewmen to rustle up some bottles to pass around the *Whydah* and *Ann Galley*. Unfortunately, they had some trouble getting into the *Mary Anne*'s hold: the heavy anchor cables were piled over the entrance. For now, the men of the *Whydah* would have to settle for the five bottles of fresh wine the pirates had found in Crumpsley's cabin. No matter, they would take the *Mary Anne* with them and find time to plunder her later. Between the decks, the pirates' morale was presumably lifted by the prospect of a wine-fueled party on the shores of an out-of-the-way Maine island.

First, there would be a short stop on Cape Cod, for after the *Mary Anne*'s capture, Bellamy ordered all three vessels to follow a course of north by northwest. This took them not to the islands of Midcoast Maine, but straight for Provincetown and, by extension, Eastham. According to surviving accounts by those present, Bellamy told his crew they would be stopping on the Cape to stock up on fresh food and provisions. But according to Eastham folklore, his real aim was to reunite with young Miss Hallett and show her and her family just how much he had made of himself.

At about three in the afternoon, a fog settled around the *Whydah* and her two prizes, so dense and impenetrable that the pirates had trouble keeping the vessels together. Without a pilot for each, Bellamy knew it would be too dangerous to approach the treacherous shores of Cape Cod; if his great ship ran aground on one of the many unmarked shoals, they would be sitting ducks for the Royal Navy or any other armed authority. Despite his desire to get to Provincetown's anchorage, Bellamy ordered the vessels to come to a stop. Their sails flapping idly in the wind, the three vessels bobbed amid the eerie mist, waiting for visibility to improve.

Not half an hour later, the pirates had a stroke of luck. Drifting through the fog, straight into their midst, came a small trading sloop, the *Fisher*, on her way from Virginia to Boston. Clearly the sloop's captain knew these waters well enough to be willing to traverse them in these conditions; just the man the pirates needed. Bellamy hailed her, asking, "whether the master was acquainted here" with the coast. The *Fisher*'s captain, Robert Ingols, replied, "he knew it very well." Bellamy insisted Ingols row over to lead the way. By five o'clock, Ingols and his first mate were standing on the *Whydah*'s quarterdeck under heavy guard, advising Bellamy on how best to proceed up the long, harborless shore of the outer Cape.

Bellamy happily ordered his three prizes to follow the *Whydah* as Ingols guided her through the fog toward the unseen coast. It would soon be dark, as well as foggy, so they placed a large lamp on the stern of each vessel to make it easier for them to keep track of one another. They proceeded to the north: Bellamy in the *Whydah* with over 130 of the pirates and most of the captives, Noland and seventeen pirates in the *Ann Galley*, the wine-loaded *Mary Anne* under the control of eight of Bellamy's men, and a prize crew of four pirates guarding captives in the *Fisher*.

Aboard the *Mary Anne*, seven of the eight pirates promptly went for the casks of wine in the hold. Thomas South, one of the carpenters forced from the *St. Michael* five months earlier, remained sullen, quiet, and unarmed, keeping his distance from the rest of the pirates. While the others shoved aside the piled-up anchor cables on top of the hatches, South whispered to one of the *Mary Anne*'s captive crewmen that he was plotting to escape from the pirates as soon as possible. Meanwhile the rest of the pirates continued taking turns at the helm while the others broke open the first barrels of Madeira wine and started what they intended to be a very long night of drinking. It wasn't long before the *Mary Anne* began falling behind the rest of the vessels. Bellamy, aboard the *Whydah*, noticed this and slacked off long enough to let the wine-laden pink catch up. He yelled at the leaders of the *Mary Anne* pirates, Simon Van Vorst and John Brown, to "make more haste." Brown, already tipsy, swore he would make the vessel "carry sail till she carried her masts away." He and the other men ordered their captives to help them handle the sails and, when they realized that the *Mary Anne* had a leaky hull, to do the backbreaking work of manning the pumps. They damned the vessel herself, saying they "wished they had never seen her." By the time darkness fell, they turned the helm over to one of their captives, freeing up another pirate for the critical task of drinking wine. Brown declared himself captain, while another pirate, Thomas Baker, began bragging to the captives, telling them that their company had a privateering commission from King George himself. "We will stretch it to the world's end," Van Vorst chimed in.

At about ten at night, the weather began turning ugly. Heavy squalls of rain began to fall, the pitch black sky was shattered by bolts of lightning. Worst of all, the wind had shifted so that it was coming from the southeast and east, driving the vessels toward the unseen shore of Cape Cod. The drunken pirates aboard the *Mary Anne* soon lost sight of the other vessels. Baker, perhaps distressed, began cursing the *Mary Anne*'s cook, Alexander Mackconachy, who was manning the helm and had apparently steered her closer to land. He "would make no more to shoot him, then he would a dog," Baker howled, musket in hand. "You will never go on shore to tell your story!"

Not long thereafter, the shore presented itself, as if rebuking Baker. The *Mary Anne* was now being battered by twenty to thirty foot seas, which broke in cascades of foam all around her. Everyone realized they might run aground at any moment and be dashed to pieces by the angry sea. Mackconachy begged the pirates to swing her around, bow to the beach, to give her the best chance of surviving the inevitable collision with the bottom. Just after they had swung around the *Mary Anne* struck, shaking the hull violently and sending wine casks tumbling about the decks. Baker grabbed an axe and began hacking away at her masts, as bringing them down would reduce the stress on the creaking hull. With two of the three masts down, another of the pirates cried out in terror, "For God's sake, let us go down into the hold and die together!" The men, captives and pirates alike, huddled on deck and in the hold, expecting to be drowned at any moment. The illiterate pirates begged Mackconachy to read from the Book of Common Prayer. As they listened to the prayers in the cook's Gaelic accent, lightning flashed in the sky, wind screamed through the rigging, and the wooden hull shuddered in the surf.

The crews of the other prize vessels were more sober and, possibly as a result, more fortunate. As the storm built, Richard Noland in the *Ann Galley* lost sight of the *Whydah*'s lantern, but he kept close to the little *Fisher*. The mountainous waves were pushing them toward the breakers, which they could hear crashing on the Cape's deserted shore. Noland realized their only chance was to drop their anchors and hope that the great iron hooks held firm enough to keep them off the beach until the storm subsided. He swung the *Ann* around and the men flung the anchors overboard. He screamed and gesticulated to the *Fisher* to do the same. On both vessels, pirates and captives alike watched anxiously as the anchor cables played out, stiffened and, miraculously, pulled the wooden ships to a stop a few hundred yards off the beach. If prayers were said during the night, they were undoubtedly directed at the anchors, clinging to the sandy bottom as the Atlantic vented its fury.

A few miles to the north, the *Whydah* was also being driven inexorably toward shore. As the huge seas tossed the ship closer and closer to the crashing surf, Sam Bellamy may well have remembered the wrecks of the Spanish treasure fleet, great hulls battered into kindling by violent, storm-driven surf. Bellamy knew where he was. In flashes of lightning, he could see the great cliffs of Eastham looming a hundred feet above the exploding waves. If they crashed here, there would be few survivors. The surf washed nearly to the feet of the cliffs, which rose precipitously to the tablelands, that windswept, sparsely inhabited plain separating the villagers of Eastham and Billingsgate from the sea. By midnight, he knew the *Whydah*'s half-ton anchors were the only hope of saving her.

The men struggled to follow the order as waves rolled over the deck. The helmsmen, their feet wide apart, spun the wheel, bringing the great ship's bow face-to-face with the wind. The anchors splashed into the water and their heavy ropes began to play out. Everyone held their breath as the lines grew taught. There may have been a moment's pause, as the *Whydah* briefly stopped drifting toward the foamy chaos behind them, but then they could feel the anchors dragging. The *Whydah* was doomed.

There was one last chance to save the crew, to do just as the men on the *Mary Anne* had done. They had to try to bring the vessel ashore gracefully, bow first, hopefully making it far enough through the violently tossing surf to give a swimmer some hope of getting ashore. Bellamy yelled out to the men to cut the anchor cables. As soon as the last strokes of their axes had fallen—the thick anchor ropes snapping free—Bellamy ordered the helmsmen to swing her all the way back around, to run face first into the beach. But the vessel didn't turn. All watched in terror as the ship slipped backward, stern first, over thirty foot waves towards the white, misty chaos at the foot of the cliffs.

The *Whydah* ran aground with shocking force. The jolt likely shot any men in the rigging out into the deadly surf, where they were alternately pounded against the sea bottom, then sucked back away from the beach by the undertow. Cannon broke free from their tackles and careened across the lower decks, crushing everyone in their path. One pirate was thrown across the deck so hard his shoulder bone became completely embedded in the handle of a pewter teapot. Little John King, the nine-year-old pirate volunteer, was crushed between decks, still wearing the silk stockings and expensive leather shoes his mother had dressed him in aboard the *Bonetta* months earlier. Within fifteen minutes, the violent motion of the surf brought the *Whydah*'s mainmast crashing down over the side. Waves broke over the decks and water poured into the bedlam of crashing cannon and barrels of cargo below decks. At dawn the *Whydah*'s hull broke apart, casting both the living and dead into the surf.

As the storm raged on through the morning hours, the ebbing tide left more and more bodies piled on the shore. Amidst the bloated, mangled corpses only two men stirred. One was John Julian, the Mosquito Indian who had served with Bellamy aboard his periaguas. The other was Thomas Davis, one of the carpenters forced from the *St. Michael*. Samuel Bellamy and some 160 other men—pirates and captives, whites, blacks, and Indians—had perished in the storm.

❧

Ten miles to the south, the pirates aboard the *Mary Anne* were thankful to be alive. At daybreak they could see they had run aground on a half-drowned island in the middle of a small, protected bay. The crew of the *Mary Anne* probably recognized the place: Pochet Island, south of Eastham. With the tide down, half of the *Mary Anne* lay high and dry against the island, and the men could get ashore without getting their feet wet. They tarried about on the beach for several hours, eating sweetmeats and drinking more wine.

At about ten in the morning, two local men who had noticed the wrecked vessel rowed over in a canoe and brought the castaways to the mainland. The locals, John Cole and William Smith, apparently weren't suspicious, even when the pirates got into heated discussions in a mix of English, French, and Dutch. They could overhear that a number of the shipwrecked sailors wanted to get to Rhode Island as fast as possible—presumably to seek shelter among Williams's people. The others seemed more subdued, sitting quietly by the fire in John Cole's home until, all of a sudden, one of them spoke up. This was Alexander Mackconachy, who blurted out that the other eight were ruthless pirates, members of "Black Sam" Bellamy's infamous company. The pirates knew it was time to go. They took their leave of the flabbergasted family of John Cole and scurried out into the rain.

They got as far as the Eastham Tavern before justice of the peace John Doane and his men caught up with them. Alerted by John Cole, Doane had headed straight for the tavern, one of the few places where strangers might procure horses. Soon Doane had all the *Mary Anne's* complement—pirates and captives alike—under armed guard, walking down the muddy road toward the Barnstable jail.

⁓⁀⁓

The pirates aboard the *Ann Galley* and the *Fisher* were luckier than the rest. Through good fortune—or perhaps by dint of the lightness of their vessels—their anchors held through the night. At ten in the morning, the rain still coming down in sheets, the wind shifted back to the west, blowing away from the land rather than into it. With great relief Noland ordered the sails and anchors raised. With the wind at their backs, they sailed away from the surf, bound for the coast of Maine, where they hoped to find the *Whydah* and her store of treasure.

Ten miles out, Noland decided it was time to rid themselves of the *Fisher*. The pirates transferred all of the crew and valuables aboard the *Ann* and left the *Fisher* floating in the open sea, crewless and with hatches open to the storm.

Two days later, on April 29, the *Ann* dropped anchor in the lee of Monhegan Island, a high, rocky island ten miles off the coast of Maine. Monhegan had been inhabited by Englishmen on and off since 1614, and was the site of one of New England's first year-round fishing stations. But on that blustery day in 1717, there may not have been anyone on the island to greet the pirates. The majority of Maine's settlements had been destroyed by Wabanaki Indians, who were allied with the French. The central and eastern portions of the coast were still contested by France and Britain, including Monhegan and other offshore islands like Damariscove and Matinicus. Monhegan had a water supply and easy access to some of the best cod-fishing grounds in the Americas. It might lack a cozy harbor, but for outlaws on the run, it was a safe place to linger and wait for the *Whydah, Marianne*, and *Mary Anne* to arrive.

Days passed, with no sign of them. Noland and the other men began to fear the worst, that they were all that remained of the greatest pirate fleet in the Americas.

～～～

Thomas Davis, one of the two survivors of the *Whydah* wreck, had dragged himself out of the surf and, shivering and exhausted, stumbled through the darkness in search of shelter. He trod down the beach a short way, pelted with rain, impassable cliffs of sand hemming him in against the sea. Illuminated by flashes of lightning, the wall of sand appeared to go on forever in both directions. There was only one way to escape. Davis began to climb.

Fortunately he was a young man, twenty-two, and presumably in good health, for despite cold and exhaustion, he somehow managed to reach the top of the 100-foot wall of sand. He must have rested a bit at the summit, an eerie plain of grass stretched out before him in the mist. Behind him, down in the surf, the shattered remains of the *Whydah* flashed in the lightning like a ghostly apparition. Finally he stumbled forward, shivering in the wind and rain, away from the sea.

At five in the morning, Davis finally arrived at the farm of Samuel Harding, two miles from the wreck site. In some form, Davis related his story to the Eastham native. Harding's ears must have pricked up when he heard of the shipwreck, for almost immediately he retrieved his horse. Davis, half-drowned, found himself stuck on its back and led to the beach by the farmer.

Harding circled the cliffs and, guided by Davis, proceeded to the wreck site. The two halves of the *Whydah* had separated by now, battered further and further apart by the storm, and bits and pieces of the ship, her cargo, and crew were spreading along the base of the cliff. They lashed anything of value to the horse and, fully loaded, proceeded back to Harding's farmhouse. Harding immediately turned around and repeated the trip, multiple times through the early morning hours.

By ten in the morning, Harding was joined by his brother Abiah, neighbors Edward Knowles and Jonathan Cole,* and some seven other men, scooping up valuables as quickly as possible, knowing the authorities could arrive at any time. They may have picked through the increasing number of storm-battered corpses piling up on the beach, more than fifty by that afternoon, relieving the dead of silver buttons and buckles, jewelry, and coins. As it turned out, they had plenty of time. Eastham's justice of the peace, Joseph Doane, was tied up for the entire day, intercepting and arresting the *Mary Anne*'s crew on the other side of town and escorting them to Barnstable. Doane didn't make it to the wreck site until the following morning, Sunday the twenty-eighth, at which point he found "all was gone of value." Doane later claimed he then "commanded the inhabitants" of the area to "save what they could for the King," while the local coroner—Jonathan Cole's father-in-law—oversaw the burial of sixty-two drowned men, collecting "several things belonging to the [Wreck]" in the process. The total value of the items set aside for the king came to only £200, suggesting that many thousands of pounds of valuables made their way into the hands of the good people of Eastham. It could hardly have been otherwise. Within a couple of days, two hundred people—most of the able-bodied inhabitants of the town—were out plundering the wreck, cutting up bits of sail and taking "riches out of the sand."

---

* Jonathan was the son of John Cole, one of the two men who rowed out to rescue the *Mary Anne* pirates that morning, ten miles to the south. It's possible that the son had sent word of the wreck to his father, and alerted him to the possibility of other wrecked pirate vessels in the area, which might explain the elder Cole's apparent nonchalance at the castaways' appearance and behavior.

A strange occurrence was later reported to authorities sent in from Boston. On Monday the twenty-ninth, less than three days after the *Whydah* wrecked, a "very great sloop" arrived off the beach. The mysterious vessel approached the largest piece of the *Whydah*, then lowered a boat into the water. A number of its crewmen rowed over and examined the weather-battered remains. She chased off several local fishing vessels before sailing off into the open sea. Colonial authorities assumed it to have been the *Whydah*'s consort, an error they passed on to history.

～≈≈～

On April 29, Paulsgrave Williams was 140 miles to the southeast, cruising for prizes near the entrance to Long Island Sound, still unaware of the *Whydah*'s destruction.

The day before, his company had plundered a sloop from Connecticut, taking three bushels of salt and two of their sailors. One of the sailors, Edward Sargeant, knew the immediate area well and was forced to act as their pilot as they lurked in the waters between Montauk and Martha's Vineyard. Unfortunately, no captures came their way that day and for several days after that, causing much dissatisfaction among the crew.

On May 3, near the desolate island called No Man's Land, south of Martha's Vineyard, they took two trading sloops inbound from North Carolina. From the *Hannah and Mary* they seized items to help in the overhaul of the *Marianne* and a Devonshire man living in Boston who could guide them safely around Cape Cod and on to Maine. The second sloop, a smaller vessel from Portsmouth, New Hampshire, had nothing of value. Such paltry pickings could not have mollified the crew; grumbling undoubtedly continued as the *Marianne* failed to catch any worthwhile prizes. Another week passed, then two, all without plunder. At this point they cruised directly for Maine, where they hoped to find Bellamy and the *Whydah*: A trusted commander and an unstoppable ship would set things right.

Guided by her captive pilot, the *Marianne* stayed well offshore of Cape Cod on a course set straight for Cape Elizabeth, a prominent headland in southern Maine that could be seen for miles out at sea. They had no way of knowing that at that very moment the *Whydah* lay scattered in the surf just over the western horizon

At noon on May 17, 1717, some seventy-five miles offshore, they intercepted a fishing sloop, the *Elizabeth*, bound from Salem, Massachusetts, to the great cod fishing grounds of Georges Bank. There was no gold on this paltry prize, of course, just sixteen huge barrels filled with salt, bait, and food. The sloop was tiny, but Williams thought it to be about the right size to help careen the *Marianne* when they finally found their way to Damariscove. The pirates forced the *Elizabeth's* skipper to come aboard, putting some of their own number on the fishing sloop, and continued on to Maine.

After daybreak on Sunday the eighteenth, Williams's men spotted the bold outline of Cape Elizabeth. Their pilot not knowing the way to Damariscove, the pirates decided to sail the *Marianne* straight to the nearest harbor, to kidnap a local mariner. In a few hours they came to anchor between Cape Elizabeth and Richmond Island, where the docks and associated detritus of a seventy-year-old fishing station stared blankly out at them. The station's fishermen were long gone, but there was a farmhouse on the mainland shore, a small sloop anchored in the harbor, and an open boat or two pulled up on the seaweed-strewn beach. Certainly, Williams reasoned, a pilot could be found here.

Up at the farmhouse, Dominicus Jordan could smell trouble. He had been born on the shores of the little anchorage, but had seen more warfare and violence than most pirates. At the start of the War of Spanish Succession, a band of Indians had occupied his parents' fortified home; Dominicus's father, a giant of a man with a fearsome reputation, put a hatchet through an Indian's head. The other Indians killed the father and carried nineteen-year-old Dominicus, his mother, and five younger siblings into captivity in the Canadian wilderness. The family spent the next thirteen years with the Indians, learning their language and many of their ways, before being released in 1715. Dominicus took one look at the heavily manned sloop-of-war and knew enough to get away. He grabbed his wife and three-year-old son, and with the servants, fled into the woods.

Williams's men spent the day and night at Cape Elizabeth, rifling through the Jordans' possessions. At one point, the pirates detained a hapless fishing boat that had entered the anchorage. One of the fishermen admitted knowing the way to Damariscove and Monhegan and was pressed into service as a pilot. His young assistant was set free ashore and ran through the woods to alert the nearest town, Falmouth, of the pirates' presence.

That afternoon they sailed thirty miles eastward to Damariscove Island, off what is now Boothbay Harbor. A long rocky island with a snug cove nestled in its southern end, Damariscove had been a rendezvous for fishermen for more than a century. Following the devastation of the Indian wars, the island was unoccupied, apart perhaps from occasional visits by fishermen needing a place to sleep after a long day spent pulling four- and five-foot-long codfish up from the cold waters of the Gulf of Maine. Anchored securely in the cove, the tops of the *Marianne*'s masts were nearly hidden from view by the brambly ridges that rose from each side. It was, indeed, a safe place to hide out, rest, and repair the sloop. Of the *Whydah*, however, there was not a sign that she had ever graced the island with her presence.

Williams stayed at Damariscove for five days, vainly hoping that Bellamy would suddenly appear, ship and treasure intact. He did his best to get the *Marianne* into shape, unloading her cargo, taking out her broken mast, and careening the underside of her hull. Those not at work gathered at the gravely beach at the head of the cove, grimly taking stock of their paltry treasure hoard: ten cannon; some bails of wool and linen cloth; a bit of scavenged iron; some barrels of food, salt, and water. As the days passed and it became clearer that the *Whydah* was not coming, the image of the great heap of gold and jewels piled in her hold must have haunted the weary men.

Though they were but fifteen miles from Monhegan, Williams's company apparently never encountered their fellow pirates on the *Ann*

Galley and the *Fisher*. Like the crew of the *Marianne*, Noland and company had tarried on the outer islands of Midcoast Maine for a time, repairing their vessels and plundering the little fishing vessels that came across their path. These pirates, intimately aware of the dangers the storm had presented to the *Whydah*, had probably already given up hope and headed south for the safety of the Bahamas.

On May 23, Williams, too, was forced to accept that his friend had missed their rendezvous. With a sense of foreboding, the crew voted to start the long, dangerous trip back to Nassau. They sailed south to Cape Elizabeth, where they released the *Elizabeth* and the other fishing vessels, then set course for Cape Cod.

In the late morning of the twenty-fifth, within sight of the tip of Cape Cod, Williams's men finally learned of the *Whydah*'s fate. The bearer of the ill news was Samuel Skinner, master of the schooner *Swallow* of Salem, Massachusetts, whom the pirates detained just inside Massachusetts Bay. The destruction of the *Whydah* was by now on everybody's lips, from Portsmouth to Newport and beyond, Skinner could have told them, and carried in the pages of the *Boston News-Letter*. The *Whydah*, the treasure, and Williams's friend and accomplice were all gone, destroyed by the sea itself. Williams, presumably reeling from the news, released the *Swallow* and sailed out of the bay.

❧❧

In Boston, the greatest city on the British American mainland, the destruction of the *Whydah* had brought little solace. Every few days another ship arrived in New England's ports bearing tales of pirate attacks: fishing boats in Maine and the open gulf; trading sloops off Connecticut, Rhode Island, Martha's Vineyard, and the Cape. For the first time since the outbreak of piracy, nowhere in New England waters seemed safe from men of the black flag.

Massachusetts Governor Samuel Shute put the colony on a wartime footing. Unable to trust the safety of the sea-lanes, he ordered the nine surviving pirates transported overland from Barnstable to Boston "under a strong guard and sufficiently bound from . . . county to county and sheriff to sheriff." For the first few days after the wreck, Boston remained without naval protection. Even after May 2, when the fifth-rate frigate HMS *Rose* finally arrived from the West Indies, Shute remained concerned about the safety of commerce. On the ninth, he dispatched the frigate to Cape Cod, where she spent nearly three weeks patrolling for pirates, including a day spent off the wreck site itself. News of the *Marianne*'s landings at Cape Elizabeth reached the governor on May 21, and unnerved him sufficiently to order a weeklong closure of Boston Harbor. He armed a sloop, the *Mary Free Love*, and sent her out as a privateer to hunt down Williams and Noland. He even allowed the captain of the *Rose* to press twenty of Boston's men, to be sure he wasn't overwhelmed by pirates while patrolling the coast. All of New England stood on a knife's edge.

Nobody was in a greater state of fear than the captive pirates themselves. They had arrived in Boston on May 4, were marched up the hill past the Town House, and then dumped in the cages of Boston's decrepit prison. In addition to the seven men from the *Mary Anne*, the prisoners included Thomas Davis and John Julian, who had been apprehended by Justice Doane before they had gotten far from the beach. Soon afterward, Julian was separated from the rest, destined, by dint of his dark skin, for the slave market.* The other eight prisoners may have wished for the first time that they weren't white, because unless some of their colleagues came into Boston to free them, they all knew they were likely to die on the gallows. Maybe they hoped, as they lay in their cages, that their brethren back in the Bahamas had heard of their fate and were coming to the rescue.

---

* It's possible that John Julian became a slave to the family of a future president. Around this time, a man named John the Indian was sold to John Quincy of Braintree, great-grandfather of president (and abolitionist) John Quincy Adams, and grandfather of President John Adams's wife, Abigail.

CHAPTER EIGHT

BLACKBEARD

May–December 1717

WHEN BLACKBEARD AND HORNIGOLD returned to the Bahamas from the Spanish Main in possession of the *Bonnet*, a fine sloop-of-war, and £100,000 in plunder, their reputations soared. Hornigold was now an undisputed leader of the pirate republic, taking his place alongside his rival, Henry Jennings. Blackbeard, who was perhaps thirty-seven at this time, was regarded as one of the finest captains in the archipelago, brave and effective. Unlike Bellamy, Blackbeard had no intention of pushing his commodore aside, especially given that Hornigold had become less reluctant to take English vessels.

Word had gotten around that young Sam Bellamy had captured a ship-of-force and taken her north to intercept those colonies' spring shipments from Europe and the Caribbean. Several other pirate companies were preparing to follow suit, and were busy loading their sloops with the necessary supplies. The French pirate Olivier La Buse was back in Nassau and had acquired a powerful ship of his own that, at 250 tons and with twenty guns, was nearly as strong as the *Whydah*. The Frenchman was busy recruiting additional crewmen; when he got to 150 he intended to cruise to New England, reconnoiter with Bellamy, and continue on as far as Nova Scotia and Newfoundland. Jennings, however, had no interest in sailing north; alone among the pirate captains, he continued to refuse to attack British vessels, the only sort one could expect to encounter with any regularity there. Charles Vane, for his part, also appeared to have no interest in cruising to cooler climes; like many of Jennings's company, he seemed content to enjoy his wealth and freedom on shore.

After a short break, during which time Hornigold refit the *Bonnet* into a proper sloop-of-war, Blackbeard and Hornigold left to cruise, though they stayed much closer to home. In early July, they lurked off eastern Cuba in their respective sloops, hoping to intercept some well-laden transatlantic ships. Instead, they took a sloop under one Captain Bishop, bound from Havana to New York with a cargo of flour. It wasn't gold, true, but flour was always in demand in the Bahamas, where the pirates grossly outnumbered the few remaining farmers. They took the time to transfer 120 barrels of the stuff on board their own sloops before letting Captain Bishop continue on his way. A week or so later, a bit to the west, they captured another New York-bound trading vessel under a Captain Thurbar, several days out of Jamaica; the pirates found nothing of interest aboard her apart from "a few gallons of rum," which they absconded with before releasing the vessel. Slim pickings, the pirate company must have thought. Perhaps they should be following their colleagues northward after all.

By August, Thatch and Hornigold were back in Nassau, their flour ensuring that nobody would want for bread for many months to come. They presumably spent the next few days unloading this cargo and preparing for a longer expedition up the eastern seaboard. Their brethren seemed nearly invulnerable, their control of the sea-lanes from Jamaica to New York virtually uncontested by any authority. As they shared intelligence gathered from captives and the merchants of Harbour Island with the other pirate captains, they concluded that the Royal Navy was helpless to stop them. HMS *Shoreham* had only recently returned to Virginia and was said to be in such poor condition that her captain didn't dare leave the protection of Chesapeake Bay. Sam Bellamy's men had so terrorized the British Leeward Islands that the mere rumor of their return had caused the colony's governor to abandon a tour aboard HMS *Seaford* for fear he would be captured. Out on Barbados, the

Scarborough's crew was said to be all but incapacitated by disease. Outside of Jamaica, that left but two or three ships to protect thousands of miles of coastline from Barbados to Maine. There were rumors that reinforcements were on their way from England, but for the time being, it seemed, the Americas belonged to them.

Some of the pirates, particularly Scotsmen and ex-Governor Hamilton's privateers, had started expressing wider aspirations. These individuals loathed King George and had been frustrated by the failure of the 1715 Jacobite rebellion against him. Feeling their power, these pro-Stuart pirates discussed volunteering their services to the Pretender, the would-be Stuart king James III, who was living again in exile in France. This faction, which probably included Jennings, Vane, and a number of Blackbeard's and Williams's men, were developing contacts with Jacobite sympathizers in England, through whom they hoped to one day secure privateering commissions from the Stuart king. The ragtag republic of pirates was ready to take a place on the world stage, and to take sides in the great geopolitical struggle of the time.

Then bad news came.

The *Marianne*, her sails ragged and her mast jury-rigged, limped into Nassau Harbor, followed by the storm-damaged *Ann Galley* under Richard Noland. Paulsgrave Williams could be seen on the *Marianne's* quarterdeck, but Sam Bellamy, his inseparable companion, was nowhere to be seen.

Williams and Noland related the tragic news of the *Whydah's* destruction, how nine survivors were said to be awaiting trial in Boston with little hope of acquittal, and that Bellamy was not among them. The governors of Massachusetts and Rhode Island had outfitted at least three privateers to hunt Williams down, forcing the pirates out of New England waters. Williams had continued plundering vessels as he worked his way down the coasts of New Jersey, Delaware, and the Carolinas, scoring enough wine and provisions to keep his men alive. Through death or desertion, his company was down to just over thirty men. Noland, who he had reunited with along the way, had some twenty men aboard. Of the 125 or more pirates who had left the southern Bahamas with Bellamy early that spring, only fifty remained.

Blackbeard was particularly incensed by the news. His friend Bellamy was dead, and the pious fools in Boston were bent on executing the last of the survivors. This could not be allowed to happen, and if it did, Blackbeard would exact a terrible revenge on the people of New England. While conversing with Williams and Noland, he likely contemplated the possibility of attacking Boston and breaking the captives out of its aging prison. To carry out such a bold plan, Blackbeard would need his own ship-of-force.

At the end of August, an unfamiliar vessel entered the harbor, her sails and rigging frayed, her decks scarred with the telltale wounds of a prolonged battle. She was a sloop-of-war flying the black flag, but nobody in Nassau had ever seen her before. When her captain showed himself, onlookers were aghast. Clad in a fine dressing gown, his body patched with bandages, was a plump gentleman who looked as if he'd hardly spent a day at sea in his life. None of the people who saw this genteel landsman hobble across the deck would ever have imagined that he was destined to become Blackbeard's leading accomplice.

❦

Stede Bonnet, the man in the dressing gown, was the most unlikely of pirates. He had been born on Barbados twenty-nine years earlier, in 1688, to an affluent family of sugar planters. The English had settled Barbados in the late 1620s, a generation earlier than Jamaica or the Bahamas, and Stede's great-grandfather, Thomas, had been among its pioneers. In the nine decades since then, the Bonnets had cleared hundreds of acres of lowland jungle to the southeast of the colony's capital, Bridgetown, planting it first with tobacco and, more successfully, with sugarcane. Like other successful planters, they had purchased African slaves to tend the crops and the sweltering tubs of cane syrup in the sugarhouses. By the time of Stede's birth, the Bonnets had one of the most prosperous estates on the island, 400 acres of sugar with two windmills and a cattle-operated mill to grind the syrup from the cane. Stede's early years were spent on the sprawling plantation, his family attended to by three servants and ninety-four slaves. His life was not without tragedy. In 1694, when he was just six years old, his father passed away, and his mother appears to have died not long thereafter. The estate was placed in the care of his guardians until he came of age. He became an orphan child with a small army of servants and slaves.

Bonnet was groomed to take his place among the Barbadian aristocracy. He received a liberal education, served as a major in the island's militia, and courted the daughter of another leading planter, William Allamby. In 1709, when Bonnet was twenty-one, he and young Mary Allamby were married in Bridgetown's St. Michael's Church, a stone's throw from the sparkling surface of Carlisle Bay. They set up house just south of Bridgetown Harbor, where Bonnet was "generally esteemed and honoured." Then everything began to go wrong.

Their first child, Allamby Bonnet, died in early childhood. This had a lasting impact on Stede Bonnet. Three more children followed— Edward, Stede Jr., and Mary—yet Bonnet's spirits did not rise. He fell into depression, even insanity. His friends felt he suffered from "a disorder in his Mind, which had been but too visible in him [for] some time," and which was supposedly caused "by some discomforts he found in a married state."

Toward the end of 1716 he reached a breaking point. His fellow planters were in an uproar over the depredations of Bellamy and Williams, who had caused much damage to the trade of the nearby Leeward Islands. Bonnet became enchanted. Though he was a landsman through and through and entirely unversed in the arts of seamanship and navigation, he decided to build his own warship. He contracted a local yard to construct a sixty-ton sloop-of-war capable of carrying ten cannon and seventy or more men. He must have told the authorities that he intended to use it as a privateer, claiming he would go to Antigua or Jamaica, where he might expect to be granted a commission to hunt down the pirates. In reality, he wished to become one himself.

When the sloop was completed, Bonnet christened her the *Revenge* and set about hiring a crew. Betraying his ignorance of privateer and pirate custom alike, he paid the men a cash salary instead of shares. He would have to pay his officers well, as he would be entirely reliant on them to operate his vessel. The crewmen may have had political reasons for joining the eccentric planter; they included an unusually large number of Scotsmen and, in the months to come, some of them would express Jacobite proclivities. While the officers set about ordering appropriate arms, stores, and provisions, Bonnet concentrated on the matter he thought most important to successful buccaneering: equipping his cabin with an extensive library.

One night in the late spring of 1717, he boarded the *Revenge* and ordered his hired hands to make ready for departure. Under cover of darkness, the sloop sailed out of Carlisle Bay, leaving Bonnet's wife behind with his infant daughter and young sons, aged three and four. He would never see any of them again.

Fearing, perhaps, he would be recognized in the Leeward Islands, Bonnet ordered his quartermaster to take the *Revenge* straight to the North American mainland. His hirelings told him he could expect to find ample prizes at the approaches to Charleston, South Carolina. Presumably nobody would recognize Bonnet there, but on the way he told his crew to refer to him as Captain Edwards, just in case.

Though separated by 1,900 miles of ocean and islands, Barbados and Charleston were remarkably alike. Charleston had been founded less than fifty years earlier by a group of Barbadian planters who had successfully replicated their West Indian slave society in the coastal swamps of southern Carolina. A compact, walled city of 3,000, Charleston's streets and low, swampy shoreline were lined with Barbadian-style homes, high-ceilinged frame structures with large windows, balconies, and tiled roofs. Outside the walls, rice and sugar plantations spread for miles up and down the Ashley and Cooper rivers, their sweltering fields tended by armies of black slaves overseen by a handful of armed whites. As in Barbados, the colony's whites were outnumbered by their slaves, in this case, by a ratio of two to one. By land, the town was entirely isolated from the rest of English America, all communication taking place by sea. South Carolina was, effectively, a West Indian slave island stranded on the swampy shores of North America.

Charleston, the only proper town in all of South Carolina, was particularly vulnerable to naval attack. It was located on a peninsula at the confluence of two rivers, five miles from the sea. The entrance to this estuary was partially blocked by a long sandbar, and three pilots were kept busy guiding vessels over it as they passed to and from the ocean. The coast itself, where "thousands of mosquitoes and other troublesome insects [were] tormenting both man and beast," was sparsely populated. Adjacent North Carolina was barely governed at all, there being only a handful of villages and fewer than 10,000 impoverished souls scattered over thousands of square miles of swampy, slow-moving creeks and bayous between Charleston and the Capes of Virginia.

For a pirate, this was a prefect setup. They could patrol the entrance of the bar, spiderlike, collecting all vessels in their web. When the time came to find a refuge to plunder the vessels and evade the law, there were hundreds of miles of creeks, inlets, and islands on the North Carolina coast to hide among, places with entrances too shallow or convoluted for a large warship to follow them. For a novice pirate with a powerful vessel, the Carolinas provided a perfect sandbox in which to learn the trade.

Bonnet's men guided the *Revenge* to the outside of the Charleston Bar in late August 1717 and waited for their prey. On August 26 it came in the form of a brigantine under Captain Thomas Porter, from Boston. The *Revenge*, her decks crammed with men and guns, overtook Captain Porter and compelled him to surrender. Bonnet's prize crew was disappointed to find the brigantine devoid of worthwhile plunder, but they held her just the same so that Porter couldn't alert the town to their presence. A few hours later, they spotted a sloop approaching from the south. They closed in on her and rolled out their guns, compelling her prompt surrender. Bonnet ordered the sloop searched while he consulted with her captain. Bonnet had been telling everyone that he was Captain Edwards, but the sloop's captain, Joseph Palmer, was not fooled; he was from Barbados and was probably surprised to find Major Stede Bonnet in command of a pirate sloop. Bonnet, engaged in piracy for less than a day, had already had been found out.

Palmer's sloop turned out to be carrying a small but valuable cargo of Barbados's primary exports: sugar, rum, and slaves. The *Revenge*, her holds still nearly full of supplies, couldn't carry more, nor did Bonnet wish to cram slaves aboard his crowded sloop. Bonnet, perhaps advised by his quartermaster, resolved to take control of both vessels and sail to North Carolina to sort things out. A few days later, the *Revenge* anchored in the slack brown waters of one of that colony's inlets, probably on Cape Fear, a famous refuge of the buccaneers and corsairs of the previous century. They unloaded Palmer's sloop and, after using it to careen the *Revenge*, set her on fire. Palmer, along with his crew and slaves, was put aboard Porter's brigantine, which the pirates relieved of anchors and most of her sails and rigging. By reducing her means of propulsion, the pirates intended to give themselves a long head start, delaying Porter's ability to get to Charleston and sound the alarm. They may have overdone it: the brigantine was so slow that Porter was forced to put most of the slaves ashore "else they would have all been starved for want of provisions." South Carolina wasn't to learn of Bonnet's piracies until September 22, four weeks after they had taken place. By then he was long gone.

"The Major was no sailor," a historian would write of Bonnet a few years later, "and therefore [was] obliged to yield to many things that were imposed on him . . . for want of competent knowledge in maritime affairs." The first such imposition took place as the *Revenge* sailed out of her North Carolina refuge. Bonnet was already beginning to lose his grip on the crew, who argued openly about where they should cruise next. Ultimately, amid "nothing but confusion," they sailed south, into the Straits of Florida, perhaps wishing to try their luck "fishing" the famed Spanish wrecks. Instead, somewhere off Cuba or Florida, they blundered into a situation that nearly cost Bonnet his life.

Savvy pirates knew better than to engage a ship far more powerful than them, and could tell a lumbering merchant ship from a deadly man-of-war. Stede Bonnet lacked these skills. Through hubris, weakness, or incompetence, he allowed the *Revenge* to engage in a full-fledged battle with a Spanish warship. By the time his crew managed to affect a retreat, the *Revenge*'s decks were awash with blood. More than half his crew, thirty to forty men, was dead or wounded, and Bonnet himself had suffered a severe, life-threatening injury. The *Revenge* escaped, probably because she was faster and more agile than the Spanish man-of-war, suggesting that Bonnet could have avoided the incident altogether.

As Bonnet lay in his cabin among his books, racked with pain, the crew set a course for the ultimate sanctuary, New Providence Island and the fabled pirate base at Nassau.

✤

The pirates of Nassau listened attentively to Bonnet's story, and those of his men. In the discussions that followed, the pirates resolved to grant the eccentric planter refuge, at least until he recovered from his appreciable wounds. In exchange, however, they wished to make use of his fine sloop-of-war. Blackbeard, Benjamin Hornigold maintained, could do big things if placed in charge of the *Revenge*, which was far superior to the sloop he had been using. Bonnet, who was barely able to leave his bed, could continue to occupy the captain's cabin, but Blackbeard would be in charge of the ship. Bonnet, now suffering from both mental and physical pain, was hardly in a position to refuse.

Blackbeard transferred many of his men and two cannon over to the *Revenge* and commenced repairs on the newly built sloop-of-war. Within a week or two, he was ready to depart, the *Revenge* now equipped with twelve guns and 150 men, among them Hornigold's longtime quartermaster, William Howard. Hornigold had business to attend to, but first he may have arranged to meet Blackbeard off the coast of Virginia in a few weeks' time. In the middle of September, Blackbeard was sailing up the Gulf Stream, in charge of his first independent command. It would be many months before he saw Nassau again.

After Blackbeard's departure, Hornigold put his affairs in order. Some of his preparations for his forthcoming cruise were documented, providing a window into a poorly understood aspect of pirate life. He first recruited Richard Noland, quartermaster of the late Sam Bellamy, to serve as his agent at Nassau, making him responsible for recruiting men and keeping an eye on his interests on the island. He then took a large load of plundered cargo aboard his pirate ship the *Bonnet*—flour, sugar, and other surplus items—and sailed it up to Harbour Island. There he spent several days, trading and visiting with Richard Thompson and the island's other merchants, who were growing rich smuggling pirate goods into Jamaica and Charleston. While on the island, he was surprised to run into Neal Walker, the son of his old nemesis Thomas Walker. The Walkers had apparently decided that if they couldn't suppress the pirates, they might as well make money off them. Neal was busy loading his sloop with barrels of pirated sugar, which members of Hornigold's crew later spotted outside Thomas Walker's new residence-in-exile on an islet off Abaco.

In Harbour Island's snug anchorage, Hornigold also encountered a newcomer to the Bahamas, a French pirate named Jean Bondavais, whose men had already earned a reputation for "harshly treating" the island's inhabitants. Bondavais, like Hornigold, was preparing for a new pirate cruise, and the two soon found themselves competing for the same resources. His sloop, the *Mary Ann* may well have been the *Marianne*, which Williams and his company would have been happy to sell after their frightening odyssey; if so, this would have irked Hornigold, who was the pirate who had originally captured the sloop eighteen months prior. Both captains were trying to buy supplies from Harbour Island's merchants, and each needed a ship's boat and more crewmen, particularly surgeons. Hornigold had taken pity on his captive surgeon, John

Howell, and released him some weeks earlier. The poor man, who loathed the pirate life, had been unable to arrange passage off New Providence, and lived in constant fear of being pressed by one pirate crew or another. Bondavais somehow got wind of this, perhaps from Hornigold's men, and quietly sent for him in Nassau.

Howell was living with the merchant William Pindar, and both men were at home when Bondavais' men rapped on the door. Pindar opened the door to find himself face-to-face with a gang of cutlass-wielding Frenchmen. They told the merchant that they had come for Howell and "a hogshead of rum" and would "cut him with cutlass" if he did not deliver both. Pindar only had a gallon of rum, which Howell had brought from town, and when he told the pirates so, they became "very rude" and threatened to drag Howell away that instant. Howell tearfully told Pindar "that he would rather choose to go with Hornigold than [with] these Frenchmen who deal so hardly with him." Somehow he and Pindar put them off long enough for Howell to run over to the house where Richard Noland was staying. He begged Noland to recruit him, saying "he would rather serve the English than French if he was compelled to make a choice of either." Noland, pitying the man, arranged for his conscription into the *Bonnet*'s crew. Shortly thereafter, Hornigold's quartermaster, John Martin, bundled him into a boat and carried him to Harbour Island, where Hornigold could protect him.

At Harbour Island, Bondavais was upset to learn that the surgeon was now aboard the *Bonnet*. The Frenchmen approached Hornigold, demanding Howell be turned over. Hornigold slyly responded that he would be happy to comply, so long as the surgeon agreed; Howell, of course, refused. Bondavais relented, eventually sailing away without the reputed surgeon. Howell remained desperate to escape from the pirates, however, and repeatedly tried to escape, despite being placed under heavy guard. At one point he approached one of the daughters of Richard Thompson, Harbour Island's leading citizen, begging her to hide him. Nobody on the island dared to help the man, Thompson later said, "lest Hornigold should burn or destroy their houses or do some other vileness, the whole place being in such fear of Hornigold that no inhabitant dare[d] speak against or contradict any of [his] orders." When the *Bonnet* departed the Bahamas to meet Blackbeard, we know Howell was on board, forced into piracy for the second time in less than a year.

~~~~~

By this time, Blackbeard and company were a thousand miles to the north, patrolling the entrance to Delaware Bay, through which all of Philadelphia's commerce passed. During the trip from Nassau, Blackbeard had developed growing doubts about the *Revenge*'s eccentric owner. Bonnet's crewmen told stories that made it clear that the planter, even in health, was entirely unfit for command, not knowing a block from a halyard. Bonnet stuck to his cabin, for the most part. When he ventured out on deck, he wore an elegant morning gown and usually carried the book he was reading in his hands. His mental state was similarly fragile, and Blackbeard suspected it would be no great feat to lift permanent control of the *Revenge* from his tenuous grasp. He was pleasant to Bonnet, encouraging him to rest in his cabin, easy in the assurance that the sloop was in good hands.

They made one capture along the way, the forty-ton sloop *Betty* of Virginia, loaded with Madeira wine and other merchandise. On September 29, as they closed on her at the Capes of Virginia, Blackbeard donned his new, terrifying battle attire. He wore a silk sling over his shoulders, to which were attached "three brace of pistols, hanging in holsters like bandaliers." Under his hat, he tied on lit fuses, allowing some of them to dangle down on each side of his face, surrounding it with a halo of smoke and fire. So adorned, a contemporary biographer reported, "his eyes naturally looking fierce and wild, [that he] made altogether such a figure that imagination cannot form an idea of a fury from Hell to look more frightful." The crews of merchant ships would take one look at this apparition, surrounded by an army of wild men bearing muskets, cutlasses, and primitive hand grenades, and would invariably surrender without firing a shot. That was exactly what Blackbeard intended. Through terror, he eliminated the need to deplete men and ammunition in battle and ensured that the vessels he captured remained undamaged and, thus, of maximum possible value to his company. The *Betty*, a humble vessel that regularly worked the wine run from Virginia to Madeira, surrendered, and the pirates looted the best of her cargo. Not wanting to allow her to alert all of Virginia and Maryland to their presence, Blackbeard ordered all the captives brought over to the *Revenge*. William Howard, his quartermaster, drilled holes in *Betty's* hull and, as she sank, climbed aboard a rowboat and returned aboard the *Revenge*.

It was now early October, and the *Revenge* stood off the high sandy capes of Delaware, five cannonballs stored alongside each of her guns, waiting for prey. The next to run afoul of Blackbeard's men was a heavily loaded merchant ship flying British colors. The ship, it turned out, was just completing the ten- to twelve-week journey from Dublin to Philadelphia, with 150 passengers crowded below her decks along with cargo. Almost all of the passengers were indentured servants and, as such, were probably in a miserable state. Disease ran rampant in the immigrants' crowded, poorly ventilated quarters, where they faced "want of provisions, hunger, thirst, frost, heat, dampnes, anxiety, want, affliction, and lamentations, together with . . . lice [that] abound so frightfully . . . they can be scraped off the bottom." Such passengers would have been desperate to make land; instead, they found themselves prisoners of a wild man with fire and smoke pouring from his head.

Under Hornigold, Blackbeard had conducted himself with restraint, taking only what he needed from the vessels he captured. Now, he was free to propose his own agenda to his crew, one far more ambitious than that of his mentor. Hornigold had limited his operations to maritime theft, but in the wake of Bellamy's death, Blackbeard sought to bring as much damage to British commerce as possible, short of the unnecessary taking of human life. He appears to have declared war on the British Empire and would use piracy and terror to bring it to its knees.

The servants aboard the passenger ship had little to fear from this more radical approach to piracy, but the merchants sailing aboard her had plenty to lose. Like other pirates, Blackbeard's men took what cargo and valuables they fancied: things like coins, jewelry, rum, food-stuffs, ammunition, and navigational instruments. Unlike Hornigold or Bellamy, however, they dumped the rest of the cargo into the sea. One merchant aboard the ship watched £1,000 of his personal cargo go over the side; he begged to be allowed to keep enough cloth to make just one suit of clothes, but the pirates refused, throwing the last bolt of textiles overboard. By the time they released the ship, nothing remained of its cargo.

Over the next two weeks, Blackbeard brought a tide of terror and destruction to the mid-Atlantic coast such as had never been seen in peacetime. The *Revenge* cruised about the Capes of Delaware and the approaches to Bermuda, the Chesapeake and New York Harbor, never staying more than forty-eight hours in a single place. They captured vessels coming from all directions: vessels bound for Philadelphia from London, Liverpool and Madeira; sloops traveling between New York and the West Indies; Pennsylvania merchantmen outbound to England and beyond. Blackbeard took at least fifteen vessels in all, and, in the process, became the most feared pirate in the Americas practically overnight.

Traumatized captains poured into New York and Philadelphia bearing tales of woe. Captain Spofford told how, not a day out of Philadelphia, he had been forced to watch Blackbeard's men dump a thousand barrel staves into the sea, and then fill his cargo hold with the terrified crewmen of the *Sea Nymph*, a snow from Bristol they had captured as it started its journey to Portugal. One of the *Sea Nymph*'s men, the merchant Joseph Richardson, had been "very barbarously used" by the pirates, who threw his cargo of wheat into the sea. Captain Peter Peters told how the pirates had seized his sloop, stolen twenty-seven barrels of Madeira wine, hacked away his mast, and left him to run aground. The pirates left Captain Grigg's sloop at anchor at the mouth of the bay, his masts chopped off and his cargo of thirty indentured servants whisked away. The pirates took all the wine from a Virginia-bound sloop before sinking her. Captain Farmer's sloop had already been looted by other pirates on its way from Jamaica, but Blackbeard's men insisted on unrigging it and removing her mast and anchors to serve as spares for the *Revenge*, before they put thirty servant captives aboard and left her to drift ashore near Sandy Hook, New Jersey. Captain Sipkins was relieved of his command of a "great sloop" from New York, which Blackbeard's men kept as a consort, mounting her with thirteen guns.

The swaggering pirates had boasted how they were awaiting their consort, "a ship of thirty guns," and that once she arrived they intended to sail up the Delaware and lay siege to Philadelphia itself. Others bragged that they planned to sail down to the Capes of Virginia, to capture "a good ship there, which they very much wanted." Blackbeard made a special point of terrorizing captives from New England on behalf of the surviving members of Bellamy's crew, then rotting in the Boston Prison, telling them that if "any of their fellow pirates suffer [in Boston] that they will revenge it on them."

Blackbeard garnered considerable intelligence from his captives. The survivors from Bellamy's wrecks, they learned, were to be tried at any time, and likely faced the gallows. If Blackbeard intended to rescue them, he was dissuaded by news that King George had ordered "a proper force" to suppress piracy in the Americas. Two frigates were said to be at Boston, HMS *Rose* and *Squirrel*. HMS *Phoenix* had arrived at New York, and in Virginia, the sixth-rate *Lyme* was now backing up the decrepit *Shoreham*. One of Blackbeard's captives, Peter Peters, told him that while he was loading his wine at Madeira, off the coast of Africa, two Royal Navy frigates had come into the harbor, one en route to New York, the other to Virginia.* If they had not arrived already, Peters reported, they soon would be. Blackbeard recognized that the east coast

---

* These were, in fact, two forty-gun fifth-rates, HMS *Pearl*, bound for Virginia to relieve the troubled *Shoreham*, and HMS *Diamond*, headed to fleet headquarters in Jamaica.

of North America was becoming a risky place for a pirate sloop. It was time to conclude their business and head south to the islands of the Caribbean, indefensible in their multitude, at least until he could gain control of a ship-of-force.

Toward the end of October, Blackbeard's sloop and prizes were spotted sailing along the outside of Long Island, in the direction of Gardiner's Island or Block Island. They may have been going to one or the other to pick items left behind by Williams, or perhaps to drop off some of their own treasure. Whatever the reason for their trip, the pirates headed south very soon afterward, sailing for the islands of the eastern Caribbean.

✤✤✤

Contrary to many popular accounts, Blackbeard did not return to the Bahamas on his way to the Caribbean, nor is there compelling evidence that he joined forces with Benjamin Hornigold, who appears to have been working his way north at this time in his "great sloop" named, confusingly enough, the *Bonnet*. Blackbeard had so terrorized the coast that his men were ascribed to a number of attacks that they could not possibly have taken part in, as more detailed and credible accounts place him hundreds or thousands of miles away at the time they occurred. Several of these erroneous reports had placed him operating with Hornigold, suggesting that his old mentor may have in fact been responsible, but operating with a new consort similar to the *Revenge*.* If so, Hornigold was sailing north while Blackbeard and his men were sailing south, probably well offshore, on their way to the far eastern Caribbean, where the Windward Islands brace themselves against the open Atlantic.

Increasing the confusion, Blackbeard was now operating two sloops

---

* This would place Hornigold well offshore of the upper North Carolina coast on October 17, 1717 (when he captured two vessels) and off the Capes of Virginia on November 26, 1717 (where he captured a Maryland-bound ship). On 17 October, Thatch appears to have still been operating around the Delaware Capes, where he took a number of vessels between October 12 and 22, before sailing north to Long Island. On November 26 (English or Julian calendar), Thatch was 2,000 miles to the southeast, near St. Vincent, in the Windward Islands.

himself: the *Revenge* and one of his prizes, a forty-ton Bermuda-built sloop, most likely the vessel taken from Captain Sipkins. This second sloop, which the surviving documents fail to name, now carried eight guns and some thirty pirates; the larger *Revenge* had twelve guns and 120 men. Mariners had been conditioned to expect Blackbeard and Hornigold to be operating together, each in his own sloop; now that each was operating separately, but with two vessels each, it's not surprising that each man's victims wrongly assumed that the other was in charge of the second sloop.

Like Bellamy before him, Blackbeard was looking to capture a ship-of-force that would allow his pirate gang to take on even the frigates of the Royal Navy. With two sloops-of-war at his disposal, the pirates knew they had a reasonably good chance of overwhelming one, and Blackbeard knew just the place to look. Out in the sea, just beyond the arc of the Windward Islands that marks the leading edge of the Caribbean, the transatlantic shipping lanes converged. One could find ships bound from France to Martinique and Guadeloupe, from England to Barbados, and from Spain to the Spanish Main, through the deepwater passages between the islands. There, Blackbeard's men decided, was where they would cast their net.

It was a good choice. On November 17, within days or even hours of arriving, the lookout let out a cry. There, on the horizon, were the sails of an approaching ship.

✥

Pierre Dosset, captain of the French slaver *La Concorde*, could not have been happy to see two large sloops approaching from the west. He knew it meant trouble. Because of the prevailing winds, many ships sailed to the Caribbean at this latitude, but nobody sailed in the opposite direction. *La Concorde* was a large, swift, powerful vessel: a 250-ton ship-rigged slaver, with a strong oaken hull and enough gun ports to accommodate up to forty cannon. Dosset's crew, however, was in no condition to go into battle.

The Frenchmen had left their homeport of Nantes eight months earlier, with a crew of seventy-five and a hold full of goods to trade with the kings and princes of Whydah, on Africa's Bight of Benin. *La Concorde's* owner, the merchant Réne Montaudoin, had given Captain Dosset a competitive advantage over the captains of rival slavers, a cargo the Africans would pay many slaves to possess. The people of the Kingdom of Whydah had a penchant for the colorful cotton prints produced in India. Montaudoin, the richest man in Nantes, had built his own textile factory near the mouth of the Loire, which turned out knockoffs of the Calico and Indiennes patterns. His ship full of colorful cotton, Dosset looked forward to a smooth and profitable journey.

Things went badly from the start. A few days from Nantes, Dosset encountered a pair of powerful storms that damaged his ship, causing the loss of an expensive anchor and the death of a crewman. He arrived in Whydah in July after seventy-seven days at sea, and succeeded in trading his goods for 516 slaves and a small quantity of gold dust. He also picked up enough tropical microbes and bacteria to sicken many of the crew members. Sixteen crewmen died during their three-month stay in Africa or during the six weeks they had been crossing the Atlantic. Thirty-six others were sick with "scurvy and the bloody flux." Sixty-one slaves had also died. Now Dosset feared he might not make it to the slave markets of Martinique at all.

With 70 percent of his crew dead or incapacitated, Dosset lacked the manpower to handle the ship's cannon and rigging at the same time. A captain in his situation could bluff, displaying his guns to ward off the attackers, but on this occasion Dosset was deprived of that option as well. Because he was carrying an unusually large number of slaves—nearly a hundred more than in any of *La Concorde's* previous trips—he had to increase his cargo capacity by mounting only sixteen guns. If the strangers turned out to be pirates, Dosset knew he was in trouble.

As the sloops closed within range, he and his lieutenant, François Ernaud, must have felt a growing sense of terror. A spyglass revealed two sloops-of-war, with guns run out of their ports, and their decks jammed with men. Any further doubt about their intentions vanished when the sloops displayed a black flag with a death's head, and smoke and fire began to swirl around the head of the fearsome bearded man on the biggest sloop's quarterdeck.

Puffs of smoke appeared along the length of one of the sloops as she fired a full volley of cannon at *La Concorde*. Cannonballs splashed in the water and flew over the deck, followed shortly by a cascade of musket balls. Dosset stayed his course and tried to rally the crewmen, but a second volley of cannon and musketry sapped the last bit of morale from them. Dosset ordered the flag struck and the helmsman swung *La Concorde* into the wind, and she drifted slowly to a stop. Monsieur Montaudoin was going to be very angry.

❧

As he looked over his new prize, Blackbeard knew he had finally found a proper flagship. *La Concorde* was as big, fast, and powerful as Bellamy's now infamous *Whydah*, maybe more so. With such a vessel, Blackbeard knew his men could cause more havoc than the rest of the old Flying Gang put together. All the French slaver needed was a little refitting and a change of name.

The pirates took *La Concorde* to Bequia, a hilly, forested island with a large protected anchorage located nine miles southeast of St. Vincent. Blackbeard knew they were unlikely to be bothered there, for unlike most of the surrounding islands, St. Vincent and Bequia were not controlled by Europeans, but by the mixed-race descendents of Carib Indians and the African survivors of the 1635 wreck of two slave ships.* These people, the Garifuna, had tenaciously defended their land from the Europeans, but their naval operations were limited to a handful of

---

* The Garifuna people survive today, though the British deported them from St Vincent in the late eighteenth century. Today they have their own communities in the Bay Islands of Honduras and around Placencia, in southern Belize.

Carib-style war canoes. Even if they did show up in force, they were likely as not to be pleased with the pirates for stopping a slave ship from reaching its destination.

The hundreds of slaves in *La Concorde*'s hold had little reason to celebrate, however. While Blackbeard had several crewmen of African descent, they had probably been born in the West Indies, men familiar with European customs, language, and technology. Most Africans Blackbeard's men encountered "straight off the boat" appear to have been treated as cargo, creatures from an alien culture who were ineligible to join the pirates' ranks. The vast majority of the 455 slaves chained in *La Concorde*'s hold were turned over to Captain Dosset, whose men guarded them on the shore of Bequia. Blackbeard kept sixty-one slaves aboard *La Concorde*, probably for use as laborers, although a few may have been inducted into his company. On this point, sadly, the historical record has little to say.

The pirates forced ten of Dosset's crewmen, and their choice illustrates their company's needs: the chief surgeon and his deputy, a pilot, both gunsmiths; the master carpenter and his deputy, an expert in the art of caulking hulls; a cook; and one seaman with unspecified skills. In addition, four of Dosset's men begged the pirates to let them join, including the coxswain and both of his cabin boys. The boys, fifteen-year-old Louis Arot and slightly older Julien Joseph Moisant, were the worst-paid members of the slaver's crew, receiving a paltry five and eight livres (£0.2 and £0.35) a month respectively. Young Arot may have had reason to dislike Dosset and his officers, as he went out of his way to cause them harm, informing the pirates that they had a secret stash of gold dust hidden somewhere on the ship or their persons. Blackbeard's men interrogated Dosset and his officers, threatening to cut their throats if they failed to turn over the gold. The Frenchmen complied, and were rewarded with the pirates' small, forty-ton sloop; the pirates were keeping *La Concorde* for themselves. The pirates also gave them "two or three tons of beans" to prevent the slaves from starving. Dosset dubbed this sloop the *Mauvaise Recontre*, the "Bad Encounter," and used it to transport his crew and slaves back to Martinique, a task that took two separate voyages.

Blackbeard oversaw the transfer of his personal effects from the *Revenge* to *La Concorde*, along with cannon and supplies from the forty-ton sloop, and much of the pirate company. Stede Bonnet had recovered from his battle wounds and, despite his inexperience, was allowed to resume command of the *Revenge* and a crew of at least fifty men. From eyewitness accounts a few days later, we know that *La Concorde* now carried twenty-two guns and 150 men, indicating that at least some of the Africans retained by the pirates had been inducted into the crew. The pirates also gave *La Concorde* a new name: *Queen Anne's Revenge*. The choice of names suggests Jacobite political leanings among Blackbeard's crew, evoking the name of the last Stuart monarch and promising vengeance in her name against King George and his Hanoverian line.

Now in command of a powerful warship, Blackbeard was ready to make his mark. He was, by now, aware of the relatively weak state of the European colonies in the Lesser Antillies, which Sam Bellamy's men would have attested to on the basis of their raids the year before. He proposed to the company that they sweep the 1,400-mile island chain from end to end, raiding ships and harbors alike until they reached the Windward Passage, where they might snare a Spanish galleon carrying the payroll to Cuba. This strategy agreed upon, the *Revenge* and *Queen Anne's Revenge* sailed out of the harbor to the south, a course set for Grenada, the first island in the chain. When they reached the French island, they would backtrack their way to St. Vincent and continue north, hopping from island to island and stripping them of valuables as if they were walking through a row of fruit trees.

This first leg of the journey, which lasted but two days, was of mixed success. Despite, or possibly because of the presence of their French pilot, the pirates managed to run one of their vessels aground on Grenada. They were able to get her off whatever reef she had struck, and while it didn't suffer any serious damage, the pirates did find it necessary to abandon a number of the slaves. (Dosset was later able to recover them, in part because he had branded them with *La Concorde's* initials.) But they also made their first capture: a large brigantine, a seaworthy, two-masted vessel, armed with ten guns. No account of the capture of this vessel survives, so there is no way of knowing where she came from or what was onboard, but the pirates kept her as a third member of their fleet. Presumably a few of her crew were forced into service and the remainder released on one of the ship's boats or put ashore on St. Lucia. In any event, the pirates acquired this brigantine between the time they left Captain Dosset on Bequia and when they encountered their next quarry a day or so later, in the deepwater passage north of St. Vincent.

This was the *Great Allen* of Boston, a very large merchant ship en route from Barbados to Jamaica. Blackbeard, still furious with Massachusetts authorities, allowed the crew to rough up the *Great Allen's* captain, Christopher Taylor, to get him to reveal the whereabouts of his valuables. The shackled captain either refused to tell or denied there were any riches, apart from whatever they had found in the *Great Allen's* hold. The pirates didn't believe him, and whipped him soundly. Whether he confessed or not, the pirates ended up with a cup of such exquisite value and workmanship that future captives would remember it above all the riches they saw aboard Blackbeard's ships. Taylor then had to watch as the pirates burned his huge ship to the waterline. The next day, Taylor and his crew were put aboard a boat and were rowed to a sparsely inhabited shore on Martinique.

It would take three months for word of the attack to reach the *Great Allen's* homeport of Boston. By then, the fate of Bellamy's crewmen had already been sealed.

Blackbeard's men confirmed they had little to fear from French authorities in that part of the Caribbean. Martinique, a sugar colony with a population of 9,400 whites and over 29,000 slaves, was the center of France's West Indies empire, but it had no naval protection of any kind. Blackbeard would have been dissuaded from attacking the harbor itself by the presence of Fort Royal, her thick walls and heavy guns providing ample protection. However Guadeloupe, Martinique's sister colony, seventy-five miles to the north, was not so strongly fortified, a fact the pirates would have learned when interrogating Dosset and his crew. It was there that Blackbeard would make the first of many brash incursions into the very capitals of Europe's American colonies.

We know only a few details of the attack on Guadeloupe town, which likely took place on the night of November 28, 1717. The pirates sailed straight into the harbor, guns blazing, before the ships at anchor could get underway. They seized control of a large French ship that had just finished taking on a cargo of sugar, raising her sails and hacking away her anchor lines to make a quick escape. Then, in the most outrageous move made by a Caribbean pirate to date, they set the town ablaze, probably by firing red-hot cannonballs into its rows of neat wooden homes. As they sailed out of the port, a growing plume of smoke rose behind them. By the time the island's residents were able to get the conflagration under control, half of Guadeloupe town lay in ashes.

The morning of the twenty-ninth found the pirates sailing north on a light wind with their big French sugar ship, creeping into the forty-mile wide passage that separated French Guadeloupe from the neighboring English islands of Montserrat, Antigua, and Nevis. A large merchant vessel appeared bearing English colors. Before they had an opportunity to attack, however, several of the ship's men were seen climbing into their longboat. To the pirates' surprise, instead of trying to escape, the boat began rowing straight up to the nearest of their three vessels, Stede Bonnet's *Revenge*. Bonnet luffed his sails, allowing the boat to come alongside. He looked over the rail and was greeted by a man who introduced himself as Thomas Knight, an officer of the *Montserrat Merchant*. Knight's commanding officer, Bonnet soon learned, had mistaken the *Revenge* and *Queen Anne's Revenge* for a pair of English slavers arriving from Africa and had sent him over to inquire if they were carrying letters bound for Montserrat or the British Leeward Islands. Bonnet, who must have looked the part of an aristocratic slave trader, introduced himself as Captain Edwards and told Knight he was bound from Barbados to Jamaica. He said they did indeed have something for them, and insisted they come on board. At this point in the conversation, Knight finally noticed the death's head flag hanging from the *Revenge*'s stern. Trying to conceal his discomfort, Knight politely declined. Bonnet then changed his tone, ordering Knight and his boat crew to come aboard, else he would sink them right then and there. The hapless men did as they were told, scampering onto the deck amid a crowd of armed men. Knight later recalled that "when we went on board, the first words they said to us were that we were welcome aboard the pirates," meaning their vessel.

For the next few hours, Knight and his men were kept in a state of terror and confusion. First, Bonnet's men invited them to a meal. Knight declined. The pirates extended the invitation a second time, this time adding that if it was refused "they would do [them] mischief." During this compulsory meal, Bonnet and his crew interrogated their guests, gathering intelligence about the British Leeward Islands. How big was Montserrat's fort at Kinsale? How many guns protected the island's principal harbor, Plymouth, and how strong were the ships anchored there? Knight told them what he knew: Kinsale's sixty-year-old fort had four guns, but there were another seven guarding the entrance to Plymouth. No other ships were armed with anything greater than personal firearms. Then he begged the pirates to release him and his men, or at least put them ashore on Guadeloupe or Montserrat, as the captain of their ship had by now figured out the situation and fled the scene. Bonnet's men refused, saying the captives "must go and speak with the Man-of-War"—the *Queen Anne's Revenge*—before they would be discharged.

As the day wore on, Bonnet caught up to the *Queen Anne's Revenge* and the French sugar ship. He came alongside Blackbeard's flagship, close enough to yell a question to his commodore: What should he do with the men they had captured? The word came back to send the captives over in a boat. Knight and his men rowed to the powerful man-of-war, which looked to them to have been built with Dutch lines, fast and agile. As they grew near, someone aboard the great pirate ship hailed them through a speaking trumpet. The message was the same as before: "Welcome aboard the Pirate."

Once on the deck of *Queen Anne's Revenge*, Knight's party was invited to yet another meal. This time they did not refuse. The pirates bragged about their conquests but concealed their commanders' names, calling Bonnet "Edwards" and claiming Blackbeard's name to be "Kentish." Blackbeard did not join them, however, and the captives soon learned that he was ill, probably from a disease carried from Africa in his ex-slave ship. The captain would speak to them later. In the meantime, they were put to work as temporary laborers aboard the ship.

The pirates sailed through the night, leaving Montserrat unmolested in favor of Nevis, the second most important island in Britain's Leeward Islands colony, a volcanic peak soaring 3,200 feet out of the shimmering ocean. They reached Nevis at daybreak and Blackbeard ordered a course for the main anchorage on the island's western shore.

A few hours later, the pirate squadron reached Nevis Harbor, but Blackbeard was so ill he could barely leave his quarters. William Howard, his quartermaster, inspected the vessels anchored against the sugarcane-fringed shores. There were a variety of merchant vessels for the taking—sloops, sailing canoes, and a few large brigantines or ships—but there was also a large frigate, which Howard took to be the warship assigned to the Leeward Islands, the sixth-rate HMS *Seaford*. The pirates reacted with excitement, not fear. The consensus was that they should pounce on the frigate where she lay, storm her decks, cut her anchor line, and before authorities ashore could react, sail her out to sea. Howard proposed this bold plan to Blackbeard, but the pirate felt too weak to take part in the risky attack and talked the company out of it. There would be other opportunities, he told them, once they were more familiar with their ship and her capabilities; instead they should concentrate on easy targets. His argument won out, and Howard ordered the flotilla to sail for Antigua, the capital of the British Leeward Islands, which they hoped was without naval protection.

The pirates sailed under English colors, doing their best to appear to be simple merchant vessels going about their business. En route to Antigua, their three vessels sailed among a pair of unsuspecting merchant ships. Perhaps not wishing to arouse a general alarm, the pirates did not attack. Instead, they sent Bonnet a bit ahead of the other ships in the *Revenge* to gather more information. As the day progressed, a merchant sloop happened to pass alongside her. Bonnet or one of his officers hailed it, claiming they were from Barbados. A man aboard the sloop responded that he was Richard Joy, captain and owner of the *New Division*, on her way from St. Christopher to Antigua. The pirates said he must come aboard their vessel, and promised to do him no harm. "When I went on board they asked me to eat and drink, and enquired what vessels were along the shore," Joy later recalled. "[I] could not tell."

While Joy was consuming his meal, some of Bonnet's men climbed aboard the *New Division*, took control of the quarterdeck, and forced all its crew back aboard the *Revenge*. They continued to interrogate Joy, demanding to know what vessels were in St. Christopher harbor. At first the merchant pleaded ignorance, but when the pirates threatened to burn his sloop, he told them everything. There were two ships, one newly arrived from Liverpool with a cargo of English foodstuffs. The pirates were pleased at the news, but announced they would sink the *New Division* all the same. Joy approached Bonnet, begging him to let him have his vessel. "[I] told him it was all I had to support my family." Bonnet took pity on the man and told his crew to let him have his sloop, but not to release him until after nightfall. When the *New Division* finally parted from the pirates, Blackbeard's quartermaster, William Howard, allowed Thomas Knight and his men to leave with them. As their captives sailed off, the pirates drew their vessels together for a consultation, and, based on their new intelligence, resolved to attack St. Christopher rather than Antigua. The three vessels turned around again, heading northwest toward their new target.

Blackbeard's flotilla arrived on December 1. The English settlers could not have been happy to see the three ships sailing into Sandy Point, black flags flying from the rigging. The settlers, who still hadn't recovered from a severe French attack during the war, were unable to keep up the island's defenses. The guns were rarely in working order, and powder, ammunition, and skilled gunners were in short supply, even at the island's principal fort on Brimstone Hill, overlooking the anchorage. The militia had presumably been called up to man what cannon they did have, but were unable to stop Blackbeard's men from seizing and plundering a number of trading sloops. (The Liverpool ship was nowhere to be seen.) In a symbolic show of contempt for the king's fort, Blackbeard had his men sail their big French sugar ship right under the fort's guns and set her on fire right at the foot of Brimstone Hill. The ship, still loaded with sugar, turned into an inferno, a great plume of acrid smoke drifting over the fort's stone battlements. As the *Revenge* and *Queen Anne's Revenge* pulled out of the harbor, the pirates also burned several trading sloops, leaving Sandy Point looking as if the French had raided it anew.

Blackbeard and Bonnet continued up the Leewards, their vessels laden with silver, gold dust, and sugar. Blackbeard had stolen another six cannon, and as they sailed for the Virgin Islands, his crew mounted them on gun carriages and rolled them into place behind the *Queen Anne's Revenge*'s spare gun ports. Blackbeard's flagship now had twenty-eight two- and six-pound cannon, with room for another twelve. Blackbeard himself had recovered his health, and perhaps regretted not attacking what he took to be HMS *Seaford* back in Nevis.

In truth, the *Seaford* had not been at Nevis. While Blackbeard and Bonnet were prowling Nevis and St. Christopher, the *Seaford* was sailing in the Virgin Islands, carrying Governor Walter Hamilton on a tour of his colony's far-flung possessions. The little frigate had just turned around to begin her return trip to Antigua, putting her on a collision course with Blackbeard and Bonnet.

Governor Hamilton and the *Seaford's* captain, Jonathan Rose, were already concerned about their safety. The *Seaford* was the only warship assigned to the sprawling Leeward Islands colony, but she was one of the Navy's smallest frigates. The twenty-year-old vessel was just ninety-three feet long and 248 tons, with twenty-four guns and a crew of eighty-five; as usual, many of her men were incapacitated by one tropical disease or another. Governor Hamilton and Captain Rose were both aware she would be no match for a heavily armed pirate sloop and frigate, especially if they were boarded. Indeed, when Sam Bellamy passed through the colony the year before, they had been forced to cancel Governor Hamilton's tour of the Virgins. Finally they were making the tour, but had already suffered a brush with danger. Just a few days earlier, they had encountered a pirate ship "of about 26 guns and 250 men" off St. Thomas. The ship flew a "white ensign with a figure of a dead man spread in it" and, according to Captain Rose, was commanded by none other than Olivier La Buse. Despite being outgunned and out-manned, the *Seaford* chased after La Buse, but was unable to catch him, being out-sailed by him as well.

Blackbeard's men spotted the *Seaford* near St. Thomas on or about December 2, and from some distance away. They identified her with certainty, probably recognizing the navy's distinctive ensign flying from her rigging. A discussion ensued. They knew they had to outman the frigate, but to realize this advantage they would need to board her. It was relatively easy to board a vessel if you surprised it at anchor, which is what the pirates had considered at Nevis, but it was far more risky to do so in a running battle at sea. Royal Navy gunners were well trained, able to fire their cannons twice as fast as their French and Spanish competitors; if they got off a well-timed broadside of grapeshot, they could cut down a hundred men in a few seconds. On the *Revenge*, veteran crewmen recalled the horrific carnage they witnessed when Bonnet had attacked a Spanish man-of-war, an engagement which Bonnet had only recently recovered from. In the end, they voted against the attack, which struck them as unnecessarily risky. As the pirates would later tell a captive, "They had met the man of war of this station, but said they had no business with her, but if she had chased them they would have kept their way." They stuck to their course and watched the *Seaford* disappear.

Aboard the *Seaford*, Captain Rose and Governor Hamilton thought they had just passed a slave ship and merchant sloop, not realizing how near they had come to danger until later that day. Approaching the island of St. Eustacius, they were hailed by a sloop "sent express from St. Christopher's" ten miles to the southeast. The sloop's crew informed the governor of the pirates' identity and their raid on Sandy Point two days earlier. The attack, Governor Hamilton later recalled, "gave the people of St. Christopher's . . . just apprehensions [for] my safety," prompting them to voluntarily outfit a six-gun sloop to escort the *Seaford* back to Antigua. A hundred militiamen volunteered to man her, and ten more came aboard the *Seaford* to bolster her crew in the event of a boarding by pirates. As the flustered governor sailed back to Antigua, he wrote a letter to Captain Francis Hume in Barbados, begging him to immediately bring HMS *Scarborough* to the Leewards to help the *Seaford* hunt down the pirates.

Future generations of historians would report that Blackbeard fought the *Scarborough* to a draw, an event seen as one of the most fantastic of his many accomplishments. The fight never happened, however, as proven by a thorough examination of the logbooks of the *Scarborough* and *Seaford* and the letters of Captains Hume and Rose. The *Scarborough* and *Seaford* pursued the pirates, tracking Blackbeard and Bonnet's movements across the Antillies for nearly a month; but they were always more than a week behind them. They never caught up with the pirates. Instead, the naval captains received a false report that Blackbeard had been seen at Dominica, near St. Vincent, which sent them on a 300-mile wild goose chase in the wrong direction.

Somehow, accounts of the *Seaford's* close encounter with Blackbeard got mixed up with those of the *Scarborough's* engagements with John Martel and other pirates, and exaggerated into an all-out naval battle that never took place.

In reality, after passing the *Seaford* on the morning of December 2, Blackbeard and Bonnet sailed to St. Croix, the pirate rendezvous used by Martel and Bellamy the year before. En route they captured two sloops, one Danish and one English, which they took into St. Croix's harbor. There they stayed for a night or two, regenerating their water and firewood supply and mounting more captured cannon aboard the *Queen Anne's Revenge*, bringing her to thirty-six guns. For recreation, they also burnt the English sloop, adding her hulk to the burned-out bones of John Martel's pirate ship and sloops. Again, the crews of these trading vessels were not harmed. When Blackbeard was ready to leave, he put the captives aboard the Danish sloop, along with "an Indian and a Negro belonging to Bermuda." The latter individuals had probably been captives for a couple of months, apparently ingratiating themselves with the pirates, for they were carrying fifteen ounces of gold dust. (It was stolen from them by the captains of the Danish and English sloops during their trip to Tortola.)

Blackbeard and Bonnet continued east and on December 5 were off the eastern end of Puerto Rico. That day they captured one final Leeward Islands' sloop, the *Margaret* of St. Christopher, after the *Queen Anne's Revenge* fired a single shot over her bow. The *Margaret's* captain, Henry Bostock, was ordered to row over to the pirate flagship with five of his men. Bostock later gave English authorities one of the most detailed accounts of Blackbeard and his ship. The pirates "did not seem to want provisions," but they did seize a number of the live cattle and hogs Bostock was carrying in his sloop, as well as his books, navigational instruments, cutlasses, and firearms. Blackbeard, Bostock reported, "was a tall spare man with a very black beard which he wore very long." His crew numbered three hundred, and his flagship was a "Dutch built . . .

French guinea man" with thirty-six guns. There was a great deal of silver on board, as well as the "fine cup" taken from Captain Taylor. The pirates didn't abuse Bostock or his men, but they did force three of them to serve aboard their ship. A fourth, Robert Biddy of Liverpool, joined them voluntarily.

Blackbeard interrogated Bostock and his crew, wanting to know what other merchant vessels were trading on the Puerto Rican coast. Bostock refused to talk, but Biddy and other crewmembers told him of French and Danish sloops they had passed on their way. Bonnet was sent ahead in the *Revenge* to chase them down, while Blackbeard's men finished transferring squealing hogs and unhappy cattle onto the *Queen Anne's Revenge*. The pirates bragged about meeting the *Seaford* and burning various ships and sloops. Bostock overheard them discussing their intention to sail for Samana Bay, Hispaniola (now within the Dominican Republic), where they would careen and "lye in wait for the Spanish Armada" they expected would sail from Havana "with money to pay the garrisons" on Puerto Rico. "They think we are gone," Blackbeard said of the Spanish, "but we will soon be at their backs unawares."

For some reason, Blackbeard and his men were extremely eager to learn the whereabouts of one Captain Pinkentham, whom the pirates "inquired often" about. Pinkentham, a sea captain with ties to Jamaica and Rhode Island, had been a privateer during the War of Spanish Succession, commanding a swift vessel with a crew of 160 men; Blackbeard would certainly have known him, and may have even served on his crew, which raises the possibility that his motives for finding Pinkentham may have been more complicated than simply wanting to loot the man's vessel. Bostock's men told Blackbeard that they had last seen Pinkentham at St. Thomas, one of the Danish-controlled Virgin Islands, in an eight-gun sloop; he planned to sail to Jamaica and then on to Florida to dive the Spanish wrecks and already had official British permission to do so. Blackbeard probably hoped to catch up to Pinkentham on his way to Jamaica. (They didn't succeed; Pinkentham's sloop was later captured by a Bermudan pirate named Grinnaway; Pinkentham's crew of "10 men, 2 boys and 6 Negros" later managed to over-power their captors and escape.)

～⊱⊰～

Bostock had one other piece of information, one that would turn the pirates' world upside down. George I was believed to have issued an Act of Grace pardoning all pirates for their crimes, provided they surrender. The actual proclamation had not reached the authorities in the Leeward Islands, but there were mariners who had seen the decree back in England, where it had been published in the *London Gazette* eleven weeks earlier. A copy of the decree would arrive any day, Bostock told them. The pirates, Bostock later reported, listened to this news, "but they seemed to slight it." The information was unsettling; it could not be otherwise. Every one of the nearly 400 men in Blackbeard's flotilla had thought they'd taken an irrevocable step into criminality and rebellion, only to discover a possibility of a second chance. Each man, Blackbeard included, must have thought about quitting piracy and retiring with their ill-gotten gains.

If Blackbeard's pirates discussed this news with one another, the content of their debates has been lost to history. In fact, Henry Bostock was the last Englishman to see Blackbeard for nearly three months. After Blackbeard let Bostock go, the pirates sailed deeper into French and Spanish territory, and the intelligence collected by the captains of HMS *Scarborough* and HMS *Seaford* dried up. The last reports they received placed the pirates at Mona Island, between Puerto Rico and Hispaniola, and finally near Samana Bay. There, Blackbeard faded out of the English records, and into a Spanish world where nobody knew his name.

CHAPTER NINE

BEGGING PARDON

December 1717–August 1718

H ENRY BOSTOCK had not lied to Blackbeard. As part of his plan to suppress the pirates, King George I had, indeed, issued a royal proclamation on September 5, 1717 decreeing that any pirate who surrendered to a British governor within one year would be pardoned for all piracies committed before January 5, 1718. As Blackbeard sailed down the Greater Antilles, copies of this Proclamation for Suppressing of Pirates were on their way from England aboard merchant ships bound for Boston, Charleston, and Barbados. When the ships reached their destinations, even jailed pirates would be freed.

The pardons had been conceived of and promoted by Woodes Rogers and were intended to reduce the number of active pirates prior to King George's counteroffensive. It was hoped that those pirates who took advantage of the Act of Grace would return to being productive, law-abiding subjects. Holdouts would be hunted down without mercy. King George had ordered all military and colonial personnel to seize such dead-enders, providing a reward of £100 for every pirate captain captured, plus £50 for senior pirate "officers," and £20–30 for other members of a pirate vessel's crew. Between captures and pardons, the king's advisors reasoned, the pirates of the Caribbean would be too weak to resist Rogers when he finally arrived to reestablish control of the Bahamas.

Official word of the pardon reached Boston first, and the text of the proclamation was published in the *Boston News-Letter* of December 9,

1717. It arrived too late for the surviving members of Bellamy's crew. Through the spring and summer of 1717, the eight prisoners waited in vain for rescue from their cages at Boston Prison. They were brought to trial in late October, in the second-floor courtroom of Boston's four-year-old Town House, one hundred yards down the street from the prison.* The two carpenters forced from the *St. Michael*—Thomas South and Thomas Davis—were found not guilty and released. The other six men were sentenced to hang.

The condemned men spent their final two weeks in the company of perhaps the most influential man in all of New England, the Puritan preacher Cotton Mather. Mather, the fifty-nine-year-old scion of a family that had dominated the spiritual and political life of Massachusetts since its foundation, took an interest in the pirates. He visited them in their cells, where he subjected them to long-winded sermons, condemning their vile behavior and accusing them, falsely, of murdering all their captives as their ship wrecked against Cape Cod. Throughout these meetings one captive, Simon Van Vorst, maintained his innocence, noting that he had been a forced man. "Forced! No," Mather admonished the man at the time. "Better [to] have died a martyr by the cruel hands of [the pirates] than have become one of their brethren." Upon his return home, however, Mather scrawled a "to do" note in his diary: "Obtain a reprieve and, if it may be, a pardon for one of [the] Pyrates, who is not only more penitent, but also more innocent than the rest." If he indeed tried to obtain this pardon, the effort was unsuccessful.

On the afternoon of November 15, Mather accompanied the condemned prisoners as they walked from the prison to the Charles River ferry landing. After he heard their final confessions, the sheriffs led them out to gallows that had been erected on the tidal flats. An enormous crowd watched as the men made their final speeches. According to Mather, most were "distinguishingly penitent," particularly Van Vorst,

---

* Boston Prison, where Captain Kidd was also detained in 1699, was located at what is now 26 Court Street, a stone's throw uphill from the Town House (1713), now known as the Old State House. The prison is described, somewhat fancifully, in Nathaniel Hawthorne's *The Scarlet Letter*.

who read a psalm in his native Dutch before exhorting "young persons to lead a life of religion . . . keep the Sabbath, and carry it well to their parents." Then the men were hanged until they were dead. "Behold," Mather wrote in a published account* of their final hours, "The End of Piracy!"

The Golden Age of Piracy was far from over.

≈≈≈

From Boston, news of the king's pardon slowly spread in all directions. A bitter snowstorm delayed the postal riders who carried word to Rhode Island and New York, but an unnamed merchant vessel brought the news to Bermuda in little more than a week, and into the hands of Governor Benjamin Bennett. Bennett, who had long been advising his superiors in London to do something about the pirate republic in the Bahamas, took it upon himself to inform the pirates of the pardon's existence. He had copies of the proclamation printed and asked his own son to deliver them to Nassau in a swift Bermuda sloop.

The governor's son was walking into the mouth of the lion, armed only with a stack of printed paper. The pirates had captured many of his countrymen's vessels and even threatened to attack Bermuda itself. If they reacted badly, young Bennett could wind up dead.

By now, so many merchants were smuggling goods back and forth to the Bahamas the pirates probably didn't give the unfamiliar sloop a second thought. Although he was the first official visitor to the island in nearly two years, the pirates may not have been aware of Bennett's presence until he stepped ashore and started handing out copies of the king's offer of pardon. They were passed on to the literate among them who read out their contents to those who could not. Within hours, everyone on the island must have known they had been offered a second chance.

---

* One week after the executions, Mather wrote in his diary: "May I not do well to give the Bookseller something that may render the condition of the pirates, lately executed, profitable?" The result was his *Instructions to the Living, from the Condition of the Dead*, published shortly thereafter in Boston.

Nassau's pirates promptly broke into two contending factions. At least half of the pirates were ecstatic, greeting young Bennett as their hero and savior. This group was exemplified by Henry Jennings, who had never intended to become an outlaw in the first place, and it included Leigh Ashworth, Bellamy's old quartermaster; Richard Noland; veteran pirate sloop captain Josiah Burgess; and Jean Bondavais, the French pirate who had previously tried to take the captive surgeon John Howell from Hornigold. Hornigold himself was at sea when Bennett arrived, but his sympathies lay with them. This camp consisted of the more moderate pirates—former sailors and privateersmen who had fallen into piracy with profit in mind. This pro-pardon crowd was eager for the chance to regain legitimacy, free to invest their plunder in commercial trade. Backed by the dozens of captives and forced men on the island, they celebrated by climbing to the top of Fort Nassau, where they raised the Union Jack in a display of submission to the Crown.

The other camp was infuriated by this action. They were the diehard outlaws, bitter, angry men who saw themselves not as businessmen or thieves, but as rebels or guerilla insurgents in a war against ship owners, merchants, and, in many cases, King George himself. This anti-pardon crowd included many of the pirates who held pro-Stuart or "Jacobite" sympathies and had been disappointed by the collapse of the 1715 uprising against King George and the House of Hanover. This faction included Paulsgrave Williams, the ruthless sloop captains Christopher Winter and Nicholas Brown, and several ambitious young men whose names would soon become infamous: Edward England, Edmund Condent, and "Calico Jack" Rackham. Their undisputed leader was Charles Vane.

Up until now, Vane had been in the background, one of the hundreds of low-ranking pirates who caroused in the streets of Nassau, drinking, gambling, fighting, and womanizing. He had been living off his earnings while serving with Henry Jennings, particularly his shares of the plunder stolen from the Spanish wrecks in 1716. He may have gone on short cruises with other pirate captains, but it seems that he spent most of the intervening year and a half as Jennings had: resting on his laurels ashore and appreciating the freedoms offered by the existence of the Bahamian pirate republic. The news of the pardon threatened to put an end to the pirate's nest, as did rumors that King George had appointed a new royal governor for the Bahamas. Vane, who had Jacobite sympathies, could not have been pleased when he read King George's proclamation. He was furious when he saw his less-committed colleagues celebrating atop the fort beneath the newly raised British flag.

Vane's faction rallied to the main square, which soon filled with hundreds of armed and angry men. They rushed the walls of the adjacent fort, evicted the revelers within, and pulled the Union Jack down from the flagpole. In its place they hoisted a flag that left no ambiguity about their allegiance: "the Black Flag with the Death's Head in it."

Vane's faction tried to attract outside support as well. Through their network of smugglers and Jacobite contacts in England, these pirates passed a message to Captain George Cammocke, a Royal Navy captain who had defected to the Pretender's cause and was now living in France. In the message, the pirates "did with one heart and voice proclaim James III for their King" and were "resolved to prosper or perish in their bold undertaking" against George I. As Cammocke would later tell it, the pirates wrote that "they have rejected with contempt the said pardon"; they "humbly desired" that the Stuarts would "send to them such a person as has borne some character in the Royal Navy of England" to serve as the Jacobite "Captain General of America, by Sea and Land," with the power to commission the pirates as privateers and to help organize their resistance to the Hanoverian King. With such guidance, they said they could mount a successful surprise attack on Bermuda and secure the colony for the Stuarts.

This extraordinary proposal reached Cammocke via supporters in England in just three months. The veteran naval officer enthusiastically embraced the pirates' plan and immediately volunteered to go to Nassau himself. In a letter sent on March 28, 1718, to James Stuart's mother, the deposed Queen Mary of Modena, Cammocke proposed to purchase a fifty-gun warship in Cádiz for £15,000, crew her with English Jacobites, and sail to the Bahamas as a Stuart admiral. Once in Nassau, Cammocke would, with James III's permission, issue a pardon for all the pirates, commissioning them as privateers instead. He would set up scheduled mail-boat service between Nassau and Spain so that the exiled Stuart court could be kept in close communication with the pirates. "Employing them against the common enemy will be the only means to make way for a Restoration" of the House of Stuart, Cammocke wrote. "For if we can destroy the West India and Guinea trade, we shall make the English merchants . . . rather desire a Restoration then [to allow] that [the reign of George,] the Duke of Brunswick should continue." Events in the Bahamas, however, would overtake Cammocke's plan before it ever got off the ground.

The situation in Nassau remained tense throughout January 1718. Several pirate vessels returned with a number of well-laden prizes that served as a reminder of the benefits of piracy. These included the *Mary Galley* of Bristol, her holds packed with bottled liquor, and three large French ships carrying brandy, white wine, and claret. Hornigold brought in two well-armed Dutch merchant ships taken off Vera Cruz, Mexico; one had twenty-six guns, enough to reinforce Fort Nassau, while the other, the *Younge Abraham* of Flushing, Netherlands, had forty, as well as a large parcel of poorly cured animal hides whose influence would soon gravely effect life on Nassau.

The pirates held a general council to resolve their differences but, in the words of *A General History of the Pyrates*, "there was so much noise and clamour that nothing could be agreed on." Vane's camp argued that they should fortify the island, forcing King George to negotiate while they awaited word from James Stuart's court-in-exile. Jennings, on the other hand, insisted that they should take the pardon and surrender "without more ado," turning the island over to the royal governor whenever he showed up. The divisions "so disconcerted" the assembled pirates "that their Congress broke up very abruptly without doing anything."

After that, almost everyone on New Providence seemed to be packing up. The diehards began fitting out the ships and sloops in the harbor, preparing for what could be long and arduous cruises. Christopher Winter and Nicholas Brown were sailing to Cuba to shelter themselves among the Spaniards. Edmund Condent and ninety-seven other men signed aboard the sloop *Dragon*, which they fit out for a cruise to Africa and Brazil. Vane and sixteen followers acquired control of the sloop *Lark* and hid her in a secluded anchorage nearby where they modified her for pirate service. Meanwhile, other residents were sailing to take the pardon in neighboring British colonies. Jennings and fifteen of his men went to Bermuda in the *Barsheba* and received pardons from Governor Bennett. Others booked passage on merchant sloops bound for South Carolina, Rhode Island, and Jamaica. Hornigold stayed in Nassau, but sent a sloop to Jamaica with eighty of his men; he must have feared for his safety among the antipardon pirates, because he instructed the departing men to ask naval authorities in Port Royal to send a warship to Nassau for "protection."

By then, a Royal Navy frigate was in fact on its way, but from New York rather than Jamaica.

≈≈≈

Captain Vincent Pearse, commander of the sixth-rate HMS *Phoenix*, received word of the proclamation on Christmas Day, during a heavy snowstorm that had slowed the postal riders from Boston. While the captains of other naval vessels took in the news of the proclamation passively, carrying on with business as usual, Pearse was young, ambitious, and ready to take the news directly to the pirates. He received the blessing of New York's governor and immediately began readying his ship, which was hunkered down for the winter, rolling guns back into place, securing supplies, and remounting topmasts and other rigging.

Pearse knew his frigate would need every advantage if the pirates proved hostile. The *Phoenix* was one of Britain's smallest frigates. At 273 tons and ninety-three feet in length, she was no bigger than a large pirate ship like the *Whydah* or *Queen Anne's Revenge*, and she carried less firepower. During the previous year, the Admiralty had removed the four quarterdeck guns she had carried in wartime, leaving the frigate with only twenty six-pound cannon. She was also vulnerable to boarding, having a peacetime complement of only ninety men. Nor was she particularly well built. As her name suggests, the *Phoenix* was originally built as a fireship, intended to be filled with combustibles, set on fire, and sailed into an enemy's battle fleet, her crew planning to get away at the last moment in an escape boat. As he set sail for Nassau on the afternoon of February 5, Captain Pearse must have hoped he wasn't getting in over his head.

On the morning of February 23, the *Phoenix* arrived at the main entrance to Nassau harbor, her men glancing nervously at the guns of the decaying fort and the death's head flag flying from its mast. Anchored in the harbor were fourteen vessels flying the colors of many nations: Dutch, English, French, Spanish, and the black or red flags favored by the pirates. Five were large ships, including the well-armed Dutch prizes brought in by Hornigold, as well as the *Mary Galley*, the unarmed French wine ship, and a small English merchantman. The other nine, Pearse later wrote in his log, "were traders with these pyrates, but pretended they never did it till [after] the Act of Grace was published."

Pearse ordered his lieutenant, Mr. Symonds, to assemble a landing party to take copies of the proclamation ashore. As the *Phoenix's* long boat slowly made its way into the harbor, Symonds holding aloft a white flag of truce, the pirates had a moment of reckoning. They could easily drive off the *Phoenix*; in addition to the guns in the fort, pirates were already onboard the thirty-six-gun *Younge Abraham* and the other twenty-six-gun Dutch ship. If they did so, there would be considerable loss of life, and none of the survivors would have any chance of obtaining a pardon. Hornigold, the most experienced and influential pirate on the island at the time, counseled a conciliatory approach. Those who wished to take the pardon and return to civilized society could do so; those who did not could still take the pardon, using it to their advantage to buy themselves more time. The rank-and-file agreed. When Symonds stepped onto the beach, proclamation in hand "he was received by a great number of Pirates with much Civility," Pearse's logbook attests. The lieutenant read the now-familiar proclamation aloud to the pirates, who greeted it with what he took to be "a great deal of joy."

Symonds was ashore for a few hours, during which time he was briefed by members of the pro-pardon faction. They wished to rid themselves of the inflammatory Charles Vane more than anyone else in the antipardon camp, and told the lieutenant how to find his secret anchorage. The pro-pardon pirates must have taken pleasure in watching the *Phoenix* sail out of the harbor in pursuit of their nemesis; Vane's allies watched with trepidation.

Pearse found Vane's sloop tucked in behind a little islet called Buskes Cay, just where his informants said it would be. He placed the *Phoenix* so that it blocked the entrance to the anchorage, then gave the order to commence firing on her.

Aboard the *Lark*, Vane's company had little choice but to surrender. As six-pound cannonballs splashed around their little vessel, the sixteen men concocted a cover story. They would tell the *Phoenix's* commander that they had been preparing not to go pirating, but rather to sail to Nassau to see him and learn about the king's pardon. With this in mind, Vane and his new quartermaster, a fearless Irishman named Edward England, sailed to the *Phoenix* and surrendered.

Pearse was not fooled by Vane's story and seized the *Lark* in the name of King George, taking Vane and company into custody. Although the sun was setting, Pearse felt confident they could find their way back to Nassau, so the *Phoenix* sailed through the night, arriving in the morning. He dropped anchor in thirty feet of water, the *Lark* anchoring nearby. Following the protocol of the day, the pirates aboard the two Dutch ships fired their guns in salute of His Majesty's ship, a sign that they recognized its authority.

Shortly thereafter, a number of boats rowed out from town, carrying what Pearse described as "their commanders and ringleaders": Hornigold, Francis Lesley, Josiah Burgess, and Thomas Nichols. Pearse recalled their conversation in his logbook later that day. They "informed me that my taking the sloop had very much alarm[ed] all, the Pyrats in general believing that [Vane and the other] men taken in her would be executed." The pirate commanders assured Pearse that if he set Vane's company free, it "would be a very great means to induce [the inhabitants of Nassau] to surrender and accept the Act of Grace." Pearse, mindful of his tenuous position, took the pirate commanders' advice and had Vane, England, and the other fourteen men released, assuring them "of his Majesty's goodness towards them." He kept the *Lark*, however, assigning some of his men to fit her out as a trading vessel. Pearse informed the pirate commanders that Woodes Rogers, the famous circumnavigator who had captured a Manila galleon during the war, had been appointed governor of the Bahamas and was expected in Nassau that summer. He added that he was willing to give each man who wished to accept the king's pardon a signed certificate that would afford them some degree of protection until Rogers arrived, or while the pirates were in transit to other colonies to get pardons from their governors. Hornigold, Vane, and the other pirate commanders rowed ashore, promising to do their best to convince those ashore to take the pardon.

After the pirates left, it started to rain and continued throughout the following day. Pearse waited in his steamy cabin for word from shore. On the second morning, February 26, 1718, a stream of boats began rowing through the rain, each filled with pirates who wished to surrender. Pearse received them throughout the next two days, acknowledging their capitulations, signing their certificates of protection, and adding their names to a growing list of soon-to-be-pardoned pirates.

The first boatloads included Hornigold, Williams, Burgess, Lesley, and Nichols, as well as Bellamy's old quartermaster, Richard Noland, and Hornigold's quartermaster, John Martin. Pearse's list grew from fifty names to a hundred, and eventually to 209, a veritable *Who's Who* of Golden Age Pirates. It soon included most of Hornigold's original partners back in his periagua days—Thomas Terrill, John Cockram, and Daniel Stillwell; Henry Jennings's fellow privateer Leigh Ashworth; and several men whose pirate careers were far from over, including Samuel Moody and Charles Vane. At the end of his first week in the Bahamas, Pearse felt he had gained the upper hand. Instead of the several thousand pirates he had expected to find upon his arrival, there had been only 500 "young resolute fellows," in Pearse's words, "a paridor of unthinking people."

Many pirates had no intention of quitting piracy at all and soon started to show signs of their impatience with the *Phoenix*'s presence. On March 1, Pearse raised all the frigate's signal flags, decking her out in celebration of the birthday of King George's eldest son and heir, the Prince of Wales. Some Jacobite-minded pirates responded by setting an English merchant ship on fire, spoiling the festive atmosphere.

Meanwhile, Vane and his followers were quietly preparing a return to piracy. Late on the night of the sixteenth, he and sixteen men climbed into a boat on Nassau's landing beach and rowed quietly past the *Phoenix* and out past the harbor's wide western entrance. The next night, twenty-four more pirates left to rendezvous with the Bahamas' new pirate commodore.

Vane took stock of his men. Edward England, his quartermaster, was smart and courageous, a veteran mate in the merchant marine who had been forced by Christopher Winter some time earlier. He had since become a committed pirate, though he was more moderate than Vane himself. "England was one of these Men who seemed to have such a share of reason as should have taught him better things" than to turn pirate, the author of the *General History of the Pyrates* wrote of him. "He had a great deal of good nature and did not want for courage. He would have been contented with moderate plunder and less mischievous pranks . . . but he was generally over-ruled and, as he was engaged in that abominable society, he was obliged to be a partner in all their vile actions." Vane's "abominable society" consisted of forty men. John Rackham stood out from the rest because of his strange habit of wearing clothes made from brightly printed Indian Calico; the other men had already taken to calling him Calico Jack. All Vane's company had were two boats and a pile of small arms but, then, that was all Hornigold, Blackbeard, and Bellamy had had when they started out. If Captain Pearse and Governor Bennett thought piracy in the Bahamas was over, Vane had some surprises in store for them.

For several days, Vane's company lurked east of Nassau, waiting for an opportunity. On March 21, perfect conditions presented themselves. The wind was light and kept changing direction, making it possible for the pirates to overtake a sailing vessel with their rowboats. A trading sloop from Jamaica came around the eastern end of New Providence, slowly drifting toward the narrow, eastern entrance of Nassau harbor. As she passed nearby, Vane's men rowed the boats out of their hiding place and, with ropes and grappling hooks, swarmed aboard the little sloop. Her crew surrendered without a fight. The pirates now needed somewhere secure to plunder and refit their prize. They decided on Nassau Harbor, right under the nose of the troublesome Captain Pearse.

Vane's men were to exploit the peculiar geography of Nassau Harbor. One of the reasons the pirates had chosen Nassau as their base was that in addition to its main entrance to the west, the harbor offered a back door—a narrow but passable channel at its eastern end, through which a knowledgeable navigator might pass in a sloop. Near this entrance, a low sandbar called Potter's Cay split the harbor nearly in two: Any vessel drawing more than eight feet of water could not pass over the sandy shoals on either side of this islet. The *Phoenix* was anchored on the western side of this shoal and was too large to cross. The pirates could sail their sloop through the eastern passage and plunder their prize behind Potter's Cay in full view of Captain Pearse.

It was political theater par excellence. The renegade pirates came into the harbor, a red or "bloody" flag flying from the top of their mast, dropped anchor in the secure basin, and began boisterously plundering their prize in full view of the *Phoenix*. Vane put the sloop's crew ashore on Potter's Cay, from where they could swim to town, but they kept her captain, promising to return his little vessel as soon as they captured another more to their liking. They celebrated through the evening, the sounds of their revelry beckoning the pirates ashore to resume their illicit trade.

Captain Pearse knew he was being made to look the fool. All of the Bahamas knew that he had released Vane from captivity and signed his certificate of pardon. Now he had the audacity to taunt him. Something had to be done, and quickly. He called his officers together and outlined a plan.

At one in the morning, after the sound of the pirates' festivities had died down, Pearse armed a contingent of his men and ordered them into the largest of the *Phoenix*'s boats. As silently as possible, they rowed across the darkened harbor, around Potter's Cay, and on toward the pirate sloop, hoping to catch her by surprise. Vane had posted a watch, however, and as the naval party came within musket range they were greeted with a fusillade of small-arms fire. The *Phoenix*'s men returned fire, but after a few exchanges it was clear that the pirates were far too strong for them, and they had to make a hasty retreat. The Royal Navy had tried to flex its muscles but had been forced to run instead.

This brief engagement greatly boosted the morale of Nassau's pirates. Suddenly the man-of-war looked vulnerable, and Vane's men heroic. Overnight the mood shifted from resignation to defiance. "I several times summoned the inhabitants together in His Majesty's name and used all the arguments possible to prevail with them to assist me in suppressing the said pirate," Pearse later wrote. "But they always rejected all methods I proposed. [They] entertained and assisted [Vane's company] with provisions and necessaries, and on all occasions showed no small hatred to government."

From then on, Pearse's situation deteriorated. On the evening of March 23, he left the harbor to convoy four sloops safely out of the Bahamas; he had a personal interest one of them, Vane's sloop, the *Lark*, which he had crewed with sailors from the *Phoenix* for a private for-profit trading mission to St. Augustine. When he returned six days later, he discovered a further affront to his authority. Nassau's pirates had burned the *Younge Abraham* and the *Mary Galley*, and had run the twenty-six-gun Dutch ship aground on Hog Island. On March 31, Vane returned to his sanctuary in the eastern basin of Nassau Harbor to taunt Pearse with his latest prize, the *Lark*, which he had captured despite Pearse's efforts. Most worrisome, three of the Royal Navy sailors he had put aboard the *Lark* had defected to Vane's crew. Not only was Pearse outmanned and outgunned, he had to worry that his own sailors were regarding the pirates as heroes.

As they transferred cannon and supplies to the *Lark*, Vane's men yelled insults at the *Phoenix*, which Vane loudly threatened to burn. Then they boldly rowed across the western basin to town, passing near the man-of-war. Pearse opened fire at the boat with both cannonballs and partridge shot and ordered the pirates to come aboard the *Phoenix*. They ignored these orders and the ordnance splashing in the water around them and proceeded to town.

In just three days, Vane's gang grew from nineteen to upward of seventy-five. During this time he also captured two more sloops whose captains, unaware of the danger, had anchored alongside the pirates. Pearse tried to warn the sloops by hoisting his topgallant sails "with sheets flying," but to no avail.

On April 4, Vane raised a black flag to the masthead of the *Lark*, and sailed out to sea. With a nimble six-gun sloop and a proper company of men, Vane was in a position to bring all commerce in the Bahamas to a standstill. He had little sympathy for his victims, especially the merchant-smugglers of Harbour Island, who had capitulated to

Pearse the moment he showed the British ensign. They would pay a price for their disloyalty to the pirate republic.

Even with Vane gone, Captain Pearse found himself in an untenable position. The pirates "have altered their treatment and sent threateningly to the Captain . . . to be gone or it should be worse for him," Governor Bennett reported after debriefing pirates who sought pardon in Bermuda. "I conclude all have surrendered that intends [to] and . . . I fear they will soon multiply for too many [sailors] are willing to join with them when [their vessels are] taken."

Pearse did his best not to show weakness, but on April 6 his carpenter accidentally set the *Phoenix* on fire while boiling tar in the galley. The crew quickly got the fire under control, but the symbolic damage was irreparable. Two days later, the *Phoenix* raised its anchors and, in the company of five merchant sloops, sailed out of the harbor, bound for New York. In a final embarrassment to the captain, he ran aground on the way out. For a few hours, the residents of Nassau watched the *Phoenix*'s men work to free her. Then she was gone, leaving Nassau in pirate hands once again.

❧❧

Blackbeard and Bonnet spent the winter of 1717–18 in Spanish territory, their movements and activities lost to British authorities. Spanish mariners told their Jamaican counterparts that a pirate known only as "the Great Devil" was cruising the Gulf of Mexico, his ship filled with "much treasure." Not long thereafter, Bonnet and Blackbeard were reported to be "cruising about" the Mexican gulf port of Vera Cruz with four sloops and "a ship of 42 guns." They were said to be hunting for a galley called the *Royal Prince*, and to have boasted that "they would have the Adventure man-of-war if they can." It was quite a boast: the thirty-six-gun HMS *Adventure*, a 438-ton fifth-rate based in Jamaica, was the most powerful Royal Navy frigate in the entire Western Hemisphere at the time.

By late March, Blackbeard and Bonnet had separated in the Bay of Honduras. Blackbeard took the *Queen Anne's Revenge* to Turneffe Island, a great ring of mangroves and islets of coral sand located twenty-five miles off the coast of what is now Belize, and a popular rest spot for English merchantmen. Bonnet sailed the *Revenge* a hundred miles further south and was cruising for prizes off the Bay Islands, three coral-ringed islands off the coast of what is now Honduras.

On March 28, 1718, Bonnet's men spotted a large ship near Roatán, the largest of the Bay Islands. The ship, the *Protestant Caesar* of Boston, was an enormous 400-ton merchantman, the muzzles of twenty-six cannon protruding from her gunports. She was more than four times the size of the *Revenge*, which carried just ten guns and fifty men. Despite the odds, Bonnet and his crew decided to attack, risking a replay of the eccentric planter's disastrous engagement with the Spanish man-of-war the year before. They caught up to the *Protestant Caesar* at nine at night, cleverly cutting behind the big ship's vulnerable stern. Bonnet's men fired five cannon and a volley of musket shot, only to be answered by two stern guns and a hail of bullets. As the smoke cleared, Bonnet yelled out that if the ship fired another gun, they would give "no quarter," a threat to kill everyone aboard. The *Protestant Caesar*'s veteran captain, William Wyer of Boston, knew a bluff when he saw it. He let off another salvo of his cannon. The running battle continued for three hours, cannon flashing in the night, until Bonnet finally gave up and retreated into the darkness.

Bonnet's men were disgruntled: Clearly their commander had learned little from his yearlong apprenticeship with Blackbeard. They voted to travel to Turneffe, where they could recuperate from their ill-advised battle. They also made it clear to Bonnet that his command was on very thin ice.

On April 2, the *Revenge* sailed into Turneffe's five-mile-wide lagoon. To the crew's relief, the *Queen Anne's Revenge* was anchored inside. A number of them begged Blackbeard to use his influence to terminate Bonnet's command. Blackbeard asked Bonnet's men to call a meeting of their company, where he proposed they replace Bonnet with one of Blackbeard's officers, a man named Richards. The men accepted the plan, whereupon Bonnet was transported to the *Queen Anne's Revenge*. There Blackbeard reportedly told his wayward colleague that "as he had not been used to the fatigues and care of such a post," it would be better for him to stay with Blackbeard, where he could "live easy, at his pleasure, in such a ship as [this], where he would not be obliged to perform the necessary duties of a sea voyage." Bonnet had been placed under house arrest and would remain so for many months to come.

The pirates stayed at Turneffe for several more days, recuperating, gorging on fish and sea turtle, and capturing wayward vessels. Their first prize was an eighty-ton logwood-cutting sloop from Jamaica called the *Adventure* that had blundered into Turneffe lagoon. The pirates found the sloop to their liking and kept it, and made its commander, David Herriot, a prisoner aboard the *Queen Anne's Revenge*. Blackbeard's mate, Israel Hands, took control of the *Adventure* in his stead. A few days later they seized at least four more sloops, three from Jamaica and one, the *Land of Promise*, from Rhode Island. Blackbeard's men burned one of the Jamaican sloops because of a grudge against its captain, but they raised red flags aboard the others and added them to what was now a five-vessel fleet. Around April 6 they left Turneffe, Blackbeard telling one of his captives that they were "bound to the Bay of Honduras to burn the ship Protestant Caesar" to ensure that Captain Wyer "might not brag when he went to New England that he had beat a pirate."

On the morning of April 8, the pirates found the *Protestant Caesar* at anchor off the coast of Honduras, her holds half-filled with freshly cut logwood. When Wyer spotted the pirates—"a large ship and a sloop with Black Flags and Deaths Heads and three more sloops with bloody flags"—he called all his men on deck to ask if they were willing to defend the ship from the attackers. According to Wyer, his men answered that "if they were Spaniards they would stand by him as long as they had life, but if they were pirates they would not fight." When it became clear that the attackers were the sloop they had fought earlier, now backed by the infamous Blackbeard, Wyer's men "all declared they would not fight, and quitted the ship, believing they would be murdered by the sloop's company." For three days, Captain Wyer and his men sheltered amid the jungle foliage and piles of logwood on shore, watching the pirates plunder their massive ship. On April 11, Blackbeard sent a messenger to Wyer, telling him that if he surrendered peacefully, no harm would come to him. Blackbeard had a fearsome reputation among the merchant captains of the Americas, but the pirate had never been known to go back on his word and, as far as anyone knew, had never killed a man. Wyer decided to trust him, and surrendered. He was taken to Blackbeard, who told him he had been smart not to burn or sabotage the *Protestant Caesar*, "else his men on board his sloop would have done him damage for fighting with them." Unfortunately Blackbeard also had some bad news. He had to burn the *Protestant Caesar* because she was from Boston, and his gang was committed to destroy all Massachusetts vessels in revenge "for executing the six pirates" who had survived the Cape Cod shipwrecks. The next day Wyer watched as the pirates went aboard his ship and set her alight, logwood and all. True to his word, Blackbeard released Wyer and his men unharmed, along with the crew of the sloop *Land of Promise*; all the captives eventually got back to Boston.

Blackbeard's company also resolved to head north. Spring was in the air, and the time had come to shift their raids to the eastern seaboard of North America. First, however, they would stop in at New Providence Island and check up on the status of their pirate brethren.

⌘

After humiliating Vincent Pearse, Vane and his band didn't return to Nassau for three and a half weeks, during which time they unleashed a reign of terror on the Bahamian archipelago. Unlike Bellamy and Blackbeard, who avoided unnecessary force, Vane presided over an orgy of violence and cruelty that helped royal authorities paint all the Bahamian pirates as monsters. In this single cruise, which lasted from April 4 to

28, 1718, his modest band captured a dozen merchant vessels, all surrendering without a fight. Nonetheless, they treated most of their captives barbarously.

The worst treatment was reserved for crews hailing from Bermuda, which accounted for seven of the twelve prizes. Bermudans visited the Bahamas regularly to rake salt—the primary food preservative in those days—among the uninhabited Turks and Caicos islands, which comprised the eastern part of the archipelago. As they tended to follow the same routes to the islands, they made an especially easy target. Vane's men had recently developed a particular animus toward them, apparently because their governor had recently detained a pirate named Thomas Brown, on suspicion of piracy. Brown had been released— probably for lack of evidence—but Vane wished to retaliate all the same. It was as if someone had messed with a "made" man in the Mafia; his colleagues were bound to mete out a lesson to the neighborhood.

Edward North's sloop *William & Mary* fell into Vane's hands off Rum Cay on April 14. On boarding the vessel, Vane's men immediately began beating North, his passengers, and crew, insisting they give up all their treasures. The little vessel had little of value aboard: seventeen Spanish pistoles (£17), some foodstuffs, and ten ounces of ambergris, a hard substance produced in the heads of some whales that often washed up on Bahamian beaches and was collected to make jewelry. Dissatisfied with the take, Vane seized one of North's sailors, bound his hands and feet, and lashed him to the topside of the *William & Mary*'s bowsprit. The pirates then stuck a loaded musket in the sailor's mouth and burning matches inside the helpless sailor's eyelids; if he didn't confess what money was hidden onboard, they would let the matches burn down to his eyeballs and blind him, after which he would be shot. After this, Vane felt confident that they had gotten everything of value, save for North's black crewman, whom they seized as plunder.

Even as these interrogations were taking place, Vane's company captured a second Bermuda sloop, the *Diamond*, and brought her alongside the *William & Mary*. As before, they began beating Captain John Tibby and his crew and picked out one of his sailors for further torture. They tied up the unlucky man, Nathaniel Catling, put a noose around his neck and hoisted him up the mast, kicking and gagging. There he hung, face turning blue, until he passed out. The pirates cut him down and left him for dead on the deck. Some time later, Catling began to regain consciousness. One of the pirates drew his cutlass and slashed the prostrate seaman across his collarbone. He raised his cutlass to continue hacking the man to death, but one of the other pirates stopped him, saying, as Catling later recalled, that it was "too great a cruelty." The pirates looted the *Diamond* of valuables—300 pieces of eight (£75) and "a negro man"—and forced all her crew aboard the *Lark*, which the pirates were now calling the *Ranger*. Then they hacked down both of the Bermudan vessel's masts and set the *Diamond* on fire. Before letting the men go on the crippled *William & Mary*, they bragged about mistreating the crews of two other Bermuda sloops the week before. They told North and Tibby that when they got home to Bermuda, they should tell Governor Bennett that the pirates "will join all the forces they can and come and take [his] country" and "make a new Madagascar out of it." During their drunken celebrations, North and other witnesses recalled Vane's men toasting "damnation to King George," the government, and "all the Higher Powers," while threatening to occupy Bermuda that very summer. Vane's men, it seems, were well apprised of the appeals the pirates had forwarded to the exiled James Stuart, and were optimistic they would soon be receiving support from that quarter.

By the time he returned to Nassau on April 28, Vane had taken three more sloops from Bermuda, three from Jamaica, one from New York, and a Boston-bound ship. In the process, his crew had swelled to ninety or more, most recruited from the Jamaican vessels, whose sailors may have known Vane from his Port Royal days. They had probably garnered only £1,000 or so in treasure, but their actions had snuffed out legitimate trade into the Bahamas. If the pirates weren't in control of the archipelago's commerce, Vane reasoned, then nobody would be.

Vane must have been pleased to find that HMS *Phoenix* had withdrawn from Nassau, leaving the pirates' control of the island uncontested. He was even happier when a massive warship came into the harbor a few days later, the death's head flag at her masthead, accompanied by a pirate sloop-of-war and two prize sloops. Blackbeard had returned.

Blackbeard was in command of some 700 men, which nearly quadrupled the pirate population of New Providence Island overnight. For a few short days, the streets of Nassau returned to life as Blackbeard traded stories with Vane, Paulsgrave Williams, and the city's other diehard pirate captains. His company likely divided their plunder at this point, as some three hundred of his men left his company. Some undoubtedly planned to wait until Governor Rogers arrived to take the king's pardon. Others, including Blackbeard's gunner, William Cunningham, wanted to enjoy himself ashore before returning to piracy. Some may have been Jacobite stalwarts who wished to stay behind with Vane to await reinforcements from the Stuart court-in-exile. A few may have snuck off with Paulsgrave Williams, who let it be known that he was soon to leave the island for Africa to prey on European slaveships.

One can imagine Williams and Blackbeard sharing a drink under the sailcloth awnings of one of Nassau's open-air alehouses, exchanging the stories of the destruction of the *Whydah*, the capture of the *Queen Anne's Revenge*, and close encounters with His Majesty's warships. They likely compared notes on their former commodore, Benjamin Hornigold, then in Jamaica, wondering if he had really given up piracy. Blackbeard heard that a fellow Bristolian, Woodes Rogers, was to be the new governor of the Bahamas. If Edward Thatch was indeed a pseudonym to protect Blackbeard's family, this news ruled out any possibility of accepting the pardon in Nassau, as Rogers would recognize him. Blackbeard had two choices: stay with Vane and try to resist Rogers or leave Nassau for good.

A day or two later, Blackbeard called all hands aboard his five-vessel fleet. A few new faces appeared, pirates who had no intention of giving up life "on the account," including Hornigold's old quartermaster, John Martin. The greatest pirate fleet afloat weighed anchor from Nassau, sails set for the Straits of Florida, Palmar de Ayz, and the Spanish wrecks.

⤞⤝

At virtually the same moment, thousands of miles away, another fleet was weighing anchor in the River Thames, south of London, the one that would carry Woodes Rogers to the Bahamas.

It was an impressive expedition, one that had taken Rogers many months to assemble. There were seven vessels in all, five of them the property of Rogers and his business partners. He sailed on the *Delicia*, his 460-ton private man-of-war, with a crew of ninety and thirty guns, accompanied by the 300-ton transport *Willing Mind* (twenty guns, twenty-two crewmen); the 135-ton ship *Samuel* (six guns, twenty-six crewmen); and the private sloop-of-war *Buck* (six guns, twelve men). Together these four vessels carried the Independent Company of one hundred soldiers, many of them recently discharged from the Chelsea military hospital; 130 male colonists with their wives and children, most of them Protestant refugees from France, Switzerland, or Germany's Palatinate; food and supplies to feed and clothe all of these people for fourteen months; all of the necessary tools and materials to, in the words of Roger's coinvestors, "build forts & houses," clear fields, and plant them with "sugar, ginger, indigo, cotton . . . and tobacco for snuff equal to that of Havana." Rogers, convinced the pirates would respond to spiritual teachings, had even brought aboard a parcel of religious pamphlets from the Society for Promoting Christian Knowledge. Altogether, the expedition represented an investment by the Copartners of £11,000, toward which Rogers had contributed £3,000.

In addition to the soldiers, crew, and colonists, Rogers was accompanied by several gentlemen who intended to help him bring order to the fallen colony. Chief among them was Sir William Fairfax, a twenty-six-year-old nobleman whose family owned 5.3 million acres of Virginia, who intended to serve as Rogers's chief justice. Fairfax, like his aristo-cratic colleagues, considered the Bahamas too dangerous for his wife to join him for the time being. "Though I expect to be [but] a little while separated from my wife . . . I trust in God she will not want anything to comfort her sorrows," he wrote his mother from aboard the *Delicia* just before departing.

Escorting Rogers's vessels to Nassau were three Royal Navy war-ships: the fifth-rate frigate HMS *Milford* (420 tons, thirty guns) under Commodore Peter Chamberlaine; the sixth-rate HMS *Rose* (273 tons, twenty guns) and the sloop-of-war *Shark* (113 tons, ten guns), each of which carried 100 men. These men-of-war represented the most con-centrated naval force ever deployed against the Bahamian pirates. Taken with Rogers's well-armed vessels, they represented an overwhelming force: seven armed ships manned by 550 soldiers and sailors. As they sailed out of the mouth of the Thames on the twenty-second of April 1718, few aboard the ships had any doubt that the Republic of Pirates was about to meet its end.

Blackbeard had come to a decision that he hadn't shared with his crew: The time for overt piracy was coming to a close. King George's pardon had split the pirates' ranks, causing the surrender of a great many of their best leaders and the scattering of so many others. He may have been impressed at Charles Vane's commitment to hold down the pirate base at all costs, but Blackbeard was too prudent a strategist to commit to a lost cause. Unless they received reinforcements from the Stuart king, the few hundred pirates in Nassau had little hope of repelling a concentrated military force of the kind Governor Rogers could be ex-pected to have with him. Blackbeard wasn't like Vane. He didn't want to go out in a blaze of glory. Blackbeard would rather be the pirate who got away with it all, perhaps setting himself up as an eighteenth-century version of *The Godfather*: a wealthy and powerful crime boss operating with the collusion of some authorities, his role undetectable or impossible to prove to the rest. He had a good idea where to set himself up in this role. First, however, he needed one more big score.

The disgraced Stede Bonnet could have given him the idea to blockade Charleston, whose commerce was forced to travel over a shoal and through the narrow mouth of the harbor. Bonnet had blockaded the South Carolina capital in the *Revenge* the year before, but had to confine himself to a hit-and-run operation, fleeing the scene before the city's residents came after him in their own sloops. With his powerful fleet, however, Blackbeard had nothing to fear from the little armed sloops of Charleston's merchants. The Royal Navy had no permanent presence in the Carolinas, and even if a frigate happened to be in the harbor, it would be grossly outgunned by the *Queen Anne's Revenge* and her three consort sloops. The pirates could bring the entire colony to its knees and might even consider plundering the town itself. The pirates agreed to set a course for Charleston.

As they sailed north, some of the men came down with an unspecified ailment, possibly syphilis acquired from the prostitutes of Nassau. Their surgeon lacked the medicines considered necessary for treatment, and their acquisition was quickly becoming a priority. The pirate fleet took several vessels in the Florida Straits, including two sloops and a brigantine, hoping to garner intelligence as well as plunder. They hit pay dirt. Two of these were commanded by members of the old Flying Gang. Josiah Burgess, one of Nassau's veteran pirate sloop captains, was sailing back to the Bahamas from Charleston in the ten-ton sloop *Providence* with bottled ale and two earthenware plates, two products apparently in demand at the pirates' lair. Burgess was happy to share what he knew of Charleston, where he had spent several weeks after receiving his pardon. He'd traveled there with a number of their pirate friends, many of whom were there now, and would be happy to see their old pals. Blackbeard was pleased to hear there were no naval vessels in the harbor, but there were a number of merchant ships preparing to depart for London and New England. Blackbeard's men bought all of Burgess's cargo and sent him back to Charleston to act as their eyes and ears ashore; South Carolina's customs records show that he returned in Charleston only a few days after he had departed, his vessel empty, just hours before Blackbeard's fleet cut off the harbor.

A few days after meeting Burgess, the pirates also intercepted the thirty-five-ton sloop *Ann* of Jamaica, commanded by another reformed pirate, Leigh Ashworth. Ashworth had sailed a different vessel from Nassau to Charleston a few weeks earlier that had been filled with contraband. Taking the pardon, Ashworth had purchased the *Ann* in a family member's name and filled her hold with barrels of tar, pitch, and beef to sell in Port Royal. He was ready to retire to his Jamaican manor, he told Blackbeard. Ashworth may have stiffened Blackbeard's resolve to slip into semilegitimacy, but not before raiding Charleston.

The pirate fleet arrived off Charleston Bar, nine miles south of town, on May 22, 1718, and seized the pilot boat before it could sail to town to raise an alarm. Then they spread their four vessels out across the approaches to the bar and waited, spiderlike, for ships to fall into their web. Within a few days they captured at least five vessels: two ships outbound to London, two ships inbound from England, and a tiny eight-ton sloop, the *William*, headed home to Philadelphia.* The captain of the latter, Thomas Hurst, was a familiar face: He had been in Nassau recently, where he had purchased eight "great guns" from the pirates there, guns that were still in his little sloop's hold. One day he was trading with pirates, now he was their prisoner.

The first of these captures proved the most valuable. The 178-ton ship *Crowley* had been headed out of the river, bound for London. Her holds were stuffed with over 1,200 barrels, but these turned out to be filled with pitch, tar, and rice, Carolina exports that weren't particularly useful to the pirates. In her cabins, however, the *Crowley* carried a number of paying passengers, among them many of the most distinguished citizens of Charleston. While the pirates looted the *Crowley* of provi-

---

* These vessels were the ship *Crowley* (Captain Robert Clark); the fifty-ton ship *Ruby* of Charleston (Jonathan Craigh); the sloop *William* of Philadelphia; the sixty-ton ship *William* of Weymouth, England (Naping Kieves); and the eighty-ton ship *Arthemia* of London (Jonathan Darnford).

sions and supplies, the frightened passengers were rowed over to the *Queen Anne's Revenge*, where they were thoroughly interrogated: who were they, what was their vessel carrying, and what other vessels were at anchor in Charleston? One turned out to be Samuel Wragg, a member of the colony's governing council who owned 24,000 acres in the province, and was returning to England with his four-year-old son, William. Blackbeard realized these captives were worth more to the pirates than the cargo in the *Crowley's* hold. It was time to call a general council to decide their fate.

In preparation for the meeting, all the pirates' captives—a total of eighty people from various vessels—were stuffed into the *Crowley's* hold and locked in darkness. "This was done with [such] hurry and precipitation that it struck a great terror in the unfortunate people, verily believing they were then going to their destruction," the author of the *General History of the Pyrates* later wrote, apparently after speaking with witnesses. Wragg and the other passengers, having heard bloodthirsty tales of the pirates, expected their captors would light the ship on fire, "and what seemed to confirm them in this notion was that no regard was had to the qualities of the prisoners," with "merchants, gentlemen of rank, and even a child of Mr. Wragg's" being confined with common servants and sailors, a harbinger of death in their minds.

As the captives cowered in the hold "bewailing their condition," the pirates met aboard their flagship to devise a plan. They would send a boat into Charleston and demand ransom for their captives; if they were refused, they would threaten to not only kill all the captives and burn their vessels, but also to sail into Charleston Harbor, sink all the ships there, and perhaps attack the town itself. Whatever disease the pirates had contracted, it must have become extremely worrisome, for the only ransom they demanded was a chest containing a list of medicines drawn up by their surgeon, with a total value of about £400. The meeting concluded, Blackbeard had the prisoners brought before the assembled pirates and informed them of the plan. Wragg begged the pirates to send one of the captive gentlemen in with whomever delivered the ransom demand, so that they could impress on the governor how serious the situation was. The pirates agreed, with some suggesting they send Wragg himself, while keeping his son hostage. Blackbeard, always the strategist, was against this tactic; he didn't want to lose possession of his most valuable bargaining chip because if his bluff was called, he had no intention of actually murdering young William Wragg and the other captives. Instead, the pirates chose another captive, a Mr. Marks, to travel with their emissaries. If the entourage didn't return with the medicines in two days, the pirates said they would make good on their threats.

The boat departed, carrying Marks and two pirates, on what would prove a farcical journey. On the way to town, a sudden squall capsized their little boat. The three men managed to swim to safety on an uninhabited island and awaited rescue for much of the day, well aware that the clock was ticking. The next afternoon, hungry and bedraggled, they realized they would have to rescue themselves. They found a large wooden hatch cover on the shore, but it wasn't buoyant enough to support all of them. Lacking other options, Marks got onto the hatch and the pirates pushed it out into the water; when they got over their heads they clung to the edge of the hatch and swam hard, pushing the makeshift raft toward Charleston, nine miles away. They paddled this way throughout the night, making little progress. By morning they were sure they were all going to die, but were saved by some passing fishermen who brought them to their camp. Marks, realizing the captives' time was already up, paid the fishermen to go tell Blackbeard what had happened. Meanwhile, he hired a second boat to take the three of them to Charleston.

By the time the fishermen found the pirates, Blackbeard was in a fury. The deadline had come and gone more than a day earlier, and the pirate commodore had threatened Wragg and the others, "calling them villains a thousand times and swearing that they should not live two hours." Though he did his best to terrify the captives, he hadn't harmed them in any way. When the fishermen related Marks's mishap and asked, on his behalf, for two additional days, Blackbeard consented.

However, when two more days passed and the emissaries did not return, Blackbeard's gang still didn't kill anyone. Instead, they resolved to sail to Charleston and terrorize the town.

Meanwhile, in Charleston, Marks was desperately searching for the two pirates he had traveled with. As soon as they had gotten to town, he had rushed to the home of Governor Robert Johnson, who had immediately agreed to Blackbeard's demands. The two pirates, however, had gone out drinking and, in the process, ran into some of their old colleagues. There were upward of a dozen Nassau pirates in town who had come to take the king's pardon. As the two pirates wandered the streets of the walled city, they discovered that many common people admired them. Enjoying the celebrity and the company of old friends, they had gone from one house to another, drinking until they forgot the time. They didn't remember their mission until, a day or two later, they heard screaming on the streets outside. Blackbeard's fleet had arrived in the harbor, frightening the inhabitants so badly that "women and children ran about the street like mad things." The two drunken pirates stumbled to the waterfront, preventing their colleagues from exacting retribution on the town.

Marks rowed out to the pirate man-of-war with the chest of medicines and a message from Governor Johnson offering to pardon Blackbeard if he wished to lay down his arms. Blackbeard rejected the overture but released all his captives and their vessels, although local officials reported they had "destroyed most of their cargoes . . . and did some damage to the ships all for pure mischief sake." In the end, the pirates left with only the medicines, provisions, a few barrels of rice, 4,000 pieces of eight (£1,000) and the clothes of their gentlemen captives, whom they had stripped before releasing. They left Charleston with only one prize: a Spanish sloop they had taken off Florida. Blackbeard had paralyzed an entire colony for over a week but, for reasons unknown, was willing to settle for plunder probably worth less than £2,000.

As they sailed north, the pirate fleet detained two more South Carolina-bound vessels, the sixty-ton ship *William* of Boston, loaded with lumber and corn; and the forty-five-ton brigantine *Princess* of Bristol, carrying a cargo of eighty-six African slaves from Angola. From the *Princess*, the pirates took fourteen of what a Charleston official called "their best Negroes," adding to an already substantial number of Africans aboard the pirate fleet's four vessels. (As the slaves were transferred, Blackbeard told the *Princess*'s commander, Captain John Bedford, that he "had got a baker's dozen," suggesting that he regarded these particular blacks as commodities, rather than recruits.) As for the *William* and her cargo, the pirate company's last words upon leaving Charleston had been that they would "swear revenge upon New England men and vessels" for executing Bellamy's men. However, it was the *Revenge* that actually captured the *William*, and for some reason her commander, Blackbeard's lieutenant, Mr. Richards, let the *William* go. Afterward, captives overheard Blackbeard raging at Richards for "not burning said . . . vessel, because she belonged to Boston."

Blackbeard soon put aside his anger, as there were more important matters to attend to. He had secretly decided that the time had come to break up his company, but with no intention of sharing the recent plunder with all 400 men. While in Central America, some of the rank-and-file pirates had become mutinous after the rum supply had run out. "Our company somewhat sober," Blackbeard wrote at the time in his journal.* "A damned confusion amongst us! Rogues a plotting [and] great talk of separation." Fortunately the fleet's next prize had "a great deal of liquor onboard" that "kept the company hot, damn'd hot, [and] then all things went well again." Blackbeard never forgave the plotters, however, and had no intention of rewarding such behavior. He developed a plan to rid himself of them, along with the incompetent Stede Bonnet and his loyalists. He shared it with only a few trusted colleagues, including his quartermaster, William Howard, and boatswain Israel Hands, who was in command of one of the fleet's vessels, the

---

* This journal later fell into the hands of the Royal Navy but, sadly, was subsequently lost. This appears to be the only excerpt ever recorded.

eighty-ton prize sloop *Adventure*. These men helped him convince the company to sail into one of North Carolina's sparsely populated bays to careen, supposedly in preparation for intercepting the annual Spanish treasure fleet in the Florida Straits.

Six days after leaving Charleston—sometime around June 3, 1718— Blackbeard's fleet turned into what is now called Beaufort Inlet, halfway up North Carolina's low, swampy coast. To avoid the sandy, uncharted shoals, the vessels had to negotiate a narrow, comma-shaped channel created by a tidal creek, whose sluggish mouth provided a quiet anchorage. Although this harbor was located right in front of the hamlet of Beaufort, the pirates had nothing to fear from the handful of families living there, who had no practical way to send for help overland. The sloops—the *Adventure*, *Revenge*, and the small Spanish prize—went in first, crossing the fifteen-foot-deep outer bar and proceeding up the curving channel to the anchorage. Blackbeard safely sailed the *Queen Anne's Revenge* over the outer bar, but as he approached the entrance to the tidal channel under full sail, he apparently ordered the helmsman to maintain a course that took her straight onto the shoals. The great ship shuddered to a stop, the force of the collision so powerful it threw men off their feet and snapped the lines of one of the ship's bow anchors, which splashed into the water. According to plan, Blackbeard sent William Howard up the channel in a boat to tell Israel Hands to come down with the *Adventure*, supposedly to help get the *Queen Anne's Revenge* off the shoal before the tide went out. Hands sailed the *Adventure* straight into the shoal a gunshot away from the flagship, tearing enormous holes in her hull. By the time the *Revenge* and the Spanish sloop reached the scene, Blackbeard's ship had started listing to port, her holds filling with water. The pirates rowed one of the *Queen Anne's Revenge*'s anchors four hundred yards into the channel, set it, and tried to drag the ship off the shoal with their anchor winch, but the effort failed. The company realized that their *Queen Anne's Revenge* was doomed. Everyone transferred to the *Revenge* and the Spanish sloop, which took them up to Beaufort.

As the pirates took stock of the situation, Blackbeard set the next part of his plan into motion. Stede Bonnet had been in a state of utter depression for weeks, declaring to one and all that he would gladly give up piracy, but on account of his actions was so "ashamed to see the face of any English man again" that he would have to "spend the remainder of his days" living incognito in Spain or Portugal. Accordingly, the pirates must have been very surprised when Blackbeard announced that he was returning command of the *Revenge* to the pathetic fellow.

Bonnet, hardly able to believe his ears, decided to secure a pardon as soon as possible. Beaufort's villagers could have told him that the governor of North Carolina, Charles Eden, lived in the tiny village of Bath, a day's sail up the sound and Pamlico River. Bonnet and a handful of loyalists hopped in a shallow-draft boat and sailed immediately, promising to return shortly for the rest of his men.

No sooner had Bonnet left then Blackbeard and his hundred or so co-conspirators drew their weapons and took their shipmates into custody. They stranded sixteen of them—and the *Adventure*'s captain, David Herriot—on Bogue Bank, a sandy uninhabited island a mile from the mainland. Another 200 pirates were left to fend for themselves in Beaufort. Blackbeard and his colleagues—"forty white men and sixty Negroes"—clambered aboard the Spanish sloop and departed, taking all the company's plunder with them, about £2,500. "'Twas generally believed the said Thatch run his vessel a-ground on purpose," Herriot later told authorities, so that he could "break up the Companies and to secure what moneys and effects he had got for himself." When Bonnet returned with his pardon three days later, the *Revenge* was waiting for him in Beaufort, but the treasure was gone. He rescued the Bogue Bank castaways and vowed to avenge himself on his double-crossing mentor.

Little did Bonnet know, but Blackbeard had also sailed to Bath, taking the outer passage around the barrier islands rather than the shallow sound inside them. As Bonnet was sailing back to Beaufort, his nemesis had been just on the other side of the barrier islands, headed in the opposite direction. About the time Bonnet discovered his treachery, Blackbeard's eight-gun sloop was making its way up a narrow creek leading to North Carolina's unassuming capital.

Although Bath was North Carolina's administrative center, oldest town, and official port of entry, it was little more than a village: three long streets, two dozen homes, a grist mill, and a small wooden fort set along Bath Creek, whose cypress-covered banks were so low, flat, and marshy it was impossible to tell where the water ended and land began. Blackbeard's sloop came into the wind and anchored in the brown, tannin-stained water, the town on one side, a wharf and plantation house on the other. Bath's hundred or so residents couldn't help but take notice of their visitors: With their arrival, the town's population doubled. Upon coming ashore, the pirates may well have asked where to find the courthouse or seat of government, and residents would have informed them that North Carolina had neither; the governing council was migratory, meeting at one member's home or another, sometimes many miles from the village. To take the king's pardon, Blackbeard was advised to row over to the wharf across the creek; Governor Charles Eden's house was at the end of it.

No eyewitness accounts of the initial meeting between Blackbeard and Governor Eden have survived, but apparently it went well. Eden, forty-five, was a wealthy English noble with a 400-acre estate, but he governed an impoverished colony, a pestilent backwater populated by aggrieved Indians and penniless settlers. Blackbeard's men had money— £2,500 in Spanish coin in addition to whatever they had saved from their previous year of piracy—and the means and inclination to bring in more, as long as the governor refrained from asking too many questions about where it was from. They came to an understanding. Eden would issue pardons to all of Blackbeard's men, most of whom would disperse. Blackbeard and a handful of his closest lieutenants would settle down in Bath, building homes and leading what might appear, on the surface, to be honest lives. In reality, they would quietly continue to detain vessels heading up and down the eastern seaboard or to and from nearby Virginia, whose haughty leaders had long looked down their noses at their backward southern neighbors. Eden and his friends would fence their goods, and the pirates would benefit from their protection. North Carolina would become, in effect, the new Bahamas, only better in that it had a sovereign government, and was therefore not subject to a British invasion.

Most of Blackbeard's company promptly left North Carolina for Pennsylvania and New York. William Howard went to Williamsburg with two slaves, one taken with *La Concorde*, the other from the brigantine *Princess*. Blackbeard and twenty other men, including at least six free black pirates, stayed in Bath. According to local tradition, Blackbeard took up residence on Plum Point, a promontory on the edge of the village. According to the author of *A General History of the Pyrates*, Blackbeard promptly married "a young creature of about sixteen years of age, the Governor performing the ceremony," allegedly his fourteenth wife, whom he "would force . . . to prostitute herself" with "five or six of his brutal companions" as he watched. The story is greatly embellished. Blackbeard would not have found the time to marry fourteen women given the amount of time he had spent at sea. With his remarkably humane track record as a pirate, it's doubtful that he would have arranged for his teenage bride to be regularly gang raped. Blackbeard did marry someone in Bath, however, as his nuptials were later remarked on by a Royal Navy captain based in neighboring Virginia, who had been keeping tabs on his activities. Local lore holds that this bride was Mary Ormond, daughter of a future sheriff of Bath, a story supported by at least one of Ormond's early-twentieth-century descendents. Another Blackbeard story in the *General History* rings true: "He often diverted himself with going ashore among the planters, where he reveled night and day. By these [people] he was well received, but whether out of Love or Fear, I cannot say."

Like Henry Avery, Blackbeard had bought the loyalty of a colonial governor, but had yet to accumulate the sort of fortune that would allow him to live like a king for the rest of his days. Therefore, after a few weeks of rest, he returned to work.

❧❀❧

Back in the Bahamas, Charles Vane had no intention of taking his activities underground. After his April cruise, he had spent nearly a month stewing in Nassau, waiting for Jacobite reinforcements. These were not to come; shortly after George Cammocke forwarded his Bahamian plan to James Stuart's mother, Queen Mary of Modena, she passed away, the plot apparently dying with her. As the weeks passed, Vane realized that Woodes Rogers, George I's governor, was going to beat the Stuarts to Nassau. The pirate republic, he was coming to realize, was likely doomed. Hornigold and other reformed pirates who had returned to Nassau intended to place themselves in Governor Rogers's service. Jennings had gone further than that, having taken a privateering commission from Governor Bennett to hunt Vane down and bring him back to Bermuda to be tried for his crimes; he was said to be fitting out two or three sloops to come to Nassau for that purpose. Vane wished to continue piracy, but was aware that the walls were closing in on him.

By late May, Vane could wait no longer. He went around Nassau calling up his old crew. Seventy-five like-minded diehards agreed to join him on the *Lark*, including Edward England and "Calico Jack" Rackham. The plan was to go out on one last cruise before Governor Rogers showed up and, hopefully, acquire a larger pirate vessel, one capable of operating without a home port for long periods of time. If Vane was to be pushed out of the pirate's nest, he wanted to be ready to fly as long and as far as necessary to find another.

Vane's first capture was an audacious one. On May 23, 1718, near Crooked Island, Bahamas, 200 miles southeast of Nassau, they overtook a familiar vessel. The fourteen-ton sloop *Richard & John* had been a fixture in Nassau for many years, bringing supplies to the pirates from Charleston and Jamaica and trading them for pirate plunder. Vane and everyone else aboard the *Lark* knew it belonged to Richard Thompson, the leading citizen of Harbor Island, and his son-in-law John Cockram, one of the founders of the pirate republic, who had sailed canoes with Hornigold back in 1714. The *Richard & John* had always been off-limits to pirates, but not this time. Cockram had been a leading member of the pro-pardon camp and was no friend to Vane and his men. They fired on the *Richard & John*, forcing her captain, Cockram's brother Joseph, to come into the wind and surrender. Vane's crew dumped him on the forlorn shores of Crooked Island and sailed away with his sloop. Vane was making a clear statement: In his book, reformed pirates were fair game.

In the first half of June, Vane captured several more vessels, including a two-masted boat and a twenty-gun French ship. The two-masted boat was turned over to Edward England, and the crew voted the flamboyantly dressed John Rackham to replace him as the company's quartermaster. The French ship, a substantial 200 to 250-ton vessel, was well suited to piracy and Vane adopted it as his new flagship. (After being disarmed, the *Lark* was apparently given to the Frenchmen.) On June 23, cruising outside the French port of Leogane, near modern-day Port-au-Prince, Haiti, they seized another French vessel, the brigantine *St. Martin* of Bordeaux, carrying sugar, indigo, brandy, claret, and white wine. Vane dumped her captain and several passengers on the shore, but kept the *St. Martin* and thirteen of her crewmen. Satisfied with these prizes and fortified with drink, Vane's company agreed to return to Nassau: Vane in his French ship, England in the two-masted boat, and the *St. Martin* and *Richard & John* sailed by prize crews.

With these large vessels, the pirates were forced to take the deep-water passage around Harbour Island and Eleuthera. This route took longer than cutting directly across the Bahama Bank, but it proved fortuitous. On the morning of July 4, the pirate flotilla found themselves among a small swarm of trading sloops heading in and out of Harbour Island. In just a few hours, the pirates captured three of them: the *Drake* of Rhode Island (Captain John Draper), carrying wine, spirits, and rum; the *Ulster* of New York (John Fredd), loaded with tropical timber from Andros Island; and the *Eagle* of Rhode Island (Robert Brown), with sugar, bread, and two barrels of nails. No treasure fleet, this, but the sloops would make good tenders, and the alcohol would keep the men happy for a few days, at least. That evening, Vane's convoy of prizes arrived in Nassau, where his men promptly seized two more sloops, the *Dove* (William Harris); and the *Lancaster*, commanded by none other than Neal Walker, the son of former justice Thomas Walker, whose family Hornigold had driven off New Providence in 1716. Vane had left Nassau with a single sloop six weeks earlier, but was now in control of at least nine vessels.

He quickly consolidated control over the island. He is said to have stormed ashore with his sword drawn, threatening "to burn the principal houses of the town and to make examples of many of the people." Vane moved against Benjamin Hornigold and other reformed pirates, making "examples of many of the people" and acting "extremely insolent to all who were not as great villains as himself," according to the author of *A General History of the Pyrates*, who had excellent sources in Nassau. "He reigned here as governor [for] 20 days, stopped all vessels which came in and would suffer none to go out . . . He swore [that] while he was in the harbor, he would suffer no other Governor than himself."

His opponents cowed, Vane and his men set to work transferring cargo from the *St. Martin* to various sloops, and shifting additional cannon aboard the big French ship. His gang intended to sail for the coast of Brazil, where they could hope to join forces with La Buse, Condent, and other die-hard pirates. Maybe another pirate republic could be built on the shores of South America, beyond the reach of the Hanoverian king, and the pirates could regroup.

On the evening of July 24, 1718, with Vane's men just three or four days from departure, the cry went out: The sails of a Royal Navy frigate had been spotted coming 'round the backside of Hog Island.

Woodes Rogers had arrived.

CHAPTER TEN

BRINKSMANSHIP

July–September 1718

WOODES ROGERS stood on the quarterdeck of the *Delicia*, cane in hand to support his bad foot, and peered out across the sea. His great ship heeled gently to starboard, her sails set close to the wind, the shadowy outline of New Providence Island three miles off her bow, dominating the southern horizon. Commodore Peter Chamberlaine's flagship, HMS *Milford*, sailed alongside, lookouts atop her mainmast and thirty heavy guns at the ready. Behind, in the *Delicia's* sizzling wake, the transport *Willing Mind* rode low in the waves with her heavy load of soldiers and supplies, with the private sloop-of-war *Buck* sailing nearby. From time to time Rogers peered through his looking glass to pick out the frigate HMS *Rose*, a lighted lantern hanging in her mizzenmast, now rounding the western end of Hog Island, three miles away. He could see the sloop-of-war HMS *Shark* hanging a half mile behind her. In the wee hours of the morning, Commodore Chamberlaine had put local pilots aboard the *Rose* and *Shark* and sent them ahead to Nassau to scout out the scene. Now, fifteen hours later, the moment of reckoning had come. The *Rose* was entering the harbor. Rogers and Chamberlaine, lacking pilots for their large, deep-draft ships, planned to spend the night sailing back and forth out in the deep water. Until daybreak, they could only wait, watching and listening, for reports from the *Rose* and *Shark*. Rogers felt a sinking feeling when, a few minutes later, he heard the unmistakable sound of cannonfire echoing from inside Nassau's harbor.

At six thirty P.M., the captain of the *Rose*, Thomas Whitney, ordered the frigate's anchors dropped just inside the harbor's main entrance. She swung into the easterly wind so that her twenty guns pointed, uselessly, at stretches of unoccupied shoreline: the tip of Hog Island to port, the shrubby, overgrown fields outside of Nassau to starboard. The main anchorage lay dead ahead, a scene of desolation. The remains of some forty captured vessels were strewn on the shore, some burnt, and all of them ruined—Dutch ships, French brigantines, sloops of various sizes and nationalities—fittings and sails missing and stray ends of rigging blowing in the wind. In the middle of the anchorage, a large twenty- to thirty-gun ship, French-built by the look of her, rode at anchor, a St. George's flag flying from her mainmast, a sign of allegiance to Old England rather than the decade-old nation of Great Britain. Sloops and other vessels were anchored all around her, some flying the death's head flag. The same flag could be seen flapping over Fort Nassau, whose seaward-facing walls were so decrepit their cracks were visible from a distance. The wind carried the sickening smell of putrefying flesh across the harbor, as if the carcasses of a thousand animals were rotting somewhere on the shore.

Suddenly, to Whitney's alarm, a flash of fire and a puff of smoke appeared from the stern of the big ship—Charles Vane's ship—in the center of the harbor. The sound came moments later—the report of a stern-mounted cannon—followed by the splash of a cannonball on the surface of the water, not far from the *Rose*. Two more cannonballs passed over his head, at least one tearing through some of the *Rose*'s rigging, before Whitney raised a white flag of truce. Clearly, the young captain must have thought, this was not going to be easy.

With the pirate ship appearing to accept the flag of truce, Whitney sent his lieutenant into the harbor in a boat to, in his words, "know the reason" for the pirates' hostility. The lieutenant went alongside Vane's ship and hailed her captain, inquiring why he had fired on the king's ship. "His answer," Whitney wrote in his logbook, "was [that] he would use his utmost endeavour to burn us and all the vessels in the harbor."

Vane also gave the lieutenant a letter addressed to Governor Woodes Rogers, on the outside of which was written: "We await a speedy Answer." The letter, which may or may not have been delivered to Rogers that evening, read:

July 24th, 1718

Your Excellency may please to understand that we are willing to accept his Majesty's most gracious pardon on the following terms, viz:

That you will suffer us to dispose of all our goods now in our possession. Likewise, to act as we think fit with every Thing belonging to us, as his Majesty's Act of Grace specifies.

If your Excellency shall please to comply with this, we shall, with all readiness, accept of his Majesty's Act of Grace. If not, we are obliged to stand on our own defence . . .

Your Humble Servants,
Charles Vane, and Company.

Vane was simply trying to buy a little time, to find a way to escape from New Providence with his new ship and all his loot. His ship was too large to pass over the Potter's Cay bar and through the harbor's shallow eastern passage. The *Rose* was anchored in the western entrance, bottling him in the harbor. Any thought of trying to run past her guns—exchanging comparable broadsides—was put to rest when, a few minutes later, the ten-gun HMS *Shark* sailed into the harbor and anchored just ahead of the *Rose*, followed by the twenty-gun transport *Willing Mind* and the ten-gun privateer *Buck*. Vane's ship was trapped, her men at the mercy of Governor Rogers's forces. The sun set, plunging the harbor into darkness.

Vane stewed for a few hours until he finally decided Rogers did not intend to honor him with a reply. His company agreed that the warships at the harbor's entrance seemed to speak for themselves. The ship was doomed, Vane told them, but there was still a way to escape the governor's clutches. The ninety men in his crew listened intently as he outlined a daring escape plan.

At two A.M., Captain Whitney was awakened in his cabin by a breathless subordinate. The pirates were attacking; the *Rose* was in danger. He rushed onto deck and was greeted by a horrific sight: Vane's ship, enveloped in flames, was heading straight for the *Rose* and her consorts. In the middle of the night, Vane's men had unloaded their ship and soaked its decks and rigging with pitch and tar. They had rolled all her guns out of their ports, every one packed with powder and two cannonballs. Weighing anchor, they had quietly towed her in the direction of the interlopers. As the distance closed, one pirate stayed on the helm, keeping the ship aimed directly at the anchored *Shark* and *Rose* while others dashed about the doomed ship, lowering sails and setting the pitch-soaked decks and rigging alight. If all went to plan, the ship would collide with the Royal Navy vessels, consuming them in the resulting conflagration.

As the last pirates abandoned their ship, sailors were rushing about the decks of the *Rose*, *Shark*, *Buck*, and *Willing Mind*, some loosening sails, others hacking away at the anchor lines with axes, trying to free the endangered vessels. As soon as the anchors came free, Whitney and the other captains swung their ships around—wind to their backs—toward the open sea. There was a frightening few minutes as the fireship drew closer, the first of her double-loaded guns discharging as their gunpowder charges ignited in the heat. Then, slowly, the *Rose* and the other vessels gained momentum and pulled away from the approaching inferno.

Vane himself watched these events from the deck of the *Katherine*, a swift Bermuda-built sloop that he had commandeered from another pirate in the middle of the night. *Katherine*'s owner, a minor pirate named Charles Yeats, remained onboard and was none too happy about having his vessel taken from him. Vane's men had loaded their possessions into the sloop and augmented her armament to ten or twelve guns. They watched with disappointment as the *Rose* and *Shark* escaped out to sea, but the action had bought them time. In the four hours remaining until sunrise, they would have the run of Nassau. Vane sent men into town, to seize anything they thought useful: equipment, supplies, weapons, valuables, and the island's best pilot and carpenter, whom they roused out of bed and carried aboard the *Katherine*. Then they waited, black flag at the mast, for the dawn.

At seven A.M., shortly after daybreak, Rogers's entire fleet appeared at the entrance to the harbor. The governor's first glimpse of his new capital was of the smoldering timbers of a large ship bobbing in the middle of the channel, embers hissing, the boneyard of ruined vessels on the shore, and a pair of pirate vessels anchored up the harbor, just behind Potter's Cay. If he had wished to make a dignified entrance, Rogers was disappointed. On their way into the harbor, both the *Delicia* and *Milford* ran aground on a sandbar and had to wait two hours for the rising tide to lift them off. Vane's men presumably had a good laugh, watching ships bearing the governor and commodore's personal flags loll on the Hog Island sandbar. The laughing stopped around ten o'clock when, with the tide now high, the shallow-drafted *Buck* and another sloop began sailing around Potter's Cay bar, their decks filled with soldiers. Vane knew they had lingered long enough. He ordered anchors lifted and sails raised. The *Katherine* turned and headed out the narrow eastern entrance of the harbor, with the *Buck* in hot pursuit.

The winds blew strong from the south-southeast that morning, and the chase proceeded close on the wind. Vane had a worried few hours, as the *Katherine* proved slower than her pursuers on this point of sail. He was relieved when they finally rounded the eastern end of New Providence, let out their sails, and began gaining ground. Vane's men fired their guns in defiance, and the *Buck* was forced to give up the chase and return to Nassau. Vane and his men were to remain at large, but New Providence Island, for the time being at least, would be in the possession of Governor Rogers.

On the morning of the twenty-seventh, Rogers landed ashore, an event punctuated by much pomp. The *Rose* and *Shark* fired eleven-gun salutes as Rogers's boat hit the beach, where, to his considerable relief, he was joyously received by pro-pardon residents. Thomas Walker, who had returned to the island in recent weeks, was the first to greet the governor, along with his old nemesis, Benjamin Hornigold. These two men—the "pirate governor" and the former justice—led Rogers and his entourage to the crumbling mass of Fort Nassau. Along the way the crews of several pardoned pirate captains—Hornigold, Josiah Burgess, and others—formed orderly lines on either side of the road, each man firing his musket into the air as Rogers walked past, creating a running salute all the way to the fortress gates.

Rogers climbed to the top of the fort to address the gathering crowd. He could see in an instant that the fort was in terrible disrepair. The seaward facing bastion looked like it might collapse at any moment, having, as Rogers put it, "only a crazy crack'd wall in its foundation." The parade ground was overgrown with weeds, and instead of longhouses for the garrison it contained a single hut, in which a pathetic old man was living. The pirates had absconded with the cannon, leaving behind a single nine-pounder, which explained why Vane hadn't tried to hole up in the fort. By the time Rogers reached the roof, William Fairfax, Walker, and Hornigold at his side, and a group of soldiers behind, some three hundred people had assembled in the square below. Rogers unrolled a scroll and read aloud the king's commission, appointing him governor of the Bahamas. The people, Rogers said, "showed many tokens of joy for the re-introduction of government."

Rogers spent the next few days consolidating control of the island and surveying its conditions. His 100-man Independent Company took control of Fort Nassau, constructing shelters out of sticks and palmetto leaves, while the sea-weary colonists set about building tents made from sails borrowed from the *Delicia*, *Buck*, and *Willing Mind*. Sailors from the *Rose* secured in the name of the king the *St. Martin*, *Drake*, *Ulster*, *Dove*, *Lancaster*, and other vessels that happened to be in the harbor. Rogers moved into the old governor's house—one of the only buildings that had survived the War of Spanish Succession. In his makeshift office he held consultations with various residents, looking for "inhabitants who had not been pirates . . . that were the least encouragers of trading with them" to serve on his twelve-man governing council. His initial appointees, announced on August 1, included Harbour Island smuggling king Richard Thompson and several men who had come with Rogers, including Fairfax (the new justice) and the *Delicia*'s captain and first mate. The council met at Rogers's house that very day and spent hours accepting the surrenders of some two hundred pirates who had not yet taken the king's pardon.

The pirate population on the island was estimated at 500 to 700, suggesting that a great number of those who had left Nassau to accept pardons in other colonies had come back. Another 200 nonpirates were also on the island, people who, in the words of one of Rogers's officials, "had made their escape from ye Spainards" during the war and now "lived in the woods destitute of all neccessarys." Rogers set all of these people to work clearing a thick layer of vegetation the pirates had allowed to smother buildings, yards, and fields. Others were recruited to assist the soldiers in arming and repairing the fort and in setting up a separate battery to guard the harbor's eastern entrance. The last vessel in Rogers's fleet, the supply ship *Samuel*, finally arrived, safe and sound in the harbor, her capacious hold filled with food and supplies. After the first week of his governorship, Rogers was likely optimistic for success.

Reports of piracy in the surrounding waters shattered the mood. First came a message from Charles Vane, who had detained two inbound vessels and said that he would join with Blackbeard, planning, as Rogers described it, "to burn my guardship and visit me very soon to return the affront I gave him on my arrival in sending two sloops after him instead of answering him." Shortly thereafter, on August 4, a Philadelphia mariner named Richard Taylor arrived with more ominous news. Taylor had been captured in the southern Bahamas by Spanish privateers who, despite the peace, had proceeded to sack the English villages on Catt Island and Crooked Island. The leader of the privateers had told Taylor that a new Spanish governor had arrived in Havana "with orders from King Phillip to destroy all the English settlements in the Bahama Islands"; he had five warships and upward of 1,500 men to accomplish this task. If the English surrendered, Taylor explained, the Spanish governor had instructions to deport them to Virginia or the Carolinas, "but in case of resistance to send them to Havana and thence [as prisoners] . . . to Old Spain."

Facing simultaneous threats from Charles Vane and the king of Spain, Rogers knew he needed to complete his fortifications as quickly as possible. Unfortunately, his labor supply began to disappear. First, the soldiers, sailors, and colonists he brought with him fell ill by the dozens. The unidentified disease—and the putrid stench that had hung over the town for weeks—was blamed on the huge piles of rotting animal hides the pirates had abandoned on the shore. Although the illness had broken out two weeks before Rogers's arrival, he wrote it was "as if only fresh European blood could . . . draw the infection"; longtime residents "quickly became free" of contagion while the newcomers were "seized so violently that I have had above 100 sick at one time and not a [single] healthful officer." Eighty-six of Rogers's party died, as did six crewmen from the *Rose* and *Milford* and two of the locals who served on Rogers's governing council. Rogers himself came down with "intestine commotions and . . . contagious distempers" and, by mid-August, was unable to attend council meetings. Most of the island's cattle also perished, striking a blow to the food supply.

Longtime Nassau residents resisted not only the illness, but Rogers's efforts to put them to work. "Most of them are poor and so addicted to idleness that they would choose rather almost to starve than work," Rogers reported home. "They mortally hate it, for after they have cleared a patch that will supply them with potatoes and yams and very little else [and] fish being so plentiful and either turtle or [iguanas available] on the neighboring islands, they eat [them] instead of meat and covet no stock or cattle; thus [they] live poorly [and] indolently . . . and pray for nothing but [ship]wrecks or the pirates . . . and would rather spend all they have in a punch house than pay me [a tax] to save their families and all that is dear to them." The locals proved unreliable militiamen as well. "These wretches can't be kept to watch at night and when they do they come very seldom sober and rarely [stay] awake all night, though our officers or soldiers very often surprise their guard and carry off their arms and punish, fine, or confine them almost every day," the governor complained. "I don't fear but they'll all stand by me in case of any [invasion] attempt, except [one by] pirates. But should their old friends have strength enough to designe to attack me, I much doubt whether I should find one half to join me."

It was at this time that Commodore Chamberlaine announced that his three men-of-war were leaving. Rogers was flabbergasted. The colony was at its most vulnerable, its defenders ill and its fortifications unfinished. The *Milford, Rose, Shark* and the three hundred men serving on them were essential to its defense. Chamberlaine was adamant however: He had cleaned his vessel's hull, taken his share of the loot seized from pirate prizes in the harbor, and, frankly, "had no orders" to stay any longer. Rogers had no power over naval personnel and so was forced to beg the commodore not to abandon the colony. Begrudgingly, Chamberlaine agreed to leave the twenty-gun *Rose* behind for three weeks longer, at which point Rogers said he "was in hopes my men and the fortification would be in a better state" to stand alone against the pirates and Spaniards. Accordingly, at nine thirty A.M. on August 16, the *Milford* and *Shark* departed for New York.

Rogers's situation deteriorated. Over the next few days, the Bahamas were racked with lightning, thunder, and rain, and Captain Whitney, expecting a hurricane, had his men take down the *Rose's* topmasts. Rogers tossed and turned in his humid bedroom, with wrenching guts and a high fever. Progress on the fort moved at a snail's pace, Rogers's lieutenants barely able to get the reformed pirates to clear the scrub from around the fort, better yet to take part in the strenuous labor of salvaging cannon from the Hog Island wrecks and transporting them to the fort's bastions. The rain continued for two weeks, toward the end of which a boat arrived carrying men who, on examination, turned out to be members of Vane's company. These men confessed that Vane, in a brigantine, was headed north, but had promised to meet them around September 14 at Abaco, one of the Bahama Islands, sixty miles from Nassau. Was he headed north to join forces with Bonnet or Blackbeard? If so, was he preparing to make good on his threat to attack Nassau? On September 8, there was more bad news. A boat arrived carrying John Cockram's brother Phillip, and several other men who had been held captive by Spanish *guardas costas* for two months. During that time they had been forced to serve as pilots for the Spaniards as they sailed around Abaco and New Providence, gathering intelligence for an imminent invasion. They had released Cockram and his colleagues so that they could bring Rogers a message: Prove to us that you are a legitimate governor and not a pirate, or expect the worst.

Rogers quickly drew up a letter to the governor of Havana, while his lieutenants set about loading the *Buck* with goods to trade in Cuba. The sloop-of-war departed on September 10, in the company of a smaller sloop, the *Mumvele Trader*. The *Buck*, however, never made it to Havana. En route, her crew—a mix of reformed pirates and Rogers's sailors— turned pirate. A number of the sailors who had come from England with the *Buck* apparently found piracy attractive. The motivations of one of these men, Walter Kennedy, were later recorded. Kennedy, the young son of a Wapping anchorsmith, had served in the Royal Navy during the War of Spanish Succession, where he "had occasion to hear of the exploits of the pirates . . . from the time of Sir Henry Morgan . . . to Captain Avery's more modern exploits at Madagascar." Inspired by these tales, Kennedy thought "he might be able to make as great a figure as any of these thievish heroes, whenever a proper opportunity offered." Kennedy seized that opportunity, apparently killing the *Buck*'s captain, Jonathan Bass, and other resistors before sailing away to Africa.

With the loss of the *Buck*, Rogers implored Captain Whitney to stay and help protect the island from Vane, who was now expected any day. Whitney delayed his departure by a week, but in the early morning hours of September 14, over Rogers's strong objection, the *Rose* left Nassau. Whitney promised Rogers he would return in three weeks. It was a promise he had no intention of keeping. Rogers watched as his last naval escort vanished over the horizon on a southwesterly breeze.

A few hours later another boat came into the harbor bearing alarming news: Charles Vane had arrived at Abaco.

※※※

After escaping from the *Buck* on the evening of July 26, Vane's exact movements remain sketchy. His company appears to have continued sailing south with the sloop *Katherine*, whose original pirate captain, Charles Yeats, remained aboard, resentful and disgruntled. The pirates appear to have spent the first half of August bouncing between the southern Bahamas and the Cuban coast. On July 28 they captured a sloop from Barbados, which was given to Yeats and his men under the condition that they continue sailing in consort with Vane. Two days later, another sloop, the *John & Elizabeth*, fell into their clutches, and not long after that a brigantine, which Vane took command of. A London paper later reported that at about this time two London-bound ships were set upon as they left Nassau by a pirate who, based on his behavior, was very likely Vane. The London *Weekly Journal* reported that the pirate captain had wanted to sink both ships "with their commanders and men," but that his crew would not consent "to such an inhuman piece of barbarity." The pirates kept their captives for five days, during which time their captain promised to capture two more London ships that were expected to come to Nassau, saying he would "cut 'em into pound-pieces." While these pirates drank and cleaned their vessels at some secluded Bahama hideaway, another vessel arrived with supplies for them, plus "news [of] where other pirates cruiz'd and what Men of War [were] out in chase after them." The captain was heard to brag "that if there came two Men-of-War to attack him, he would fight 'em and if he could not escape them, he would go into his Powder

Room and blow up his ship, and send [any of] them on board and himself to Hell together."

In mid-August Vane sent several men to Nassau to gather information and provisions, which they were to bring back to him at a secluded anchorage near Abaco. Vane appears to have been biding his time, observing his enemy and hoping to eventually join forces with Blackbeard or Bonnet to attack the island; he may have even hoped that the Spaniards would attack, weakening or destroying Rogers's forces, creating a vacuum into which the pirates could return. In the meantime, he counted on old friends to buy his goods, smuggle vital provisions to his gang, and keep him abreast of happenings on New Providence.

Toward the middle of August, his company's morale may have started to flag, because he decided to take a short cruise to Charleston in the hopes of filling the crewmen's purses. The pirates blockaded the harbor on August 30, 1718, Vane in his twelve-gun brigantine with ninety men and Yeats in a sloop—presumably the *Katherine*—of eight guns and twenty men. The merchants of South Carolina had to have been appalled to be at the mercy of pirates once again, as vessel after vessel fell into their clutches. Over a thirty-six-hour period, Vane and Yeats took eight in all, from the little fifteen-ton sloop *Dove* of Barbados to the 300-ton ship *Neptune* of London. From the eighty-ton brigantine *Dorothy* of London, Vane seized ninety slaves from Guinea and forced them aboard Yeats's sloop, which he intended to use as a floating warehouse. Yeats, however, had other plans. His sloop full of valuable human cargo, he took off in the other direction, intending to make his escape from his overbearing commander. Vane put up a chase and got off at least one broadside, but was unable to prevent his underling's escape. Yeats hid his vessel in Edisto Inlet, thirty-five miles south of Charleston, and sent a messenger to that city offering to surrender if the governor would grant his men pardon. The governor ultimately agreed.

Vane was undoubtedly furious about Yeats's defection, but two other prizes gave him consolation. These were the fifty-ton ship *Emperor*

and the *Neptune,* both bound for London with pitch, tar, rice, and tur-
pentine. These cargoes would find a ready market in the Bahamas, but
they comprised 2,900 large barrels, far too bulky to transfer to Vane's
modest brigantine. Instead, Vane's company resolved to take both ships
to the Bahamas, where they could plunder at their leisure. They would
go to their hideaway near Abaco, where they expected their informants
and suppliers from Nassau to be waiting.

Vane's men left Charleston not a day too early, for a posse was setting out to bring them to justice. The merchants of South Carolina had
fitted out two well-armed, well-manned sloops under the command of
militia colonel William Rhett, a wealthy merchant who had lost a good
deal of money to the pirates over the years. By the time Rhett's vessels
got out of Charleston's harbor, Vane was nowhere to be seen. Rhett decided to snoop around the North Carolina coast, hoping to find the pirates in one of their hideaways. On the afternoon of September 27, he
found some in Cape Fear harbor—not Vane's crew, who were halfway
to the Bahamas by then, but another pirate company that just couldn't
seem to catch a break.

∾≈∾

Poor Stede Bonnet. After Blackbeard had double-crossed him at Top-
sail Inlet, vanishing with the Spanish prize sloop and much of the company's treasure, Bonnet spent much of June 1718 trying to hunt him
down. When he heard a rumor that Blackbeard was at Ocracoke Inlet,
fifty miles up the North Carolina coast, he sailed there in the *Revenge,*
only to find a couple of deserted, sandy islands.

Bonnet fell into despair. He had been a pirate for more than a year
and had little more than what he had started out with: his sloop *Revenge,*
a crew of forty men, and, thanks to the pardon from the governor of
North Carolina, a clean legal record. As a pirate captain, he had been a
total failure, his poor decisions having cost the lives of many of his men
and the rest of his treasure. Any hopes he might have had to take part
in a Jacobite uprising against King George had been dashed: The "true"

king, known to them as James III, could barely help himself, better yet the pirates of the Americas. Bonnet had a ruinous reputation in both respectable and outlaw circles, and he could not bear the humiliation of returning to either his old life among the slave plantations of Barbados or living among his pirate peers in the Bahamas. He would have to live on the fence. While getting his pardon in Bath, Bonnet learned that the king of Denmark—one of Britain's minor allies in the War of Spanish Succession—was still at war with Spain. Perhaps if Bonnet were to go to St. Thomas, Denmark's principal Caribbean colony, he could persuade its governor to grant him a privateering commission. His company thought it a good idea; some of the pirate's former captives, like Captain David Herriot, signed up for the plan.

When they left Beaufort Inlet, the pirates elected Robert Tucker as their quartermaster. Tucker was a mariner from Jamaica whom Blackbeard had seized from a merchant sloop some weeks earlier. Like many other captives, he found that he liked the pirate's life and had become a popular member of the crew. He had little respect for Bonnet and wasn't particularly interested in returning to being a law-abiding subject. When the crew discovered that the *Revenge* had but ten or eleven barrels of food aboard—Blackbeard having stolen the rest—Tucker resolved that they should simply seize more from the next merchant vessel they encountered. Bonnet was opposed to this plan and even threatened to resign and leave the *Revenge*, but the crew didn't seem to mind the thought of losing him, and a majority threw their votes behind Tucker. The pirates seized the very next vessel they encountered, taking provisions. Then they took another. Pretty soon they were off the Capes of Virginia taking every vessel they could lay their hands on.

Bonnet tried to keep the company from invalidating his pardon. To conceal his identity, he insisted that he be called Captain Edwards or Captain Thomas, a ruse that didn't fool all their captives. To hide their tracks further, the pirates renamed the *Revenge* the *Royal James* in homage to James Stuart. Bonnet also insisted that the pirates give their captives "payment" for the goods they stole, so that they might later claim that they were traders, not pirates. Their first two victims received small parcels of rice, molasses, and even an old anchor cable in exchange for the barrels of pork and bread that were taken from them. After a week or two, however, most of the pirates refused to participate in this subterfuge, and some of Tucker's clique took to threatening and abusing captives instead. On July 29, off Cape May, New Jersey, Tucker boarded the fifty-ton sloop *Fortune* and "fell to beating and cutting people with his cutlass and cut one man's arm," according to an eyewitness. Two days later they boarded a sloop anchored in the harbor of Lewes, Delaware, and threw themselves a party in the captain's cabin, eating pineapples, drinking rum punch, singing songs, and toasting the health of James Stuart, saying they "hoped to see him King of the English nation," according to one of the sloop's crewmen. Tucker was, by now, captain in everything but name, and the pirates had even taken to referring to him as their "father."

Not all of the men aboard the *Royal James* wished to return to piracy, and took great risks to escape Tucker's clutches. Seven men successfully escaped on July 21 by stealing a prize sloop, which they took to Rhode Island; authorities there imprisoned them but five managed to escape before being brought to trial. When, after taking at least thirteen vessels off New Jersey, Delaware, and Virginia, the pirates returned to Cape Fear to wait out the hurricane season, several forced men fled into the woods. Unable to find food, shelter, or inhabitants in the swampy wilderness, the men had no choice but to return several days later and were put to work "among the Negroes" cleaning the *Royal James*. One of the captives, a mulatto, lamented to another that "he was not able to bear any longer, but was forced to comply with [the pirates], for they told him they would have no regard for the colour [of his skin] but would make a slave of him." On another occasion, a pirate told the same mulatto captive that he "was but like a negro, and they made slaves of us all of that colour if they did not join" with the pirates. In Bonnet's company, it seems, blacks could choose between slavery and piracy.

Bonnet did not try to escape from the *Royal James* when the company returned to piracy. The pirates planned to continue on to St. Thomas after hurricane season had passed, so he may have held out hope that he could still become a legitimate privateer in the service of Denmark.

On September 27, 1718, the two South Carolina pirate-hunting sloops under Colonel William Rhett found the *Royal James* at anchor behind Cape Fear. The pirates were outnumbered by nearly two to one, Rhett having the sloops *Henry* (eight guns, seventy men) and *Sea Nymph* (eight guns, sixty men) against Bonnet's ten-gun, forty-five-man sloop. Rhett lost the element of surprise, though, when he ran aground and was forced to take on the pirates in a full-on naval battle. Bonnet's company raised anchor and attempted to run straight between the South Carolinian sloops to the open sea. Instead, all three sloops ran aground, the *Royal James* and *Henry* within short range of each other. The pirates had the advantage as the *Royal James* happened to list on the starboard side so that her raised rail protected the pirates during the musket battle that followed. Colonel Rhett's *Henry*, by contrast, listed to port, exposing her entire deck to the pirates' fire. The two parties exchanged fire for the next five hours until the rising tide lifted the *Henry* free. Still immobilized and facing the *Henry*'s cannon, the pirates surrendered. Nine died as the result of wounds received in the battle, as did fourteen of Colonel Rhett's men.

Bonnet, who had survived unscathed, was brought into Charleston on October 3 and placed in armed custody, to the considerable joy of some, but not all, of the colony's inhabitants. He was the first prominent pirate captain to be captured by British authorities.

❧❧❧

By late July 1718, Blackbeard decided it was time to get back to work. He and his men had been involved in minor thefts: Witnesses reported that he was "insulting and abusing the masters of all trading sloops and taking from them what goods or liquors he pleased." In their drunken revelries, he and his men had committed "some disorders" in Bath itself, according to North Carolina Governor Charles Eden, who perhaps encouraged Blackbeard to take his men to sea for a time. Governor Eden had already granted Blackbeard undisputed ownership of the Spanish prize sloop in which he had come from Beaufort; now he signed customs papers clearing him to take the sloop—which Blackbeard unoriginally renamed *Adventure*—to St. Thomas, where he could keep his men occupied as privateers if he so desired. As it turns out, he didn't.

Instead of going to St. Thomas, Blackbeard and his men apparently sailed up the Delaware River, 250 miles north, where he quietly went ashore at Philadelphia to sell some select treasures. Pennsylvania Governor William Keith later reported that Blackbeard had been seen on the city's streets, and that he was well known among many people there because of visits to the city years earlier while serving as a mate on a Jamaican vessel. In the early 1840s a number of elderly Philadelphians would tell historian John Watson that in their youth they or their relatives had encountered Blackbeard and members of his crew, one of whom had been "an old black man" who lived with the family of the brewer George Gray. According to their accounts, Blackbeard visited a store at 77 High Street where "he bought freely and paid well." He also was said to frequent a High Street inn, always wearing "his sword by his side." Nobody dared arrest him for fear that his crew would come ashore "and avenge his cause by some midnight assault."

By the second week of August, the pirates having accomplished their business, the *Adventure* slipped out of Delaware Bay and into the open sea. It was time to refill their coffers far from their familiar stomping grounds. They sailed straight into the Atlantic, in the direction of Bermuda, looking for foreign ships whose crews would be unlikely to be able to finger them for their crimes. They may have taken some vessels along the well-traveled sailing route from Philadelphia, but their first documented captures were on August 22, 1718, to the east of Bermuda. The victims were a pair of French ships, one heavily laden, the other largely empty, on their way home to France from Martinique. The French put up a fight, damaging the *Adventure* and wounding some of her men, but were ultimately overwhelmed by the pirates. Blackbeard's crew transferred all of the cargoes to one ship, which they kept, and all the French crewmen to the other, which was sent on its way. As Blackbeard began sailing back to North Carolina, he had no idea how much trouble this incident was to bring him.

Around September 12, they anchored their prize behind the sandy mass of uninhabited Ocracoke Island and began to unrig her, stripping the valuable masts, spars, and lines, and unloading the cargoes of sugar and cocoa. Blackbeard refused to allow anyone to board his vessels, a passing mariner later reported, "except a doctor to cure his wounded men," who claimed to have been injured when a cannon shifted in rough seas.

Leaving both vessels at Ocracoke on the afternoon of the thirteenth, Blackbeard and four black sailors headed up the Pamlico to Bath in one of their boats. He carried sweetmeats, loaf sugar, a bag of chocolate, and some mysterious boxes found aboard the French ship, all presents for Governor Eden's next-door neighbor, Tobias Knight, North Carolina's chief justice and His Majesty's collector of customs. According to his four black crewmen, Blackbeard arrived at Knight's plantation "about twelve or one o'clock in the night," gave Knight his gifts, and went into the house with him "till about an hour before the break of day," at which point he ordered the men to head back down to Ocracoke. Three miles down the Pamlico River, Blackbeard noticed a periagua tied up at the landing of an isolated farmhouse with two men and a boy aboard. Blackbeard decided to plunder this trading canoe, and ordered his men to row alongside.

William Bell, the owner of the periagua, had spent the night at John Chester's landing and had seen Blackbeard's boat pass by earlier that evening. Bell's crew consisted only of his young son and an Indian servant, so when the five pirates came alongside his boat, he knew resistance would be difficult. At first, Blackbeard simply asked if Bell had anything to drink, to which Bell answered that "it was so dark he could not well see to draw any" from the cask. Blackbeard turned to one of his black sailors, who handed him a sword. He then jumped into the periagua and commanded Bell "to put his hands behind him in order to be tyed" and "swearing damnation seize him, he would kill [Bell] if he did not tell him truly where the money was." Bell, who was from Currituck, near the Virginia border, did not recognize Blackbeard and demanded to know who he was. "Thache [sic] replied that he came from Hell and he would carry him presently [there]," Bell was able to tell authorities, despite having been foolish enough to have grabbed Thatch and tried to force him from the periagua. Blackbeard called to his men, who quickly subdued Bell. They then rowed the periagua out to the middle of the river with them and plundered her of pistols, brandy, a box of clay pipes, £66 in cash, and "a silver cup of remarkable fashion." Blackbeard then threw Bell's oars and sails overboard and, in retribution for his resistance, beat him with the flat end of his sword until it broke. Blackbeard continued on his way to Ocracoke. Bell must have gotten replacement oars at Chester's landing, because two hours later he was at Tobias Knight's house in Bath to report the crime. Knight, Bell would later testify in court, listened patiently and filed a report, but never mentioned that the perpetrators had spent the night at his house.

On September 24, Blackbeard sailed up to Bath in the *Adventure*, where he reported to Governor Eden, under oath, that the French "ship and goods were found by him as a wreck at sea." When an arch pirate comes to one's door, claiming to have "found" a vessel floating in the middle of the ocean, filled with valuables and sufficiently seaworthy to be sailed some 700 miles back to North Carolina, one might have grounds to be suspicious. Eden and Blackbeard apparently had an understanding. The governor promptly declared the French ship to be Blackbeard's property by right of salvage, and a large parcel of sugar from the wreck somehow found its way into Chief Justice Knight's barn and hid itself under a pile of hay. Eden also gave Blackbeard permission to promptly burn the French ship as a hazard to navigation, conveniently eliminating any physical evidence that piracy had taken place.

With the governor and chief justice in his pocket, North Carolina was shaping up to be a safer pirate lair than the Bahamas ever were. Blackbeard never would have guessed that the governor of another colony would have the audacity to invade.

CHAPTER ELEVEN

HUNTED

September 1718–March 1720

ALEXANDER SPOTSWOOD, the governor of Virginia, had been keeping tabs on Blackbeard for months. He had received intelligence
of his intentional grounding of the *Queen Anne's Revenge*, his accepting
the pardon from Governor Eden, and the subsequent depredations on
trading vessels in the humid creeks of North Carolina. Spotswood had
collaborated with the captain of one of the two naval frigates in Virginia,
Captain Ellis Brand of HMS *Lyme*, to send spies into North Carolina
"to make particular inquiry after the pirates." He had even seized Blackbeard's old quartermaster, William Howard, who had taken the king's
pardon and was hanging around Hampton Roads under the pretence
that he could not explain how he had acquired the £50 in his pocket or
the two African slaves in his company. On these questionable legal
grounds, Spotswood and Captain Brand had Howard forced aboard
the *Lyme* and then incarcerated in Williamsburg's tidy brick jail. By interrogating Howard and debriefing his spies, Spotswood had assembled
a detailed picture of what Blackbeard was up to, where he spent his
time, and how he had bought the protection of the senior-most officials
in North Carolina. In late October, he decided to act.

Spotswood would later argue that Blackbeard represented a threat
to Virginia's commerce, and that his presence encouraged others to
piracy. All of this was true, but was not the real reason for Spotswood's
decision to move against the pirate. Like politicians before and since,

Spotswood intended to launch a military expedition abroad to divert public attention from his own improprieties at home.

Spotswood governed the second most powerful colony on the American seaboard after Massachusetts, with a population of 72,500 whites and 23,000 blacks. It was entirely different from that northern colony. Virginia was a land of plantation manors surrounded by tobacco fields and the hovels of their servants and slaves. Each plantation had its own pier and served as a factory unto itself, its employees and human chattel producing most requisite products and services on site. As a result, there were hardly any towns or cities to speak of, the planters conducting much of their business at rural landings, churches, courthouses, and weekly markets. Even the capital, Williamsburg, was little more than an administrative center, a campus of elegant government buildings set near the brick buildings of the College of William and Mary. For most of the year Williamsburg had a population of little over 1,000: administrators, craftsmen, teachers, and students. When the colony's aristocratic legislators met at the grand brick Capitol, Williamsburg came alive. Its inns, boarding houses, and taverns were packed to the bursting point, while enthusiastic audiences gathered to watch productions at British America's only theater, a two-year-old structure on the east side of the carefully landscaped Palace Green.

In recent years, the legislators came together to criticize Governor Spotswood and the culture of corruption he had nurtured during the eight years he had overseen the colony. They drafted an official complaint over how "he lavishes away the country's money" on the nearly completed Governor's Palace, with its opulently appointed dining rooms, carved marble mantelpieces, formal orchards, gardens, and entry gates. Others were incensed at Spotswood's corrupt land dealings. He would eventually transfer 85,000 acres of public land to himself via blind trusts, in an area which came to be known as Spotsylvania County. Most legislators opposed his imperious claim to control the appointment of all priests and high officials in the Anglican Church, the official religion of the colony. In 1717, the legislature had successfully petitioned the king to repeal some of Spotswood's economic regulations and was now working to remove him from office altogether.

With so many enemies at his door, it was in strict secrecy that Spotswood met with Captain Brand of the *Lyme* and Captain George Gordon of HMS *Pearl* in early October of 1718. He asked their assistance in ridding the Americas of Blackbeard, once and for all.

❧❀❧

In Nassau, Woodes Rogers was also preparing to confront pirates. On September 14, 1718, he received word that Charles Vane was at Green Turtle Cay, near Abaco, 120 miles north of Nassau. Facing a Spanish invasion and bereft of manpower or Royal Navy support, Rogers knew his only hope was to take a chance on the leaders of the pro-pardon pirate camp.

Benjamin Hornigold and John Cockram responded to the governor's call and agreed to become pirate hunters. Rogers outfitted a sloop for them—probably Hornigold's *Bonnet*—and dispatched them to gather intelligence and, if possible, confront Vane. They left Nassau four days later. Nobody saw them again for weeks.

While awaiting Hornigold's return, Rogers tried to put Nassau's defenses in order. Nassau's governing council agreed to impose martial law, setting up "a very strick't watch" and ordering the island's subjects and their slaves to help repair the fortress. Practically every night, however, pirates stole boats and fled the island, hoping to join Vane. Rogers estimated that 150 had abandoned him between the end of July and late October. As the days turned to weeks, Rogers began to fear that Hornigold "was either taken by Vaine or [had] begun his old practice of pirating again." Most islanders concurred. But three weeks after his departure, Hornigold's sloop sailed back into the harbor with a prize and a handful of pirate captives.

Hornigold told everyone how he and Cockram had spent most of the time hiding out near Green Turtle Cay, observing Vane and waiting for an opportunity to ambush him when away from his main force. Unfortunately, that chance never presented itself, and Hornigold and Cockram judged Vane's company too powerful to take on directly. In addition to his pirate brigantine, Vane had the *Neptune* and *Emperor* with him, the two ships he had captured at the Charleston bar, and his party spent most of their time plundering these ships and careening their vessels. After nearly three weeks had elapsed, the pirates said good-bye to the captive crews of the *Neptune* and *Emperor*, "wishing them a good voyage home," but as they sailed from the anchorage they spotted another sloop coming in. This, Hornigold was able to report, was the thirty-ton sloop *Wolf*, which had sailed out of Nassau a few days earlier with Rogers's permission to hunt sea turtles. In reality, the *Wolf*'s captain, a pardoned pirate named Nicholas Woodall, was smuggling ammunition, supplies, and intelligence to Vane. Vane dropped anchor and consulted with Woodall, who gave him a detailed description of Rogers's activities and defenses. Vane, perhaps hoping his fellow pirates had risen up against the governor, was apparently disappointed. When one of the captives asked the pirates what news they had of Nassau, they replied, "none good," and told them not to ask too many questions. The pirates, "being very much disturbed with the news," voted to maroon the captives and destroy the *Neptune* by hacking down her masts and rigging and then firing a gun "double loaded with shot" straight into her hold. Vane's pirates left the harbor in the brigantine and the *Wolf*, at which point Hornigold sailed in to give the captives provisions and to let them know that help had arrived. That night, Hornigold sailed out in pursuit of the pirates and, a few days later, intercepted the *Wolf* and brought her with him to Nassau.

Hornigold's capture of the *Wolf* boosted Rogers's morale. "Captain Hornigold having proved honest," Rogers wrote his superiors in London, "disobliged his old friends . . . divides the people here, and makes me stronger than I expected." Unsure of his authority to try Woodall, Rogers kept him in irons and sent him back to England on the next outward-bound ship. With the change in seasons, the weather also improved, and Rogers's people began recovering from their sickness. A convoy of trading sloops left the island to trade with friendly contacts in Cuba, from whom they hoped to secure additional supplies. With the fort almost complete and one of the leading pirates on his side, Rogers felt a growing sense of security.

On November 4, Rogers received word that the crews of all four trading sloops he had sent to Cuba had gone pirate and were intending to join Vane. The renegades were said to be at Green Turtle Cay, however, and might still be caught. Rogers again turned to Hornigold and Cockram, who sailed to the island and engaged the recidivists in an all-out battle. The pirates-turned-pirate hunters came back to Nassau on November 28 with ten prisoners—including Blackbeard's former gunner, William Cunningham—and the corpses of three more. Rogers was ecstatic. "I am glad of this new proof [that] Captain Hornigold has given the world to wipe off the infamous name he has hereto been known by," he wrote the British secretary of state, "though in the very acts of piracy he committed most people spoke well of his generosity."

The pirate prisoners presented a challenge, as Rogers lacked the men to ensure they stayed locked up. Trying and executing them in Nassau might spark an uprising. He called a secret session of his governing council, which now included the former chief justice, Thomas Walker, and laid out the options. More than anything, the councilors worried that Vane, tipped off by his numerous informants, might attempt to free the captives. "If any fear be shown on our part," they resolved, "it might animate several [pirates] now here to incite the pirates without to attempt the rescue of those in custody. Therefore . . . to prevent the designs of Vane the pirate," the council concluded they should "as soon as possible . . . bring the prisoners to trial." Lacking a jail, Rogers had the ten prisoners chained aboard the *Delicia* before setting about what he knew was to be a risky confrontation with the island's pirate sympathizers.

———

On leaving Green Turtle Cay, Vane headed north. The intelligence he had received from Woodall suggested he would need reinforcements if he were to make good on his threat to attack Nassau. Having lost hope that the Stuarts would send assistance, Vane knew he had to turn to his old comrades for help. La Buse had vanished to the south. Williams, England, and Condent had sailed for Africa and Brazil. One pirate, however, was still in the region, and everyone knew where to find him. Vane's men agreed; they would sail for North Carolina's Pamlico Sound, where they hoped to hook up with their comrade Blackbeard.

They arrived at Ocracoke Inlet in the second week of October. There, behind Ocracoke Island, they spotted an armed sloop that would later prove to be Blackbeard's *Adventure*. There must have been a few minutes of confusion until the two parties identified each other, as neither was sailing in a vessel that was familiar to the other. Somehow—probably by speaking trumpet—Blackbeard and Vane confirmed each other's identity. Vane promptly saluted his comrade, firing his brigantine's guns high in the air, Blackbeard responding in kind. Vane anchored his vessel alongside the *Adventure*. Men rowed from one vessel to the other, commencing a pirate festival that would last several days and spread to the shores of Ocracoke Island.

The two men shared their experiences over the past few months. Blackbeard was probably the first to inform Vane of Stede Bonnet's capture, an event that had been on everyone's lips from Charleston to Boston. Vane told Blackbeard about his confrontations with Pearse and Rogers at Nassau, and of the progress of the latter's government. Vane may have tried to convince his former partner to join him for a joint assault on New Providence. If so, Blackbeard, comfortable in his new situation, declined. His men were safe and sound, free to continue their piracies without fear of reprisal.

Their revelries concluded, Charles Vane and Edward Thatch took leave of each other to follow their separate paths.

———

Governor Spotswood planned his attack on Blackbeard under a cloak of secrecy. He informed neither Virginia's governing council, nor its legislature, and he certainly had no intention of airing the matter with Governor Eden. The pirates, he later explained, were simply too popular. "I did not so much as communicate to His Majesty's Council here, nor to any other person but those who were necessarily to be employed in the [project's] execution, least among the many favorers of pirates we have in these parts, some of them might send intelligence to Thatch." He had grounds to worry. A few months earlier, some of Blackbeard's men had passed through the colony on their way to Philadelphia and had tried to tempt a number of merchant sailors to join them. Local officials wanted to arrest the pirates, but reported to Spotswood that they "could find none [willing] to assist them in the disarming and suppressing [of] that gang." Spotswood did manage to arrest William Howard, Blackbeard's quartermaster, but shortly thereafter one of the judges of his own Vice-Admiralty Court, a friend of Governor Eden named John Holloway, ordered the arrest of Captain George Gordon and Lieutenant Robert Maynard of HMS *Pearl*, on which Howard had been detained. Holloway filed a civil suit against both naval officers on the pirate's behalf, seeking £500 in damages from each of them. Fearing a jury might let Howard go, Spotswood had him tried without one, a move strongly condemned by the governing council. Virginians, Spotswood sniffed, had "an unaccountable inclination to favor pyrates."

It was at Howard's trial that Spotswood unveiled his plan to Captain Brand and Captain Gordon, who had been sharing intelligence with him for months. It was the perfect opportunity to meet with the Royal Navy officers without raising suspicions, as both were in Williamsburg to serve as officers of the court. After the trial—at which Howard was found guilty—Brand and Gordon walked the four blocks from the handsome, H-shaped Capitol, through the market square and down the Palace Green to the Governor's Palace. Within one of the palace's opulent rooms, Spotswood outlined his plan. Since Blackbeard shared his time between Bath and Ocracoke, there would be a two-pronged assault. Brand, as the senior-most officer, would lead a contingent of marines overland to Bath, connecting with gentlemen sympathizers along the way. A second force would travel by sea to Ocracoke, ensuring no pirates escaped into the Atlantic. The *Pearl* (531 tons, forty guns) and the *Lyme* (384 tons, twenty-eight guns) were both far too large to negotiate the dangerous shoals of North Carolina's brackish creeks and barrier islands. Instead, Spotswood offered to purchase, at his own expense, two nimble sloops, which would be placed at the officers' disposal. Brand and Gordon agreed to man, arm, and supply the sloops and to place both under the command of Captain Gordon's first officer, Lieutenant Robert Maynard. (Gordon himself would stay behind with the frigates at Hampton Roads.) In addition to the possibility of claiming some of Blackbeard's treasure, naval personnel had an extra incentive to participate: Spotswood had just pushed a new law through the legislature rewarding a special bounty for the capture of Blackbeard or his minions. Gordon and Brand agreed to the plan. If it went well, it might prove both patriotic and profitable.

Spotswood's plan was also entirely illegal, as neither the governor nor the officers had the authority to invade another colony. Blackbeard was, legally speaking, a citizen in good standing; he had been pardoned for his previous crimes, had applied for and received legal sanction to salvage his French "wreck" from Governor Eden, and had yet to be indicted for any crime.

The expedition departed from Hampton on November 17. Maynard, who was the oldest naval officer serving in America, climbed aboard his flagship, the *Jane*, the larger of the two sloops hired by Governor Spotswood. On board the *Jane* were thirty-five men; an ample supply of muskets, cutlasses, and swords; a month's worth of provisions; but no cannon, the *Jane* being too small to bear them. The other sloop, the *Ranger*, was even smaller, carrying twenty-five sailors under the command of Midshipman Edmund Hyde of the *Lyme*. With no cannon and only sixty men, Maynard knew that if his sloops were the ones to encounter Blackbeard, they would have to surprise him at anchor. At three o'clock on that November afternoon, they raised their anchors and sailed out of the Chesapeake.

A few hours later, Captain Brand of the Lyme set out on horseback from the Hampton village with a small contingent of sailors. They rode on dirt tracks through the Virginia countryside, past empty fields and teams of slaves tending racks of tobacco leaves drying in the cool fall air. The following day the last fields, plantations, and roads fell behind them as they entered the trackless wilderness of North Carolina.

They spent three agonizing days crossing miles of pine barrens and the aptly named Great Dismal Swamp before emerging, on November 21, at Edenton, one of the colony's few settlements. Coming from the pastoral manors of Virginia, the poverty of the North Carolinians would have made an impression on Brand. "The people indeed are ignorant, there being few that can read and fewer write, even of their justices of peace," another early-eighteenth-century visitor said of the area's inhabitants. "They feed generally upon salt pork, sometimes upon beef, and their bread of Indian corn which they are forced for want of mills to beat, and in this they are so careless and uncleanly that there is but little difference between the corn in the horse's manger and the bread on their tables."

Two men were waiting for Brand in Edenton. They introduced themselves as Maurice Moore, a colonel in the colony's militia and the son of the former governor of South Carolina; and Edward Moseley, the founding settler of Edenton, a wealthy and accomplished lawyer who had once been a member of North Carolina's governing council. Captain Brand described them as "two gentlemen that have been much abused by Thach [sic]," but they were also longstanding political opponents of Governor Eden and were probably Spotswood's chief informants in the colony. Brand's party spent the night in or near Edenton, probably at Moseley's home, where the officer let it be known that he had "come in to take Thach." The next morning Moseley and Moore arranged onward transportation across Albemarle Sound and, with several other residents, accompanied Brand on his final push to Bath, thirty miles further south.

Brand and company reached the outskirts of Bath at about ten o'clock on the night of November 23, six days after leaving Hampton. Moore scouted ahead and discovered that Blackbeard was not in town, as Brand had hoped he would be, but was "expected any minute" with another load of cargo "salvaged" from the French ship. Leaving most of his men behind, Brand crossed the head of Bath Creek and went straight to Governor Eden's plantation house. There, Brand later reported, "[I] applied myself to him and let him know I was come in quest of Thach." Governor Eden must have been alarmed at Brand's surprise appearance in the company of two of his political rivals. He could only hope that Blackbeard had made his escape, and that Brand would not discover the large parcel of stolen goods hidden in the barn of his neighbor, Tobias Knight. It's easy to picture Brand sitting by Eden's fireplace until dawn, loaded musket at his side, waiting for Blackbeard to come down the stone path from Eden's dock.

Blackbeard never came.

⚓

As he sailed down North Carolina's Outer Banks, Lieutenant Maynard heard all sorts of stories about Blackbeard. His pilot, a North Carolinian hired by Spotswood, said Blackbeard had been ferrying stolen cargo between Ocracoke and Bath. At Roanoke Inlet, halfway down the Outer Banks, local mariners told them that the Monday before they had seen Blackbeard's *Adventure* aground on Brant Island, a marshy islet on Currituck Sound, thirty miles back toward Virginia. Maynard spent the rest of the day sailing back and forth the length of Currituck Sound, but saw no sign of Blackbeard or anyone else. Spotswood himself had warned that Thatch was "fortifying an island at O[cra]acock Inlet and making that a general rendevouz of such robbers." From other mariners, Maynard probably heard another disturbing story that would reach

Williamsburg a few days later: Blackbeard had "been join'd by some other pirate crews" at Ocracoke, increasing his numbers to 170 men; Maynard had no way of knowing that Vane's pirate crew had come and gone eight weeks earlier.

On November 21 at four P.M., with mounting trepidation, Maynard's small sloops reached Ocracoke Inlet, thirty miles south of Cape Hatteras. Once around the outer edge of Ocracoke Island, Maynard saw two sloops at anchor behind the island in a place now known as Thatch's Hole, one of them bearing nine guns and matching the description of Blackbeard's *Adventure*. The other sloop was unarmed and looked to be a coastal trading sloop. On the island, Maynard would have seen a large tent, the remains of bonfires, some empty kegs and barrels perhaps, but no sign of fortifications. He took note of the wind and currents and the sun, low in the sky, and gave the order for the *Jane* and *Ranger* to drop anchor. He didn't want to engage Blackbeard in darkness.

Since Vane had left, Blackbeard had indeed been traveling back and forth between Bath and Ocracoke, spending a couple of weeks overseeing twenty or so men at Ocracoke, then a couple of weeks with his wife in Bath. His return to town was, by now, overdue. Four days earlier—November 17—he had received a letter from Tobias Knight urging him to "make the best of your way up as soon as possible . . . [as] I have something more to say to you than at present I can write"; the justice had signed it "your real friend and servant, T. Knight." Blackbeard had more important matters to attend to than Knight or the two modest sloops that had just appeared in the inlet; his pirate gang was entertaining one of their merchant friends, Samuel Odell, whose trading vessel was anchored alongside the *Adventure*. While Maynard's men tried to sleep, steeling themselves for the fight ahead, Blackbeard's men drank late into the night.

At nine o'clock the following morning, Maynard gave the command to weigh anchor and sailed straight for the *Adventure*, hoping to board her before Blackbeard could roll out her cannons. As they entered the anchorage on the faintest of breezes, Midshipman Hyde's *Ranger* ran aground on a sandbar. He ordered his men to start throwing ballast stones overboard in the hopes of making the sloop light enough to get back afloat. Maynard pressed ahead in the larger *Jane*, only to run aground himself, eliminating any possibility of a surprise attack. Despite their hangovers, Blackbeard's men couldn't help but take notice of the two sloops that had clearly been trying to sneak up on them, and whose suspiciously large crews were now noisily throwing ballast and water barrels over the side in an urgent attempt to get free. When it dawned on them that they were under attack, the pirates sprang into action, rushing to loosen sails, cut the anchor cables, and ready the cannons. It happened so fast that their guest, Samuel Odell, and his three crewmen didn't have time to get off Blackbeard's vessel. Just as the *Adventure*'s sails caught their first faint breath of wind, Hyde got the *Ranger* afloat and headed straight for the pirates, with most of his twenty-five men straining at the oars.

The pirates began firing their muskets, and when the vessels had closed to within "half [a] pistol shot," Blackbeard signaled the gun crews to fire. Flames blasted from the muzzles of the *Adventure*'s cannons and, a split second later, four- and six-pound cannonballs tore across the *Ranger*'s foredeck, demolishing foresails and killing Hyde and his second in command, the *Lyme*'s coxswain, Allen Arlington. Wounded men convulsed on the *Ranger*'s blood-soaked deck as the sloop slowed to a stop. Amid the confusion, some of the sailors managed to let off a volley of small arms fire as the *Adventure* swept past. One of the musket balls severed the jib halyard, the line holding up the pirate's foresails, causing the *Adventure* to lose speed. This was a critical piece of luck for Maynard's men. Having gotten the *Jane* free, they now rowed madly toward the pirates in the hope of boarding them. Had the halyard not been hit, the *Adventure* could have escaped into the open sea. Instead, the two vessels closed to within fifty feet of each other.

At this point, Blackbeard hailed Maynard. "Damn you villains, who are you and from whence came you?" he said, according to the *General History*. "You can see by our colors we are no pirates," Maynard is said to have replied. Thatch, his beard tied in black ribbons, held up a glass of liquor and, according to Maynard, "drank damnation to me and my men, whom he styled Cowardly Puppies, saying he would neither give nor take Quarter." Maynard responded that that was fine with him. Blackbeard then signaled to his gunner, Phillip Morton, to unleash his other broadside. Morton had loaded the guns with grape and partridge shot that yielded a shotgunlike discharge that was extremely deadly at such close range. Other pirates threw improvised hand grenades they had made by stuffing gunpowder, musket balls, and bits of old iron into empty rum bottles. When the smoke lifted, the *Jane*'s deck was covered with bodies. In just a few seconds, twenty-one of Maynard's crew had been killed or wounded. Only two men were still standing on the sloop's deck. The battle, Blackbeard concluded, was won. He ordered the *Adventure* to come alongside the *Jane* and for his men to prepare to board.

Under cover of gunpowder smoke, however, Maynard had ordered a dozen or so uninjured men to hide in the *Jane*'s hold and await his signal. Crouching at the ladder, he whispered instructions to his helmsman and his first mate, Mr. Baker, telling them to lie low and to signal to him when the pirates came over the side.

When the *Adventure* banged against the *Jane*, Blackbeard was the first over the rail "with a rope in his hands to lash or make fast the two sloops." At Baker's signal, Maynard rushed up from the hold, sword in hand, a dozen crewmen behind him. In a scene that inspired many Hollywood movies, Blackbeard and Maynard faced off against each other—dashing naval lieutenant and fearsome pirate—swords drawn. Humphrey Johnson, the North Carolina mariner who carried the news of the battle to New England, described the fight this way. "Maynard making a thrust, the point of his sword went against Teach's cartridge box"—where he stored his ammunition—"and bended it to the hilt." Blackbeard then delivered a blow that shattered the guard of Maynard's sword, slicing the officer's fingers. Maynard jumped back, "threw away his sword and fired his pistol, which wounded Teach." By now, ten of Blackbeard's men had clambered aboard the *Jane* and were clashing with

Maynard's men. In the chaos, the *Jane's* helmsman, Abraham Demelt, made his way to Maynard's side and managed to slash Blackbeard across the face. The pirates aboard the *Jane* were outnumbered by Maynard's men and rapidly fell to the bloodstained deck. More men trained their pistols on Blackbeard, who staggered on, swinging his sword at Maynard and Demelt, blood gushing from his face and body. More musket balls struck his tall frame as the sailors surrounded him, swords drawn, circling for the kill.

According to Humphrey Johnson, the final blow came from a Scots highlander, who decapitated Blackbeard with a powerful swing of his sword, "laying it flat on his shoulder" attached by a bit of flesh. The author of the *General History* disagrees, saying Blackbeard expired suddenly "as he was cocking another pistol," finally succumbing to his wounds. In letters to friends and relatives, Maynard didn't say how Blackbeard died, but noted that he fell "with five shot in him, and 20 dismal cuts in several parts of his body." The melee had lasted less than six minutes, during which time all of the boarding pirates were slain without killing a single one of Maynard's men, though he reported several "were miserably cut and mangled."

The *Ranger* came alongside to help finish off the pirates remaining aboard the *Adventure*, who were outmanned by nearly three to one. Many jumped in the water, where the naval sailors picked them off. (According to Captain Gordon's postaction report, one of the pirates made it to shore, succumbed to his injuries, and was "discovered some dayes after in the reefs by [way of] the fowls hovering over him.") One of the *Ranger's* sailors had been killed by friendly fire, bringing the navy's total casualties to eleven dead and over twenty wounded. The victors had one final scare outside the *Adventure's* powder room: They discovered a black pirate named Caesar, match in hand, struggling to get free of the merchant Samuel Odell and one of his crewmen, so he could follow Blackbeard's last command: In the event of defeat, blow them all to smithereens. Caesar was successfully restrained and became one of fourteen pirate prisoners—nine white and five black—that were taken into custody. Odell, his body bearing "no less than seventy wounds," was also taken prisoner, though he was later released.

After the battle, Maynard's men searched the *Adventure*, hoping to find a horde of Spanish gold and silver. Instead they found some gold dust, a few items made of silver (including the goblet stolen from William Bell), and "other small things of plunder." They also found Tobias Knight's recent letter to Blackbeard, and a number of papers implicating Knight and Eden in Blackbeard's piracy. The tent on the shore concealed the remnants of the French ships' cargo: 140 bags of cocoa and ten casks of sugar. If Blackbeard had accumulated fantastic wealth, he had not kept it with him at Ocracoke.

Whether severed during or after the battle, Blackbeard's head was strung up in the *Adventure*'s bowsprit: a grotesque trophy that would fetch the sailors £100 bounty when they got back to Virginia. Maynard had Blackbeard's headless body thrown into Pamlico Sound, where, according to legend, it swam around the *Adventure* three times before sinking into the brackish water.

❧❧❧

Owing to a spate of rough weather, Maynard and Brand didn't meet up until November 27, when the lieutenant came up to Bath to deliver the evidence found against Knight and Eden. Brand was already furious with Knight, who he said was "making [an] abundance of difficulty . . . advising the Governor not to assist me and constantly justifying the pyrates." The chief justice had "positively denied that any [pirated] goods were about his plantation." Brand now confronted Knight with incriminating evidence from Blackbeard's letter, the "memorandum in Thache's pocket book," and statements from several witnesses who had taken part in unloading plunder. Knight finally "owned the whole matter" and showed Brand twenty barrels of sugar and two bags of cotton "covered with fodder" in his barn. Eden, seeing the game was up, ordered his marshal to deliver to Brand six slaves and sixty hogsheads of sugar that had belonged to Blackbeard or his men and had been in the governor's possession. Brand also tracked down "several pyrates lurking [in Bath]," including Blackbeard's boatswain, Israel Hands, who would ultimately agree to testify against his companions in exchange for his life. The total value of the cargo found in Bath and Ocracoke was estimated at £2,238, including the *Adventure* herself.

Lieutenant Maynard returned to Hampton Roads in the *Adventure* on January 3, 1719, Blackbeard's head still hanging from the bowsprit. As he passed HMS *Pearl*, he saluted Captain Gordon with all nine of the *Adventure's* guns. Gordon treated his lieutenant to a rare honor: an equal return salute from one of His Majesty's frigates. Gordon and Maynard presented Blackbeard's head to Governor Spotswood, who had it suspended from a tall pole on the west side of the Hampton River at a place now known as Blackbeard's Point, as a ghoulish admonition to would-be pirates.

In a few weeks, Maynard would be a household name from New England to London, Port Royal, and beyond. In Boston, thirteen-year-old Benjamin Franklin, then a printer's apprentice, wrote and published a "sailor's song" about Maynard's accomplishment, which he sold on the street. The text has been lost, save for one stanza ending with the lines

> *It's better to swim in the sea below*
> *Than to swing in the air and feed the crow,*
> *Says jolly Ned Teach of Bristol*

The expedition kept the court system busy for many years as the various parties tried to settle their scores with one another. On March 12, 1719, the prisoners were tried at the Capitol in Williamsburg and, apart from Samuel Odell, found guilty. Thirteen pirates were executed, their bodies hung in gibbets strung along the Hampton-Williamsburg road. The last, Israel Hands, was freed just prior to execution, owing to the timely arrival of a ship carrying an extension of the king's pardon, an event that also saved William Howard. Based on evidence gathered by Brand and Maynard, Tobias Knight was brought to trial in North

Carolina for colluding with the pirates; he was found not guilty, largely because he managed to have the testimony of Blackbeard's four black crewmen thrown out because, as he argued, "by the laws and customs of all America" the testimony of blacks was not of "any validity against any white person whatsoever." Governor Eden threatened to prosecute Brand for trespassing on the lands of the lords proprietor of North Carolina, and sparred for months with Spotswood over both the legality of the invasion and the ownership of plunder, though these efforts came to naught. Edward Moseley and Maurice Moore broke into an official's home in an unsuccessful attempt to find evidence linking Eden with Blackbeard, and were caught, tried, and convicted of sedition. For his part, Robert Maynard filed an unsuccessful lawsuit against Gordon and Brand after the captains decided to share Spotswood's bounty money among the crew of the *Lyme* and *Pearl*, not just those who had fought at Ocracoke; in the end, most sailors received only £1 for their part in the battle.

⤞⤝

In Charleston, the courts had not only been busy, they had literally been under siege. The inhabitants were at odds over the fate of Stede Bonnet and the other pirates Colonel William Rhett had captured at Cape Fear. Most colonists were undoubtedly pleased that perpetrators of some of the recent blockades were finally being brought to justice. This sentiment was particularly strong among merchants and planters who had lost ships and cargo in these incidents. But there were a great many people in Charleston who supported the pirates, and their passion exceeded that of their counterparts in North Carolina or Virginia. This faction included a large number of pardoned pirates and former Nassau smugglers, as well as servants, sailors, free blacks and other members of South Carolina's enormous underclass. Bonnet, they argued, was "a gentleman, a man of honour, a man of fortune, and one who has had a liberal education." His crewmen were seen as heroes, men unafraid to seize the goods of wealthy men or to drink to the damnation of Britain's so-called king. They insisted, none too quietly, that all the pirates should be freed.

Like Woodes Rogers in Nassau, Governor Johnson was not at all sure that he could keep the pirates in custody. South Carolina had just fought a major Indian war, thus manpower was in short supply. Charleston had no jail, so Johnson had been forced to incarcerate the pirates in the Court of Guard, a small two-story building that stood on the Half-Moon Battery, a fortification on the Bay Street waterfront. The structure's wooden walls had numerous windows, making it less than secure despite the presence of armed guards. As a concession to Bonnet's gentility—and to keep him from plotting with his men—Johnson had the pirate captain held at the home of Nathaniel Partridge, the colony's provost marshal, where "centinels were placed early in the evening" to guard against jailbreaks. Through these improvised arrangements, Johnson hoped to hold the pirates from October 3, when they were brought in, until October 28, when their trial was scheduled to begin.

Nonetheless, on the night of October 24, 1718, Bonnet escaped from the marshal's house with the help of Richard Tookerman, a merchant who had made a small fortune smuggling goods back and forth to the Bahamas when they were under pirate rule. Marshal Partridge may have been complicit in the escape, which apparently took place without a struggle; he was fired a few days later. Curiously, Bonnet escaped in the company of David Herriot, a forced man who would almost certainly have been acquitted, as he had turned state's evidence that very morning, giving a lengthy deposition against the pirates. He had been moved from the Court of Guard to the marshal's house as a reward for his cooperation. Yet Herriot chose to flee into the night with Bonnet. By the time the alarm was sounded, they were halfway across the harbor in Tookerman's canoe, paddled by several of his black and Indian slaves.

Not long thereafter, Charleston descended into civil disorder. The details of what came to be called "the disturbances" are unclear, but from passing references in subsequent legal documents it appears that an armed mob laid siege to the Court of Guard in an attempt to free the remaining pirates. "[We] can't forget how long this town has laboured under the fatigue of watching [the pirates], and what Disturbances were lately made with a design to release them," Assistant Attorney General Thomas Hepworth said a few days later. "We were apparently in danger of losing [our lives] in the late disturbance when, under a notion of the honor of Carolina, [the rioters] threatened to set the town on fire about our ears." The attack, Hepworth concluded, "shows how necessary it is that the law be speedily executed on them to the terror of others, and for the security of our own lives." The trials started on October 28, and when they concluded on November 5, twenty-nine of the thirty-three prisoners had been found guilty. Twenty-two were hanged three days later at White Point, a marshy tongue of land sticking out from the southern end of the Charleston peninsula.

Meanwhile, while paddling to North Carolina, Bonnet and Herriot encountered a storm that forced them ashore on Sullivan's Island, just four miles south of Charleston. There, on November 8, they were ambushed by yet another posse led by William Rhett. There was a brief exchange of gunfire in which Herriot was killed and two slaves injured. Bonnet was recaptured, carried to Charleston, and, on November 12, found guilty of piracy. By an odd coincidence, the chief justice was Nicholas Trott, nephew and namesake of the disgraced governor of the Bahamas, who had helped Henry Avery go free. If Bonnet entertained hopes that Trott's nephew might grant him leniency, he was disappointed. "You . . . shall go from hence to the place of execution," Justice Trott told him, "where you shall be hanged till you are dead."

Bonnet was said to have made such a pathetic display on hearing this sentence that a number of Charleston's citizens—most of them women—applied to the governor to spare his life. According to the author of the General History, the governor was also approached by "some of Bonnet's friends" with a proposal to send the gentleman pirate to England so "that his case might be referred to his majesty." Colonel Rhett is said to have offered to go with Bonnet and to raise funds to pay for the trip. These and other interventions prompted Johnson to delay Bonnet's execution seven times, the London *Original Weekly Journal* later reported, a situation that so angered the city's merchants that they approached the governor "in a mass" and demanded "immediate execution on the offender." Bonnet, fearing the end was near, wrote a plaintive letter to the governor, begging him to "look upon me with bowels of pity and compassion" and to "think me an object for your mercy." "[Make] me a menial servant to your honour and this government, and . . . you'll receive the willingness of my friends to be bound for my good behavior and constant attendance to your commands." The governor was unmoved.

On December 10, 1718, Major Stede Bonnet was led to the gallows at White Point and hanged.

⁂

News of the "disturbances" and the execution of Bonnet's men traveled quickly to Nassau, convincing Woodes Rogers and his governing council of the need to move quickly against the ten pirates they had in custody aboard the *Delicia*.

Rogers was, if anything, in a more vulnerable position than Governor Johnson. Until his arrival, the Bahamas had been the epicenter of Atlantic piracy, and despite the departure of so many, the pirates and their followers still constituted the majority of inhabitants of New Providence. By late November 1718, Rogers had barely enough men to keep his ten prisoners under guard, better yet to defend the colony from Vane or a Spanish invasion fleet. His Independent Company had been reduced by disease, which even killed their surgeon. Of the four vessels he had brought with him, three were gone: the ten-gun *Buck* stolen by pirates, the twenty-gun *Willing Mind* wrecked on a sandbar, and the six-gun *Samuel* on her way to London to secure more troops and supplies. The only thing standing between Rogers and his enemies were the *Delicia*, a poorly manned ruin of a fort, and the influence of Hornigold, Cockram, and Josiah Burgess. The time had come for a final test of wills between Rogers and the island's pirate sympathizers.

On December 9, the prisoners were brought to the fort and escorted to a guardroom where the trial was to be held. Robert Beauchamp, head of the Independent Company, had all sixty of his surviving soldiers guard the entrances before going inside. There he sat down with Rogers, Chief Justice William Fairfax, and five other men Rogers had appointed as justices, including reformed pirate captain Burgess (now an officer in the militia) and Thomas Walker, who was no doubt pleased to finally be sitting in judgment over the pirates of the Bahamas. The trial lasted two days, during which time numerous witnesses testified to the guilt of nine of the pirates. The last, John Hipps, proved to have been a forced man and was acquitted. The rest, including Blackbeard's former gunner, William Cunningham, were sentenced to death by hanging, with the execution set for two days thence. A few of the men begged Rogers to delay the execution, but the governor refused. According to the trial record, "the Governor told them that from the time of their being apprehended . . . they ought to have accounted themselves as condemned."

On the morning of December 12, a crowd of 300 formed at the base of the fort's northeastern rampart, a sandy shoreline where a gallows had been erected, against the water's edge. The throng consisted almost entirely of former pirates, who might have been there to interrupt the proceedings. "Few men besides the governor's adherents were spectators to the tragedy," the official trial record put it, "but [those who] had lately deserved the same fate." At ten A.M., the nine prisoners were unchained from their ad hoc cell by the provost marshal and led, under heavy guard, to the top of the rampart. The crowd's behavior was erratic. Some cheered their former brethren, others looked warily at the heavy cannon trained on them from the ramparts and the 100 armed soldiers, sailors, and officials posted there and around the perimeter of the gallows. Standing atop the rampart, most of the prisoners were cowed, including their ringleader, John Augur, who was dressed in filthy clothes and had neither washed nor shaved. In contrast, twenty-eight-year-old Dennis McCarthy and Thomas Morris, twenty-two, were dressed flamboyantly, with long blue and red ribbons adorning their wrists, necks, knees, and skulls. Morris was in good humor, smiling frequently. Mc-Carthy looked out on the crowd cheerfully before yelling out that "he knew a time when there [were] many brave fellows on the island that would not suffer him to die like a dog." He kicked each of his shoes over the wall and into the crowd, adding, "that some friends of his had often said he should die in his shoes, but that he would make them liars." The crowd buzzed, but nobody attempted to rush the well-guarded fort. At the prisoners' request, the island's Huguenot priest read several prayers and psalms "in which all present joyn'd." When the priest finished, the marshal conducted the prisoners, one by one, over the ramparts and down a ladder to the gallows. Thomas Morris paused at the top of the ladder to quip: "We have a good governor, but a harsh one." Near the foot of the ladder, nine nooses hung over a single wooden stage held up by three large barrels. Each was led to his appointed noose, "where the hangman fastened the cords as dexterously as if he had been a servitor at Tybourne," London's primary execution site, the trial record noted. With hands tied behind their backs and a noose in place, the prisoners were allotted forty-five minutes to say their final words, drink their last goblets of wine, and sing their last psalms before the boisterous crowd.

Most of the prisoners set to drinking to deaden their fear, particularly William Lewis, a former prizefighter who was eager to toast fellow prisoners and bystanders alike. When Lewis asked for more wine, one of the sullen prisoners, William Ling, shot back that "water was more suitable to them at [this] time." William Dowling, a twenty-four-year-old Irishman, became so drunk that "his behavior was very loose on stage." McCarthy and Morris hadn't given up on the crowd, exhorting them to rush the stage. According to the *General History*, Morris began "taxing [the spectators] with pusilanimity and cowardice, as if it were a breach of honour in them not to rise and save them from the ignominious death they were going to suffer." Some of "their old cohorts" and others surged forward and "got as near to the foot of the gallows as the marshal's guard would suffer them," according to the official account,

". . . but their wills saw too much power over their heads to practice anything."

The moment passed, Rogers stepped forward to announce the last minute reprieve of young George Rounsivell because, as he later explained, "I hear [he] is the son of loyal and good parents at Weymouth," in Rogers's native Dorset. The fortunate young man was untied and brought off the stage. The marshal's men then gripped the ropes tied to the barrels supporting the stage and waited for Rogers's signal. In these last moments, Morris yelled out that he "might have been a greater plague to these islands and now wished he had been so."

Rogers gave the signal, the guards heaved on their ropes, and, in the words of the official record, "the stage fell, and the eight sprang off." As the eight corpses swung from the gallows before the placid blue waters of Nassau Harbor, Rogers knew he had finally gained the upper hand.

Indeed, Rogers would realize that the executions had dealt a mortal blow to those on the island who wished to overthrow his government. Sometime after Christmas, several disgruntled residents held a secret meeting where they hatched a plot to kill Rogers and his officers "and then to deliver up the fort for the use of the pirates." But opinion in Nassau was against the plotters. Some privy to the conspiracy passed word to Rogers, who had three of the ringleaders seized "and punished . . . with severe whipping." In the wake of the executions, the coup had garnered so little support that Rogers decided his new prisoners could do him no harm. "I shall release them," he wrote the British secretary of state a few weeks later, "and be the more on my guard" in the future.

The home front was secure, but Rogers faced other threats. He was still keeping a lookout for the Spanish and also for Charles Vane and the handful of other pirates-at-large still operating in and around the Bahamas.

***

As Vane sailed south from Ocracoke in mid-October 1718, he must have felt disappointed. He had been unable to convince Blackbeard to join forces with him against Nassau and had but ninety men aboard his twelve-gun brigantine. Based on what his informants had told him, even Rogers's depleted forces at New Providence would be able to resist an attack by such a small contingent. If he were to oust the governor and restore the pirate republic, he would have to wait until he had accumulated a stronger force or hope the Spanish would once again invade, destroy the government, and abandon the island. For now he would have to content himself with smaller, softer targets. Harbour Island was also too strong for him, its fortifications well manned and maintained by Richard Thompson and the Cockrams. The farming hamlet on adjacent Eleuthera was another matter. There were only families living on the entire 200-square-mile island, and between them they could only muster a militia force of seventy. Vane proposed that they sack Eleuthera, pillage supplies, and make south for sparsely populated Hispaniola, to establish their own pirate camp and wait for events to unfold in the adjacent Bahamas. The company, which included quartermaster "Calico Jack" Rackham and first mate Robert Deal, agreed.

The raid on Eleuthera was a complete success. The pirates came ashore, plundered the inhabitants of their liquor and as much of their livestock as could be carried away. The brigantine departed as quickly as it came, her decks crowded with live pigs, goats, sheep, and poultry, the makings of many a feast. On October 23, as they made their way south through the Bahamas, they captured two prizes: a small sloop and the forty-ton brigantine *Endeavor* of Salem, on her way home from Kingston. "Vane . . . bore down on him, hoisted a black flag, and fired a shot at him," the captain of the *Endeavor*, John Shattock, later deposed. "[He] ordered him to hoist out his boat and come on board him, which [he] did." Apparently, Shattock's boat crew didn't row fast enough, because the pirates began yelling that they would "fire a volley of small shot into them if they did not make haste." The pirates kept Shattock's men aboard their vessel for two days, beating and abusing their captain while they plundered the *Endeavor* of her gunpowder, salt, and whale oil. When Shattock complained of his abuse, Robert Deal replied: "Damn you, old dog, then tell where your money is. If we find you in one lie, we'll damn you and your vessel also." The frightened captain told them what they wanted to know and, on the twenty-fifth, was put aboard the *Endeavor* and allowed to sail away. Vane kept the small sloop as a tender and took her with him to Hispaniola.

During their passage, the pirates lived "riotously on board," drinking heavily and gorging on freshly slaughtered farm animals. Perhaps as a result of these excesses, they failed to capture a single vessel for the better part of a month. As they slaughtered the last chickens and drank the dregs of their wine casks, the pirates' morale began to wane. They had forsaken the pardon in the hopes of living merry, acquiring riches, and pestering the forces of the Hanoverian king; now they found themselves sober, bored, and filled with discontent.

The sour mood lifted on November 23 when their lookouts spotted a large frigate-rigged ship downwind of their position. Vane ordered the brigantine and sloop to bear down on her, and ran a black flag up his mainmast, expecting the ship to surrender as almost everyone before her had done. Instead, the ship's captain ran up a white flag studded with tiny gold fleur-de-lis: the ensign of the French Navy. Cannon muzzles rolled out of her heretofore-unnoticed gun ports and, in a thunderous, rolling, explosion, the French man-of-war blasted Vane's brigantine with a full broadside. By concealing their guns until the last minute, however, the French gunners were apparently unable to aim them properly, as the brigantine suffered little or no damage from the opening salvo.

Vane was not one to back off from a fight, but seeing himself outgunned, he ordered his vessels to swing around and run away into the wind. The French frigate trimmed her sails and, to Vane's surprise, followed them. Then, as a captive later recalled, "the pirates quarreled among themselves" about how to proceed. Vane was for escaping, but quartermaster Jack Rackham and much of the crew wanted to take on the man-of-war, arguing "that though she had more guns and a greater weight of metal, they might board her and then the best boys would carry the day." Vane responded that "it was too rash and desperate an enterprise, the man-of-war appearing to be twice their force"—twenty-four guns—"and that their brigantine might be sunk by her before they could [get] on board." Deal and fifteen other pirates agreed, but the other seventy-five supported Rackham. Unwilling to embark on what he considered a suicide mission, Vane pulled rank, forcing the pirates to retreat by dint of his absolute power as captain while "fighting, chasing, or being chased." The company was outraged but, respecting the articles they'd signed, followed orders, tightening their sails and ultimately leaving the French frigate in their wake.

The incident cost Vane dearly. The next day the pirates were out of danger, putting an end to Vane's war powers. Jack Rackham, clad in his multicolored Indian prints, called a meeting of the ship's company to challenge Vane's rule by a vote of confidence. "A resolution passed against [Vane's] honor and dignity," the author of the *General History* wrote a few years later, "branding him with the name of coward, deposing him from command, and turning him out of the company with marks of infamy." Vane, Deal, and fifteen loyalists were put aboard the sloop the pirates had captured off Long Island, with some provisions and ammunition. Rackham, whom the pirates had elected as their new captain, sailed away in the brigantine, bound for Jamaica. Vane had been deposed from command.

❦

After all of his bravado—defying the Royal Navy, blockading cities, putting entire colonies into a state of terror—Vane's pirating career ended with a whimper.

Reduced to a single sloop, fifteen men, and a cannon or two, Vane was no longer in a position to threaten His Majesty's governments, but he tried to rebuild all the same. As they sailed south for the jungle-carpeted shores of the Bay of Honduras, he and Deal did their best to transform the puny vessel from tender to gunboat, mounting cannon, shifting ballast, and modifying the rigging. In late November they tarried several days off the northwest coast of Jamaica, capturing two periaguas and a sloop and convincing most or all of their crews to join the company. Deal took command of the second sloop and the pirates continued southwards. They reached an anchorage in the Bay of Honduras on December 16, where they surprised two merchant sloops, and kept them to help careen their vessels. A few days later, Vane made what would be his final capture: the *Prince*, a forty-ton sloop from Kittery, Maine, sailed by Captain Thomas Walden. His men now scattered among five vessels, Vane led the way to their ultimate destination: the Bay Islands, forty miles off the coast of Honduras.

The Bay Islands made the perfect nest for a pirate captain on the mend. They had served as a retreat for generations of freebooters, from Henry Morgan to John Coxon. Lush, mountainous, and out of the way, the islands had everything Vane's men needed: fresh springs, secluded anchorages, timber, game, and fish-infested coral reefs located so close to the shore one could practically wade to them. Vane set up camp at Guanaja, which had an anchorage on the southern shore with no less than seven entrances and exits between sharp reefs and sandbars. Here, from late December to early February, Vane cleaned his vessels, chatted with his men, and feasted on fish, crabs, and salt pork on the island's beaches. At the end of this peaceful interlude, Vane and Deal loaded up their respective sloops and sailed out to cruise the Spanish Main, no doubt hoping to overwhelm a "ship of force" that would get them back to the top of their game.

A few days out to sea, the pirates were overtaken by a violent hurricane. Vane and Deal lost each other amid the towering seas and screaming winds and, after being battered for two days, Vane's sloop was driven ashore on a small uninhabited island in the Bay of Honduras. The vessel was smashed to pieces and, in the process, most of her crew and all of the food and supplies aboard her were lost. Vane survived but was "reduced to great straits for want of necessaries." He lived as a castaway for several weeks, kept alive by the charity of visiting turtle hunters, who came from the mainland in dories and provided him with meat. The turtlers must have been a pathetic lot, as Vane preferred to stay on the island rather than join them in their jungle camps. He knew an English merchant vessel was bound to show up in search of water or firewood, and take him back to civilization.

He was proven right when, sometime in the late winter or early spring of 1719, a ship from Jamaica dropped anchor off his island. Vane greeted them and was surprised to learn that their captain was an old friend, a retired buccaneer by the name of Holford. But Holford knew of his old friend's reputation and refused to take him aboard. "Charles, I shan't trust you aboard my ship unless I carry you prisoner," he is said to have told the sorry pirate. Otherwise "I shall [find] you caballing with my men [to] knock me on the head and run away with my ship a' pyrating." He put Vane ashore, telling him that he would return in about a month with a load of logwood. "If I find you upon this island when I come back," he vowed, "I'll carry you to Jamaica and hang you."

Luckily for Vane, before the month was up, a different ship put in for water, one whose captain and crew did not know him. Eager to get off the island, Vane gave a false name and signed on as a crewman for the remainder of the voyage.

Holford arrived at the anchorage shortly thereafter, and the captain of the vessel on which Vane was now crewing invited Holford aboard for dinner. While making his way down the deck to the captain's cabin, Holford happened to glance down into the hold and spotted Vane at work. He went straight to the captain, a friend of his, and advised him of the castaway's true identity and reputation. Holford, who was on his way back to Jamaica, volunteered to carry him to justice. Vane soon found himself at gunpoint while Holford's crewmen clamped him into irons. The crew of a humble trading vessel had captured the most notorious pirate in the Americas.

A week or two later, Vane was home in Jamaica, a prisoner of the king he so despised. For reasons that are unclear, he was allowed to rot in jail for the better part of a year before being brought to trial in Spanish Town, the Jamaican capital, on March 22, 1721. He knew the verdict would not be in doubt. Numerous witnesses came to testify against him:

captains, crewmen, and passengers from various vessels he had captured, and even Vincent Pearse of HMS *Phoenix*, who related how Vane had made a mockery of the king's pardon. When it was Vane's turn to present his defense he called no witnesses and asked no questions. His piracy career had started aboard one of Lord Hamilton's privateers. Now it was Hamilton's successor, Governor Nicholas Lawes, who pronounced what he termed "the usual sentence": to be "hanged by the neck, 'till he was dead, and the Lord have mercy on his soul."

On Wednesday, March 29, 1721, Charles Vane was hanged at Gallows Point in Port Royal. Governor Laws had his corpse cut down, carried to Gun Cay at the harbor's entrance, where it hung in chains from a gibbet for all mariners to see. Over the months and years that followed, they watched his apparition disappear, bit by bit, ravaged by birds, insects, and the elements, until all that was left of Vane—and the Golden Age of Piracy—were the stories told by the tavern fire, or in hammocks between the decks of a thousand creaking, miserable ships.

PIRACY'S END

1720–1732

W ITH THE EXECUTION of the pirates at Nassau in December 1718, Woodes Rogers no longer feared his government would be brought down by a coup, but the threat from the Spaniards remained. Throughout the winter of 1718–1719, he did his best to put the impoverished colony on a good defensive footing, prodding his indolent subjects to shore up Fort Nassau, writing requests for reinforcements, and begging, unsuccessfully, for naval support from Commodore Chamberlaine, commander of the Jamaica squadron. In March 1719 he received official word that Britain and Spain were again at war,* and he promptly handed out privateering commissions to many of the Bahamas' former pirates, most of whom were probably eager to return to pirate-like work. When his government ran out of funds shortly thereafter, Rogers paid, fed, and supplied the colony's sailors and soldiers with money out of his own pocket, expecting to be reimbursed by his fellow investors or the Crown. Despite these efforts, Rogers knew the Bahamas were in no way ready to repel a serious invasion attempt.

A Spanish invasion fleet sailed from Cuba in May 1719 carrying 3,000 to 4,000 troops. Had it attacked New Providence as planned, it

---

* The War of the Quadruple Alliance (December 1718 to February 1720) pitted Spain against Britain, France, Austria, and the Netherlands. In this war, which one British historian aptly termed "the most forgotten of our conflicts," Spain unsuccessfully sought to add the Bahamas, Carolinas, and French Louisiana to its empire. Rogers received the official declaration of war on March 16, 1719, though he had been expecting it since the previous November.

would certainly have rolled over the islands' paltry defenses. En route, however, the Spanish commodore received word that the French—Britain's allies this time around—had captured a strategically important fortress at Pensacola. The fleet therefore turned around and sailed for that settlement on Florida's Gulf Coast, sparing the Bahamas for another nine months.

Rogers continued pushing and prodding Nassau's "very lazy" citizenry to finish the fort. A close brush with invasion prompted everyone to pitch in, but only for a couple of weeks, after which most abandoned their work sites, leaving Rogers with "a few of the best of them . . . ye Negroes, and my own men." Receiving no financial assistance from the Crown, he continued to purchase vital war supplies on credit—£20,000 worth by the end of 1719, some of it under his own name, rather than on behalf of his investment group. Many suppliers started cutting him off for nonpayment. "Having no news of my bills being paid at home, I am forced to run too much in debt," he alerted officials of the Council of Trade and Plantations in early 1720. "I must [continue doing so] or . . . we shall starve or be a sacrifice to the Spaniards." His letter went unanswered, as had every single letter he had sent them. In fact, he hadn't heard from anyone in the central government for the better part of a year. With the pirates defeated, King George's administration seemed to have forgotten the Bahamas' existence. Rogers hadn't gotten much support from the navy either, whose captains, in Rogers's words, had "little regard for this infant colony." In his first year as governor, only two men-of-war visited Nassau: one to deliver official mail, the other—Captain Whitney's *Rose*—forced in for fresh water by poor sailing conditions. "I observed a general dissatisfaction [in] the Governour," Whitney sniffed in a report to the Admiralty. Rogers was still "complaining for want of help, which I'm afraid [he and his fellow investors] will always be in 'till they have redeemed their credits"—paid their bills—"throughout America."

Even so, when a Spanish invasion fleet appeared off Nassau on February 24, 1720, Rogers was able to face them with a fifty-gun fort, the ten-gun eastern battery, the *Delicia*, 100 soldiers, and 500 armed militia-men. By fortune, the sixth-rate frigate HMS *Flamborough* (twenty-four guns) was in Nassau at the time, although Rogers had to browbeat her abrasive captain, John Hildesley, to stay and defend the island. The Spanish, by contrast, had three frigates of forty, twenty-six, and twenty-two guns, a twelve-gun brigantine, eight armed sloops, and an invasion force of 1,300 men. Rogers's defenses dissuaded the Spanish from a direct assault on the harbor. Instead, they landed on the backside of Hog Island and, in the middle of the night, attempted to cross the narrow eastern channel in small boats. A pair of heroic sentries—both free blacks—somehow managed to fire enough musket rounds to frighten the Spaniards into retreat. Ironically, two men who had probably been slaves themselves had saved Rogers, a professional slave dealer.

The Bahamas were secured, but the effort exhausted Rogers's physical and financial resources. The imperial government continued to ignore his letters, merchants denied him credit, and his colony's economy remained paralyzed for lack of productive settlers. Rogers was in such poor health that he nearly died on two occasions. In November 1720 he spent six weeks in South Carolina, hoping a rest in the cooler climate and more genteel surroundings of Charleston would repair his health. Instead, he found a city in political upheaval and, while there, was wounded in a duel with Captain Hildesley of HMS *Flamborough* relating to "disputes they had at [New] Providence." He sent one last set of letters to London before returning to Nassau, begging support and instructions. They, like many others before them, went unanswered.

By midwinter, Rogers could bear it no longer. "I can subsist no longer on the foot[ing] I have been left ever since my arrival," he wrote the Council of Trade on February 23, 1722. "I have no other satisfactions left me in this abandoned place and condition, [except] having done my duty to His Majesty and my country, though at the hazard of my entire ruin." Leaving the colony in the hands of William Fairfax, Rogers sailed for England a month later, hoping face-to-face meetings would prove more productive than his correspondence. He arrived in London in August to learn that King George had fired him, and a new governor was already on his way to Nassau. Worse, his fellow investors had liquidated the Co-partners for Carrying on a Trade & Settling the Bahama Islands, making no allowance for the £6,000 Rogers had personally advanced on their behalf. Rogers was ruined once again. His creditors moved in on him and, before long, he found himself locked in debtors prison. The man who had captured a Manila galleon, dispersed the pirates of the Caribbean, and successfully defended a critical strategic asset from an invasion force twice his strength was left behind bars.

❧❧

Many former pirates became privateers during the course of the War of the Quadruple Alliance, with varying degrees of success. Benjamin Hornigold, founder of the pirate republic, took his commission from Rogers and cruised against Spanish pirates from the familiar shelter of Nassau Harbor. In the spring of 1719, while lurking near Havana, his vessel was captured by a Spanish ship and brigantine; he either died in the engagement or in a Cuban prison, as his Bahamian colleagues never saw him again. Josiah Burgess, once Nassau's third most powerful pirate, served Rogers as a lieutenant of the Independent Company, a justice of the Vice-Admiralty Court, and a privateer. In the latter capacity, his vessel was wrecked near Abaco; Burgess drowned, along with George Rounsivell, the young man Rogers pardoned at the gallows, who had gone back into the water to try to rescue him.

Henry Jennings and Leigh Ashworth both operated privateers out of Jamaica. Jennings was particularly successful, arriving in New York in October 1719 on his trusty *Barsheba* with two brigantines and a sloop taken from the Spaniards off Vera Cruz. Jennings survived the war and returned to respectable merchant service out of Bermuda. In 1745, during the War of the Austrian Succession, his sloop was captured in the West Indies; prison may have proven fatal to a man in his early sixties. Ashworth's fate is unclear, but in May 1719 he was again stepping over the line between privateering and piracy, by attacking one of Rogers's privateers and kidnapping one of Thomas Walker's sons off Cuba.

Others jumped over the line with both feet, and none more infamously than Vane's old quartermaster, "Calico Jack" Rackham.

❧❧❧

Rackham didn't lack for courage, but perhaps for judgment. After abandoning Vane in November 1718, he convinced his band to cruise just off the shore of Jamaica, a particularly dangerous environment as the island was home to the Royal Navy's West Indies fleet and a large number of armed merchant vessels. With risk came rewards. On December 11, the pirates lay chase to the merchant ship *Kingston*, overtaking her so close to Port Royal that the townspeople watched the attack. The ship, it turned out, was carrying a cargo valued at £20,000, much of it in the form of a large parcel of gold watches hidden in the bulk cargo. Her Jamaican owners were not going to let such a brazen theft succeed. As it happened, there were no warships in the harbor, but with the governor's blessing, the owners outfitted a pair of privateering vessels to recover their ship.

Three months later, in early February 1719, the privateers finally found the *Kingston* at Isla de los Piños, south of Cuba. Rackham's brigantine was anchored alongside, but most of her crew was ashore, sleeping off hangovers under the brigantine's sails, which they'd converted into temporary tents and awnings. Surprised and in no condition to defend themselves, Rackham's company fled into the woods, hiding there until the privateers left with the *Kingston* and most of her cargo. Rackham and his men were left with two boats, a canoe, a few small arms, twenty silver watches, and several large bales of silk stockings and laced hats. After donning the finery, the pirates became divided over how to proceed. From their captives they had learned that King George had extended his pardon (the same extension that had allowed some of Blackbeard's men to escape hanging in Virginia). Rackham and six followers decided to take the pardon in Nassau, where they might claim that

Vane had forced them into piracy. They left in one of the boats and worked their way around the eastern tip of Cuba, capturing various Spanish boats along the way.

Rackham arrived in Nassau in mid-May 1719 and convinced Rogers to pardon his men. They lived in Nassau for a while, hawking watches and stockings, drinking in what taverns and brothels still remained. (Rogers, who continued to distribute Protestant religious pamphlets to the ex-pirates, presumably clamped down on some of Nassau's moral excesses.) As their money ran out, Rackham's friends shipped out on privateers or merchant sloops. Rackham, with his captain's double-share of plunder, lasted the longest. During this time, he made the acquaintance of one of New Providence's most infamous harlots, Anne Bonny, wife of James Bonny, a rank-and-file pirate who had become one of Rogers's informants. Rackham took a fancy to the fiery young woman, who swore like a pirate and had cuckolded her husband on a great many occasions. He spent the last of his money courting her, then shipped out on one of Burgess's final privateering missions, and spent his share of the proceeds on his new flame. The two fell in love and, sometime in the spring or early summer of 1720, approached James Bonny to seek an annulment of their marriage. Bonny agreed to do so in exchange for a substantial cash payment, but they would need a respectable witness to sign the appropriate papers. They chose their witness poorly. Richard Turnley, a mariner despised in some circles for having piloted HMS *Rose* safely into the harbor when Rogers first arrived, not only refused to act as witness, he informed Governor Rogers of the situation. Rogers, perhaps having read too many of the religious pamphlets he'd brought with him, told Bonny that if she annulled her marriage he would have her thrown in prison where he would force Rackham to whip her. Anne "promised to be very good, to live with her husband and keep loose company no more." She had no intention of doing any of these things.

Unable to continue their relationship ashore, Rackham and Bonny decided to take to the sea as pirates. The couple recruited a half-dozen disgruntled former pirates as well as Anne's close friend, a cross-dressing female sailor named Mary Read. The author of *A General History of the Pyrates* erroneously claimed that Bonny and Read met at sea, when Read, dressed as a man, was pressed into service aboard Rackham's pirate sloop. According to this oft-repeated account, Bonny took a liking to the fresh-faced recruit, only discovering her true gender after making the moves on her. Read is then said to have explained that her mother had raised her as a boy in order to pass her off as another man's son, that she had served as a sailor and foot soldier, and had come to Nassau when pirates captured a merchant ship she was serving aboard. Indeed, the two women may well have met after Bonny mistook Read for a handsome young man, but the encounter almost certainly took place not at sea, but in Nassau. We know this because by the time Rackham and Bonny decided to go pirating together, Mary Read was not only with them, her identity and gender were already well known to Governor Rogers, who identified the women by name in an official proclamation released to the Boston newspapers.

The account is partially correct: The women did indeed become cross-dressing pirates. Late on the night of August 22, 1720, Rackham, Anne Bonny, Mary Read, and six men stole one of the swiftest vessels in all of the Bahamas, the *William*, a twelve-ton, six-gun sloop belonging to privateer John "Catch Him if You Can" Ham.* The watch aboard the *Delicia* challenged the pirates as they left the harbor, but they talked their way out of trouble, claiming they were going to stand outside the harbor for the evening after having broken their anchor line. Instead, they took the *William* round to the backside of New Providence and began plundering fishing canoes and other vessels from locations all over the Bahamas, their numbers growing as unhappy sailors and former pirates joined their company. Rackham and Bonny also went out of their way to track down Richard Turnley, whom they knew to be

---

* *A General History* incorrectly identifies him as John Haman. Rogers, who would have known the man personally, provides more accurate information in his official proclamation of September 5, 1720.

hunting turtles on one of the Bahamas' outer cays. They destroyed his boat and pressed three of his crewmen, while Turnley and his young son hid in the woods. They left behind a fourth crewman with a message for Turnley: If Rackham and Bonny ever came across him again, they would whip him to death.

Over the next two months, Bonny and Read became inseparable and, in matters of fashion, developed a compromise between them. "When they saw any vessel, gave chase, or attacked, they wore men's clothes," as Read preferred, a former captive would later testify at their trial, "and at other times, they wore women's clothes." At a time when women sailors were unheard of, Bonny and Read actively participated in combat, running gunpowder for the men, fighting in battles, and terrorizing their captives. Dorothy Thomas, a fisherwoman detained by the pirates on the north side of Jamaica, testified that the two women "wore men's jackets and long trousers and [had] handkerchiefs wrapped around their heads . . . a machete and pistol in their hands and cursed and swore at the men, [urging] . . . that they should kill her, to prevent her [testifying] against them." Thomas added that the only reason she knew they were women "was by the largeness of their breasts." On October 20, 1720, the pirates daringly attacked the sloop *Mary & Sarah* while she lay at anchor in Dry Harbor, on the north shore of Jamaica; the vessel's captain noted that Bonny had "a gun in her hand," and that "they were both very profligate, cursing and swearing much, and very ready and willing to do anything on board."

Despite having his lover aboard, Rackham continued to pursue a reckless strategy. He spent much of October on the shores of Jamaica, hopping from harbor to harbor, stealing small vessels, and recruiting additional crewmen. Soon he was being dogged by several Jamaican privateers, including one commanded by former Bahamian pirate Jean Bondavais, who had been terrorizing Spanish shipping. Bondavais caught up with Rackham while he was collecting recruits from shore near the western tip of Jamaica. Rather than trying to conceal his identity, Rackham promptly fired on Bondavais' vessel. Bondavais retreated to report the incident to Captain Jonathan Barnet, a privateer who had been hunting for Rackham in his own well-armed sloop. Barnet chased Rackham throughout the afternoon and into the night, during which time many of Rackham's men fell to drinking. The alcohol may have affected the pirates' handling of their swift vessel because, at ten o'clock, Barnet came within hailing distance. He ordered them "to strike immediately to the King of England's colors." Somebody on Rackham's sloop responded: "We will strike no strikes," at which point Barnet's men fired a swivel gun.

At this point, most of Rackham's men fled into the hold, leaving Read and Bonny on deck. Read, according to the *General History*, "called to those under deck to come up and fight like men and, finding they did not stir, fired her arms down the hold amongst them, killing one and wounding others." Moments later, Barnet's men fired a broadside, backed by a hail of small arms fire, causing the pirates' boom to crash onto the deck, followed by the shot-ridden mainsail. Unable to maneuver their vessel, the pirates begged for quarter. Barnet's men stormed over the rails, took everyone aboard into custody, and the next morning delivered them to the militia officer ashore. Soon thereafter, Calico Jack, Anne Bonny, and Mary Read found themselves in Spanish Town jail, awaiting trial.

Among their fellow prisoners was Charles Vane. It's not known if the pirates were able to speak to one another, but if they did, Vane may have had some harsh words for his former quartermaster. Had Rackham not led the uprising against him two years earlier, Vane might have succeeded in building a pirate fleet comparable to those once commanded by Bellamy and Blackbeard. Once divided, neither man had the strength to do any serious damage to the British Empire. Rackham was among the first to be tried and found guilty. On November 18, 1720, the day of his execution, Anne Bonny was allowed to see him one last time. "I'm sorry to see you here," she is said to have told him, "but if you had fought like a man, you need not have hanged like a dog." Later that day he and four other men were executed at Gallows Point in Port Royal. His body was later placed in a gibbet on a small island in the harbor now known as Rackham's Cay; he and Vane may have been hanged separately, but their corpses swung within sight of each other across Port Royal Harbor.

As for Mary Read and Anne Bonny, they were tried on November 28, 1720, found guilty, and sentenced to death. They had a surprise for Governor Lawes and the other officials at the Spanish Town courthouse. They "plead their bellies," claiming to be "quick with child" and, thus, ineligible for execution, as it was illegal for the court to take the lives of their fetuses. Lawes ordered that the women be examined, whereupon their claim was found to be true. Their sentences were postponed and the women were presumably returned to prison. Mary Read died there from a violent fever and was buried at St. Catherine's church in Jamaica on April 28, 1721. Anne Bonny's fate is unclear, though she was apparently not executed. During her pregnancy, her long-estranged father, a South Carolina planter of some means, may have been able to obtain her release. If she died on Jamaica, the records of her burial have been lost.

✵✵✵

With the execution of Rackham and Vane, the Golden Age of Piracy was all but over. While ships would continue to be attacked—particularly off West Africa—the pirates never again had the upper hand. With few exceptions, the pirates of the 1720s spent their time playing cat-and-mouse games with the authorities; there were to be no more threats to the colonies themselves. British authorities estimated the worldwide pirate population at approximately 2,000 between 1716 and 1718, but less than 200 by 1725, a collapse of 90 percent. After 1722, most pirates had abandoned any hope of carving out their own republic or helping overthrow the Hanoverian kings of England and spent most of their time fighting for mere survival.

That's not to say that all of the Flying Gang pirates were defeated. Indeed, many of the diehards who abandoned the Bahamas in 1718 carried on for years, and a few managed to retire comfortably. Olivier La Buse, Bellamy's longtime consort, went to the Leeward Islands with his ship-of-force prior to the pirate republic's collapse. On June 12, 1718, Captain Francis Hume's HMS *Scarborough* cornered La Buse at La Blanquilla, where he had anchored to plunder a small prize sloop. As the frigate approached, La Buse and most of his crew made their escape on the faster, more nimble sloop. He eventually made his way to West Africa, meeting up with a number of Bahamian colleagues, including Edward England and Paulsgrave Williams. He had a long and generally prosperous career in Africa and the Indian Ocean until 1730, when he was apprehended by French authorities and executed on the island of Réunion. His grave is a popular tourist site there.

Paulsgrave Williams also wound up in Africa, where he was last seen in April 1720 serving as quartermaster aboard La Buse's brigantine. A man held captive on that vessel, slaver captain William Snelgrave, recalled that Williams was grouchy and despondent, threatening him with violence without provocation. "Don't be afraid of him, for it is his usual way of talking," another captive told Snelgrave. "But be sure [to] call him Captain as soon as you get aboard" his vessel. Indeed, Williams warmed to the use of his old title, as he was unhappy not being in command. Snelgrave also reported that members of the pirate fleet drank toasts to "King James the Third," suggesting continued Jacobite proclivities among Williams's associates. Williams probably sailed with La Buse for some time thereafter, possibly settling among other aging pirates in Madagascar. He never again saw his wife and children in Rhode Island, but his eldest son apparently never forgot him. When he grew up, Paulsgrave Williams Jr. became a wig-maker, specializing in the peruke his father was so fond of wearing.

The rank-and-file pirates who stole Rogers's privateer *Buck* helped spawn a new wave of outlaws who would terrorize the Atlantic and Indian Oceans. Led by Howell Davis, a fearless Welshman, they plundered vessels from Virginia to West Africa. In November 1719, he forced a carpenter named Bartholomew Roberts to serve aboard the *Buck*; after Davis was killed a short time later during an attack on a Portuguese slave fortress, Roberts presided over what was probably one of the most productive pirate companies in history, taking over 400 vessels before they were captured by the Royal Navy in February 1722. Another *Buck* mutineer was Walter Kennedy, an Irishman inspired to piracy by the tales of Henry Avery. After running his own pirate sloop for a time, he returned to London to enjoy his riches, set up his own brothel on Deptford Road, and dabbled in mugging and other petty crime. He was eventually apprehended and executed for piracy in 1721 at Wapping, where he had been born twenty-six years earlier. One of Kennedy's old shipmates aboard the *Buck*, Thomas Anstis, also became a successful pirate captain, but was killed by his own crew during a 1723 mutiny.

It was Edward England, Vane's first quartermaster, who may have come closest to living out the Avery legend. After parting ways with Vane, England specialized in attacking slave ships on the West Coast of Africa, whose demoralized crews were reliable sources of fresh manpower. He captured nine such vessels in the spring of 1719, and more than a third of their sailors defected to his company. At Cape Corso he nearly captured Lawrence Prince's new command, the 250-ton *Whydah II*, which fled under the guns of a slave fort to avoid following her namesake into piracy. He, like Avery, spent considerable time cruising the Indian Ocean. He raided the shipping of the Moghul Empire and, upon catching a thirty-four-gun ship, named it *Fancy* as Avery had done. In the end, his men deposed him for refusing to allow them to harm their captives, marooning him on one of the islands of Mauritius, east of Africa. England managed to build a raft and conveyed himself to Madagascar, where he lived the rest of his days among Avery's surviving pirates.

～≈～

For the most part, the pirates' nemeses and their high-level collaborators fared worse than the pirates themselves.

After abandoning Rogers in Nassau, Commodore Peter Chamberlaine of HMS *Milford* remained in charge of the Royal Navy's West Indies fleet until June 1720, when he received orders to escort fourteen merchant vessels back to London. On June 28, while passing through the Windward Passage, the fleet encountered a violent storm that drove every vessel ashore on the east end of Cuba. A witness later said, "the shore [was] covered with dead bodies." Two-thirds of the 450 sailors and passengers were killed, including Chamberlaine and the entire complement of the *Milford*, apart from thirty-four sailors, the purser, and a blind cook.

Francis Hume, commander of HMS *Scarborough*, who destroyed the pirate vessels of Martel and La Buse, was rewarded in 1723 with the command of the third-rate *Bedford*, one of only twelve ships of the line then in service. Nonetheless, he shot and killed himself in Scotland "on account of some private discontent" in February 1753.

Vincent Pearse's *Phoenix* was based in New York for many years, allowing him to build many lasting relationships among the leading citizens of that city. These led to his marriage to Mary Morris, the daughter of New Jersey governor Lewis Morris, who owned a vast estate in what is now the Bronx. The marriage was not a happy one. While Pearse was in England, Mary carried on a dalliance with another naval officer. Pearse didn't discover the affair until a few years later, when the couple was living in London. Enraged, he brought her to court for adultery. The scandal was voluminously documented in the Morris family's letters to one another, and descended into a soap opera of lawsuits, countersuits, abortive reconciliation, and intrigue. In 1742, while Pearse fought his wife in London, a New York court ruled against him in a £1,500 lawsuit on an unrelated matter, which likely ruined him. He was probably still quarreling with his wife when he died, in May 1745.

Shortly after killing Blackbeard, Lieutenant Robert Maynard was found to have kept a number of valuables taken from the *Adventure*, having disobeyed a direct order from Captain Gordon to return them to the inventory of seized plunder. His self-aggrandizing accounts of the battle at Ocracoke further discredited him with his superiors and Governor Spotswood, in whose letters praise for the lieutenant is conspicuously absent. Maynard was not promoted to commander for another twenty one years. He eventually made captain and was given command of the sixth-rate *Sheerness* in September 1740, when he must have been an old man. He died in England in 1750.

While cleared of wrongdoing by his governing council, Governor Charles Eden's reputation never recovered from his dealings with Blackbeard. He died of yellow fever at his home in Edenton on March 17, 1722, at the age of forty-nine. His tombstone carried the epitaph: "He brought ye country into a flourishing condition, and died much lamented."

Assisted by the fallout from his invasion of North Carolina, Alexander Spotswood's political enemies succeeded in having him replaced as governor of Virginia. In September 1722, Spotswood retired to his 45,000-acre estate, where he dabbled in iron mining and production. In the 1730s he served as deputy postmaster-general of the American colonies, established postal service between Williamsburg and Philadelphia, and selected Benjamin Franklin to be Pennsylvania's postmaster. In 1740, he was appointed major general and asked to lead a detachment of troops to fight in Spain during the War of the Austrian Succession. On June 7, 1740, while overseeing their departure, he died of fever in Annapolis, Maryland.

Ironically, Lord Archibald Hamilton, the discredited governor of Jamaica, fared better than the rest. He had left Jamaica under arrest, but despite his Jacobite scheming and encouragement of piracy, he was found innocent of all wrongdoing by British courts. In 1721, the Council of Trade and Plantations even ordered the government of Jamaica to pay Hamilton his share of the plunder seized by his privateers in 1716. He married an earl's daughter, retained estates and castles in Ireland and Scotland, and died at his comfortable home on London's Pall Mall in 1754, at the ripe old age of eighty-four, after which he was buried at Westminster Abby. He had long before given up interest in a Stuart restoration, and appears to have done nothing to assist in the final Jacobite uprising in 1745, led by James Stuart's son, Bonnie Prince Charlie.

James Stuart and his son are interred in the crypt of St. Peter's basilica in the Vatican. The descendents of King George occupy the British throne to this day.

❧❧❧

As for Woodes Rogers, he spent the twilight years of the Golden Age of Piracy in London, sickly, indebted, and deeply depressed. "For some time," Rogers later wrote, I was "very much perplexed with the melancholy prospect of [my] affairs." His fellow investors had dissolved their partnership, and neither they nor the government would honor the £6,000 in debts Rogers had incurred on its behalf. In the end, it was his creditors who took pity on him, absolving his debts and getting him out of debtors prison.

In 1722 or 1723, he was approached by a man who was researching a book about the pirates. The author needed Rogers's help to fill in details of the pirate republic that Rogers had put down and, perhaps, share copies of his official letters and reports as governor. Rogers apparently agreed, as the author included information only Rogers could have provided. The result, in May 1724, was the publication of *A General History of the Robberies and Murders of the Most Notorious Pyrates*, which, like so many books of that era, was written under an alias, in this case, "Captain Charles Johnson." English readers were captivated by the activities of the pirates, even as they were taking place. It was an enormous hit on both sides of the Atlantic, going through numerous editions. Articles and advertisements promoting it appeared in London's *Weekly Journal*, as well as the Philadelphia's *American Weekly Mercury*. The book, still in print, almost single-handedly created the popular images of the pirates that remain with us today.

Generations of historians and librarians have erroneously identified Captain Charles Johnson as Daniel Defoe, a contemporary of Rogers and the author of *Robinson Crusoe* and *Captain Singleton*. Recently, Arne Bialuschewski of the University of Kiel in Germany has identified a far more likely candidate: Nathaniel Mist, a former sailor, journalist, and publisher of the *Weekly Journal*. The book's first publisher of record, Charles Rivington, had printed many books for Mist, who lived just a few yards from his office. More importantly, the *General History* was registered at His Majesty's Stationary Office in Mist's name. As a former seaman who had sailed the West Indies, Mist, of all London's writer-publishers, was uniquely qualified to have penned the book, being well aquainted with the maritime world and the settings the pirates had operated in. Mist was also a committed Jacobite and would eventually go into exile in France, serving as a messenger between London and the Stuart court in Rome, which would explain the *General History*'s not entirely unsympathetic account of the maritime outlaws. In 1722–1723 Mist also had the motivation to try to write a bestseller: The *Weekly Journal*'s profits had been languishing for years due to increased competition from rival newspapers.

꣠ꣳ꣠

The publication of *A General History*—which highlighted Rogers's role in dispersing the Bahamian pirates—revived the deposed governor's reputation as a national hero. Readers, including many members of Britain's elite, couldn't help but wonder what had happened to Rogers and were undoubtedly embarrassed to discover how poorly he had been repaid for his patriotic service. It is probably not a coincidence that Rogers's fortunes began to recover not long thereafter. In early 1726 he successfully petitioned the king for redress. Authorities were sympathetic when they read Rogers's plea, which was written in the third person: "He has lost . . . eight years of the prime of his life, by his honest ambition and zeal in serving his country, and is left destitute of money for this surface or any new employ[ment], though no complaint has yet been made of any mal-administration or want of doing his duty." In the end, the king not only awarded Rogers with a pension equivalent to half the salary of an infantry captain, retroactive to June 1721, he also appointed him, in 1728, to a second term as the governor of the Bahamas.

Before leaving for New Providence, Rogers sat for what may have been his only portrait. The painter, William Hogarth, placed Rogers in a romanticized version of Nassau. Rogers, in white wig and an elegant full-length jacket, is seated in a comfortable armchair, his face turned in profile, concealing the disfigurement left by a Spanish musket ball. At his back is the bastion of Fort Nassau, on which an ornamental plaque can be seen which bears his personal motto: DUM SPIRO SPERO, "While I breathe, I hope." Rogers, then fifty, has a globe to his left (symbolizing his circumnavigation) and a pair of dividers in his right hand, with which he is about to take the measurements of the "Island of Providence" from a map held in his son's hand. William Whetstone Rogers, who would accompany his father to Nassau, is standing wearing the wig and elegant clothing of a gentleman. Daughter Sarah Rogers sits to the left, awaiting a servant with a plate of fruit. In the harbor behind them, a large warship lets off a multigun salute.

When Rogers and his son arrived in Nassau on August 25, 1729, Nassau wasn't quite as pleasant as Hogarth had imagined. The island had just been stricken by a hurricane, and many of its residents lay in their battered homes, weakened by contagious fever. The economy and fortifications remained a shambles, and the outgoing governor's wife had upset many of Nassau's inhabitants by trying to use her position to intimidate justices, monopolize shopkeeping, and hire away other people's servants before their terms of indenture had expired. There had been a few improvements in the eight years that Rogers had been away: a new church in the town center, a stone gatehouse at the entrance to the fort, and Government House, a two-story Georgian residence where Rogers would spend the final years of his life.

His final term was easier than the first, but less than relaxing. He wound up locked in a bitter dispute with the representatives to the colony's new governing assembly over the imposition of local taxes. Rogers wished to raise money to repair the fort; the assemblymen did not. Frustrated with their intransigence, Rogers took the extreme step of dissolving the assembly, upsetting local planters. By early 1731, the fight had worn Rogers out. He became ill and, as before, went to Charleston to recover his health. In the meantime, his son, the governing council's clerk, did his best to build the family a proper slave plantation, making several trips to West Africa to purchase the requisite labor force. (He would die from fever in the port of Whydah during such a trip in 1735, while he was serving as one of the Royal Africa Company's three chief merchants.)

Governor Rogers returned to New Providence in May of 1731, but he was never able to truly recover his health. He passed away on July 15, 1732, and was buried in Nassau. His grave has since been lost, but his name adorns the main street on the city's waterfront, and he is honored in the official motto of the Bahamas: EXPULSIS PIRATIS, COMERCIA RESTITUA, "Pirates Expelled, Commerce Restored."

AFTERWORD

Since the initial publication of *The Republic of Pirates* in 2007, I located some additional documents that help resolve a few minor mysteries in regards to the Bahamian pirates and their nemesis, Woodes Rogers. I take the opportunity to share these with readers of this revised North American edition.

Those researching the Golden Age pirates are rightly nervous about relying on *A General History of the Pyrates*. It's been shown to have passages that are either extremely accurate and or entirely fictitious, and there is a great deal of intriguing material that has yet to be shown to be one or the other. I'm pleased to be able to confirm, using more reliable sources, another of the book's iconic accounts. **Stede Bonnet** really did embark on his pirate's life nocturnally and aboard his own vessel. "There is also or has been lately over on the [North American] coast a pirate sloop from Barbados commanded by one Major Bonnet, who has an estate on that island," Captain Benjamin Candler of the HMS *Winchelsea* wrote the Admiralty in the summer of 1717. "The sloop is his own. This advice I had from a letter thence, that in April last he ran away out of Carlisle Bay in the night and had aboard 126 men and 6 guns . . . and ammunition enough."*

The following winter, Bonnet and **Blackbeard** vanished from the

* ADM 1/1471, f15: Benjamin Candler to the Admiralty, HMS *Winchelsea* off Crooked Islands, Bahamas: 19 July 1717.

historical record for several months, leaving historians to speculate as to where he was and what he was doing. While writing the book, I made the case that the two were in the Gulf of Mexico, based on previously neglected accounts in London newspapers. Fleet Street, it turns out, was well informed.

A series of letters and legal depositions forwarded to the Admiralty by another naval captain indicate Blackbeard was stalking the South Seas Company ship *Royal Prince* and her escort, HMS *Diamond*, which the documents show were in the Mexican port of Vera Cruz on a high-profile trading mission from October 1717 to February 1718. The *Royal Prince* was what we would now call a "terrorist target of symbolic importance." She was the first ship to trade in the Spanish Americas under the provisions of the Treaty of Utrecht and, at her launch, King George and his court were feted on board. Her mission was considered so critical to royal prestige that the *Diamond* had been ordered to convoy her all the way from Madera, her captain's letters show.*

Blackbeard never came across the ship, probably because he gave up prematurely. The documents place him on Roatán—in Honduras's Bay Islands—in early February 1718. There he captured several English merchant vessels and cleaned and refitted his flagship, the *Queen Anne's Revenge*. One of his captives, Martin Preston, later reported that Thatch's crew "often threatened to take his majesty's ship the *Diamond*, as they heard she was weakly manned." Blackbeard's intelligence was excellent. The letters of the frigate's commander, Captain Thomas Jacob, indicate his crew had been critically weakened by tropical diseases on their trip from Jamaica to Vera Cruz.†

Another captive, William Wade, reported that the pirates also boasted they would overwhelm another vessel, the thirty-six-gun HMS *Adventure*, the largest British warship in the Caribbean at the time. He

---

* ADM 1/1982, f4: Thomas Jacobs to Secretary Burchett, Madera: 26 August 1717.

† ADM 1/1982, f4: Thomas Jacobs to the Admiralty, Port Royal: 27 March 1718; Declaration of Martin Preston, Kingston: 20 May 1718.

also testified that 70 of Blackbeard's 250 crewmen were of African descent, further evidence that blacks aboard the *Queen Anne's Revenge* were fellow pirates, not pirate cargo.*

I've long suspected that the future revelations about these pirates will come from the largely unexplored French and Spanish archives. Mike Daniel, the underwater explorer who discovered the remains of the *Queen Anne's Revenge* off North Carolina in 1996, recently shared one such discovery with me: French eyewitness accounts of Blackbeard's last known act of piracy, the capture of two French vessels bound home with a load of Martinique sugar. In this engagement—which I described in detail in a February 2014 cover story for *Smithsonian*—Blackbeard displays some cunning tactics in the engagement, and, once again, threatens his captives without actually harming any of them. There's even a promise to throw them into the sea—a common atrocity among slave ship captains at the time—which might form the kernel of the legend of pirates having people walk the plank.†￼ I suspect we'll gain additional insights from these and other untapped archival sources in the coming decade.

I can also shed some more light on why **Woodes Rogers** lost his governorship of the Bahamas. As related in this book, in late 1720 Rogers fought a duel in South Carolina with the captain of HMS *Flamborough* over an unspecified disagreement they had had in Nassau earlier that year. On a subsequent trip to the National Archives in Kew, I located the letters of that captain, John Hildesley, which describe in detail what happened in Nassau. It's an account that puts Rogers in an extremely unfavorable light.

The *Flamborough* was the only Royal Navy warship in the Bahamas at the time of the Spanish invasion, and her young commander threw himself into the island's defense. As Hildesley later explains in his let-

---

* ADM 1/1982, f4: Declaration of William Wade, Kingston: 15 May 1718.

† Mike Daniel, president, Maritime Research Institute, personal communications, April and May 2013; Colin Woodard, "The Last Days of Blackbeard," *Smithsonian*, February 2014, pp. 32–41.

ters, during the attack he sent some of his men aboard Rogers's armed merchant ship, *Delicia*, "there being no watch aboard her." Rogers responded in the most bizarre fashion: he ordered the guns of Fort Nassau to be trained on the *Flamborough* and had Hildesley and his first officer arrested! Immediately after the invasion, Hildesley writes, Rogers challenged Hildesley to a duel, but then failed to appear at the appointed time. Rogers also allegedly encouraged "a mob" to attack the *Flamborough*'s first officer on the streets of Nassau.

In his letter to the Admiralty, Hildesley's tone is apologetic, an indication the young officer feared he—not Rogers—would be the one facing demotion. "If my ignorance of the extent of my commission had led me into any error in this affair . . . I humbly [hope] their Lordships will be pleased to excuse what I have done . . . and consider me as a young officer who may better know how to act . . ." He even enumerated the possible grievances Rogers could have had against him, all of them involving questions of whether Rogers had the right to order a naval captain around. (He did not.) Rogers may have been particularly incensed by Hildesley having refused to attack Havana, even though it would have been a suicide mission for the twenty-four-gun vessel.*

By this time, Rogers had already offended the captains of HMS *Milford*, *Rose*, and *Shark*. By threatening one of the king's ships and arresting her commander, Rogers likely prompted the Admiralty to move against him in London. It strengthens the impression that Rogers, while brave and patriotic, had an erratic streak that turned many would-be allies against him.

Freeport, Maine,
November 2014

---

* ADM 1/1880: Johnathan Hildesley to the Admiralty, Nassau: 25 March 1720.

ACKNOWLEDGMENTS

THE REPUBLIC OF PIRATES is a history and, as such, has benefited from the work of generations of historians, archivists, genealogists, scribes, and scribblers. Our understanding of the Golden Age of Piracy would be impoverished had John Campbell not founded the Boston News-Letter in 1704 and decided to regularly cover the pirates' activities in the years following the War of Spanish Succession. Some of these dispatches made their way to London, where they joined the accounts of governors and other colonial officials in the files of the Council of Trade and Plantations and of the secretary of state for America and the West Indies. The captains of Royal Navy warships also collected intelligence on the pirates, and their letters and logbooks were eventually delivered to the Admiralty. When colonial authorities succeeded in capturing pirates, copies of the resulting trials were usually sent home to London. There, much of this mountain of information was made available to the anonymous author of A General History of the Pyrates, whose account still dominates discourse on the Bahamian pirates, nearly three centuries after its publication.

The General History remains an impressive work of scholarship, skillfully integrating documentary records with material clearly gathered from interviews with Woodes Rogers and other principals. It is, however, riddled with errors, exaggerations, and misunderstandings, most of which were not detected until the twentieth century, when historians finally got around to reviewing the original records for themselves. British scholars Sir John William Fortescue (1859–1938) and Cecil Headlam (1872–1934) spent years assembling the relevant volumes of the *Calendar of State Papers, Colonial Series*, which contain excerpts and summaries of many of the most important documents in the British archives; in effect, they created a treasure map that has helped countless researchers locate and recover parts of America's past, long buried in a million sheets of quill-and-ink handwriting. I am indebted to them and to the work of historians who followed their leads, including Robert E. Lee's *Blackbeard the Pirate: A Reappraisal of His Life and Times* (1974), Robert Ritchie's *Captain Kidd and the War Against the Pirates* (1986), and Bryan Little's *Crusoe's Captain*, published in 1960 and still the finest biography of Woodes Rogers.

I have also benefited from the advice, generosity, and encouragement of several of the world's leading pirate scholars. Marcus Rediker of the University of Pittsburgh helped me locate many hard-to-find sources and shared of his firsthand experience in conducting research at the new National Archives complex near London's Kew Gardens; his *Villains of All Nations* and *Between the Devil and the Deep Blue Sea* built the foundations for the study of pirates from their own perspective, rather than from that of their adversaries. Kenneth J. Kinkor of the Expedition Whydah Museum in Provincetown, Massachusetts, knows more about Samuel Bellamy than the pirate's own parents did, and he kindly shared a great number of document transcriptions, saving me weeks of work and a good deal of gasoline. Joel Baer of Macalester College in St. Paul, the leading authority on Henry Avery, graciously entertained my queries and supplied me with missing pages from some of the hard-to-find pirate trials; researchers will welcome his forthcoming *British Piracy in the Golden Age*. My deepest thanks to all three of you: Immersing oneself in the past can be isolating, but you helped make it a congenial experience.

The same can be said for others who helped me along the way. Gail Swanson of Sebring, Florida, took the time to copy and send a package of translations of documents, from the Archive of the West Indies in Seville, relating to the Spanish treasure fleet of 1715. Also in Florida, Mike Daniel took the time to help clarify French accounts of Blackbeard's capture of *La Concorde*. Rodney Broome of Seattle shared valuable suggestions on what and whom to see in his native Bristol. Shep and Tara Smith of Norfolk, Virginia, put a roof over my head while I went to and from my sojourns in the Carolinas, while Abel Bates and my in-laws, Larry and Andrea Sawyer, arranged the same for me on outer Cape Cod. Daniel Howden introduced me to his neighborhood in London's East End, a welcome respite from days spent reading fading ink on old parchment.

I am especially grateful to the staff of the Portland Public Library, whose interlibrary loan office kept me supplied with hard-to-find volumes throughout this project, and to the people of Maine, whose tax dollars support Maine Info Net, our extraordinary statewide lending system; knowledge is power. Also in Maine, I am grateful to the Hawthorne-Longfellow Library at Bowdoin College for repeatedly loaning their bound volumes of the *Calendar of State Papers* and for access to microfilms of early English newspapers; to the Ladd Library at Bates College, for making available films of early American newspapers; and to the Maine Historical Society Research Library in Portland, the Maine State Library in Augusta, and the Fogler Library at the University of Maine in Orono. I also benefited from resources at the Dimond Library of the University of New Hampshire in Durham, and the Widener Library at Harvard University, where the few surviving copies of the *Jamaica Courant* reside on an all-too-short roll of film. In North Carolina, thanks to the staff of the Bath Museum and to David Moore and his colleagues at the North Carolina Maritime Museum in Beaufort; I hope that wreck proves to be the *Queen Anne's Revenge*. In England, my thanks to the remarkably efficient staff of the National Archives in Kew, especially Geoff Baxter for having a great stack of captains' logs waiting for me on my first day—your document retrieval system is the standard by which all others should be measured. Thanks also to the staff of the Bristol Records Office for indulging my searches for Teaches, Thatches, and Rogers on a gray December afternoon.

My friend and colleague Samuel Loewenberg in Berlin tirelessly reviewed various versions of the manuscript and provided valuable suggestions and feedback—thanks, Sam, I really needed that extra pair of eyes. Thanks also to Brent Askari of Portland for helping to smooth the edges of those rough early drafts. Any errors that remain are, of course, my own.

This book would not be possible were it not for the advice and acumen of Jill Grinberg, the finest agent in New York City; the enthusiasm and support of Timothy Bent, my original editor at Harcourt, now at Oxford University Press; and Andrea Schulz, whose skill, care, and attentiveness ensured a smooth editorial transition. I'm also grateful for the work of David Hough at Harcourt, copy editor Margaret Jones, and Jojo Gragasin, of LoganFrancis Design, who created the maps and illustrations that appear within.

Last and certainly not least, thanks to my parents for their love and support, and to my wife, Sarah Skillin Woodard, who read the manuscript countless times and helped shape it into the book you now hold in your hands; thank you, my dearest, for your patience, support, and suggestions throughout this process, and for saying "I do" along the way.

New Year's Day, 2007
Portland, Maine

ENDNOTES

ABBREVIATIONS

ADM1/1471–2649: Admiralty Records, Letters from Captains, National Archives, Kew, UK.

ADM33/298: Navy Board Pay Office, Ship's Pay Books, National Archives, Kew, UK

ADM33/311: Navy Board Pay Office, Ship's Pay Books, National Archives, Kew, UK

ADM51/606: Admiralty Records, Captain's Logs, *Milford*, 16 Jan 1718 to 31 Dec 1719, National Archives, Kew, UK.

ADM51/672: Admiralty Records, Captain's Logs, *Pearl*, 26 July 1715 to 8 Dec 1719, National Archives, Kew, UK.

ADM51/690: Admiralty Records, Captain's Logs, *Phoenix*, 8 Oct 1715 to 6 Oct 1721, National Archives, Kew, UK.

ADM51/801: Admiralty Records, Captain's Logs, *Rose*, 18 Jan 1718 to 9 May 1721, National Archives, Kew, UK.

ADM51/865: Admiralty Records, Captain's Logs, *Scarborough*, 11 Oct 1715 to 5 Sept 1718, National Archives, Kew, UK.

ADM51/877: Admiralty Records, Captain's Logs, *Seaford*, 19 Sept 1716 to 22 Sept 1720, National Archives, Kew, UK.

ADM51/892: Admiralty Records, Captain's Logs, *Shark*, 18 Jan 1718 to 23 Aug 1722, National Archives, Kew, UK.

ADM51/4250: Admiralty Records, Captain's Logs, *Lyme*, 23 Feb 1717 to 14 Aug 1719, National Archives, Kew, UK.

C104/160: Chancery Records, Creagh v. Rogers, Accounts of the Duke & Dutchess, 1708–1711, National Archives, Kew, UK.

CO5/508: Colonial Office Records: South Carolina Shipping Returns, 1717–1719, National Archives, Kew, UK.

CO5/1265: Colonial Office Records: Documents relating to Woodes Rogers's appointment, National Archives, Kew, UK.

CO5/1442: Colonial Office Records: Virginia Shipping Returns, 1715–1727, National Archives, Kew, UK.

CO23/1: Colonial Office Records: Bahamas Correspondence, 1717–1725, National Archives, Kew, UK.

CO23/12: Colonial Office Records: Bahamas, Misc. Records, 1696–1731, National Archives, Kew, UK.

CO23/13: Colonial Office Records: Bahamas, Letters from Governors, 1718–1727, National Archives, Kew, UK.

CO37/10: Colonial Office Records: Bermuda Correspondence, 1716–1723, National Archives, Kew, UK.

CO137/12: Colonial Office Records: Jamaica Correspondence, 1716–1718, National Archives, Kew, UK.

CO142/14: Colonial Office Records: Jamaica Shipping Returns, 1709–1722, National Archives, Kew, UK.

CO152/12: Colonial Office Records: Leeward Islands Correspondence, 1718–1719, National Archives, Kew, UK.

CSPCS 1696–1697: John W Fortescue, ed., *Calendar of State Papers, Colonial Series: America and the West Indies: 15 May 1696 to October1697* (Vol. 10), London: His Majesty's Stationary Office, 1904.

CSPCS 1697–1698: John W Fortescue, ed., *Calendar of State Papers, Colonial Series: America and the West Indies, 27 October 1697 to 31 December 1698* (Vol. 11), London: His Majety's Stationary Office, 1905.

CSPCS 1712–1714: Cecil Headlam, ed., *Calendar of State Papers, Colonial Series: America and the West Indies, July 1712 to July 1714* (Vol. 27), London: His Majesty's Stationary Office, 1926.

CSPCS 1716–1717: Cecil Headlam, ed., *Calendar of State Papers, Colonial Series: America and the West Indies, January 1716 to July 1717* (Vol. 29), London: His Majesty's Stationary Office, 1930.

CSPCS 1717–1718: Cecil Headlam, ed., *Calendar of State Papers, Colonial Series: America and the West Indies, August 1717 to December 1718* (Vol. 30), London: His Majesty's Stationary Office, 1930.

CSPCS 1719–1720: Cecil Headlam, ed., *Calendar of State Papers, Colonial Series: America and the West Indies, January 1719 to February 1720* (Vol. 31), London: His Majesty's Stationary Office, 1933.

CSPCS 1720–1721: Cecil Headlam, ed., *Calendar of State Papers, Colonial Series: America and the West Indies, March 1720 to December 1721* (Vol. 32), London: His Majesty's Stationary Office, 1933.

CSPCS 1722–1723: Cecil Headlam, ed., *Calendar of State Papers, Colonial Series: America and the West Indies, 1722–1723* (Vol. 33), London: His Majesty's Stationary Office, 1934.

E190/1164/2: Exchequer Records: Port Books, Bristol, 1708, National Archives, Kew, UK.

GHP: Charles Johnson, *A General History of the Pyrates*, ed. Manuel Schonhorn, Columbia, SC: University of South Carolina Press, 1972.

HCA1/54: High Court Admiralty Records: Examinations of Pirates and Other Criminals, 1710–1721, National Archives, Kew, UK.

HCA1/55: High Court Admiralty Records: Examinations of Pirates and Other Criminals, 1721–1725, National Archives, Kew, UK.

SAT: Translations of Spanish and Vatican Documents from the Archive of the West Indies, Seville, Spain; overseen by Jack Haskins, Kip Wagner, and others. Unpublished manuscript: Islamorda Public Library, Islamorda, Florida.

TEP: *The Trials of Eight Persons Indited for Piracy*, Boston: John Edwards, 1718.

TJR: *The Tryals of Captain John Rackham and other Pirates*, Kingston, Jamaica: Robert Baldwin, 1720.

TSB: *The Tryals of Major Stede Bonnet and Other Pirates*. London: Benjamin Cowse, 1719.

PROLOGUE

1 **Pirate sentiments and American Revolution:** The Golden Age pirates were, of course, long gone by 1776, but the spirit of maritime rebellion persisted throughout the century. Disgruntled sailors and African Americans led riots and mob actions against Royal Navy press gangs in Boston in 1747 and 1768; Newport, Rhode Island, and Portland, Maine, in 1764; New York in 1764 and 1765; and Norfolk, Virginia, in 1767. In the 1747 riot—which lasted for three days—slaves, servants, and seamen stormed the Boston Town House, forced the governor to flee his home, beat up the sheriff, and detained a naval officer. Sailors also led the resistance to the Stamp Act and the angry Boston mob that was fired upon by British soldiers in what became known as the Boston Massacre. See Jesse Lemisch, "Jack Tar in the Streets: Merchant Seamen in the Politics of Revolutionary America," *William & Mary Quarterly*, 3rd Series, Vol. 25, No. 3, July 1968, pp. 371–407.

2 **Disability benefits:** Marcus Rediker, *Villains of All Nations: Atlantic Pirates in the Golden Age*, Boston: Beacon Press, 2005, pp. 73–74.

4 **Kinkor quote:** Author's Interview, Kenneth J. Kinkor, Provincetown, MA: 15 June 2005.

4 **Quote from Bermuda Governor:** Benjamin Bennett to the Council of Trade and Plantations, Bermuda: 31 May 1718 in *CSPCS 1717–1718*, No. 551, p. 261.

4 **Captain of *Seaford*'s fears:** Walter Hamilton to the Council of Trade and Plantations, Antigua: 15 May 1717 in *CSPCS 1716–1717*, No. 568, p. 300.

5 **Pirate sympathizers:** Alexander Spotswood to Lord Carteret, Williamsburg, VA: 14 February 1719 in R. A. Brock (ed), *The Official Letters of Alexander Spottswood*, Vol. I, Richmond, VA: Virginia Historical Society, 1882, p. 274.

CHAPTER ONE: THE LEGEND

10 **Arrival of sloop at Nassau:** Examination of John Dann, 3 August 1696, in John Franklin Jameson, *Privateering and Piracy in the Colonial Period: Illustrative Documents*, New York: Macmillan Co., 1923, pp. 169–170.

11 **Nassau described (1696):** John Oldmixon, *The British Empire in America*, London: J. Brotherten, 1741, pp. 428–431.

11 **Rumors of French capture:** "The Case of Nicholas Trott," 25 October 1698, in *CSPCS 1697–1698*, No. 928, p. 506; Michael Craton, *A History of the Bahamas*, London: Collins, 1962, pp. 86–87.

11 **Navy not at Bahamas for years:** Oldmixon, p. 429.

11 **Fort Nassau, difficulty of manning:** Oldmixon, pp. 429–430.

12 **Contents of letter carried by Adams:** "The Trial of Joseph Dawson, Edward Forseith, William May, William Bishop, James Lewis and John Sparkes at the Old Baily for Felony and Piracy," London: 19 October 1696, in Francis Hargrave, *A Complete Collection of State Trials and Proceedings*, Volume V, London: T. Wright, 1777 p. 10; "The Case of Nicholas Trott," p. 506; Examination of John Dean, pp. 169–170; Affidavit of Phillip Middleton, London: 11 November 1696, in Jameson, pp. 171–173.

12 **Notes on the conversion of Spanish currencies to English pounds:** At the time, a Spanish peso or piece of eight was worth 5 shillings or £0.25 according to Phillip A Bruce, *Economic History of Virginia in the Seventeenth Century*, New York: MacMillan & Co., 1896, pp.

503, 507, 510–11; Each "piece of gold" is presumed to be equivalent to a Spanish pistole; according to John Condiuitt, *Observations upon the present state of our Gold and Silver Coins* (1730), a pistole was worth 32 ryals.

12 **Salary of governor:** In 1713, North Carolina, a minor colony owned by the same aristocrats who owned the Bahamas, paid their governor an annual salary of £300. Warrant from the Lord Proprietors to Daniel Richardson, St. James's Palace, London: 13 August 1713 in *CSPCS 1712–1714*, item No. 451, p. 219.

12–13 **Trott meets with his Council:** "The Case of Nicholas Trott," pp. 506–507.

13 **Trott's "very civil" letter:** Affidavit of Phillip Middleton, p. 172; Hargrave (V), p. 10.

13 **Avery's "tip" to Trott:** Affidavit of Phillip Middleton, p. 173.

13 **Trott's later claims of innocence:** "The Case of Nicholas Trott," pp. 506–507.

13–14 **Trott orders emptying of *Fancy,* crewing by Africans:** Affidavit of Phillip Middleton, pp. 172–173.

14–15 **Henry Avery's early life and career:** Joel H. Baer, " 'Captain John Avery' and the Anatomy of a Mutiny," *Eighteenth Century Life*, Vol. 18 (February 1994), pp. 3–4.

15 **Avery joins *Charles* II:** Ibid., pp. 4–5.

15 **Getting to, delays in La Coruña:** Ibid., pp. 5–6.

15–16 **Petitions to Houblon and his response:** Ibid., pp. 8–9, 11.

16 **William May's offer and Gibson's response:** Ibid., p. 9.

16 **Crews feel they've been sold to the Spanish:** Ibid., p. 9.

16–17 **Description of mutiny:** Ibid., pp. 13–14; Hargrave (V), p. 6.

17–18 **Avery speaks to Gibson, Gravet:** Hargrave (V), pp. 6–8.

18 **Meeting of the ship's company:** Baer (1994), p. 15.

18 **Privateering vs. piracy shares:** For examples see Gomer Williams, *History of the Liverpool Privateers and Letters of Marque with an Account of the Liverpool Slave Trade*, Montreal: McGill-Queen's Press, 2004, p. 31; Angus Kostram, *Privateers & Pirates 1730–1830*, Oxford, UK: Osprey Publishing, 2001, p. 20.

18–19 ***Fancy* at Moia:** Examination of John Dann, 3 August 1696, in Jameson, p. 165; Hargrave (V), p. 10.

19 **Avery declaration not to harm English:** in Declaration of Henry Avery to All English Commanders, Johanna, Comoro Islands: 28 February 1694, enclosed within Petition of the East India Company to the Lord Justices, London: July 1696, in Jameson, p. 154.

19 **Captures, atrocities en route to Red Sea:** Examination of John Dann, pp. 165–167; Hargrave (V), pp. 8–10; Examination of Peter Claus in *CSPCS 1697–1698*, No. 404ii, p. 184.

20–21 **Meeting with privateers, fleet slips past:** Examination of John Dann, pp. 167–168; Hargrave (V), pp. 9–10.

21 **Capture of the *Fath Muhmamadi*:** Examination of John Dann, p. 168; Hargrave (V), p. 10.

21 **Attack on the *Ganj-i-sawai*:** Hargrave (V), pp. 9–10.

22 **Captain Ibrahim has Turkish concubines fight:** "Khafi Khan" in H. M. Elliot and John Dawson, *The History of India as Told by its Own Historians*, Volume VII, London: Trubner, 1867–1877, pp. 421–422.

22–23 **Legendary accounts of aftermath aboard *Ganj-i-sawai*:** *The Life and Adventures of Captain John Avery*, London: 1709, pp. 30–32.

23 **Accounts of atrocities aboard *Ganj-i-sawai*:** "Abstract of East India Company Letters from Bombay," 12 October 1695 in Jameson, pp. 158–159; "Khafi Khan" in *The History of India as Told by its Own Historians*, Volume VII, pp. 421–423.

23 Split of plunder at Réunion, shares of £1,000: Hargrave (V), p. 10; Examination of John Dann, p. 169.

24 Seven men stay at Nassau: John Graves to the Council of Trade and Plantations, New Providence, Bahamas: 11 May 1698, in CSPCS 1697–1698, No. 444, p. 208.

24 Party on the Isaac, others to Charleston: Examination of John Dann, p. 170.

24 Avery's purchase of Sea Flower: Examination of John Dann, p. 170.

24 Trott disposes of Fancy: Affidavit of Phillip Middleton, p. 174.

24 Trott's claims "they could give no information," governor of Jamaica "gave no proof": "Case of Nicholas Trott . . . ," pp. 506–507.

24–25 Avery's men at Philadelphia: Robert Snead to Sir John Houblon, 29 September 1697, in CSPCS 1696–97 No. 1331, pp. 613–615; Edward Randolph to William Popple, New York: 12 May 1698, in CSPCS 1697–98, No. 451, pp. 211–212; Narrative of Captain Robert Snead, in CSPCS 1697–98, No. 451i, pp. 212–214; Information of Thomas Robinson, in CSPCS 1697–98, No. 451ii, pp. 214–215.

25 Isaac party in West Ireland: Examination of John Dann, p. 171; "Abstract of Letters from Ireland," in Jameson, pp. 160–164.

25–26 Sea Flower and Avery in North Ireland: Examination of John Dann, pp. 170–171.

26 John Dan in England: Examination of John Dann, pp. 170–171.

26 Executions: Hargrave (V), p. 18.

26–27 Legends of Avery: Charles Johnson, The Successful Pyrate, London: Bernard Lintott, 1713, pp. 3–4; The Life and Adventures . . . pp. 46–7, 57–59.

27 Account in A General History of the Pyrates: GHP, pp. 49–50, 56–57.

CHAPTER TWO : GOING TO SEA

28 Bellamy birth: Kenneth J. Kinkor, "The Whydah Sourcebook," unpublished document, Provincetown: Whydah Museum, Provincetown, MA: 2003, p. 355; Parish register printouts of Hittisleigh, Devon, England christenings, 1673–1837, FHL Film 933371, Item 4, Provo, UT: Church of Jesus Christ of Latter-day Saints Genealogical Society. Microfilm.

29 Hittisleigh described: The National Gazeteer of Great Britain and Ireland, London, Virtue, 1868.

29 Quotes on Devon soils: [Daniel Defoe] A Tour Thro' the Whole Island of Great Britain, 4th ed., London: S. Birt, et al., 1768, pp. 360–361.

29 Uses of Commons described: Jane Humphries, "Enclosures, Common Rights, and Women: The Proletarianization of Families in the Late Eighteenth and Early Nineteenth Centuries," The Journal of Economic History, Vol. 50, No. 1, March 1990, pp. 17–42.

29 Man's wages equal to dairy cow production: Ibid., p. 24.

29–30 Quotes from "traveler" and Bacon: M. Dorothy George, England in Transition, Baltimore: Penguin, 1953, pp. 12, 15.

30 Half the English population barely surviving (1689): David Ogg, England in the Reigns of James II and William III, Oxford, UK: Oxford University Press, 1969, pp. 33–34.

30 Poor half the life expectancy of the rich: Ogg, pp. 34–35.

30 Poor six inches shorter than the rich: John Komlos, "On English Pygmies and Giants: The Physical Stature of English Youth in the late-18th and early-19th Centuries," Discussion Paper 2005-06, Munich: Department of Economics, University of Munich, April 2005.

30 Vane lived in Port Royal: *TJR*, p. 27.

31 A third of pirates from London: Marcus Rediker, *Villains of All Nations: Atlantic Pirates in the Golden Age*, Boston: Beacon Press, 2004, p. 51.

31 London in 1700: Ogg, 132; Maureen Waller, *1700: Scenes from London Life*, New York: Four Walls, Eight Windows, 2000, pp. 1–4.

31 Churches crowded by trade: *New State of England*, 4th ed., London: R. J., 1702, p. 149.

32 Floating forest of masts: Ibid., p. 149.

32 Wapping on the Ooze: John Stow as quoted in Sir Walter Besant, *The Thames*, London: Adam & Charles Black, 1903, p. 110.

32 Crowded conditions, mass graves, coal in Wapping: E. N. Williams, *Life in Georgian England*, London: B. T. Batsford, Ltd., 1962, pp. 113–114.

32 Dead animals putrefy: Waller, p. 95.

32 Disease and death rates: Waller, pp. 96–102; includes a photograph, "A General Bill of all the Christenings and Burials from the 19 of December 1699 to the 17 of December 1700."

32 Baby and child survival rates: Waller, p. 62.

33 Renting out babies to beggars: *A Trip Through the Town*, London: J. Roberts, 1705.

33 Climbing boys: J. P. Andrews, *An Appeal to the Humane on behalf of the most deplorable class of society, the Climbing Boys*, London: John Stockdale, 1788, pp. 8–9, 30–31.

33 Blackguards: Edward Ward, *The London Spy*, London: The Folio Society, 1955, Originally published 1698–1700, pp. 27–28.

33 Prominent craftsmen described: *An Account of a Dreadful and Amazing Fire*, London: Edward Harrison, 1703. Pamphlet.

35 Descriptions of Wapping executions: David Cordingly, *Under the Black Flag*, New York: Harcourt, 1997, p. 224; Richard Zacks, *The Pirate Hunter*, New York: Hyperion, 2002, pp. 386–392.

35 Last words of John Sparcks et al.: *An Account of the Behavior, Dying Speeches and Execution of Mr. John Murphy, for High Treason, and William May, John Sparkes, William Bishop, James Lewis, and Adam Forseith, for Robbery, Piracy, and Felony*, London: T. Crownfield, 1696.

36 Seamen in short supply, accounting for two-thirds: R. D. Manning, *Queen Anne's Navy*, London: Navy Records Society, 1961, p. 170.

36 Navy's bounty for volunteers: Ibid., p. 170.

36 "sea for pleasure, hell for pastime": Rediker (1987), p. 13.

36 Quote on spirits: Edward Barlow quoted in Ibid., p. 81.

36 Spirits and crimps: Ibid., pp. 43, 81–82.

37 Edward Ward describes sailors: Ward (1955), pp. 249–250.

37 Sailor avoiding press quote: Christopher Lloyd, *The British Seaman 1200–1860: A Social Survey*, Rutherford, NJ: Fairleigh Dickinson University Press, 1970, p. 104.

37 Methods of avoiding the press: *A Copy of the Marquis of Carmarthen's Method for the Speedy Manning Her Majesty's Royal Navy and for Encouraging Seamen*, Speech given 12 February 1705, London: John Humfreys, 1706, pp. 3–4.

37 Sailors go abroad to avoid press: Lloyd (1970), p. 109; Marquis Carmarthen, p. 2.

37 Press leader get 20s a head: John Dennis, *An Essay on the Navy*, London: John Nutt, 1702, p. 32.

37 Press gangs break into homes: Marques Carmarthen, p. 3, Dennis, p. 32.

37 Pressing sailors from incoming ships: Lloyd (1970), pp. 108–109.

37 Sailors mutiny to avoid impressments: Ibid., pp. 142–143.

38 Whipping ship's boys on colliers: Dennis, p. 33.

38 Capturing tradesmen and quote on that: Ibid., p. 32.

38 Beggars fair game, wealthier exempt: R. D. Merriman, *Queen Anne's Navy*, London: Navy Records Society, 1961, p. 172.

38 Blackbeard's birthdate and place: *GHP*, p. 71; Robert E. Lee, *Blackbeard the Pirate: A Reappraisal of His Life and Times*, Winston-Salem, NC: John F. Blair, 1974, pp. 175–176n.

38 Bristol tax assesment of 1696: Elizabeth Ralph and Mary E. Williams, *The Inhabitants of Bristol in 1696*, Bristol, UK: Bristol Records Society, 1968. The author also examined partial tax records from the 1690s at the Bristol Records Office.

38 Thatch of Gloucester: Lease of Martin Nelme to Thomas Thatch and Charles Dymock, Bristol: 27 November 1712, Bristol Records Office, Bristol, UK, Document 00452/12b; Marriage Settlement of Martin Nelme, Bristol: 28 November 1712, Bristol Records Office, Bristol, UK, Document 00452/12a.

39 Physical appearance of Blackbeard: CO 152/12, No. 67iii: Deposition of Henry Bostock, St. Christopher, Leeward Islands: 19 December 1717.

39 Bristol described: Roger H. Leech, *The Topography of Medieval and Early Modern Bristol, Part I*, Bristol, UK: Bristol Record Society, 1997; Author visit, Bristol, November 2005; Frank Shipsides and Robert Wall, *Bristol: Maritime City*, Bristol, UK: Redcliffe Press, 1981, pp. 47–50.

40 Ogg quote on sailors: Ogg, p. 328.

40 Samuel Johnson quote: James Boswell, *The Life of Samuel Johnson*, London: 1791, p. 876.

40 Hazards presented by cargo: Rediker (1987), pp. 89, 91, 93.

40 Barlow quotes on climbing rigging: Quoted in Lloyd (1970), p. 106.

40 Large numbers died from falling, etc: Rediker (1987), pp. 92–93.

40–41 Sailor's clothes: G. E. Manwaring, *The Flower of England's Garland*, London: Philip Allan & Co., 1935, pp. 157–169; Edward Ward, *The Wooden World Dissected*, 3rd ed., London: M. Cooper, 1744, p. 70.

41 Hans Sloane on sunburns: Hans Sloane, *A Voyage to the Islands of Madera, Barbados, Nieves, St Christopher's and Jamaica*, Vol. I, London: B. M., 1707, p. 25.

41 Sailor's quarters, vermin: Rediker (1987), pp. 160–161; Stephen R. Brown, *Scurvy: How a surgeon, a mariner, and a Gentleman solved the Greatest Medical Mystery of the Age*, New York: St Martin's Press, 2003, pp. 14–15.

41 Passenger's quote on cabin conditions (1750): Gottlieb Mittelberger as quoted in John Duffy, "The Passage to the Colonies," *Mississippi Valley Historical Review*, Vol. 38. No. 1 (June 1951), p. 23.

41 Sailor's food and drink: Rediker (1987), pp. 127–128; "mouldy and stinking" Edward Barlow quoted in Lloyd (1970), p. 108; Web site on HMS *Victory* (1797) at www.stvincent.ac.uk/Heritage/1797/Victory/food.html.

41 Planned shortages of food: Rediker (1987), p. 143.

41–42 Starvation accounts: "Dispatch from *Dublin Post-Boy* of 11 March," *Boston News-Letter*, 1 May 1729, p. 1; "Boston Dispatch, November 4," *Boston News-Letter*, 6 November 1729, p. 2.

42 Brutal discipline accounts: Rediker (1987), pp. 215–221.

42 Sadistic Captain Jeane account: *The Tryal of Captain Jeane of Bristol*, London: T. Warner, 1726, pp. 5–7.

43 Royal Navy punishments: *Instructions*, London: [for the Admiralty], 1714, p. 27; Dudley Pope, *Life in Nelson's Navy*, London: Unwin Irwin, 1987.

43 Mortality in slavers, Navy: Rediker (1987), pp. 32–33, 47–48, 92–93.

43 Shortchanging sailors: Rediker (1987), pp. 144–146.

44 Navy wages: Lloyd (1970), pp. 107–108; Merriman, pp. 171–173; Rediker (1987), p. 33.

44 Woodes Rogers's childhood home in Bristol: Ralph and Williams, p. 107.

44 Rogers born in 1679: His birth records have not survived, but his younger siblings were born in 1680 and 1688. We know he was "about twenty-five" at the time of his 1705 marriage in London. See Little, p. 18.

44–45 Rogers family history in Poole: Newton Wade, "Capt. Woodes Rogers," Notes and Queries, Vol. 149, Number 22, 28 November 1925, p. 389; Manwaring (1935), pp. 92–93; Bryan Little, Crusoe's Captain, London: Odham's Press, 1960, pp. 15–17.

45 Poole oysters and fishing: A Tour Through the Whole Island of Great Britain, pp. 346–347; on the Newfoundland fish trade see Michael Harris, Lament for an Ocean, Toronto: McClelland & Stewart, 1998, pp. 42–43.

45 Woods Rogers senior in Africa: Captain [Woodes] Rogers to William Dampier, circa 1695, as excerpted in William Dampier, Dampier's Voyages, Volume II, John Masefield, ed., London: E. Grant Richards, 1906, pp. 202–203, 321–324.

45 Education, pastor Samuel Hardy: Little, pp. 17–19.

45 Rogers in Bristol in June 1696: Ralph and Williams, p. 106.

45–46 Bristol disadvantages as a port: Kenneth Morgan, Bristol and the Atlantic trade in the eighteenth century, Cambridge, UK: Cambridge University Press, pp. 29–30.

46 Pope's quote on Bristol: Ibid., p. 33.

46 Description of central Bristol, Redcliffe in 1700: Andor Gomme, Michael Jenner, and Bryan Little, Bristol: an architectural history, London: Lind Humphries, 1979, p. 94; Roger H. Leech, The Topography of Medieval and Early Modern Bristol, Part I, Bristol: Bristol Records Society, 1997, pp. xx–xxvii, 119–162; Morgan, pp. 7–9.

46–47 William Dampier, Woodes Rogers, Roebuck: Christopher Lloyd, William Dampier, Hamden, CT: Archon Books, 1966, pp. 15–16; Dampier, pp. 202–203, 321–324.; David Lyon, The Sailing Navy List, London: Conway, 1993, p. 26.

47 Dampier and Avery: Joel H. Baer, "William Dampier at the Crossroads: New Light on the 'Missing Years,' 1691–1697," International Journal of Maritime History, Vol. VIII, No. 2 (1996), pp. 97–117.

47–48 Rogers's apprenticeship: Little, p. 19.

48 Rogers in Newfoundland: We know he had traveled there in the fisheries trade prior to 1708, owing to a passing reference in Woodes Rogers, A Cruising Voyage Around the World, Originally published 1712, New York: Longmans, Green & Co., 1928, p. 99.

48 Woodes Rogers senior and Elizabeth: W. N. Minchinton, The Trade of Bristol in the Eighteenth Century, Bristol: Bristol Record Society, 1957, p. 6.

48 Trinity Bay and Poole merchants: "Poole," "Trinity Harbour," and "Old Perlican" in Encyclopedia of Newfoundland and Labrador, St. John's, Nfld.: Memorial University, 1997.

48 Whetstone's bio and command: J. K. Laughton, "Whetstone, Sir William (d. 1711)" in Oxford Dictionary of National Biography, Oxford University Press, 2004; Little, pp. 19–20.

49 House on Queen's Square (1702): Gomme, Jenner & Little, pp. 96–98; Little, pp. 22–23.

49 Whetstone's early career: J.K Laughton, "Whetstone, Sir Willaim," Oxford Dictionary of National Biography, Oxford, UK: Oxford University Press, 2004; David Syrett (ed.), Commissioned Sea Officers of the Royal Navy 1660–1815, London: Navy Records Society, 1994, p. 983.

49–50 Causes of the War of Spanish Succession, King Charles II: Wikipedia, "Charles II of Spain" and "War of Spanish Succession," online resource, viewed 10 January 2006.

50 1703 storm: G. J. Marcus, A Naval History of England, Volume I: The Formative Centuries, Boston: Little, Brown & Co., 1961, pp. 221–223.

50 Queen's Square house completed: Little, p. 22.

50–51 Marriage, Knighthood, Rear Admiral of the Blue: *Oxford Dictionary*; Syrett, p. 983; Manwaring, p. 93n.

51 Father dies: *Notes & Queries*, Volume 149, Number 22, 28 November 1925, p. 388; Newton Wade, "Capt. Woodes Rogers," *Notes & Queries*, 10th series, Number VIII, No. 207 (December 14 1907), p. 470.

51 Woodes made freeman: Manwaring, p. 93.

51 Woodes Rogers's physical appeareance: William Hogarth, *Woodes Rogers and his Family* (1729), oil on canvas painting, National Maritime Museum, London.

CHAPTER THREE : WAR

52 Purpose of ships of the line: A. B. C. Whipple, *Fighting Sail*, Alexandria, VA: Time-Life Books, 1978, pp. 12–15.

52 Size, complement of a first-rate: Merriman, p. 365.

52–53 Conditions in fleet battles: Whipple, pp. 146–165.

53–55 Naval battles in War of Spanish Succession: N. A. M. Rodger, *The Command of the Ocean: A Naval History of Britain 1649–1815*, London: W. W. Norton, 2004, pp. 166–174.

55 French privateers: Merriman, p. 338; "Letter from the Masters of six merchant vessels to the Victualling Board of the Royal Navy," Dover, 30 December 1704, reproduced in Merriman, pp. 341–342; Julian Hoppit, *A Land of Liberty: England 1689–1727*, Oxford: Oxford University Press, 2002, p. 112; G. N. Clark, "War Trade and Trade War," *Economic History Review*, Vol. 1 No. 2 (January 1928), p. 263.

55 Port Royal "height of splendor": John Taylor (1688) as quoted in Allan D. Meyers, "Ethnic Distinctions and Wealth among Colonial Jamaican Merchants, 1685–1716, *Social Science History*, Vol. 22 (1), Spring, 1998, p. 54.

57 Port Royal casualties in 1692 earthquake: Cordingly, pp. 141–142.

57 Port Royal 1703 fire: *A New History of Jamaica*, London: J. Hodges, 1740, pp. 270–272.

57–58 Port Royal as a slum with quotes, dunghill: Edward Ward, *A Collection of the Writings of Mr. Edward Ward*, Vol. II, fifth ed., London: A. Bettesworth, 1717, pp. 164–165.

58 Sources of indentured servants: George Woodbury, *The Great Days of Piracy in the West Indies*, New York: W. W. Norton, 1951, pp. 32–46.

58 Character of Jamaica as per Edward Ward: Ward (1717), pp. 161–162.

58–59 Slave population growth on Jamaica: Richard S Dunn, *Sugar and Slaves: The Rise of the Planter Class in the English West Indies, 1624–1713*, Chapel Hill, NC: University of North Carolina Press, 1972, pp. 164–165.

58–59 More slaves died than were born: Dunn, pp. 300–305.

59 Slave laws of Jamaica: *A New History of Jamaica*, pp. 217–223; Dunn, pp. 238–246.

59 Runaway slave communities and Nanny Town: Mavis C. Campbell, *The Maroons of Jamaica 1655–1796*, Granby, MA: Bergin & Gravey Publishers, 1988, pp. 49–53.

60 Spanish population seven million: Wikipedia, "Economic History of Spain," viewed 5 April 2006.

61 Weak dispostion of Royal Navy in West Indies: Ruth Bourne, *Queen Anne's Navy in the West Indies*, New Haven: Yale University Press, 1939, pp. 59–61.

61 Sixty-eight degrees: N. A. M. Rogers, *The Wooden World*, New York: W.W. Norton, 1996, p. 46.

61–62 Difficulties of communicating: Bourne (1939), pp. 66, 70.

62 No mainmasts available in West Indies: Ibid., pp. 74–75

62 Shipworm and lack of careening facilities: Ibid., pp. 73–74.

62 Jamaica squadron's condition in 1704: Ibid., pp. 75–76.

62 Leeward Islands station ship in 1711: Ibid., p. 80 (also in CSPCS 1710–11, No. 824).

63 Problems of disease: Bourne (1939), pp. 87–88.

63 Kerr's fleet (1706–7): Bourne (1939), pp. 93–95; see Josiah Burchett, A Complete History of the Most Remarkable Transactions at Sea, London: 1720, pp. 699, 701.

63 Jamaicans refuse to grow or eat produce: Dunn, pp. 273–275.

63 Constable's letter (1711): Bourne (1939), pp. 100–101; his first name from John Hardy, A Chronological List of the Captains of His Majesty's Royal Navy, London: T. Cadell, 1784, p. 29.

63–64 Buccaneers at Port Royal (1670s): Dunn, p. 185.

64 10 percent of prize to the Admiralty: Clark, p. 265.

64 1702–3 Privateering campaign against Spanish: Oldmixon, p. 340; Howard M. Chapin, Privateer Ships and Sailors, Toulon, France: Imprimerie G. Mouton, 1926, pp. 240–241.

64 1704 privateer captures and successes: Oldmixon, pp. 342–343.

64 Size of Jamaican privateer fleet: The State of the Island of Jamaica, London: H. Whitridge, 1726, p. 4.

64 Quote on Jamaican privateering: A New History of Jamaica (1740), p. 273.

65 127 Bristol privateers: Shipsides & Wall, p. 50.

65 Whetstone Galley: Powell, p. 102; Patrick McGrath (ed.), Bristol, Africa, and the Eighteenth-Century Slave Trade to America, Vol. I, Bristol, UK: Bristol Records Sociey, 1986, p. 12; Bryan Little, Crusoe's Captain, London: Odham's Press, 1960, pp. 41–42.

65–66 Eugene Prize: Powell, p. 95; Little, p. 42.

66 Dampier's Pacific travels: Summarized nicely in Gary C. Williams, "William Dampier: Pre-Linean Explorer, Naturalist," Proceedings of the California Academy of Sciences, Vol. 55, Sup. II, No. 10, pp. 149–153.

66–67 Gold and silver production in Spanish America: Timothy R. Walton, The Spanish Treasure Fleets, Sarasota, FL: Pineapple Press, 1994, pp. 136–138.

67 Treasure fleets described: Kip Wagner, Pieces of Eight: Recovering the Riches of a Lost Spanish Treasure Fleet, New York: E. P. Dutton & Co., 1966, pp. 52–54; Walton, pp. 47–55; Charles E. Chapman, "Gali and Rodriguez Cermenho: Exploration of California," Southwestern Historical Quarterly, Vol. 23, No. 3 (January 1920).

67–70 Quote on Dampier's attack on Manila Galleon: Lloyd (1966), p. 117.

70 Dampier "never gave over": Edward Cooke, A Voyage to the South Sea and Round the World, London: B. Lintott and R. Golsing, 1712, Introduction.

70 Court martial rulings against Dampier: Lloyd (1966), p. 96.

70 Dampier's performance on St. George expedition: Lloyd (1966), pp. 97–121; Donald Jones, Captain Woodes Rogers' Voyage Round the World 1708–1711, Bristol, UK: Bristol Branch of the Historical Association of the University, 1992, pp. 5–6.

70–71 Investors in Rogers's expedition: Little, pp. 45–46; Jones, p. 5.

71 Size, age of the Duke and Dutchess, Jones, pp. 4–5.

71 Officers of the Rogers expedition: Powell, p. 104n; Little, pp. 47–48.

71 Dr. Dover's use of mercury: Leonard A. G. Strong, Dr. Quicksilver, 1660–1742: The Life and Times of Thomas Dover, M.D., London: Andrew Melrose, 1955, pp. 157–159.

72 333 men aboard: Woodes Rogers, A Cruising Voyage Round the World, 2nd Ed. Corrected, London: Bernard Lintot & Edward Symon, 1726, p. 2.

72 Design flaws, crew shortcomings at outset: Rogers, pp. 2–3.

72–73 Events during Atlantic passage, including mutiny: Woodes Rogers, *A Cruising Voyage Around the World,* Originally published 1712, New York: Longmans, Green & Co., 1928, pp. 8–33.

73–74 Events in the South Atlantic in December and early January: Rogers, pp. 30–33; Cooke (1712, Vol. I), pp. 30–36; quote on dolphins: Rogers (1726), p. 103. The author has been able to fill in some from his crossings of the Drake Passage.

74–75 Scurvy symptoms, effects, age of sail casualties: Stephen R. Bown, *Scurvy: How a Surgeon, a Mariner, and a Gentleman Solved the Greatest Medical Mystery of the Age of Sail,* New York: St. Martin's Press, 2003, pp. 1–7, 33–46.

75 Scurvy deaths: Cooke (1712, Vol. I), p. 35; Rogers (1928), pp. 89–90.

75–76 Selkirk's bio: Rogers (1928), pp. 91–96; Alexander Winston, *No Man Knows My Grave: Privateers and Pirates 1665–1715,* Boston: Houghton-Mifflin, 1969, pp. 183–184.

76 Selkirk's aversion to Dampier: Edward Cooke, *A Voyage to the South Sea and Around the World,* Vol. II, London: Bernard Lintot & R. Gosling, 1712, pp. xx–xxi.

77 Rogers's quotes on Selkirk: Rogers (1928), pp. 91, 94, 96.

77–78 Privateering in late February and early March: Rogers (1928), pp. 103–113; Little, pp. 80–84; Cooke (1712, Vol. I), pp. 126, 130–132.

78 *Beginning* slave manifests: C104/160: Accounts of the Negroes now onboard the *Ascension,* Gorgona, 20 July 1709 and 28 July 1709.

78 Capture of *Havre de Grace:* Cooke (1712, Vol. I), pp. 136–8; Rogers (1928), pp. 116–7; C104/160: List of Negroes and cargo on *Havre de Grace* when captured, 15 April 1709.

78 Rogers reaction to brother's death: Rogers (1928), pp. 117–118.

78–79 Siege of Guayaquil: Little, pp. 87–100.

79–80 Activities at Gorgona: Cooke (Vol. I), pp. 164, 317; Rogers (1928), pp. 167–171.

80 Near-mutiny at Gorgona: Rogers (1928), pp. 172–177.

80 Low supplies, state of ships (December 1709): Rogers (1928), pp. 211–213; Jones, p. 14.

81 Battle with *Incarnación:* Rogers (1928), pp. 213–215.

81–82 Battle with *Begoña:* Rogers (1928), pp. 216–222; Cooke (Vol. I), pp. 346–352.

83 Rogers accused of leaving treasure at Batavia: Jones, p. 21.

84 Value of expedition's proceeds, Rogers's share: Little, pp. 149, 169.

84 Sailors impressed: Jones, pp. 19–21.

84 Charles Vane in Port Royal c. 1712: TJR, p. 37.

85 Quote on Jennings's social stature: GHP, p. 41.

85 Embargo of shipping prior to hurricane: "A letter containing an account of the most general grievances of Jamaica," Jamaica, 6 October 1712, in *The Groans of Jamaica,* London: 1714, p. 1.

85 Description of the 1712 hurricane: Oldmixon, p. 345; *Boston News-Letter,* 12 January 1713, p. 1; Burchett (1720), p. 785.

85 Peace breaks out: Word had gotten as far as Antigua by late September; see Burchett, p. 784.

CHAPTER FOUR : PEACE

86 RN demobilization and slashing of merchant wages: Rediker (1987), pp. 281–282.

86 Possession of Spanish currency as ground for seizure: Lord Archibald Hamilton, *An Answer to An Anonymous Libel,* London: 1718, p. 44.

86 Thirty-eight vessels captured by Spanish: CO137/12, folio 90(iii): A List of Some of the Many Ships, Sloops, and other Vessels taken from the Subjects of the King of Great Britain in America by the Subjects of the King of Spain since the Conclusion of the last peace, Jamaica: c. 1716.

86 Governor of Jamaica quote: Hamilton (1718), p. 44.

87 Quotes, description of the situation of seamen in Jamaica: A. B., *The State of the Island of Jamaica*, London: H. Whitridge, 1726, p. 8.

87 Hornigold amongst the first pirates: Ibid., p. 8n.

88 New Providence during the war: Oldmixon, p. 432; Craton, pp. 93–94; CO5/1265, No. 76v: Memorial of Sundry Merchants to Joseph Addison, London: 1717; CO23/1, No. 17: Testimonial of Samuel Buck, London: 2 December 1719.

88 Population, situation in Nassau and Bahamas in 1713: This surmised from remarks on eyewitness comments on the condition of the island by John Graves in 1706, as quoted by Craton, pp. 93–94. The situation was probably similar in 1713, as any advances the islanders would have made after 1706 were rolled back by subsequent French attacks; this supposition is further supported by the poor state of the island's development as late as 1718, as described by Samuel Buck in CO23/1, No. 17 and described in later chapters.

89–90 Sources for the early piracies, activities of Hornigold, Cockram, West: "Boston News Item," *Boston News-Letter*, 29 April 1714, p. 2; Henry Pulleine to the Council of Trade and Plantations, Bermuda: 22 April 1714 in *CSPCS 1712–1714*, No. 651, pp. 333–334.

91 Long Wharf and Boston harbor described: Carl Bridenbaugh, *Cities in the Wilderness: The First Century of Urban Life in America 1625–1742*, New York: Alfred A. Knopf, 1955, pp. 171–172, 151, 178–179; Justin Winsor (ed.), *Memorial History of Boston, 1630–1880*, Boston: Ticknor & Co., 1880, pp. 440–441, 496.

91 People drowning on the road to Roxbury: Winsor, p. 442n.

91 Shops of King Street: Michael G. Hall, *The Last American Puritan*, Middletown, CT: Wesleyan University Press, 1988, p. 338.

93 News-Letter and postal network: Winsor, pp. 388–390, 442–443; Bridenbaugh (1955), p. 180.

93 Royal Exchange Tavern: Winsor, p. 499.

93 Faneuil's store: Bridenbaugh (1955), p. 185.

93 Eastham environment: Henry David Thoreau, *Cape Cod*, New York: W. W. Norton, 1951, pp. 45–60.

93 Wrecking in Eastham area: Jeremiah Digges, *Cape Cod Pilot*, Provincetown, MA: Modern Pilgrim Press, 1936, pp. 134–137.

94 Legend of Bellamy and Hallett: Digges (1936), pp. 193–197. Another interpretation, somewhat dated by new evidence, was offered in Edwin Dethlefson, *Whidah: Cape Cod's Mystery Treasure Ship*, Woodstock, VT: Seafarer's Heritage Library, 1984, pp. 14–22. For a more fanciful account see Barry Clifford, *The Pirate Prince*, New York: Simon & Schuster, 1993, pp. 21–22.

95 Mary Hallett and her family: A. Otis, *Genealogical Notes of Barnstable Families*, Barnstable, MA: F. B & F. P Goss, 1888; Robert Charles Anderson, *The Great Migration*, Vol. 3, Boston: New England Historic Genealogical Society, 2003; Author's Interview, Kenneth J. Kinkor, Provincetown, MA: 15 June 2005.

95 Great Island Tavern: Kinkor (2003), p. 312; Fact Sheet, Great Island, Cape Cod National Seashore, National Park Service: online resource at www.nps.gov/caco/places/index.thml, viewed 13 May 2006.

95 Hallett will: "Last Will & Testament of Mary Hallett," Yarmouth, MA: April 19, 1734 from *Barnstable County Public Records*, Vol. 8, as appears in Kinkor (2003), pp. 295–296.

95 Paulsgrave Williams background: George Andrews Moriatry, "John Williams of New-port, Merchant, and His Family," *The Genealogical Magazine*, Nos. 1–3 (1915), pp. 4–12; *Genealogies of Rhode Island Families, Volume II: Smith—Yates*, Baltimore: Clearfield, 2000, pp. 401–406.

96 Guthrie, New Shoreham, Malcolm Sands Wilson, *Descendants of James Sands of Block Island*, Privately printed: p. 194; George R. Burgess & Jane Fletcher Fiske, "New Shoreham Town Book No. 1," manuscript transcription, 1924, p. 17.

96 Williams's family ties to organized crime: Author Interview, Kenneth J. Kinkor, 15 June 2005; Zacks, pp. 232–233, 240–241; Barry Clifford, *The Lost Fleet*, New York: Harper-Collins, 2002, pp. 108–118, 262–264.

97 Johnathan Darvell background: Jameson, pp. 141–142.

98 Hornigold et al.'s activities from Eleutheria (1714): CO5/1265, No. 17i: A List of the men's names that sailed from Iletheria and Committed Piracies Upon the Spaniards on the Coast of Cuba since the Proclamation of Peace, Nassau: 14 March 1715; CO5/1265, No. 17iv: John Chace's Receipt for Carrying Daniel Stilwell, Nassau: 2 January 1715, p. 32. Note that these accounts are more accurate than the year-old recollections of John Vickers, which muddle some of the dates and details: Deposition of John Vickers, Williamsburg, VA: 1716 in CSPCS 1716–1717, No. 240i, pp. 140–141.

98 Walker's background: CO5/1265, No. 17: Thomas Walker to the Council of Trade and Plantations, Nassau: 14 March 1715; Craton, p. 91.

99 Walker's letters: CO5/1265, No. 16i: Thomas Walker to Colonel Nicholson, New Providence: 14 March 1715; CO5/1265, No. 17: Thomas Walker to the Proprietors of the Bahamas, New Providence: 14 March 1715; Bruce T McCully, "Nicholson, Francis," in *Dictionary of Canadian Biography*, CD-ROM, Toronto: University of Toronto, 2000.

99 Bermuda governor's letter and mariners: Pulleine to the Council of Trade, 22 April 1714, p. 334.

99 Walker's capture of Stillwell et al. (January 1715): Johnathan Chace's Receipt, CO5/1265, No. 17i: Thomas Walker to Archibald Hamilton, 21 January 1715.

100 Warning of a Spanish attack: CO5/1265, No. 17v: George Hearne to Thomas Walker, Harbour Island, Bahamas: 20 January 1715.

100 Walker's mission to Havana: CO5/1265, No. 17iii: Marquis de Cassa Torres to Thomas Walker, Havana: 15 February 1715.

100–101 Stillwell rescued by Hornigold: Deposition of John Vickers, p. 141.

101 Archibald Hamilton's family: Sir James Balfour Paul, *The Scots Perage*, Vol. IV, Edinburgh: David Douglas (1907), pp. 380–385; Kinkor (2003), pp. 342–343.

102 Hamilton's Jacobite activities while in office: Samuel Page to Sir Gilbert Heathcote, London: 8 May 1716 in CSPCS 1716–1717, No. 158viii, pp. 82–83; "Representation of the Assembly of Jamaica to the King," Jamaica: Early 1716 in CSPCS 1716–1717, No. 158xi(a), pp. 83–87; An account of the mal-administration in Jamaica during the Government of Lord Hamilton, Jamaica: early 1716, CSPCS 1716–1717, No. 158xii, pp. 88–90.

102 Hamilton's later defense: Hamilton (1718), pp. 44–48.

103 Details of *Barsheba*: CO137/12, folio 16ii: A list of vessels commissioner by Governor Lord A. Hamilton, c. May 1716.

103 Jennings worth £400 a year: Hamilton (1718), p. 59.

103 Hamilton owns shares in *Barsheba*: Hamilton (1718), pp. 62–63, 68.

103 Combined treasure fleet of 1715: Wagner, pp. 55–73; up-to-date information on the names, fate, and identity of particular ships can be found on www.1715fleet.com. The storm is described in Don Miguel de Lima y Melo to Duque de Linares, Havana: 19 October 1715 (Gregorian), in SAT, pp. 32–34.

104 Ubilla the ultimate commander: Marion Clayton Link, *The Spanish Camp Site and the 1715 Plate Wreck Fleet*, 2nd corrected draft, unpublished manuscript, c. 1970, p. 2.

106 Treasure worth 7 million pesos: Walton, p. 160. Documentary research by Jack Haskins and other sailors suggests 6,486,066 pesos, in SAT, p. 94.

106 Survivors' actions: Link (c. 1970), pp. 4–6; Wagner (1966), pp. 60–73.

106 *News-Letter* report of fleet disaster: The actual editions—from the summer of 1715—have been lost, but offhanded references to the wrecks in later issues make it clear that it had been reported on.

106 Thomas Paine and wrecking: Clifford (2002), pp. 108–118, 262–264.

106 Early reports of wrecks in Jamaica: Hamilton (1718), p. 49.

106 Belcher on wrecking fever in Jamaica: ADM 1/1471, f24: P. Balcher (Captain) to the Admiralty, HMS *Diamond* at the Nore, England: 13 May 1716.

107 Hamilton approaches navy officers: Deposition of Samuel Page, Jamaica: 15 May 1716 in CSPCS 1716–1717, No. 158v, pp. 80–81.

107 Hamilton buys shares of privateers: Deposition of Walter Adlington, Jamaica: 15 May 1716 in CSPCS 1716–1717, No. 158vi, p. 81; Extract of a Letter from Don Juan Francisco de Valle to the Marquis de Montelon, Jamaica: 18 March 1716 in CSPCS 1716–1717, No. 158i, pp. 78–79.

107 Hamilton's commissions: "Instructions for Captain Jonathan Barnet," St. Jago de la Vega, Jamaica: 24 November 1715, published as Appendix II in Hamilton (1718), pp. 72–73.

107 Hamilton's directions to send them to the wrecks: Before leaving Jamaica, the privateering masters spoke openly about their true design being the wrecks and, given Hamilton's past and future actions, it's clear that he was involved in directing them toward such a mission. See ADM 1/1471 f24, Balcher letter.

107 Fourteen divers with Jennings: Testimony of Pedro de la Vega, Havana: 13 January 1716, in SAT, pp. 112–115.

107 Sloop *Eagle*: Jennings's consort is sometimes misidentified as being commanded by Edward James, who was in fact a part owner of the vessel (see ADM1/1471, f24, Balcher letter). The *Eagle*, commanded by Willis, is positively identified as Jennings's consort in the notes to the list of vessels commissioned by Hamilton (CO137/12, No. 16ii).

107–108 Jennings's movements in December: Marquis de Cassa Torres to Archibald Hamilton, Havana: 3 January 1716, as translated in Kinkor (2003), pp. 19–20. The original is in CO137/12, No. 9.

108 Capture of *San Nicolas de Vari y San Joseph*: Testimony of Pedro de la Vega, pp. 112–115; Deposition of Joseph Lorrain, Jamaica: 21 August 1716, Jamaica Council Minutes, ff. 110–111 in Kinkor (2003), p. 67.

108 Relative location of the wrecks: The *Regla* (Cabin Wreck), *Roman* (Corrigan's), *Carmen* (Rio Mar), and *Nieves* (Douglas Beach) wrecks are mapped out in Jim Sinclair et al., *Florida East Coast Shipwreck Project 2001 Season Report*, Sebastian, FL: Mel Fisher Center, 2002, pp. 61–69. The *Urca de Lima* wreck is two miles north of the *Nieves*, often referred to as the Wedge Wreck.

109 Palmar de Ayz an Indian palm grove: Link (c. 1970), p. 5.

109 **Salmon at Palmar de Ayz:** Francisco Salmon to the king of Spain, Palmar de Ayz: 20 September 1715, in SAT, pp. 6–7; Don Joseph Clemente Fernandez letter, Palmar de Ayz: 10 September 1715, a "Vatican document" translated in SAT, pp. 112–113; Marquis de Cassa Torres to Viceroy Linares of Mexico, Havana: 12 October 1715 (Gregorian) in SAT, pp. 31–32; Miguel de Lima y Melo to Duque de Linares, 19 October 1715, pp. 33–35.

109–110 **Diving technology, work of divers:** Kris E. Lane, *Pillaging the Empire: Piracy in the Americas 1500–1700,* Armonk, NY: M. E. Sharpe, 2001, pp. 161–163; Link (c. 1970), p. 7; Wagner, pp. 63–65. The use of "diving engines" or bells is confirmed in GHP, p. 35.

110 **Quantity of treasure salvaged:** Wagner, p. 66, to whose estimate should be added that sent out in the *Maricaybo*: Declaration of Antonio Peralta, Havana: [1716?], translated in SAT, pp. 115–116. Further details in Letter of Captain Don Francisco de Soto Sanchez, Havana: 29 October 1715 translated in SAT, pp. 102–103.

110 **About 350,000 pieces of eight on site:** GHP, p. 36.

111 **Jennings's raid on the Spanish Camp:** "Extract of a letter from Don Juan Francisco del Valle to the Marquis de Monteleon," Jamaica: March 18, 1716 in CSPCS 1716–1717, item No. 158i, pp. 78–79; Testimony of Pedro de la Vega, pp. 113–114; Declaration of Antonio Peralta, pp. 115–116; Link, p. 8; Deposition of Joseph Lorrain, pp. 67–68.

111 **Vane's presence in the attack:** GHP, p. 135.

112 **Torture of Spanish prisoners:** Representation of Merchants against Governor Lord A. Hamilton, Jamaica: c. May 1716 in CSPCS 1716–1717, No. 158viii, p. 82.

112 **Flying Gang rejects Treaty of Utrecht, will spare Dutch and English:** "New York Dispatch," *Boston News-Letter,* 28 May 1716, p. 2.

112 **Hornigold's actions in November 1715:** Deposition of John Vickers, pp. 140–141; CO5/1265, No. 52i: Deposition of Thomas Walker Jr., Charlestown, SC: 6 August 1716; CO5/1265, No. 52: Thomas Walker to the Council of Trade, Charlestown, SC: August 1716.

114 **Jennings goes to Nassau from wrecks:** Deposition of Joseph Lorrain, Jamaica: 21 August 1716, Jamaica Council Minutes, ff. 110–111 in Kinkor (2003), pp. 67–68.

CHAPTER FIVE: A PIRATE'S LIFE

115 **Queen's Square house transferred:** Little, pp. 169–170.

115 **Allegation of £3 million:** Little, p. 168.

115 **Creagh frees impressed men:** Jones, p. 19.

116 ***Creagh v. Rogers:*** Jones, pp. 19–22. Boxes of the original trial documents have survived and can be found in the British National Archives, C104/160.

116 **Birth, death of Woodes Rogers IV:** Powell, p. 103.

117 **Size of *Delicia*:** CO23/1, No. 31: "Memorial from the Copartners for Carrying on a Trade and Settling the Bahamas Islands," London: 19 May 1721. CO5/1265, No. 76ii: Woodes Rogers proposal to the Proprietors of the Bahamas, 1717.

117–118 **Old East India House:** John Rocque, *London, Westminster, Southwark,* First Edition, Map, 1746, Sheet E2, Section 3; "A View of the Old East India House," Engraving, 1784, British Library, shelf mark P2167; *A Tour Thro' the Whole Island . . . ,* pp. 132–149.

118 **Rogers's arrival in Madagascar:** Manwaring, p. 124; Little, 172. Both accounts draw on documents in the Archives Department, Houses of Parliament, Cape Town, South Africa.

119 Experiences with Madagascar pirates: GHP, pp. 58–62. A careful reading of GHP makes clear that the author must have known Rogers and interviewed him in detail for the preparation of his book. The facts he presents in relation to Madagascar fit perfectly with other documentary evidence, especially Rogers's immediate interest in acquiring slaves.

119 Relative cost of Malagasy slaves: Virginia Bever Platt, "The East India Company and the Madagascar Slave Trade," William & Mary Quarterly, 3rd series, Vol. 26, No. 4 (October 1969), p. 549.

120 Dutch ship Schoonouwen: Manwaring, p. 124.

120 Pirates abortive plan to seize Delicia: GHP, p. 62.

120 Madagascar pirates petition Queen Anne: Little, p. 172; Manwaring, p. 124.

120–121 Conditions on slave ships circa 1700: Malcom Cowley and Daniel P. Mannix, "The Middle Passage" in David Northup (ed.), The Atlantic Slave Trade, Lexington, MA: D. C. Heath & Co., 1994, p. 103; Wilem Bosman, "Trading on the Slave Coast, 1700," in Ibid., pp. 71–75; Captive Passage: The Transatlantic Slave Trade and the Making of the Americas, Washington: Smithsonian Institution Press, 2002, pp. 77–87.

121 Sumatra leg of Rogers' voyage: Little, p. 172.

122 Jennings in Nassau, dividing loot: Deposition of Joseph Lorrain, Jamaica: 21 August 1716, Jamaica Council Minutes, ff. 110–111 in Kinkor (2003), p. 68.

122 Jennings takes Hornigold's sloop: Deposition of John Vickers, p. 140.

122 Casa de Torres's advanced warning: Marquis de Cassa Torres to Archibald Hamilton, Havana: 3 January 1716, translated in Kinkor (2003), p. 19–20.

122 Cubans follow Jennings to Jamaica: Alexandre O. Exquemelin, The History of the Bucaniers of America, Vol. I, 5th ed., London: T. Evans, 1771, p. 6.

122 News of the 1715 uprising: Boston News-Letter, 25 December 1716, pp. 1–2; "Edinburgh Dispatches of September 21 and September 23," Boston News-Letter, 23 January 1716, p. 1.

123 Treasure brought ashore by Jennings at Jamaica: Deposition of Joseph Lorrain, Jamaica: 21 August 1716, Jamaica Council Minutes, ff. 110–111 in Kinkor (2003), p. 68.

123 Hamilton's quote regarding treasure: Hamilton (1718), p. 62; CO137/12 No. 16ii: List of Vessels Commissioned by Governor Lord A. Hamilton, Jamaica: c. 15 May 1716.

123 Hamilton signs Jennings's departure papers (laissez-passe): Hamilton (1718), pp. 57–58.

123 Jennings's departure, consorts, crew for March cruise: Deposition of Samuel Liddell, Jamaica: 7 August 1716, Jamaica Council Minutes, folios 49–50 in Kinkor (2003), pp. 56–57; Deposition of Allen Bernard, Jamaica: 10 August 1716, Jamaica Council Minutes, folios 63–68 in Kinkor (2003), pp. 58–62.

123 Carnegie's sloop named Discovery: This confirmed in A Proclamation Concerning Pyrates, Jamaica: 30 August 1716, Jamaica Council Minutes, folios 153–155 in Kinkor (2003), p. 70.

124 English at Palmar de Ayz (Jan. 1716): Captain Ayala Escobar to Governor Torres y Ayala, Palmar de Ayz, Florida: 4 February 1716 translated in SAT, pp. 56, 69.

124 Amount taken by wreckers in that period: Escobar to Cassa Torres, Palmar de Ayz, Florida: 9 February 1716, translated in SAT, pp. 56, 69.

125 Dispersed by Spanish in Feb 1716: Ibid., p. 69.

125 Baymen: Emory King, The Great Story of Belize, Vol. I, Belize City, Belize: Tropical Books, 1999, pp. 6–8; "Rhode Island Dispatch, September 16," Boston News-Letter, 12 September 1715, p. 2; "New York Dispatch, October 3," Boston News-Letter, 3 October 1715, p. 2.

125 "A Sailor": Deposition of Allen Bernard.

125 Capture of Cornelison's ship: TEP, pp. 1, 24.

125 **Capture of Young's ship:** Deposition of Allen Bernard; CO137/12, No. 411i: Deposition of Joseph Eeels, Port Royal, Jamaica: 3 December 1716.

125 **Bellamy and Williams flee Young's ship:** Deposition of Allen Bernard.

126 **Jennings at Bahía Honda:** Deposition of Allen Bernard; Deposition of Joseph Eeels; Deposition of Samuel Liddell.

127 **Details of the St. Marie:** CO137/12, No. 211i: Le Comte de Blenac (Governor of Hispaniola) to Archibald Hamilton, Leogane, Haiti: 18 July 1716; Memorial of Monsr. Moret, Jamaica: c. August 1716, Jamaica Council Minutes, folio 17–23 in Kinkor (2003), pp. 48–50.

128 **Bellamy and Williams arrive at Bahía Honda:** Deposition of Joseph Eeels; Deposition of John Cockrane, Jamaica: 10 August 1716, Jamaica Council Minutes, folio 68–69 in Kinkor (2003), pp. 62–63.

128 **Bellamy and Williams naked:** Deposition of Allen Bernard, p. 59.

129 **Account of the attack on St. Marie:** Ibid., p. 60; Deposition of Samuel Liddell.

130 **St. Marie worth 700,000 livres:** Comte de Blenac to Hamilton, 18 July 1716.

130 **D'Escoubet's letter:** "Extract of a Letter of Captain D'Escoubet to Lord Hamilton," Bay Honda, Cuba: c. 4 April 1716, Jamaica Council Minutes folios 17–23 in Kinkor (2003), pp. 50–51.

131 **Conditions in Nassau in winter, 1716:** Deposition of John Vickers, pp. 140–141.

131 **Fernandez's raids on wrecks, time in Nassau:** Deposition of Bartolome Carpenter, Havava?: 24 June 1716, translated in SAT, pp. 117–119; Deposition of John Vickers, p. 141.

131–132 **Authority, elections, sharing of plunder on pirate ships:** Rediker (2004), pp. 61–71.

132 **Marianne described:** Comte de Blenac to Hamilton, 18 July 1716.

132–133 **Bellamy and Williams rob the St. Marie:** Deposition of Joseph Eeels; Deposition of Allen Bernard.

134 **Jennings burns sloop, "cut to pieces" periagua:** Deposition of Joseph Eeels.

134 **Bellamy and Williams join Hornigold:** TEP, p. 24.

135 **Capture of the English logwood ship:** Ibid., p. 23.

135 **Capture of Spanish brigantines, careening at Isle of Piños:** Ibid.

136 **Decision to sail Benjamin to Nassau:** We know that Bellamy rid himself of the Benjamin between the end of May and the first week of July, when Musson captured her. Reports that appear to date May 1716 place a pirate vessel consistent with the Benjamin in the Bahamas. "New York Dispatch, May 31," Boston News-Letter, 21 May 1716, p. 2.

136 **Behavior of Jennings, crews at Nassau:** Deposition of Allen Bernard; Deposition of Joseph Eeels.

138 **Ownership of the Dolphin:** This is almost certainly the Bahamas-owned sloop of the same name that cleared customs in and out of South Carolina in early May and late July of 1717. CO5/508: South Carolina shipping returns 1716–1717, p. 23.

138 **Jennings's second raid on the wrecks:** "New York Dispatch, May 31," Boston News-Letter, 21 May 1716, p. 2; Deposition of John Cockrane.

139 **Slaves fleeing to Bahamas:** Hugo Prosper Leaming, Hidden Americans: Maroons of Virginia and the Carolinas, New York: Garland Publishing, 1995, pp. 128–129; Frank Sherry, Raiders and Rebels: The Golden Age of Piracy, New York: William Morrow, 1986, pp. 212–213.

139 **James and Anne Bonny:** GHP, pp. 623–624.

139–140 **Thomas Barrow's activities:** Deposition of John Vickers, p. 141.

140 **Thompson and Cockram's syndicate, other traders:** CO5/508: South Carolina shipping returns 1716–1717, pp. 16, 20, 23; CO142/14: Jamaica shipping returns 1713–1719, p. 70. For a general reference to illicit traders at Nassau see CO5/1265, No. 52: Thomas Walker to

the Council of Trade and Plantations, Charlestown, SC: August 1716 (extracts published in *CSPCS* 1716–1717, item 328, pp. 176–177).

140 **Quote on importance of traders:** CO23/1, No. 12i, Mr. Gale to Thomas Pitt, South Carolina: 4 November 1718.

140 **Jennings's men on island:** For example, Captain Forbes, in Alexander Spotswood to Lords of Trade, Virginia: 3 July 1716, in Brock (1882), pp. 170–171.

140 *Benjamin* **sold to Perrin:** Deposition of Robert Daniell, Charlestown, SC: 14 July 1716 in *CSPCS* 1716–1717, No. 267, pp. 149–150.

140–141 **Walker on loss of** *Benjamin:* Thomas Walker to Council of Trade, August 1716.

141 **Walker flees:** Ibid.

141 **Further news on Jacobite rebellion reaches Americas:** "News item via Barbados and Rhode Island," *Boston News-Letter,* 12 March 1716, p. 1; "Whitehall Dispatch, November 16," *Boston News-Letter,* 12 March 1716, p. 1; "New York Dispatch, March 12," *Boston News-Letter,* 12 March 1716, p. 2; "Whitehall Dispatch, December 10," *Boston News-Letter,* 30 April 1717, p. 1.

141–142 **Official complaints against Hamilton:** *CSPCS* 1716–1717, No. 158i–xv, pp. 77–90.

142 **Diplomatic complaints against Hamilton's privateers:** *CSPCS* 1716–1717, items 158i, iii, pp. 77–90. CO137/12, No. 21iii: Michon to Governor Hamilton, Leogane, Haiti: 18 June 1716; Comte de Blenac to Governor Hamilton, Leogane: 18 June 1716; CO137/12, No. 21iv: Comte de Blanc to Governor Hamilton, Leogane: 25 July 1716; Memorial of Mnsr. Moret.

142 **Manifest, path of St. Marie:** *TEP,* pp. 18, 23.

143 **Hamilton's removal:** General Heywood to the Council of Trade, Jamaica: 11 August 1716 in *CSPCS* 1716–1717, No. 308, pp. 163–165; Draught of H. M. Commission revoking the Commission of Governor Lord A. Hamilton in *CSPCS* 1716–1717, No. 159i, p. 91.

143 **Jennings on the lamb by late August:** Archibald Hamilton to the Governor in Council, Jamaica: 24 August 1716, Jamaica Council Minutes, folio 126 in Kinkor (2003), pp. 69–70.

143 **Royal proclamation against pirates:** A Proclamation concerning Pyrates, Jamaica: 30 August 1716, Jamaica Council Minutes, folio 153–155 in Kinkor (2003), pp. 70–71.

CHAPTER SIX: BRETHREN OF THE COAST

144 **Members, composition of Bellamy's crew:** *TEP,* pp. 23, 25; CO5/1318, No. 16ii: Information of Andrew Turbett and Robert Gilmore, Williamsburg, Virginia: 17 April 1717; CO137/11, No. 45iii: Deposition of Abijah Savage, Antigua: 30 November 1716.

144–145 **Bellamy and La Buse's captures in June–July 1716:** Examination of Richard Caverley, New York: 15 June 1717, *Records of the Vice-Admiralty Court of the Province of New York 1685–1838* as appears in Kinkor (2003), p. 150; Examination of Jeremiah Higgins, New York: 22 June 1717, *Records of the Vice-Admiralty Court of the Province of New York 1685–1838* as appears in Kinkor (2003), p. 154.

145 **Hornigold deposed as commodore:** *TEP,* p. 23; Examination of Jeremiah Higgins, p. 154.

145–146 **Bellamy and La Buse's minor captures c. August 1716:** Examination of Jeremiah Higgins, pp. 154–155.

146 **Battle with French ship:** Ibid., p. 154; Examination of Richard Caverley, p. 151.

147 **Captures in the Virgin Islands:** *TEP,* p. 23.

147 **Forced unmarried, let married free:** Ibid., p. 25.

147 *Bonetta* capture, Bellamy's intentions to capture ship: Deposition of Abijah Savage; "death's head" flag described: testimony of Thomas Baker in *TEP*, p. 24.

147 Wickham an Antigua planter: Will of John McLester, Antigua: 9 December 1730, in ROE Book, Box 187, 1676–1739 Item No. 1, LDS Film 1855671.

148 St. Croix: careening, escapees, Hoff whipped: *TEP*, pp. 24–25; Deposition of Abijah Savage.

148 Robin Hood's men: *TEP*, p. 11.

148 Indian boy, Negro, John King taken by pirates: Deposition of Abijah Savage; Michael Levinson, "Remains are Identified as a boy pirate," *Boston Globe*, 2 June 2006; Thomas H. Maugh II, "A Pirate's Life for Him—at Age 9," *Los Angeles Times*, 1 June 2006. (Kenneth Kinkor of the Expedition Whydah Museum attributed a bone found on the *Whydah* wreck—a fibula clad in an expensive shoe and stocking—to John King; archeologists say it belonged to a child between eight and eleven years of age.)

149 Capture of the *Sultana*: Examination of Jeremiah Higgins, p. 155; Examination of Richard Caverley, p. 151.

150 "Cries of grief" of captured men: *TEP*, p. 25.

150 Walter Hamilton's letter to Barbados: Walter Hamilton to the Council of Trade and Plantations, Antigua: 14 December 1717, *CSPCS 1716–1717*, No. 425, p. 230. Savage got to Antigua by 30 November.

151 French sloops captured: Walter Hamilton to Council of Trade, 14 December 1717, p. 230.

151 Events at La Blanquilla: Ibid., p. 18–19.

151 *Marianne's* armament increased to 14 guns: Walter Hamilton to the Council of Trade, 14 December 1717, p. 230.

152 Ultimate plan to capture larger vessel: *TEP*, p, 24.

152 Treasure location and practices: Ibid., p. 24.

152 Day-to-day weather in Windward Islands (Dec. 1716–Jan. 1717): Reconstructed based on the log entries of HMS *Scarborough*, which was at Barbados and the Virgin Islands during this period. ADM 51/865: Logbooks of HMS *Scarborough*, entries of 1 December 1716–31 January 1717.

152 Storm, anchoring at St. Croix: *TEP*, p. 25.

153 Details of battle, pirate wrecks at St. Croix: ADM 1/1689 f5: An Inventory of Several Goods Taken from the Pirates at St. Cruze by His Majesty's Shipp Scarborough, c. Summer 1717; ADM 51/865: entries of 16–22 January 1717; Lyon, p. 36; Walter Hamilton to the Council of Trade and Plantations, Antigua: 1 March 1717 in *CSPCS 1716–1717*, item No. 484; *GHP*, pp. 65–69.

153 Sources re. blacks on slave and pirate vessels: Kenneth J. Kinkor, "Black Men Under the Black Flag" in C. R. Pennell, *Bandits at Sea: A Pirates Reader*, New York: New York University Press, 2001, pp. 200–203.

155 Spanish Town description, population: List of dutiable inhabitants of Spanish Town, Spanish Town, Virgin Gorda: c. 15 November 1716 in *CSPCS 1716–1717*, No. 425iv, p. 231; Deputy Governor Hornby to Walter Hamilton, Spanish Town, Virgin Gorda: 15 November 1716 in *CSPCS 1716–1717*, No. 425v, p. 231; Captain Candler (HMS *Winchlsea*) to Secretary Burchett, 12 May 1717 in *CSPCS 1716–1717*, No. 639i, pp. 339–340.

155 Bellamy at Spanish Town: Captain Candler to Burchett, p. 340; *TEP*, pp. 11, 25.

156–157 Lawrence Prince and *Whydah*: CO142/14: Jamaica Shipping Returns, "An account of goods exported from the Island of Jamaica since the 29th day of September 1713 and the 25th day of March 1715 and the goods and Negroes Imported, Kingston," No. 58;

Examination of Jeremiah Higgins, p. 155; Examination of Richard Caverley, p. 151; T70/19, No. 63, Letter of David Welsh to the Royal Africa Company, Williams Fort, Whydah, Ghana: 22 February 1717 as printed in Kinkor (2003), p. 89; Donovan Webster, "Pirates of the Whydah," *National Geographic*, May 1999; "Proclamation of Gov. Samuel Shute," *Boston News-Letter*, 13 May 1717, p. 1.

158 **Stern guns fired at Marianne:** TEP, p. 23.

158 **Pirates' weapons:** "Manifest of Recovered Artifacts from the pirate ship Whydah," in Barry Clifford, *The Pirate Prince*, New York: Simon & Schuster, 1993, pp. 207–208 (on armament); Author Interview, Kenneth J. Kinkor, Provincetown, MA: 15 June 2005.

159 **Captured Spanish vessel used as guardship:** Matthew Musson to the Council of Trade and Plantations, London: 5 July 1717 in CSPCS 1716–1717, No. 635, p. 338; Peter Heywood to the Council of Trade and Plantations, Jamaica: 3 December 1716 in CSPCS 1716–1717, No. 411, p. 213.

159 **Capture of one of the ships sent to "dislodge" pirates:** CO23/1, No. 31: Memorial from the Copartners for Carrying on a Trade & Settling the Bahamas Islands, London: 19 May 1721. This was the *Sarah*, Captain William Taylor, which sailed with the *Samuel*, Captain Edward Hampton. Samuel Buck was the primary owner of both ships.

159 **Bahamas as sanctuary for mulattos and escaped slaves:** Hugo Prosper Leaming, *Hidden Americans: Maroons of Virginia and the Carolinas*, New York: Garland Publishing, 1995, pp. 128–129.

159 **Bermuda governor on slaves and pirates:** Bennett to the Council of Trade, 31 May 1718, p. 261.

159–160 **Henry Jennings (March 1717):** Matthew Musson to the Council of Trade, 5 July 1717, p. 338.

160 **Jennings and Hamilton Galley incident:** "New York Dispatch, October 29," *Boston News-Letter*, 29 October 1716, p. 2.

160 **Abaco, Harbour Island (March 1717):** Ibid.; Council of Trade and Plantations to Secretary Joseph Addison, Whitehall, London: 31 May 1717 in CSPCS 1716–1717, No. 596, p. 321.

161 **Thatch's first command:** "New York Dispatch," *Boston News-Letter*, 29 October 1716, p. 2; GHP, p. 71.

161 **Thatch's appearance (c. 1717):** GHP, pp. 84–85.

161 **Thatch as a mulatto:** Leaming, p. 125.

161 **Up-and-coming rivals to Hornigold:** Musson to the Council of Trade, 5 July 1717, p. 338. Vane's role is surmised from his subsequent behavior and the knowledge that he spent much of 1717 spending the fruits of past piracies as noted in GHP.

162 **Sick mulatto and taking of John Howell:** CO23/1, No. 42iii: Bahamas Council Minutes (Trial of John Howell), Nassau: 22 December 1721.

162–163 **Capture of the Bonnet, Revenge:** Testimony of Robert Brown in CO23/1, No. 42iii; Bennett to the Council of Trade and Plantations, Bermuda: 30 July 1717 in CSPCS 1716–1717, No. 677, p. 360.

164 **Hans Sloane biography:** Arthur MacGregor, "Sir Hans Sloane (1660–1753)," in *Oxford Dictionary of National Biography*, Oxford, UK: Oxford University Press, 2004.

164 **Rogers's letter to Hans Sloane:** British Museum, Sloane Collection, MS No. 4044, folio 155 as printed in Manwaring (1935), p. 125.

164–165 **Contact with the S.P.C.K.:** Little, p. 173.

165 **Madagascar scheme squelched by East India Company:** An entirely believable theory put forth in Little, p. 174.

165 *Swift* fears capture by pirates: General Peter Heywood to the Council of Trade and Plantations, Jamaica: 3 December 1716 in *CSPCS 1716–1717*, No. 411, p. 212.

165 *Seaford* fears capture by Bellamy: Walter Hamilton to the Council of Trade and Plantations, Antigua: 15 May 1717 in *CSPCS 1716–1717*, No. 568, p. 300.

165 *Swift, Seaford* specifications (in notes): Lyon, pp. 28, 32.

165–166 Diplomats' letter to Addison: Council of Trade and Plantations to Secretary Joseph Addison, Whitehall, London: 31 May 1717 in *CSPCS 1716–1717*, No. 596, p. 321.

166 Copartners and Samuel Buck: CO23/1, No. 31: Memorial from the Copartners for Carrying on a Trade & Settling the Bahamas Islands, London: 19 May 1721; Little, p. 180.

166 Petitions to the King: CO5/1265, No. 76iii: Woodes Rogers Petition & Proposal to the King to Govern the Bahamas Islands, London: c. July 1717; CO5/1265, No. 76iv: Petition to the King from Merchants, 1717; CO5/1265, No. 76v: Memorial to Joseph Addison from Sundry Merchants, 1717; CO5/1265, No. 76vii: Petition of Merchants of Bristol to the King, Bristol: 1717.

166–167 Petition to the King and his decision: "Letter of Secretary Joseph Addison to the Council of Trade and Plantations," Whitehall, London: 3 September 1717 in *CSPCS 1717–1718*, No. 64, p. 25.

167 Arguments to Lords Proprietor: CO5/1265, No. 76ii: Woodes Rogers's proposal to the Lords Proprietor of the Bahamas, 1717; Little, pp. 179–180; Letter of Richard Shelton to Mr. Popple, London: 6 November 1717 in *CSPCS 1717–1718*, No. 183, p. 97; Copy of the Surrender from the Lords Proprietor of the Bahama Islands to the King of their right of civil and military government, London: 28 October 1717 in *CSPCS 1717–1718*, No. 176, pp. 85–87.

167 Purchases for the expedition: "Memorial from the Copartners . . ."

168 Lords' Proprietor document completed: "Copy of the Surrender . . . ," pp. 85–87.

168 St. James's Palace described: John Roque, *London, Westminster and Southwark*, Map, 1st edition, 1746, Sheet B2, section 8; Thomas Bowles, *A View of St. James Palace, Pall Mall & etc.*, Engraving, 1763.

168 King's instructions to Rogers: His Majesty's Commission to Woodes Rogers to be Governor of the Bahama Islands, Court of St. James, London: 16 January 1718 in *CSPCS 1717–1718*, No. 220i, pp. 110–112; His Majesty's Instructions to Governor Woodes Rogers, London: 16 January 1718, in *CSPCS 1717–1718*, No. 220ii, pp. 112–113.

CHAPTER SEVEN: BELLAMY

169 Plundering of *Whydah*, treatment of Prince: TEP, pp. 23–24.

170 Peter Hoff's remarks: Ibid., p. 25.

170 Cargoes for Prince loaded: Ibid., p. 25.

171 Capture of the *Tanner* frigate: Ibid., pp. 11, 23, 25.

171 Condition, description of *Marianne* (c. April 1717): CO5/1318, No. 16iii: Deposition of John Lucas before John Hart, Annapolis, MD: 13 April 1717; CO5/1318, No. 16iv: Deposition of Joseph Jacob before John Hart, Annapolis, MD: 13 April 1717.

173 Capture of Beer's sloop: "Rhode Island Dispatch, May 3," *Boston News-Letter*, 6 May 1717, p. 2.

173 Bellamy's speech to Beer: GHP, p. 587.

175 *Marianne, Whydah* separated in fog: TEP, p. 23; Examination of Richard Caverley, p. 151.

175 **Capture of *Agnes*, *Endeavor*, *Anne Galley*:** *TEP*, pp. 16, 23–24; CO5/1318 No. 16ii: Deposition of Andrew Turbett, Williamsburg, VA: 17 April 1717.

176 **William's appearance:** Deposition of John Lucas.

176 **Capture of *Tryal*:** Deposition of John Lucas; Deposition of Joseph Jacob.

177 **HMS *Shoreham*:** ADM51/4341 pt 6: Logbook of *Shoreham*; Lyon, p. 26.

177 **Pirates on lookout for *Shoreham*; attempted captures on 13 April:** CO5/1318 No. 4: Anonymous letter to Council of Trade and Plantations, Rappahannock, VA: 15 April 1717.

178 **Sails to Block Island:** Examination of Richard Caverley, p. 151; Examination of Jeremiah Higgins, p. 155.

178 **Rhode Island described:** Bridenbaugh, pp. 149, 153–154; J. A. Doyle, *English Colonies in America, Volume V: The Colonies Under the House of Hanover*, New York: Henry Holt & Co., 1907, p. 18.

179 **Gardiner's Island:** Zacks, pp. 235–237, 241–242; Robert F. Worth, "Robert D. L. Gardiner, 93, Lord of His Own Island, Dies," *New York Times*, 24 August 2004; Guy Trebay, "The Last Lord of Gardiners Island," *New York Times*, 29 August 2004; "New York Dispatch, 19 April," *Boston News-Letter*, 5 May 1717, p. 2.

180 **Capture of *Mary Anne*:** Deposition of Thomas Fitzgerald and Alexander Mackonochie, Boston: 6 May 1717 in Jameson, pp. 296–297; *TEP*, p. 9.

180 **Course set for Cape Cod:** Ibid.

181 **Capture of *Fisher*:** Deposition of Ralph Merry and Samuel Roberts, Boston: 16 May 1717 in Jameson, pp. 301–302.

181 **Lights placed astern, proceed northwards:** Ibid.; Deposition of Thomas Fitzgerald and Alexander Mackonochie; *TEP*, p. 9.

182 **Events on *Mary Anne*:** *TEP*, pp. 9–11; Deposition of Thomas Fitzgerald and Alexander Mackonochie, pp. 301–302.

183 **Events on *Ann Galley* and *Fisher*:** Deposition of Ralph Merry and Samuel Roberts, pp. 301–302.

184 **Events on *Whydah*:** *TEP*, p. 24; Cyprian Southack to Governor Shute, Eastham, MA: 8 May 1717, Massachusetts Archives item 51: 289, 289a as printed in Kinkor (2003), pp. 121–122; Cyprian Southack to Governor Shute, Provincetown, MA: 5 May 1717, Massachusetts Archives item 51: 287, 287a, as printed in Kinkor (2003), pp. 108–110; Colonel Buffett to Governor Shute in *Boston News-Letter*, 29 April 1717, p. 2; Author's Interview, Kenneth J. Kinkor. The shoulder blade, still embedded on the teapot handle, is on display at the Whydah Museum.

185 **Fate of the *Mary Anne* pirates:** *TEP*, p. 9; Deposition of Thomas Fitzgerald and Alexander Mackonochie.

186 **Fate of the *Ann Galley* and *Fisher* pirates:** Deposition of Ralph Merry and Samuel Roberts, pp. 301–302.

187 **Thomas Davis and the Eastham beachcombers:** Cyprian Southack to Governor Shute, 8 May 1717; Cyprian Southack to Governor Shute, 5 May 1717.

189 **Capture of Connecticut sloop:** This was the *Elizabeth* of Weathersfield, Captain Gersham, on their way home from the Salt Tortugas. Deposition of Edward Sargeant, New York: 3 June 1717, *Records of the Vice-Admiralty Court of the Province of New York 1685–1838*, no. 36–3 as printed in Kinkor (2003), pp. 147–148; Examination of Richard Caverley, p. 151.

189 **Captures off Martha's Vinyard:** "New London Dispatch, May 10," *Boston News-Letter*, 13 May 1717, p. 2; Deposition of Zachariah Hill, Boston: 11 May 1717, Suffolk Court Files of the Massachusetts Archives, folio no. 11945 as printed in Kinkor (2003), p. 127.

190 **Capture of Elizabeth:** Deposition of Paul Mansfield, Salem, MA: 25 May 1717 in Suffolk Court Files of the Massachusetts Archives, folio no. 11945 as printed in Kinkor (2003), p. 136.

190 **Dominicus Jordan and Cape Elizabeth:** John Lane to Governor Shute, Winter Harbor [Falmouth], ME: 19 May 1717 in James Phinney Baxter ed., *Documentary History of the State of Maine*, Vol. IX, Portland, ME: Lafavor-Tower Co., 1907, p. 357; Tristram Frost Jordan, *The Jordan Memorial*, Somersworth, MA: New England History Press, 1982, pp. 131–155; Deposition of Paul Mansfield; "Piscataqua Dispatch, May 24," *Boston News-Letter*, 27 May 1717, p. 2.

191 **Williams at Damariscove:** Deposition of Paul Mansfield; "Piscataqua Dispatch, May 24," *Boston News-Letter*, 27 May 1717, p. 2.

192 **Williams learns of Whydah disaster:** Deposition of Samuel Skinner, Salem, MA: 26 May 1717, Suffolk Court Files of the Massachusetts Archives, folio no. 11945 as printed in Kinkor (2003), p. 138.

192–193 **Shute's actions:** "Boston Notice, May 27," *Boston News-Letter*, 27 May 1717, p. 1; Warrant by Governor Shute to the Sheriff of Barnstable County, Boston: 29 April 1717, Massachusetts Historical Society, Belknap Collection, item 161.A.22 as printed in Kinkor (2003), p. 102.

193 **Movements of Rose and pressing of Bostonians:** ADM 51/801: Logbook of the *Rose*; Action of the Massachusetts General Court, Boston: 11 June 1717, Massachusetts Court Records 21 June 1706 to 11 November 1720, p. 144 as printed in Kinkor (2003), p. 150.

CHAPTER EIGHT: BLACKBEARD

194 **La Buse's ship and plans:** "Piscataqua Dispatch, July 19," *Boston News-Letter*, 22 July 1717, p. 2.

195 **Blackbeard and Hornigold's spring 1717 cruise:** "New York Dispatch, July 29," *Boston News-Letter*, 5 August 1717, p. 2; this appears to have been the source for an inferior account in *GHP*, p. 71.

196 **Williams and Noland's raids down the coast:** "Philadelphia Dispatch, June 20," *Boston News-Letter*, 1 July 1717, p. 2; "New York Dispatch, June 17," *Boston News-Letter*, 24 June 1717, p. 2; "New York Dispatch, June 3," *Boston News-Letter*, 9 June 1717, p. 2.

197 **Stede Bonnet's family background:** St. Michael's Parish: v. 1A–2A baptisms, burials 1648–1739, Barbados Parochial Registers, Series A, 1637–1680, Microfilm, Salt Lake City, Utah: Genealogical Society of Utah, 1978, Batch M513951, Source 1157923; Joanne McRee Sanders, *Barbados Records: Wills and Administrations, Volume I: 1639–1680*, Marceline, WI: Sanders Historical Publications, 1979, pp. 37–38; Lindley S. Butler, *Pirates, Privateers & Rebel Raiders of the Carolina Coast*, Chapel Hill, NC, University of North Carolina Press, 2000, pp. 54–55.

198 **Bonnet's plantation:** Richard Ford, *A New Map of the Island of Barbados*, Map, 1674 as detailed in Dunn, p. 94.

198 **Bonnet's early life, social standing, mental illness:** *GHP*, p. 95; John Camden Hotten, ed. *The Original Lists of Persons of Quality*, New York: G. A. Baker & Co, 1931, p. 451.

199 **Bonnet's crew, library, presence of Scots:** *GHP*, p. 104.

199 **Charlestown and Barbados connections:** Bridenbaugh, p. 150n.

199 **Charlestown and South Carolina described:** John Lawson, *A New Voyage to Carolina*, originally published 1709, Chapel Hill, NC: University of North Carolina, 1967, pp. 13–14; Bridenbaugh, pp. 143, 150–151; Doyle, pp. 46–48.

200 North Carolina described: Doyle, pp. 46, 48.

200 Captures off Charlestown bar: "By letters from South Carolina, 22 September," *Boston News-Letter*, 28 October 1717, p. 2; *GHP*, p. 96.

201 Dissension within crew departing North Carolina: *GHP*, p. 96.

202 Encounter with Spanish Man-of-War: "Philadelphia Dispatch, October 24," *Boston News-Letter*, 11 November 1717, p. 2.

202 Hornigolds's preparations to cruise: CO23/1: Trial of William Howell, Bahamas Council Minutes, Nassau: 22 December 1721.

203 Bondavais's first name: *GHP*, p. 637.

205 Bonnet's dressing gown and books: "Philadelphia Dispatch, October 24," *Boston News-Letter*, 11 November 1717, p. 2.

205 Blackbeard's appearance in battle: *GHP*, pp. 84–85.

206 Capture, sinking of the *Betty*: Indictment of William Howard, Williamsburg, VA: 29 October 1718 in Lee, p. 102; CO5/1442: Wines imported and exported from Madera, March 1716 to March 1717. (The latter contains numerous references to the *Betty*, which regularly made the wine run; coincidently, she was usually captained by John Perrin, the man who bought Hornigold's sloop.)

206 Conditions aboard immigrant ships: Gottleib Mittelberger quoted on his voyage from Europe to Philadelphia in 1750 in John Duffy, "The Passage to the Colonies," *Mississippi Historical Review*, Vol. 38, No. 1 (June 1951), p. 23.

207 Blackbeard's captures, activities off Midatlantic coast: ADM 1/1472, f11: Ellis Brand to the Admiralty, *Lyme*, Elizabeth River, VA: 4 December 1717; "Philadelphia Dispatch, October 24," *Boston News-Letter*, 11 November 1717, p. 2; "New York Dispatch, October 28," *Boston News-Letter*, 11 November 1717, p. 2; "Philadelphia Dispatch, October 31," *Boston News-Letter*, 11 November 1717, p. 2; "New York Dispatch, November 4," *Boston News-Letter*, 11 November 1717, p. 2; Indictment of William Howard, p. 102.

208 What Blackbeard's men told captives: "Philadelphia Dispatch, October 24," *Boston News-Letter*, 11 November 1717, p. 2; "Philadelphia Dispatch, October 31," *Boston News-Letter*, 11 November 1717, p. 2.

208 What Blackbeard learned from captives: On the vessels at Madera, "Philadelphia Dispatch, October 24," *Boston News-Letter*, 11 November 1717, p. 2.

208 King's decision to suppress pirates: "Whitehall Dispatch, September 15," *London Gazette*, 17 September 1717, p. 1.

209 Dispositions of Royal Navy vessels in Americas: "A List of His Majesty's Ships and Vessels employed and to be employed, at the British Governments and Plantations in the West Indies," *London Gazette*, 17 September 1717, p. 1.

209 Blackbeard spotted off Long Island: "New York Dispatch, October 28," *Boston News-Letter*, 11 November 1717, p. 2.

209 Hornigold's probable activities in October and November 1717: "Philadelphia Dispatch, December 10," *Boston News-Letter*, 6 January 1718, p. 2; "Philadelphia Dispatch, November 14," *Boston News-Letter*, 25 November 1717, p. 2.

210 Blackbeards' vessels, armament, crew size: David D. Moore and Mike Daniel, "Blackbeard's Capture of the Nantaise Slave Ship La Concorde," *Tributaries*, October 2001, pp. 24–25. Moore and Daniel cite and quote from French documents at the Centre des Archives d'Outre Mer in Aix-en-Provence, France.

210 Date of Blackbeard's encounter with *La Concorde*: Depositions of Pierre Dosset and Francoise Ernaud as related in Moore and Daniel (2001), p. 24. Dosset and Ernaud note that

they were attacked on 28 November 1717 as per the Gregorian calendar used in France. This date corresponds to 17 November under the Julian calendar, which remained in use by Britain and her colonies until 1752.

211–212 **Description of** *La Concorde* **and capture by Blackbeard:** Moore and Daniel (2001), pp. 18–19, 24; Richard W. Lawrence and Mark Wilde-Ramsing, "In Search of Blackbeard: Historical and Archeological Research at Shipwreck Site 0003BUI," *Southeastern Geology*, Vol. 40, No. 1 (February 2001), p. 2; Bulter, p. 34; Author's Interview, David Moore, North Carolina Maritime Museum, Beaufort, NC: 17 April 2005.

212 **Bequia and Garifuna described:** "Minutes of the Assembly . . . with a view to determining the measures needed to destroy the Caribs of St. Vincent and Dominica," Cul-de-sac du Marin, Martinique: 27 August 1679; Susie Post Rust, "The Garifuna," *National Geographic*, September 2001.

212 **Pirates at Bequia:** Moore and Daniel, p. 25, "Muster roll of Concorde's crew, March 1717," Ibid., pp. 22–23.

214 **Armament, crew of Blackbeard's vessels (c. 25 November):** CO152/12, No. 67ii: Deposition of Thomas Knight, Antigua: 30 November 1717.

214 **Running aground, abandoning slaves at Grenada:** Moore and Daniel, pp. 21, 27.

215 **Existence of brigantine, capture of the** *Great Allen:* "New York Dispatch, February 24," *Boston News-Letter*, 10 March 1718; CO152/12, No. 67iii: Deposition of Henry Bostock, St. Christopher: 19 December 1717.

216 **Capture of** *Montserrat Merchant,* **events in Nevis:** Deposition of Thomas Knight.

219 **Capture, release of the** *New Division:* Deposition of Thomas Knight; Co152/12, No. 67i: Deposition of Richard Joy, Antigua: 30 November 1717.

219 **Condition of St. Christopher:** Extract of Letter of Lt. General Mathew to Governor Walter Hamilton, St. Christopher: 29 September 1720 in *CSPCS 1720–21*, No. 251i, pp. 166–167.

220 **Raid on St. Christopher:** Walter Hamilton to the Council of Trade and Plantations, Antigua: 6 January 1718 in *CSPCS 1717–1718*, No. 298, p. 149; Deposition of Henry Bostock.

220 **Guns added to** *Queen Anne's Revenge:* ADM1/2378 f12: Captain Jonathan Rose to the Admiralty, HMS *Seaford* at Antigua: 23 December 1717; size of guns based on archeaological evidence from Author Interview, Mark Wilde-Ramsing, Queen Anne's Revenge Project, Moorehead City, NC: 17 April 2005.

221 *Seaford's* **size, location, encounter with La Buse:** Jonathan Rose to the Admiralty, 23 December 1717; Walter Hamilton to the Council of Trade, 6 January 1718; Lyon, p. 28.

221 *Seaford's* **close encounter with Blackbeard:** Walter Hamilton to the Council of Trade, 6 January 1718, p. 149.

222 **St. Christopher residents reinforce** *Seaford:* Jonathan Rose to the Admiralty, 23 December 1717; Walter Hamilton to the Council of Trade, 6 January 1718, pp. 149–150.

222 *Scarborough* **and** *Seaford's* **pursuit of Blackbeard:** ADM 1/1879 folio 5: Francis Hume to the Admiralty, *Scarborough*, Barbados: 16 February 1718; ADM1/2378 f12: Jonathan Rose to the Admiralty, *Seaford* at Barbados: 18 February 1718; ADM51/865: entries of 1 November 1717 to 31 March 1717; ADM51/877: entries of 1 November 1717 to 31 March 1717.

223 **Blackbeard at St. Croix:** Deposition of Henry Bostock; Francis Hume to the Admiralty, 16 February 1718; Jonathan Rose to the Admiralty, 18 February 1718.

223 **Capture of the** *Margaret:* Deposition of Henry Bostock.

224 **Captain Pinkentham:** "New York Dispatch, May 28," *Boston News-Letter*, 4 June 1711, p. 2; "Philadelphia Dispatch, July 24," *Boston News-Letter*, 11 August 1718, p. 2.

225 **Blackbeard's subsequent movements:** Francis Hume to the Admiralty, 16 February 1718; Jonathan Rose to the Admiralty, 18 February 1718.

CHAPTER NINE: BEGGING PARDON

226 **The Royal Proclamation:** George I, "A Proclamation for Suppressing of Pirates," Hampton Court: 5 September 1717 in *London Gazette*, 17 September 1717, p. 1.
226 **Pardon reaches Boston first:** Some historians have suggested that news of the pardon arrived prior to the execution of the Bellamy pirates on November 15, but this allegation is not supported by evidence. The following documents demonstrate that news reached Boston between December 1 and 9, Bermuda on or prior to December 19, HMS *Phoenix* in New York on December 25, and HMS *Pearl* in Virginia on January 3. Word was slow to get across the Atlantic, in part because no Royal Navy vessels made the trip between the time the king issued the proclamation and the arrival of Woodes Rogers in the Bahamas in July 1718. Sources: ADM 1/1472 f11: Ellis Brand to the Admiralty, *Pearl* at Virginia: 10 March 1718; ADM 1/2282 f13: Vincent Pearse to the Admiralty, *Phoenix* at New York: 4 February 1718; "A Proclamation for Supressing of Pirates," *Boston News-Letter*, 9 December 1717, p. 1; Benjamin Bennett to the Council of Trade and Plantations, Bermuda: 3 February 1718 in *CSPCS 1717–1718*, No. 345, p. 170.
227 **Trial of the Bellamy pirates:** *TEP.*
227 **Location of courtroom, Boston Prison:** The courtroom occupied the western or uphill end of the new brick Town House, its windows looking out toward the prison. Sinclair and Catherine F. Hitchings, *Theatre of Liberty: Boston's Old State House*, Boston: Boston Safe Deposit & Trust Company, 1975, pp. 1–6; "Old Boston Prison," Commemorative Plaque, 26 Court Street, Boston, MA.
227–228 **Cotton Mather's involvement, quotes:** Cotton Mather, "The Diary of Cotton Mather 1681–1724" in *Collections of the Massachusetts Historical Society*, Series 7, Vol. 7, Boston: Massachusetts Historical Society, 1911, pp. 448, 483, 490; Cotton Mather, *Instructions to the Living from the Condition of the Dead: A Brief Relation of Remarkables in the Shipwreck of above One Hundred Pirates*, Boston: John Allen, 1717, pp. 17–18, 37–38.
228 **Bennett forwards pardons to Nassau:** Bennett to the Council of Trade, 3 February 1718; "Bermuda Dispatch, February 16," *London Gazette*, 12 April 1718, p. 1.
229 **Pirates react to proclamation:** "Extract of a Letter from South Carolina," 2 February 1718 in London *Weekly Journal or British Gazetteer*, 3 May 1718, p. 1,033.
230 **Antipardon pirates' proposal to James III; Cammocke's letter:** George Cammocke to Queen Mary of Modina, St. Germaine, France: 28 March 1718 in Stuart Papers 29/49.
230 **Jacobite letter to Cammocke:** Craton, p. 100.
231 **Prizes brought into Nassau December 1717–January 1718:** Extract of a Letter from South Carolina, 2 February 1718; "Jamaica Dispatch, March 28," The [London] *Weekly Journal or British Gazetteer*, 7 June 1718, p. 1; Lord Carteret to Governor Burnet, Whitehall, London: 22 August 1722, *CSPCS 1722–1723*, item 267, p. 128; ADM 1/2282 f13: Vincent Pearse to the Admiralty, *Phoenix* at New York: 3 June 1718; HCA 1/54: Deposition of Benjamin Sims, London: 28 September 1721.
231 **General council of the pirates:** *GHP*, p. 41.
232 **Pirates scatter (Winter and Brown):** Clinton V. Black, *Pirates of the West Indies*, Cambridge, UK: Cambridge University Press, 1989, p. 120; Black incorrectly states that Winter, Brown,

and Blackbeard accepted the pardon at Nassau; Peter Earle, *The Pirate Wars*, New York: St. Martin's Press, p. 162.

232 **Pirates scatter (Condent):** ADM 1/2282 f13: Vincent Pearse to the Admiralty, *Phoenix* at New Providence, Bahamas: 4 March 1718; Pearse to the Admiralty, 3 June 1718; GHP, pp. 581–582.

232 **Vincent Pearse obtains pardon:** ADM 1/2282 f13: Pearse to the Admiralty, *Phoenix* at New York: 4 February 1718. Pearse says he received word of the proclamation "the 25th of last month," but I am assuming he meant the month of December, as it seems impossible that the proclamation, printed by the *Boston News-Letter* on 9 December, would take nearly two months to reach New York.

232 **Storm of 24–25 December 1717:** News item, *Boston News-Letter*, 6 January 1718, p. 2. Winter storms also delayed the departure of the weekly postal rider on the week of 9 December.

232 **Pearse background:** Hardy, p. 34.

233 **Pearse refits the *Phoenix*:** ADM 51/690: entries of December 1717–February 1718. Pearse notes in the log that he departed New York "having partially re-rigged."

233 ***Phoenix* specifications, history:** Lyon, pp. 37–38; ADM 33/298: HMS *Phoenix* Pay Book, 1716–1718.

233 ***Phoenix* departs New York:** Pearse to the Admiralty, *Phoenix* at New York: 4 February 1718; ADM 51/690: entry of February 6, 1718.

233 ***Phoenix* arrival at Nassau:** ADM 51/690: entries of 22–24 February 1718; Pearse to the Admiralty, 3 June 1718.

233 **Lt. Symonds's identity, trip ashore:** Abstract of a Letter of Robert Maynard to Lt. Symonds, North Carolina: 17 December 1718 in [London] *Weekly Journal or British Gazette*, 25 April 1719, p. 1,339.

234 ***Phoenix* confronts Vane, takes *Lark*:** ADM 51/690: entry of 24 February 1718.

234 **Vane and the *Lark*:** ADM 51/690: entry of 24 February 1717.

235–236 **Pearse meets with pirate leaders, releases Vane:** ADM 51/690: entry of 24 February 1718.

236 **Pardoning of pirates, list thereof:** ADM 51/690: entries of 24–28 February 1718; ADM 1/2282 f13: A List of the Names of such Pirates as Surrendered themselves at Providence to Capt. Vincent Pearse, Nassau, Bahamas: 26 February to 11 March 1718.

236 **Pearse estimates 500 pirates, optimistic comments:** Pearse to the Admiralty, 3 June 1718; Pearse to the Admiralty, 4 March 1718.

236 **Edward England described:** GHP, p. 114.

236 **Several sloops come and go from Nassau:** ADM 51/690: entries of 1–7 March 1718.

236 **Events of March 1:** Ibid., entry of 1 March 1718.

236 **Pirates scatter (Jennings):** Bennett to the Council of Trade, 3 February 1718; "Bermuda Dispatch, February 16," *London Gazette*, 12 April 1718, p. 1.

236 **Pirates scatter (on merchant vessels):** "Philadelphia Dispatch, March 5," *Boston News-Letter*, 17 March 1718, p. 2; Francis Leslie to Bennett, Nassau: 10 January 1718 in *CSPCS 1717–1718*, No. 345iii, p. 171.

237 **Jack Rackham described:** GHP, pp. 148, 620.

237 **Vane captures Jamaica sloop:** Ibid., p. 141; ADM 51/690: entry of 21 March 1718.

237 **Orientation of Nassau harbor:** Nassau Harbor, map, in Little, p. 183; Pearse to the Admiralty, 3 June 1718.

238 **Vane plunders sloop in harbor, Pearse counterattacks:** GHP, p. 141; ADM 51/690: entry of 22 March 1718; Pearse to the Admiralty, 3 June 1718.

238 Quotes on change of mood in Nassau: ADM 51/690: entry of 22 March 1718; Pearse to the Admiralty, 3 June 1718.

238 Pirates burn ships at Nassau: ADM 51/690: entry of 29 March 1718.

238 Hornigold's men, request for man-of-war: "Rhode Island Dispatch, March 28," *Boston News-Letter*, 31 March 1718, p. 2; "New York Dispatch, March 10," *Boston News-Letter*, 18 March 1718, p. 2; Vincent Pearse to the Admiralty, 4 March 1718.

239 Vane slips out of Nassau, joined by 24 others: Ibid., entries of 18–19 March 1718; *GHP*, p. 141.

239 Vane returns with *Lark*, threatens *Phoenix*, rows ashore: Ibid.: entries of 31 March and 1 April 1718; *GHP*, p. 141; Pearse to the Admiralty, 3 June 1718.

239 Growth of Vane's crew: *GHP*, p. 141; Pearse to the Admiralty, 3 June 1718.

239 Vane captures two sloops in Nassau Harbor: ADM 51/690: entry of 2 April 1718.

240 Bennett on Pearse's deteriorating situation: Bennett to the Council of Trade, 31 May 1718, p. 260.

240 *Phoenix* catches fire, runs aground: ADM 51/690: entries of 7–10 April 1718.

240 Defection of *Phoenix*'s men: Pearse to the Admiralty, 3 June 1718; ADM 1/2282 f13: Pearse to the Admiralty, *Phoenix* at Plymouth, England: 21 January 1722.

240 "Great Devil" in Gulf of Mexico: "Jamaica Dispatch, March 28," London *Weekly Journal or British Gazetteer*, 7 June 1718, p. 1.

240 Blackbeard, Bonnet near Vera Cruz, threaten *Adventure*: "From a letter of *Crown Galley* of Jamaica," London *Weekly Journal or British Gazetteer*, 27 September 1718, p. 1,161.

240 *Adventure* specifications, largest frigate: Lyon, p. 25; "A List of His Majesty's Ships and Vessels employed and to be employed at the British Governments and Plantations in the West Indies," *London Gazette*, 17 September 1717, p. 1.

241 Bonnet engages *Protestant Caesar*: "Report on William Wyer, May 31," *Boston News-Letter*, 16 June 1718, p. 2.

241 Blackbeard deposes Bonnet: *GHP*, p. 22; "The Trials of Major Stede Bonnet and Thirty-three Others," in Francis Hargrave, *A Complete Collection of State Trials and Proceedings for High Treason*, 4th Ed., Vol. VI, London: T. Wright, 1777, p. 183.

242 Capture of *Adventure*, *Land of Promise*: "Report of Thomas Newton," *Boston News-Letter*, 16 June 1718, p. 2; *TSB*, pp. 44–45.

242 Capture of *Protestant Caesar*: Report of William Wyer; *GHP*, p. 72; *TSB*, pp. 44–45.

244 Vane captures twelve vessels: CO 37/10, No. 10viii: Deposition of John Tibby, Bermuda: 24 May 1718. The seven Bermuda sloops were, in order of capture: two unnamed sloops commanded by Daniel Styles and James Borden; the *William & Mary* (Edward North); *Diamond* (John Tibby); *Penzance* (William Hall); *Samuel* (Joseph Besea); and an unnamed sloop under Captain John Penniston. The others were the *Betty* of Jamaica (Benjamin Lee); a Jamaica sloop under John Gainsby; the twenty-six-foot sloop *Fortune* of Jamaica (George Guy); a sloop from New York (Samuel Vincent); and a Boston ship under Captain Richards.

244 Bermuda vessels in Bahamas: Bennett to the Council of Trade, 31 May 1718.

244 Thomas Brown motivates abuse by Vane: CO 37/10, No. 10i: Deposition of Samuel Cooper, Bermuda: 24 May 1718; CO 37/10, No. 10v: Deposition of Nathaniel Catling, Bermuda: 17 May 1718; CO 37/10, No. 10vi: Deposition of Joseph Besea, Bermuda: 28 May 1718.

244 Tortures aboard *William & Mary*: CO 37/10, No. 10ii: Deposition of Edward North, Bermuda: 22 May 1718; CO 37/10, No. vii: Deposition of Nathaniel North, Bermuda: 22 May 1718.

245 **Tortures aboard** *Diamond*: Deposition of Nathaniel Catling; Depostion of Samuel Cooper.

245 **Threaten to attack Bermuda**: Bennett to the Council of Trade, 31 May 1718; Deposition of Samuel Cooper.

245 **Damnation to King George**: Deposition of Edward North; Deposition of Samuel Cooper.

245 **Other captures, growth in crew**: *TJR*, pp. 38, 40; CO 37/10, No. 10iv: Deposition of James Mack-Cuelle, Bermuda: 16 May 1718; Deposition of Edward North.

246 **Blackbeard, Bonnet arrive in Nassau**: Hargrave (VI), p. 164.

247 **Composition, contents of Rogers's fleet**: CO 23/1, No. 31: Memorial from the Copartners for carrying on a trade and settling the Bahamas Islands, London: 19 May 1721.

247 **S.P.C.K. documents**: Little, p. 180.

247 **Overall investment, six partners, Rogers portion**: Memorial from the Copartners . . . , 19 May 1721; Little, p. 180; CO 23/12/2: Woodes Rogers's Appeal to the King, 1726.

247–248 **William Fairfax bio, quotes**: Donald Jackson, ed., *The Diaries of George Washington*, Vol. 1, Charlottesville, VA: University Press of Virginia, 1976, p. 3n; William Fairfax to Anna Harrison Fairfax, *Delicia* at the Nore, England: 19 April 1718 in Edward D Neill, *The Fairfaxes of England and America in the Seventeenth and Eighteenth Centuries*, Albany, NY: Joel Munsell, 1868, pp. 70–71.

248 **Specifications of HMS** *Rose*, *Milford*, *Shark*: Lyon, pp. 26, 37.

248 **Date of departure (from the Nore)**: ADM 51/892 pt. 2: entry of 22 April 1718; ADM 51/801: entry of 22 April 1718.

249 **Stopped at Florida Wrecks**: *TSB*, p. 45.

249 **Captures en route to Charleston**: *GHP*, p. 74; Hargrave (VI) p. 164.

249–250 **Movements of Burgess, Ashworth**: CO 5/508: South Carolina Imports for the 25th March to the 24th June 1718, pp. 51, 54; CO 5/508: South Carolina Exports for the 25th March to the 24th June 1718, pp. 59–61.

250 **Arrival at Charleston, seize pilot boat**: Governor Johnson to the Lords Proprietor of Carolina, Charlestown, SC: 18 June 1718 cited in Edward McGrady, *The History of South Carolina Under the Proprietary Government, 1670–1719*, New York: Macmillan Company, 1897.

250 **Vessel captures at Charleston bar**: CO5/508: South Carolina Imports . . . , p. 54; CO 5/508: South Carolina Exports . . . , p. 60; "South Carolina Dispatch, June 6," *Boston News-Letter*, 7 July 1718, p. 2; "Philadelphia Dispatch, June 26," *Boston News-Letter*, 7 July 1718, p. 2; CO 5/1265: Letter to the Lord Proprietors of Carolina, Charlestown, SC: 13 June 1718; Testimony of Ignatius Pell, p. 164; *GHP*, p. 74.

251 **Interrogation of Wragg, pirates' council and demands**: *GHP*, pp. 88–89.

251 **Prisoners number eighty**: *GHP*, p. 91.

251 **Events at Charleston**: *GHP*, pp. 89–91; Letter to the Lord Proprietors of Carolina, 13 June 1718.

253 **Pirates are seen as heroes in Charleston**: Hargrave (VI), p. 163.

253 **Blackbeard offered pardon by Johnson**: Spotswood to Lord John Cartwright, Williamsburg, VA: 14 February 1718 in R. A. Brock (1882), p. 273.

253 **Plunder taken, cargoes destroyed, keeping Capt Hurst**: "South Carolina Dispatch, June 6," *Boston News-Letter*, 7 July 1718, p. 2; "Philadelphia Dispatch, June 26," *Boston News-Letter*, 7 July 1718, p. 2; Letter to the Lords Proprietor of Carolina, 13 June 1718.

254 **Capture of the** *Princess*, *William* of Boston: Letter to the Lords Proprietor of Carolina, 13 June 1718; CO5/508: South Carolina Imports . . . , pp. 54–55; *TSB*, p. 44.

254 "Baker's dozen": *TSB*, p. 48.

254 Swearing revenge on New Englanders: "South Carolina Dispatch, June 6," *Boston News-Letter*, 7 July 1718, p. 2.

254 Blackbeard angry at Richards for not burning William: *TSB*, p. 44.

254 Quotes from Blackbeard's journal: *GHP*, p. 86.

255 Alleged plan to intercept Spanish treasure fleet: *TSB*, p. 45.

256 Beaufort Inlet, channel, and village in 1718: John T. Wells and Jesse E. McNinch, "Reconstructing Shoal and Channel Configuration in Beaufort Inlet," *Southeastern Geology*, Vol. 40, No. 1 (February 2001), pp. 11–18; Charles L. Paul, "Colonial Beaufort," *North Carolina Historical Review*, Vol. 42, 1965, pp. 139–152; Author's Visit, Beaufort, NC: 17 April 2005.

256 Blackbeard runs *Queen Anne's Revenge* aground: Richard W. Lawrence and Mark Wilde-Ramsing, "In Search of Blackbeard: Historical and Archeological Research at Shipwreck Site 0003BUI," *Southeastern Geology*, Vol. 40, No. 1 (February 2001), pp. 7–9. *TSB*, p. 46; "Philadelphia Dispatch, June 26," *Boston News-Letter*, 7 July 1718, p. 2.

256 Blackbeard doublecrosses Bonnet, other pirates: Hargrave (VI), pp. 163, 167; "New York Dispatch, July 14," *Boston News-Letter*, 21 July 1718, p. 2.

257 Bath described: Herbert R. Paschal Jr., *A History of Colonial Bath*, Raleigh, NC: Edwards & Broughton Co., 1955, pp. 32–38; "Historic Bath Walking Tour" (pamphlet), Bath, NC: Historic Bath Historic Sites; Author's Visit, Bath, NC: 16 April 2005.

257 Charles Eden background, home: Wilson & Fiske, Vol. 7, p. 301; Lee, pp. 55–65.

258 Blackbeard's men disperse: Spotswood to Lord John Cartwright, 14 February 1718; Spotswood to the Council of Trade and Plantations, Williamsburg, VA: 22 December 1718 in *CSPCS* 1717–1718, No. 800, p. 430.

258 Blackbeard at Plum Point: Lee, p. 62 (citing interviews with elderly Bath residents during a 1966 research trip).

258 Blackbeard marries in Bath: *GHP*, p. 76; Lee, pp. 74–75; ADM 1/1826 f2: George Gordon to the Admiralty, London: 12 September 1721.

258 Blackbeard revels with planters: *GHP*, p. 77.

259 Death of Mary of Modena; collapse of Stuart plan: Hector McDonnell, *The Wild Geese of the Antrim McDonnells*, Dublin: Irish Academic Press, p. 81.

259 Jennings takes Bennett's commission: "Piscatiqua (Portsmouth, NH) Dispatch, July 4," *Boston News-Letter*, 7 July 1718, p. 2.

259 Vane departs with seventy-five men: *GHP*, p. 141.

259 Capture of *Richard & John*: *TJR*, pp. 38, 40.

260 Capture of French ship and two-masted vessel: *GHP*, pp. 141–142. The ship was not yet in Vane's possession when he captured the *Richard & John*, but is referred to regularly in regard to the events of July 4, so was presumably his flagship during the capture of the *St. Martin*.

260 Capture of *St. Martin*: ADM 1/2649, f11: Vice Admiralty Court Proceedings, Nassau: 7–9 August 1718 (especially Testimony of Jacques Blondez); *GHP*, p. 141; Note that Blondez cites a "New Style" or Gregorian calendar date (July 1) in his testimony; ADM 1/2649 f11: An account of the Wines, Flower & Beef belonging to the Brigantine called the St. Martin of Bordeaux.

260 Capture of sloops off Harbour Island, Vane in Nassau July 4–24: *GHP*, p. 142; ADM 1/2649, f11: Vice Admiralty Court Proceedings, Nassau: 7–9 August 1718 (testimonies of Robert Brown, William Harris, John Draper, John Fredd).

261 Rogers arrives: ADM 51/801: entries for 24–25 July 1718.

CHAPTER TEN: BRINKSMANSHIP

262 Disposition of Rogers fleet, night of July 24: ADM 1/2282 f2: George Pomeroy to the Admiralty, New York: 3 September 1718; ADM 51/406 pt. 4: entries of 23–25 July 1718; ADM 51/801 pt. 4: entries of 24–25 July 1718; ADM 51/892: entries of 24–25 July 1718.

263 Vane fires on *Rose*, scene in harbor: ADM 51/801 pt. 4: entry of 25 July 1718; GHP, p. 143; CO 23/1, No. 31: Memorial from the Copartners for carrying on a trade and settling the Bahamas Islands, London: 19 May 1721; CO 23/1, No. 17: Testimonial of Samuel Buck on the State of the Bahama Islands, 2 December 1719.

263 Lieutenant meets with Vane: ADM 51/801 pt. 4: entry of 25 July 1718.

264 Vane's letter: Charles Vane to Woodes Rogers, Nassau: 24 July 1718 in GHP, p. 142.

265 Vane's fireship: ADM 51/406 pt. 4: entry of 25 July 1718; ADM 51/801 pt. 4: entry of 25 July 1718; ADM 51/892: entry of 25 July 1718; GHP, p. 143.

265 Vane takes *Katherine*, collects supplies, men from town: GHP, p. 143; CO 23/1, No. 10viii: Deposition of Richard Taylore, Nassau: 4 August 1718; ADM 51/406 pt. 4: entry of 25 July 1718.

266 Smoldering timbers: Rogers to the Council of Trade and Plantations, Nassau: 31 October 1718 in CSPCS 1717–1718, No. 737, p. 372.

266 *Delicia*, *Milford* run aground: ADM 51/406 pt. 4: entry of 25 July 1718; Rogers to the Council of Trade, 31 October 1718, p. 372.

266 *Buck*, another sloop, pursue Vane: ADM 51/801 pt. 4: entry of 25 July 1718; ADM 51/892: entry of 25 July 1718; GHP, p. 143; George Pomeroy to the Admiralty, 3 September 1718; Rogers to the Council of Trade, 31 October 1718.

267 Rogers's landing and reception: Rogers to the Council of Trade, 31 October 1718, p. 372; GHP, pp. 616–617.

267 Condition of the fort: Rogers to the Council of Trade, 31 October 1718, p. 374; GHP, p. 615.

267 Accommodations for soldiers, colonists: GHP, pp. 617–619.

268 Governing council named: CO 23/1, No. 10ii: Council Minutes for 1 August 1718; Woodes Rogers to the Council of Trade, 31 October 1718, pp. 372–373.

268 Pirate and nonpirate population: Testimonial of Samuel Buck on the State of the Bahama Islands, 2 December 1719.

268 Rogers's work plans: CO 23/1, No. 10ii: Council Minutes for 5, 20 & 28 August 1718.

268 *Samuel* arrives: ADM 51/892: entry of 1 August 1718.

268 Vane's message: Rogers to the Council of Trade, 31 October 1718, pp. 376–377.

268 Richard Taylor's report: Deposition of Richard Taylore.

269 Disease strikes Nassau: Rogers to the Council of Trade, 31 October 1718, pp. 373–374; ADM 51/801 pt. 4: entries of 8–9 August 1718; ADM 51/406 pt. 4: entries of 6–13 August 1718; CO 23/1, No. 10i: A general list of soldiers, sailors and passengers deceased since we arrived at Providence, Nassau: October 1718; Testimonial of Samuel Buck.

269 Rogers's sickness: CO 23/1, No. 10ii: Council Minutes for 29 August 1718; CO 23/12/2: Woodes Rogers' Appeal to the King, London: 1726.

269 Rogers on locals' laziness: CO 23/1, No. 15: Rogers to the Council of Trade, 29 May 1719; Rogers to the Council of Trade, 31 October 1718, p. 374.

270 Rogers negotiates with Chamberlaine: Rogers to the Council of Trade, 31 October 1718, p. 376.

270 *Milford*, *Shark* depart Nassau: ADM 51/406 pt. 4: entry of 16 August 1718.

271 **Vane's men in boat, Joseph Cockram's news:** Rogers to the Council of Trade, 31 October 1718, pp. 376; CO 23/1, No. 10iii: Deposition of Thomas Bowlin and four others, Nassau: 8 September 1718.

271 **Loss of Buck, story of Walter Kennedy:** ADM 51/801 pt. 4: entry of 10 September 1718; CO 23/1, No. 31: Memorial from the Copartners for carrying on a trade and settling the Bahamas Islands, London: 19 May 1721; ADM 1/1597 f11: Peter Chamberlaine to the Admiralty, *Milford* at New York: 20 November 1718; Arthur L. Hayward (ed.), *Lives of the Most Remarkable Criminals*, London: George Routledge & Sons, 1927 (originally published London: John Osborn, 1735), pp. 35–36.

271–272 **Negotiations with, departure of Whitney:** Rogers to the Council of Trade, 31 October 1718, pp. 376; ADM 51/801 pt. 4: Logbook of the *Rose*, entry of 14 September 1718; CO 23/13: Rogers to Secretary Craggs, Nassau: 24 December 1718.

272 **News of Vane's arrival:** Rogers to the Council of Trade, 31 October 1718, p. 376.

272 **Capture of *John & Elizabeth*:** TJR, pp. 26, 35, 37.

272 **Capture of Barbados sloop *John & Elizabeth*:** GHP, p. 135.

272 **Pirate account from *Weekly Journal*:** "News from a ship newly-arrived from South Carolina," London *Weekly Journal or British Gazetteer*, 27 December 1718, p. 1,238.

273 **Vane's captures at Charleston:** "Rhode Island Dispatch, October 10," *Boston News-Letter*, 20 October 1718, p. 2; Governor and Council of South Carolina to the Council of Trade and Plantations, Charlestown, SC: 21 October 1718 in *CSPCS 1717–1718*, No. 730, p. 366; CO 5/508: South Carolina Imports for the 24th June to the 29th September 1718, p. 64.

273 **Yeats' defection:** "Rhode Island Dispatch, October 10," *Boston News-Letter*, 20 October 1718, p. 2.

273–274 **Catching the *Emperor* and *Neptune*:** "Protest of Captain King, Commander of the *Neptune*," Nassau: 5 February 1719 in *GHP*, p. 144; Deposition of Joseph Aspinwall, London: 28 July 1719 in Peter Wilson Coldham (ed.), *English Adventurers and Emigrants 1661–1733*, Baltimore: Genealogical Publishing Inc., 1985, p. 150; CO 5/508: South Carolina Exports for the 24th June to the 29th September 1718, p. 68. The *Neptune* was a 300-ton ship under Captain John King, the *Emperor* a fifty-ton vessel under Arnold Powers.

274–275 **Bonnet seeks privateering commission:** Bonnet even went so far as to obtain clearance papers from Governor Eden, officially endorsing his departure for St. Thomas. Hargrave (VI), pp. 164, 185.

275 **Robert Tucker elected, overrules Bonnet:** Ibid., pp. 162, 164, 184–185.

275 ***Revenge* has only 10–12 barrels of provisions:** Ibid., p. 167.

275 **Bonnet's aliases, renaming *Revenge*:** Ibid., p. 161; TSB, p. 46.

275–276 **Trading goods for plunder:** TSB, p. 46; GHP, p. 98.

276 **Tucker cuts victims:** Hargrave (VI), p. 173.

276 **Toasting James Stuart in Lewes, Tucker "their father":** Ibid., p. 166.

276 **Pirates escape to and from Rhode Island:** "Rhode Island Dispatch, August 8," *Boston News-Letter*, 11 August 1718, p. 2; TSB, p. 46; "Rhode Island Dispatch, August 15," *Boston News-Letter*, 18 August 1718, p. 2.

277 **Account of battle at Cape Fear:** Governor and Council of South Carolina to the Council of Trade, 21 October 1718, pp. 366–367; GHP, pp. 100–102.

277 **Captives' abortive escape at Cape Fear:** Hargrave (VI), p. 178.

278 **Quotes on status of blacks:** Ibid.; TSB, p. 48. The mulatto captive, Thomas Gerrat, was later tried and found not guilty of piracy.

278 **Pirates intend to go to St. Thomas:** TSB, p. 47.

278 **Blackbeard's men plundering trading vessels:** ADM 1/1472 f11: Brand to the Admiralty, *Lyme* at Virginia: 6 February 1719.

278 **Blackbeard's men cause trouble at Bath, Blackbeard cleared to St. Thomas:** Deposition of Governor Charles Eden to North Carolina Council, Chowan, NC: 30 December 1718 in William L Saunders, *Colonial Records of North Carolina*, Vol. II, Raleigh, NC: P. M. Hale, 1886, p. 322.

278 **Blackbeard at Philadelphia:** John F. Watson, *Annals of Philadelphia and Pennsylvania*, Vol. II, Philadelphia: John Pennington & Uriah Hunt, 1844, pp. 216–218; Lee, p. 78.

278 **Blackbeard captures French ships near Bermuda:** Alexander Spotswood to Secretary Craggs, Williamsburg, VA: 26 May 1719 in Brock (1882), pp. 316–319; North Carolina Council Minutes, Chowan, NC: 27 May 1719 in Saunders (1886), p. 341; Spotswood to the Lords of Trade, Williamsburg, VA: 26 May 1719 in Brock (1882), p. 323.

279 **Plundering of French ship, wounded men at Ocracoke:** "Rhode Island Dispatch, November 14," *Boston News-Letter*, 17 November 1718, p. 2; Brand to the Admiralty, 6 February 1719.

280 **Blackbeard's attack on William Bell:** Ibid., p. 342; Testimony of William Bell, Chowan, NC: 27 May 1719 in Saunders (1886), pp. 342–343.

280 **Blackbeard goes to Bath:** North Carolina Council Minutes, 27 May 1719, p. 341.

280 **Blackbeard meets with Knight:** Ibid., pp. 341–342.

280 **Blackbeard comes to Bath, claims French ship was wreck:** Spotswood to the Lords of Trade, Williamsburg, VA: 26 May 1719 in Brock, p. 323; Testimony of Tobias Knight, Chowan, NC: 27 May 1719 in Saunders (1886), p. 347.

280 **Pirated sugar in Knight's barn:** Abstract of testimony of Ellis Brand given in Virginia, 12 March 1718, North Carolina Council Minutes, Chowan, NC: 27 Mary 1719 in Saunders (1886), p. 346; ADM 1/1472 f11: Brand to the Admiralty, Galleon's Reach, England: 14 July 1719.

280 **French ship burned:** Spotswood to the Council of Trade and Plantations, Williamsburg, VA: 11 August 1719 in *CSPCS 1719–1720*, No. 357, p. 207.

CHAPTER ELEVEN: HUNTED

283 **Virginia population, description:** Brock (1882), p. xi; Doyle, pp. 32–39.

283 **Williamsburg described:** Samuel Chamberlain, *Behold Williamsburg*, New York: Hastings House, 1947, pp. 3, 9; A. Lawrence Kocher and Howard Dearstyne, *Colonial Williamsburg: Its Buildings and Gardens*, Williamsburg, VA: Colonial Williamsburg, 1949, pp. 3–17.

283 **Governor's Palace:** Instructions to William Bird, Agent for the Colony of Virginia, Williamsburg, VA: 20 November 1718 in *CSPCS 1717–1718*, No. 808iib, p. 435; Kocher and Dearstyle, pp. 21, 52–55.

283 **Spotswood's land dealings:** Lee, pp. 97–99.

283 **Spottswood's other dealings:** Address of the House of Burgesses of Virginia to the King, Williamsburg, VA: 20 November 1718 in *CSPCS 1717–1718*, No. 808iia, p. 434; Instructions to William Bird, pp. 434–435.

284 **Rogers dispatches Hornigold, Cockram:** Rogers to the Council of Trade, 31 October 1718, p. 376.

284 **Rogers's activities awaiting Hornigold's return, 150 pirates abandon island:** Woodes Rogers to the Council of Trade, 31 October 1718, pp. 376–377.

284 **Hornigold and Vane's activities at Green Turtle Cay:** Protest of Captain King, in *GHP,* pp. 145–146; Deposition of Joseph Aspinwall, in Coldham, pp. 150–151.

285 **Woodall's capture effects pirate morale:** Rogers to the Council of Trade, 31 October 1718, pp. 376–377.

286 **Capture of pirates at Green Turtle Cay:** CO 23/1: Trial & Condemnation of Ten Persons for Piracy at New Providence, Nassau: 10 December 1718; Rogers to the Council of Trade, 31 October 1718, pp. 377–378; Rogers to Secretary Craggs, 24 December 1718.

286 **Council meets to decide prisoners' fate:** CO 23/1, No. 18: Private Consultation Minutes, Nassau: 28 November 1718.

287 **Vane, Blackbeard at Ocracoke:** *GHP,* 138; ADM 1/1826: Spotswood to George Gordon, Williamsburg, VA: 24 November 1718; in the letter, Spotswood informs Gordon that "the Pyrats at Okracock have been join'd by some other Pyrat crews, & are increased (as 'tis said) to 170 men."

288 **Spotswood's secrecy, Virginian pirate sympathizers:** Spotswood to Lord Carteret, Williamsburg, VA: 14 February 1719 in Brock (1882), p. 274; Spotswood to the Council of Trade and Plantations, Williamsburg, VA: 22 December 1718 in *CSPCS* 1717–1718, No. 800, pp. 430–432; ADM 1/1472: Ellis Brand to the Admiralty, Whorstead, England: 8 April 1721.

288 **Brand, Gordon meet Spotswood after Howard trial:** Brand to the Admiralty, 6 February 1719.

289 **Size of *Lyme, Pearl*:** Lyon, pp. 26, 36.

289 **Bounty for Thatch:** Spotswood to Council of Trade, 22 December 1718, p. 432.

289 **Gordon's orders; size, complement of *Jane, Ranger*:** ADM 51/672 p3: entry of 17 November 1718; Abstract of Letter of Robert Maynard to Mr. Symonds of the Phoenix, North Carolina: 17 December 1718 in London *Weekly Journal or British Gazette,* 25 April 1719, p. 1,339.

289 **Maynard as oldest officer:** ADM 1/1826 f2: George Gordon to the Admiralty, *Pearl* at Carlisle Bay, Jamaica: 10 March 1718.

289 **Edmund Hyde:** Abstract of Letter of Robert Maynard to Mr Symonds, p. 1,339; Hyde's full name and rank is found in ADM 33/311: Paybook of the *Pearl,* where he is listed as "Killed in taking Pirate Teach."

290 **Hour of 17 November departure:** Brand to the Admiralty, 6 February 1719.

290 **Edenton (Chowan) area described:** William Gordon to the secretary, London: 12 May 1709 in Saunders (1886), pp. 711–714; Doyle (1907), pp. 44–47.

290 **Maurice Moore, Edward Moseley:** Lee, pp. 157–160.

290 **Brand in Edenton, Bath:** Brand to the Admiralty, 6 February 1719.

291 **Maynard at Roanoke, Currituck Sound:** Brand to the Admiralty, 6 February 1719.

291 **Blackbeard "fortifying Ocracoke," backed by 170 men:** Spotswood to the Council of Trade, 22 December 1718, p. 430; ADM 1/1826: Spotswood to George Gordon, Williamsburg, VA: 24 November 1718.

292 **Maynard arrives at Ocracoke:** Ellis Brand to the Admiralty, 6 February 1719.

292 **Blackbeard's travels, Knight's letter, drinking with Oddell:** ADM 1/1826 f2: George Gordon to the Admiralty, London: 14 September 1721; Tobias Knight to Edward Thatch, Bath, NC: 17 November 1718 in Saunders (1886), pp. 343–344; *GHP,* pp. 80, 83.

293–296 **Account of the battle:** Ibid.; Abstract of Letter of Robert Maynard to Mr. Symonds, p. 1,339; "Rhode Island Dispatch, February 20," *Boston News-Letter,* 2 March 1719, p. 2; *GHP,* pp. 79–83; Letter of George Gordon to the Admiralty, 14 September 1721; ADM 33/311: Paybook of the *Lyme* (for identity of slain coxswain Allen Arlington).

296 Goods found by Maynard: Brand to the Admiralty, 6 February 1719; George Gordon to the Admiralty, 14 September 1721.

296 Blackbeard's severed head, body: Abstract of Letter of Robert Maynard to Mr Symonds, p. 1339; ADM 51/672 p5: Entry of 3 January 1719; Lee, 124.

296 Maynard comes to Bath: Brand to the Admiralty, 6 February 1719; GHP, p. 83.

296 Brand on Knight: Brand to the Admiralty, 14 July 1719; Abstract of testimony of Ellis Brand given in Virginia, Saunders (1886), p. 344.

296 "Memorandum in Tache's pocket book," other evidence: Ibid.

296 Knight shows Brand stolen goods: Ibid.

296 Eden turns over slaves, sugar: ADM 1/1472 f11: Brand to the Admiralty, Lyme at Virginia: March 1719; Brand to the Admiralty, 6 February 1719.

297 Maynard's return to Virginia: ADM 51/672 pt. 5: entry of 3 January 1719.

297 Head given to Spotswood, hung from pole: Extract of some letters from Virginia, London Weekly Journal or British Gazette, 11 April 1719, p. 1,229; Watson (II, 1844), p. 221.

297 Benjamin Franklin's ditty: Lee, pp. 228–229.

297 Trial, execution of Blackbeard pirates: The trial records have sadly been lost, apparently in the fire that engulfed Virginia's Capitol in 1747. Fragmentary accounts of the trial survive in GHP, p. 86, and Saunders (1886), pp. 341–344. See also Lee, pp. 136–142.

297–298 Trial of Tobias Knight: The full trial record is found in: Minutes of North Carolina Governing Council, Chowan, NC: 27 May 1719 in Saunders (1886), pp. 341–349.

298 Eden versus Brand, Spotswood: Spotswood to Secretary Craggs, 26 May 1719 in Brock (1882), pp. 316–319.

298 Moore and Moseley's troubles: Lee, pp. 161–167.

298 Maynard's lawsuit: George Gordon to the Admiralty, 14 September 1721; Lee, p. 139.

298 Bonnet's escape, Richard Tookerman: HCA 1/55: Information of William Rhett, Jr., London: 28 September 1721; GHP, p. 102; Hargrave (VI), pp. 162–163; Shirley Carter Hughson, The Carolina Pirates and Colonial Commerce, 1670–1740, Baltimore: The Johns Hopkins Press, 1894, pp. 99–101.

299 Disturbances to free pirates: Hargrave (VI), p. 164.

300 Trial, execution of Bonnet's men: Ibid., p. 183.

300 Rhett recaptures Bonnet: Information of William Rhett, Jr.; GHP, pp. 102–103; GHP, pp. 102–103; CO 23/1, No. 12i: Mr Gale to Thomas Pitt, Charlestown, SC: 4 November 1718; "Rhode Island Dispatch, December 9," Boston News-Letter, 29 December 1718, p. 2.

300 Trott's sentence: Hargrave (VI), p. 188.

301 Interventions to save Bonnet's life: GHP, p. 111.

301 Bonnet reprieved seven times; merchants angered: "By Letters from Carolina of December 8," Applebee's Original Weekly Journal, London: 28 February 1719, p. 1,363.

301 Bonnet's letter to Johnson: Stede Bonnet to Governor Johnson, Charlestown, SC (November or December): 1719 in GHP, pp. 112–113.

301 Charleston events influence Rogers: Private consultation minutes, Nassau: 28 November 1718.

301 Independent Company surgeon dies: James Buett was dead by early January 1719, when he was replaced by John Howell, the surgeon previously coveted by Hornigold and Bondavais. CO 23/13, No. 47: Bahamas Council Minutes, Nassau: 12 January 1719.

301 Loss of Willing Mind, Departure of Samuel: The Samuel departed for England on November 11, while the Willing Mind was lost while carrying salvaged cargo back from Green

Turtle Cay. CO 23/13, No. 20: Woodes Rogers to Secretary Craggs, Nassau: 24 December 1718; Protest of Captain King, in GHP, p. 147.

302 Trial of the Nassau pirates. CO 23/1. Trial and Condemnation of Ten Persons for Piracy at New Providence, Nassau: 10 December 1718 (hereafter: Trial at New Providence).

302 Pirates on the ramparts of Fort Nassau, gallows: Ibid.: GHP, p. 43.

304 Rogers reprieves Rounsivell: Rogers to Secretary Craggs, p. 24 December 1718.

304 Morris's final words, execution: Trial at New Providence.

304 Coup attempt against Rogers: CO23/13, No. 28, Rogers to Secretary Craggs, Nassau: 24 January 1719.

305 Strength of Eleuthera, Vane's attack: Rogers to the Council of Trade, 31 October 1718, p. 375; GHP, p. 620.

305 Capture of *Endeavor*: CO 142/14: A List of all the ships and vessels that have called at Kingston in His Majesty's Land of Jamaica from the 29th day of September to the 25th day of December 1718; TJR, p. 24.

306 Vane's men live "riotously": GHP, p. 620.

306 Cruising in Windward Passage: TJR, p. 24; GHP, p. 138.

306-307 Encounter with French man-of-war: TJR, p. 24; GHP, pp. 138-139.

307 Vane deposed, replaced by Rackham: TJR, p. 24; GHP, p. 139.

307 Vane's final captures: TJR, pp. 24-25; CO 142/14: A List of all the ships and vessels that have called at Kingston in His Majesty's Land of Jamaica from the 29th day of September to the 25th day of December 1718; GHP, p. 139.

308 Vane at Guanaja (Bonaca): TJR, p. 25; GHP, p. 139, Chris Humphrey, *Moon Handbooks: Honduras*, 3rd edition, Emeryville, CA: 2000, p. 154.

308 Vane shipwrecked: GHP, pp. 139-140.

309 Vane's capture: GHP, pp. 140-141.

310 Vane's trial, execution: TJR, pp. 36-40; "New York Dispatch, May 1," Philadelphia *American Weekly Mercury*, 4 May 1721, p. 2.

EPILOGUE: PIRACY'S END

311 Rogers learns of war, commissions privateers: CO 23/1, No. 14ii: Bahamas Council Minutes, Nassau: 31 March 1719.

311 "Most forgotten conflict," Spain's war aims: Little, p. 191.

311 Rogers pays colony's debts: CO23/12/2: Rogers Appeal to the King, 1726.

312 Spanish invasion fleet diverted to Pensacola: Little, p. 191; Rogers to Secretary Craggs, Nassau: 27 May 1719 in CSPCS 1719–1720, No. 205, p. 97.

312 Rogers's comments on work at Nassau: Rogers [to Secretary Craggs?], Nassau: 24 January 1719 in CSPCS 1719–1720, No. 28, pp. 8–9.

312 Rogers's credit problems, lack of contact with London: Rogers to the Council of Trade and Plantations, Nassau: 20 April 1720 in CSPCS 1720–1721, No. 47, p. 30; Governor and Council of the Bahamas to Secretary Craggs, Nassau: 26 November 1720 in CSPCS 1720–1721, No. 302, p. 201.

312 Naval visits; Whitney's comments: ADM 1/2649 f111: Thomas Whitney to the Admiralty, *Rose* at Port Royal, Jamaica: 26 October 1719; Rogers to Craggs, 27 May 1719, p. 97.

313 Rogers's defenses, 1720 invasion: Rogers to Council of Trade, 20 April 1720, p. 29;

Nicholas Laws to the Council of Trade and Plantations, Jamaica: 31 March 1720 in *CSPCS 1720–1721*, No. 35, p. 21; Little, p. 193; Lyons, p. 36.

313 **Rogers to Charleston, fights a duel:** John Lloyd to Secretary Craggs, Charleston, SC: 2 February 1721 in *CSPCS 1720–1721*, No. 372, p. 252.

313 **Rogers quits, sails home:** Rogers Appeal to the King; Little, p. 198.

314 **Rogers deposed, goes to debtor's prison:** Little, pp. 198–201.

314 **Hornigold's fate:** ADM 1/2649 f11: Thomas Whitney to the Admiralty, *Rose* off Cape Canaveral, Florida: 3 June 1719.

314 **Burgess's fate:** *GHP*, pp. 640–641.

314 **Jennings's fate:** "Shipping News, New York, Oct. 10," *Boston Gazette*, 17 October 1720, p. 4; "New York Dispatch, August 15," *American Weekly Mercury*, 18 August 1720, p. 2; "New York Dispatch, October 23," *American Weekly Mercury*, 19 October 1721, p. 2; Report via Captain Styles of Bermuda, *Pennsylvania Gazette*, Philadelphia: 4 July 1745.

314 **Ashworth's piracies:** CO 23/13, No. 53: Deposition of William South, Nassau: 27 May 1719.

315 **Rackham captures *Kingston*:** Nicholas Lawes to Council of Trade and Plantations, Jamaica: 31 January 1719 in *CSPCS 1719–1720*, No. 34, p. 18; *GHP*, p. 622.

315 **Kingston recaptured, Rackham to Nassau:** "Port Royal Dispatch, February 10," *Weekly Jamaica Courant*, Kingston, 11 February 1719, p. 3; *GHP*, pp. 622–623; Nicholas Lawes to Council of Trade and Plantations, Jamaica: 24 March 1719 in *CSPCS 1719–1720*, No. 132, p. 64.

316 **Rackham at Nassau, romance with Bonny:** *GHP*, pp. 623–624.

317 **How Read and Bonny were said to have met:** *GHP*, pp. 153–158.

317 **Bonny and Rackham steal Ham's sloop:** "Woodes Rogers' Proclamation," Nassau: 5 September 1720 in *Boston Gazette*, 17 October 1720, p. 3; Lt. Lawes to Captain Vernon, 20 October 1720 in *CSPCS 1720–1721*, No. 527xxxiv (e), p. 344; "New Providence Dispatch, September 4," *Boston Gazette*, 17 October 1720, p. 2; *GHP*, pp. 624–625.

317 **Rackham terrorizes Turnley, attacks fishing vessels:** *TJR*, pp. 8–10; *GHP*, pp. 625–626.

318 **Eyewitness descriptions of Read and Bonny:** *TJR*, pp. 18–19.

318 **Bondavais and Barnet encounter Rackham:** Ibid., pp. 10–11.

319 **Pirates flee to hold, Bonny and Read stay:** Ibid., p. 32–33; *GHP*, p. 156.

319 **Bonny's words to Rackham:** *GHP*, p. 165.

319 **Rackham's execution:** "St. Jago de la Vega Dispatch, November 22," *Boston News-Letter*, 27 February 1721, p. 2; Black, p. 115.

320 **Bonny and Read's pregnancies:** *TJR*, p. 19; "New York Dispatch, January 31," *American Weekly Mercury*, Philadelphia: 7 February 1721, p. 2; *GHP*, p. 165.

320 **Read's death, burial:** Black, p. 116; *GHP*, p. 159.

320 **Bonny not executed:** *GHP*, p. 165; Black, p. 116.

320 **90 percent collapse in pirate population:** Rediker (2004), pp. 29–30.

321 **La Buse and the *Scarborough*:** ADM 1/1879 f5: Deposition of Thomas Heath, St. Christopher: 5 July 1718; ADM 1/1879 f5: Francis Hume to the Admiralty, *Scarborough* at St. Christopher: 6 July 1718.

321 **La Buse in Africa, Indian Ocean:** Letter from Captain Mackra, Bombay: 16 November 1720, in *GHP*, pp. 118–120; Adrien D'Epinay, *Renseignements pour servier a L'Histoire de L'Ile de France*, Ile Maurice (Mauritius): Nouvelle Imprimerie Dupuy, 1890, p. 88; Madeleine Philippe & Jan Dodd, *Mauritius Reunion & Seychelles*, Victoria, Australia: 2004, pp. 194–195.

321 Williams at Sierra Leone: William Snelgrave, *A New Account of Some Parts of Guinea and the Slave Trade*, London: James, John & Paul Knapton, 1734, pp. 216–217, 257–259.

321 Williams's son a peruke maker: *Genealogies of Rhode Island Families*, Vol. II, Baltimore: Clearfield, 2000, pp. 405–406.

321 Howell Davis and *Buck*: "New York Dispatch, November 17," *Boston News-Letter*, 24 November 1718, p. 2; "Piscataqua Dispatch, April 17," *Boston News-Letter*, 13 April 1719, p. 2; *GHP*, pp. 167–176, 191–193.

321 Roberts's 400 vessels, capture: Rediker (2005), pp. 53, 169–170.

322 Kennedy's fate: Hayward, pp. 34–38.

322 Anstis' fate: *GHP*, pp. 288–296.

322 England's career: *GHP*, pp. 114–134; "London Dispatch, April 9," *American Weekly Mercury*, Philadelphia: 30 June 1720, p. 4; CO 142/14: A List of all the ships and vessels that have called at Kingston in His Majesty's Land of Jamaica from the 29th day of September to the 25th day of December 1718.

322 Chamberlaine's fate: "New York Dispatch, July 25," *Boston Gazette*, 1 August 1720, p. 3; John Hardy, *A Chronological List of the Captains of His Majesty's Royal Navy*, London: T. Cadell, 1794, p. 25.

323 Hume's fate: Hardy, p. 33; John Charnock, *Biographia Navalis*, Vol. IV, London: R. Faulder, 1796, p. 46.

323 Pearse's fate: Charnock, p. 58; Lewis Morris to Mary Morris Pearse, Trenton, NJ: 22 May 1742, in Eugene Sheridan (ed.), *The Papers of Lewis Morris*, Vol. III, Newark, NJ: New Jersey Historical Society, 1993, pp. 192–194; Lewis Morris to Vincent Pearse, 1 May 1742 in Ibid., pp. 186–189; Lewis Morris to Euphemia Morris Norris, Trenton, NJ: 14 May 1742 in Ibid., pp. 189–192; Eupehmia Morris Norris to Lewis Morris, Bois, Buckinghamshire, England: 15 June 1742 in Ibid., pp. 196–204.

323 Maynard's fate: Syrett, p. 614; Hardy, p. 44; Lyons, p. 50.

324 Eden's fate: Lee, pp. 63–65.

324 Spotswood's fate: James Grant Wilson and James Fiske, *Appleton's Cyclopedia of American Biography*, Vol. V, New York: D. Appleton & Co., 1888, pp. 635–636; Brock (1882), pp. xii–xvi.

324 Hamilton's fate: "London News Item," London *Weekly Journal or British Gazetteer*, 31 August 1717, p. 321; Minutes of the Commissioners for the Trade and Plantations, London: 6 June 1721 as appears in Kinkor (2003), p. 266; Sir James Balfour, ed., *The Scots Peerage*, Vol. IV, Edinburgh: David Douglas, 1907, p. 7.

325 Woodes Rogers in London: Woodes Rogers Appeal to the King.

325 Mist as author of A *General History*: Arne Bialuschewski, "Daniel Defoe, Nathaniel Mist, and the *General History of the Pyrates*," *Papers of the Bibliographical Society of America*, Vol. 98 (2004), pp. 21–38; Advertisement for the *General History*, *American Weekly Mercury*, 29 December 1724, p. 2.

326 Rogers's petition, redress: "Rogers Appeal to the King," 1726; Little, pp. 202, 208.

327 Hogarth portrait of Rogers: Hogarth, *Woodes Rogers and his Family*, 1729.

327 Rogers's final term: Little, pp. 210–222.

328 Motto of the Bahamas: Little, p. 210n.

INDEX